The

MAKING OF THE AMERICAN REPUBLIC

1763–1815

Paul A. Gilje

University of Oklahoma

PEARSON

Prentice
Hall

Upper Saddle River, New Jersey 07458

Library of Congress Cataloging-in-Publication Data

Gilje, Paul A.
   The making of the American Republic, 1763–1815 / Paul A. Gilje.
      p.   cm.
   Includes bibliographical references (p.) and index.
      ISBN 0-13-183667-6
      1. United States—History—Colonial period, ca. 1600–1775.   2. United States —History—
Revolution, 1775–1783.   3. United States—History—1783–1815.   4. United States—Economic
conditions —To 1865.   5. Capitalism—United States—History.   6. Individualism—United States—
History.   I. Title.

E301.G55 2006
972.2'5—dc22   2005053463

Editorial Director: Charlyce Jones-Owen
Executive Editor: Charles Cavaliere
Associate Editor: Emsal Hasan
Editorial Assistant: Maria Guarascia
Production Liaison: Joanne Hakim
Director of Marketing: Heather Shelstad
Marketing Assistant: Jennifer Lang
Manufacturing Buyer: Benjamin Smith
Cover Art Director: Jayne Conte
Cover Design: Bruce Kenselaar
Cover Illustration/Photo: Edward Savage,
Liberty. Hand-colored engraving on paper.
22 3/4×14 5/8" from the collection of Gilcrease
Museum, Tulsa, Oklahoma.

Director, Image Resource Center:
Melinda Reo
Manager, Rights and Permissions: Zina Arabia
Manager, Visual Research: Beth Brenzel
Manager, Cover Visual Research
& Permissions: Karen Sanatar
Image Permission Coordinator:
Richard Rodrigues
Photo Researcher: Diana Gongora
Full-Service Project Management: Dennis
Troutman/Stratford Publishing Services
Composition: Integra Software Services
Pvt. Ltd.

Cover Photo Caption: "Liberty in the form of the Goddess of Youth Giving Support to the Bald Eagle."
Edward Savage's 1798 engraving combined several symbols. In the eighteenth century the female figure
frequently represented nations and continents. A warlike Britannia symbolized Great Britain. In American
hands the female figure became a youthful representation of liberty. The nubile young woman in Savage's
picture has trampled upon symbols of royalty, is bedecked in garlands, stands in front of a classical structure,
and feeds from a golden chalice the bald eagle—the U.S. In the background are dark clouds and a storm
over a port city. At the top of the picture is the American flag and liberty cap amid a blue sky. In all, the
picture is a wonderful metaphor for the making of the American republic.

Credits and acknowledgments borrowed from other sources and reproduced, with permission, in this
textbook appear on pages 329–330.

Pearson Education LTD., London
Pearson Education Singapore, Pte. Ltd
Pearson Education, Canada, Ltd
Pearson Education—Japan
Pearson Education Australia PTY, Limited

Pearson Education North Asia Ltd
Pearson Educación de Mexico, S. A. de C.V.
Pearson Education Malaysia, Pte. Ltd
Pearson Education, Upper Saddle River, New Jersey

ISBN 0-13-183667-6

To my teachers,
colleagues who study the early republic,
the amigos, and my students

CONTENTS

5 Contested Republic 122

6 The Revolution of 1800 152

7 The New Society 176

8 Frontier Expansion 211

9 Free Trade 241

10 The Debacle of War 273

PREFACE

The *Making of the American Republic* began in the classroom. In 1986 I taught a course on the early republic molded around the relationship between the first years of American independence and the rise of American capitalism. Since that year I have taught variations of this course many times, including in the spring of 2004 while I was writing this book. When Charles Cavaliere began to discuss with me an upper-division text on the early republic I knew how I wanted to approach the subject: I did not want to simply write a narrative of events; I wanted to provide an interpretive text—a book that would cover the essential details with a larger thesis that tied the entire period together. Given the way that I have taught the early republic for almost twenty years, and the fact that I edited a book of essays on the subject (*Wages of Independence: Capitalism in the Early American Republic,* 1997), that larger thesis had to center on how the creation of the United States helped to foster the aggressive individualism and the dynamic economic patterns that we associate with American capitalism.

The early republic is an exciting period that has attracted a great deal of attention from historians. Although there have been at least six Pulitzer Prizes awarded to books on the subject in recent years, and best-selling biographies of men such as John Adams and Alexander Hamilton, the period is often given short shrift in university course catalogs. Frequently, it is taught either as the follow-up to the American Revolution, or as the precursor to the age of Jackson. At a quick glance, this volume may appear to have taken the first approach because it starts with the colonial period and moves through the Revolutionary War. However, first impressions can be deceiving. Obviously, it is my hope that the book will be used in courses that cover both the revolution and the early republic, but the focal point remains the latter. The book begins by asking if colonial America was capitalistic, both in an effort to offer an explanation for the American Revolution and to present a starting point for the greater changes that come to fruition in the 1790s and early 1800s. I also write about the Revolutionary War because we cannot understand the full meaning of what happened in the early republic without understanding the experience of living through that conflict. Yet it is the new society that emerges out of independence that is my real concern.

It is a humbling experience to write this type of synthetic book. In providing a text for the entire period it has not been easy to cover everything that I would have liked. As a social historian, I wanted to make sure that the story of the common person would be included. I have striven to show how ordinary people were both affected by and, in turn, had an effect on the larger events. I also wanted to make sure that African Americans, Native Americans, and women would not simply be tagged on to the story to meet some sort of quota of political correctness. I wanted to include them as important players in the larger drama. But, at times, I had to let the great men have their due. In writing this book, I came to realize as I never had before that men like George Washington and Thomas Jefferson, whatever their faults, made a difference. I therefore have striven to balance the larger political and diplomatic history with the nitty-gritty of social and economic history. I have written about both Washington and Jefferson, as well as other leaders, but offer some sense of the dimensions of everyday life, too. In the end, it is my hope that the reader will come to a fuller appreciation of the early republic and how it contributed to the America we know today.

A Note on Citations

I have cited mainly material that I have quoted directly either from a primary source or from a book or article quoting a primary source. In the notes the reader will find a number of Internet sources. Although most of the quotations taken from the Internet can also be found in traditional book form, I decided to use the Internet notes as a guide to student readers to demonstrate how easy it is to access the documents for themselves. The Internet is an incredible research tool, but it can also be somewhat unstable. What is online one day, might be taken offline the next. I tried to refer the reader to Internet locations that should be around for some time. I should also point out that many more references in my notes can also be found on the Internet. The Library of Congress has placed on the Internet the *American State Papers* and the *Annals of Congress.* In addition, many university libraries now have access to early American books and newspapers online. This collection is not fully digitized, but within a few years it will be possible through university library portals to access every book and pamphlet published before 1820 and most newspapers in the colonial and early republic periods.

Acknowledgments

This book has been in the "making" for over twenty-five years. Since my years as a graduate student I have focused my studies on the early republic broadly defined. During the course of my professional career I have accumulated numerous intellectual debts to teachers, colleagues, and students. Among my teachers I must single out Gordon Wood, whose kindness and scholarship I only hope to emulate. I feel particularly fortunate to be part of an active and exciting scholarly community that has transformed our understanding of the early republic. Without the growing body of books and articles on the early republic I could never have written this book. The suggested reading list and notes only scratch the surface of my intellectual debts. On a more personal level, at countless professional meetings, especially the summer gatherings of the Society for Historians of the Early American Republic, I have made many friends who have enriched my life both personally and professionally. To these friends and "amigos" I want to say thank-you. I have now taught at least two generations of students at the University of Oklahoma—a student recently informed me that her father told her that if he could survive my class many years ago, she certainly could do so now. The great thing about teaching is that you never learn anything better than when you have to explain it to others. Explaining the subject matter in this book to students has not only helped me to learn it, but has forced me, often as the result of piercing questions, to think and rethink it countless times. I owe more to my students than they will ever know.

I also appreciate the encouragement and support I have had from Charles Cavaliere at Prentice Hall. Thanks, too, to James Henretta, University of Maryland, Gordon S. Wood, Brown University, Cynthia Kierner, University of North Carolina, Charlotte, and Jonathan Earle, University of Kansas, for comments on a draft of several chapters of the book.

At the University of Oklahoma, I want to thank Dean Paul Bell, Provost Nancy Mergler, and President David Boren for creating and sustaining an academic atmosphere conducive to scholarship. I would especially like to thank Robert Griswold for his friendship and support. As chair of the Department of History he provided me with valuable time off from teaching that facilitated the completion of this book. As Dean of the Honors College, he asked me to teach a course on the rise of American capitalism in the spring of 2004 and provided funding for me to bring four guest speakers into the classroom. Three of these individuals, Douglas Egerton, John Larson, and Alan Taylor, came from other institutions. The fourth, Catherine Kelly, has an office across the hall from me at the University of Oklahoma. I am grateful to all four for visiting my class and for sharing their special knowledge of the early republic with me and my students at a crucial time during my writing. I would also like to thank Josh Piker, another colleague at the University of Oklahoma, for reading the entire manuscript and suggesting ways I could strengthen my argument.

As always, I owe the most to my family. My daughter, Karin, has helped me in tangible ways by checking the notes, indexing, and in being the incredible young women that she has become. My son, Erik, had a less direct hand in the book, but has always been supportive of everything I do. My wife, Ann, is my life partner, who, with our children grown and out of the house, is eager for our next great adventure—whatever that may be.

ABOUT THE AUTHOR

Paul A. Gilje is a leading social historian of the revolutionary era and early national period. Born in Brooklyn, he attended Brooklyn College as an undergraduate and earned his Ph.D. from Brown University in 1980. Since then he has taught at the University of Oklahoma where he is Professor of History and was awarded a Samuel Roberts Noble Foundation Presidential Professorship in 2000. He is the author of *Liberty on the Waterfront: American Maritime Society and Culture in the Age of Revolution, 1750–1850* (Philadelphia: University of Pennsylvania Press, 2004), *Rioting in America* (Bloomington, Indiana: Indiana University Press, 1996), and *The Road to Mobocracy: Popular Disorder in New York City, 1763 to 1834* (Chapel Hill, N.C.: University of North Carolina Press for the Institute of Early American History and Culture, Williamsburg, 1987), and has edited or co-edited five other books. He has authored over thirty articles and essays. His work has won several prizes and honors including the Society for Historians of the Early American Republic's Best Book Award for 2005 for *Liberty on the Waterfront*. He has lectured extensively in this country and abroad at a variety of professional meetings and institutions, including Oxford University, Edinburgh University, the University of Glasgow, University of Pennsylvania, and Johns Hopkins University. He has also held prestigious fellowships at Johns Hopkins University and Washington University in St. Louis. In addition he has been awarded several grants for research and teaching from the National Endowment of the Humanities and other organizations.

Capitalism and the American Revolution

Was Colonial America Capitalistic?

Roots of Rebellion

Resistance to Imperial Regulation

Was Colonial America Capitalistic?

Benjamin Franklin was the most famous colonial American of his day. Born in Boston in 1706, his life spanned much of the eighteenth century. His *Autobiography* reads like a textbook for any would-be entrepreneur. Franklin described how, through hard work and thrifty living, he amassed a fortune. In the nineteenth century the book became a gospel to the developing middle class. His tale is so compelling that his autobiography continues to be read and his life has been the raw material for countless biographies. His list of thirteen moral virtues could apply to many of the self-help guides you can find in a bookstore today. Franklin went so far as to use a chart to measure his success in keeping to his program of self-improvement. If his *Autobiography* were not enough to indicate that "lightning Tamer" Ben were a capitalist, then his little pamphlet, "The Way to Wealth," which first appeared in the front of Franklin's *Poor Richard's Almanac* in 1757, would certainly provide proof. In this essay, Franklin strung together a series of popular sayings emphasizing industry and frugality that he had spread throughout his almanacs in twenty-five years of publishing. Franklin drove home these points relentlessly with a barrage of pithy quips:

> *Sloth makes all Things difficult, but Industry all easy, as Poor Richard says; and He that riseth late, must trot all Day, and shall scarce overtake his Business at Night. While Laziness travels so slowly, that Poverty soon overtakes him,* as we read in *Poor Richard,* who adds, *Drive thy Business, let not that drive thee; and Early to Bed, and early to rise, makes a Man healthy, wealthy, and wise.*[1]

1

1 52   *A New Guide*

A Bird in the Hand is worth two in the Bush.

FABLE XII. *Of the Fisherman and the Fish.*

A Fisherman having cast his Line into the Water, presently after drew up a Fish.
The little Captive entreated the Fisherman that he would spare her (she being but small) till she was grown larger; then she would suffer herself to be taken by him again.

No, no, replies the Fisherman, I am not to be so served: If I let you go, I must never expect to see you any more; neither should I have caught you now, if you had known there was a Hook within the Bait: And I was always of that Temper, that whatever I could catch, I had rather take it away than leave it behind me.

The Interpretation.

Never let go a Certainty for an Uncertainty.

FIGURE 1–1 *Poor Richard's Almanac* In the mid-eighteenth century Benjamin Franklin urged frugality, honesty, and self-improvement, values later associated with capitalism, in his almanac and his essay "The Way to Wealth."

Poor Richard and Honest Ben are misleading. Yes, as a scion of the Enlightenment, Franklin believed in the perfectability of mankind and thus encouraged self-improvement. But his career was not nearly as independent as he would make us think. Crucial to his success in printing were extensive political and personal connections that brought him patronage and employment. Franklin claimed it was his skill as a printer and his hard work that brought the contracts, but it was his skill in developing appropriate relationships within the social hierarchy that brought him these favors. After he "retired" and devoted himself to public service, he continued to operate in a world of aristocracy. His trips to England from 1757 to 1762 and 1764 to 1775 were largely to seek favor at court, in hopes of a title and in pursuit of large land grants. Ultimately he failed in these efforts, although he did manage to obtain the governorship of New Jersey for his illegitimate son, William Franklin. It was largely in reaction to his failure to become Duke Ben of Franklin that he picked up his pen and retold the story of his humble birth and his march from rags to riches through what he now saw as the dint of his own labor.

Of course, there were elements of capitalist enterprise in Franklin's life. If we focus on these elements only we would fail to understand the absence of an important part of the capitalist mind-set—the idea that one is concerned solely with the investment of capital to produce more capital. The American Revolution helped to remove the last shackles that had kept men like Franklin striving to rise within a social aristocracy, and allowed them to trumpet, instead, their own humble origins. It is no coincidence that almost as soon as he returned to the colonies, Ben became a vocal revolutionary. It is also no coincidence that his son William, whose appointment as New Jersey's governor could be seen as a great success within the old world order, became a Loyalist.

Men like Ben Franklin can best be viewed as conflicted and being pulled in several different ways simultaneously. Yes, they participated in capitalist enterprise, but they operated in a hierarchical and aristocratic world and sought recognition by their social betters. Until 1773, Franklin hoped that his own achievements, which made him one of the most famous Britons—not simply a colonial American—would bring a just reward. As late as 1768, Franklin responded enthusiastically to a suggestion from Lord Frederick North, the Chancellor of the Exchequer, that the king might find a position for him in government by declaring that he would "stay with pleasure" if he "could any ways be useful to government."[2] When he did not succeed he seized on a new identity, the Ben Franklin we know from his autobiography. There were elements of this new Franklin in the publisher of the sayings of Poor Richard. But he needed not just the independence movement of 1776, but also the new world of equality of the early republic, to unleash his capitalist identity.

The contradictions evident in Ben Franklin extended throughout the colonies. Partially modern and capitalistic, and partially traditional and anticapitalistic, British North America stood on the brink of great changes. Social and economic problems erupted into conflict within the colonies themselves, creating a tinderbox ignited into rebellion by new efforts at imperial regulation. The subsequent revolution was more about the character of American society than about the relationship between the king and his colonial subjects.

To understand Franklin—and the significance of the American Revolution—we need to look at just how different the colonial world was from the world of the early republic. The key to comprehending this difference is the concept of equality. Before the revolution nearly everyone assumed that all men were created *unequal*. With the advent of the revolution the world began to change and the idea that "all men are created equal" gathered force. The history of the early republic, indeed the history of America from that point on, is the history of how the ideal of equality expanded to include more and more people and how it came to be the basic assumption holding the American political, social, and economic world together. Equality also became the major impetus behind the growth of capitalism in the United States. Capitalism—an economic system based on the investment and accumulation of capital that facilitated production and the open exchange of goods through market and impersonal, price-driven relations—thrived in the charged egalitarian atmosphere created by the American Revolution. Before we get to the story of how the American Revolution led to the spread of the ideal of equality and the rise of capitalism we need to understand the assumptions challenged by these changes.

The great divide in the traditional Anglo-American society was between patrician and plebeian, or the gentry and ordinary folk. Later, after the leveling effect of the egalitarianism of the revolution, every man became a gentleman. But to be a gentleman in colonial America meant you were a breed apart from the common people. Gentlemen did not work with their hands, nor did they earn their bread from the sweat of their brows. A gentleman was supposed to live off an income derived from the land. In reality, gentry in England and America often had to actively manage their estates, involve themselves in commerce, and oversee agricultural and even industrial production. The American gentry did not reach as high, nor could they distance themselves as much from those below, as their English counterparts. Yet the yawning gap persisted between those who rode on horseback and those who traveled afoot. As one poor colonist admitted, "what were called *gentle folks*" were "beings of a superior order."[3] The very sight of a gentleman, distinguished by the cut of his clothing, his wig, and his bearing, would send a commoner stuttering or speechless. Shoemaker George Robert Twelves Hewes was "scared all the while . . . 'almost to death'" as he later confessed, when he visited the Boston home of the great merchant John Hancock to pay respect and homage on a holiday.[4] Even George Washington, who grew up among the gentry, studied when to pull off his hat before a superior and noted in his copybook the way to bow "according to the Custom of the Better Bred and Quality of the Person" and "give to every Person his due title According to his Degree."[5]

Crucial to the notion of hierarchy was the idea of a corporate society—the belief that all elements of society, just like a corpus or human body, shared a single, identifiable interest. Today we assume that there are many competing interests in the political arena. In the eighteenth-century world of Anglo-America, competing interests were an anathema and were something to be protected against. Everyone was supposed to work for a greater good. Distinctions were acceptable because everyone understood that all levels of society had their special functions. Patrician and plebeian were therefore bound together: The gentry served at the head; the people composed the body, the arms, and the legs. Without all parts of the body politic operating together, everything would be akimbo and nothing would ever get done. As William Shakespeare explained, "take but degree away"—social differences—"untune that string, and, hark, what discord follows!"[6]

The cement that held the society together was paternalism and deference. Paternalism was the action by those higher in society to protect those below; deference was the action of those below to concur and follow the lead of those above them in society. Perhaps one of the clearest American statements in the eighteenth century of how paternalism and deference was supposed to work came from the pen of J. Hector St. John de Crèvecoeur. Although Crèvecoeur is most famous for asking "What, then, is the

FIGURE 1–2 J. Hector St. John de Crèvecoeur This French-born aristocrat moved to British America after the French and Indian War and settled as a farmer in New York. As author of *Letters of an American Farmer* and *Sketches of Eighteenth-Century America*, he praised the American as a "new man, who acts upon new principles," yet expressed continued faith in the king and hierarchy in government and society.

American, this new man?" and thereby asserting what many historians perceive as a new American national character, his vision of society was backward looking and his sympathies during the Revolutionary War were with the crown.[7] In Crèvecoeur's essay "The American Belisarius" the main character, S. K., goes into the wilderness to establish his own plantation. A natural aristocrat and leader, S. K. acts the true paternalist by assisting others in settling nearby, providing wheat and hay for those who need it, and allowing a poor man to use his horse. He benefits from this largesse by having his less well-off neighbors assist him with the harvest for no monetary reward. This "princely farmer"—a phrase used by Crèvecoeur—becomes "a father to the poor of this wilderness." When approached by wheat dealers from abroad to export his harvest for higher and immediate profits, S. K. responds with an anticapitalist mantra that English historian E. P. Thompson would have labeled the moral economy: "I have no wheat," S. K. proclaims, "for the rich; my harvest is for the poor." S. K. then asks "What would the inhabitants of these mountains do were I to divest myself of what superfluous grain I have?" From this perspective profit was irrelevant. What counted was the greater good of the corporate community and it was the duty of community leaders to safeguard the public welfare.[8]

Crèvecoeur struck the same theme in his more famous discussion of American national identity in *Letters from an American Farmer*. Letter III, "What is an American," has often been misread and cited only as an example of the opportunity afforded the "new man" in North America. Like Franklin's *Autobiography*, it has been viewed as a part of the American gospel of wealth and a statement of our capitalist origins. This reading misses the mark. Crèvecoeur's example of the great American success story is Andrew the Hebridian, who through "honesty," "sobriety," and "industry" works his way from being an impoverished immigrant from Scotland to becoming an independent American freeholder. What is usually overlooked is the fact that Andrew succeeds only because of the intervention of the narrator, who acts as a benefactor, finding jobs for Andrew and his family, and even arranging for Andrew to lease a farm. The benevolent paternalist is just as crucial to Andrew's success as are his own abilities and the bounties of the American environment.[9]

Perhaps more important to our understanding of capitalism in colonial America was Crèvecoeur's definition of success. In the colonies, "the idle may be employed, the useless become useful, and the poor become rich." Lest we misunderstand Crèvecoeur again, he immediately clarified himself: "but by riches I do not mean gold and silver—we have but little of those metals; I mean a better sort of wealth—cleared lands, cattle, good houses, good clothes, and an increase of people to enjoy them." This wealth had a specific end. The idea was not to accumulate capital to make more capital. Nor was the goal to obtain luxuries and a high lifestyle. Nor was it even the eighteenth-century goal of Benjamin Franklin to move up the social hierarchy. Instead, it was to gain "a pleasing uniformity of decent competence." Nature, in other words, promised the European who came to North America that "If thou wilt work, I have bread for thee; if thou wilt be honest, sober, and industrious, I have greater rewards to confer on thee—ease and independence."[10] The immigrant thereby gained fields and clothes, as well as a warm fireside and decent bed. The aim of this competence was simple enough—to pass on to the next generation the fruits of the farmer's labor—a rich homestead and comfortable living.

Not every colonist, as the life of Franklin demonstrates, limited his goals to simply achieving competence. But if we take Andrew the Hebridian as one end and we put Benjamin Franklin at the other end, we see a spectrum of possible goals for colonial Americans. The axis of that spectrum hinged on the acceptance of hierarchy in a corporate world bound together by paternalism and deference. These contours of a traditional society held not only for Andrew and Ben of Pennsylvania, but for all the colonies despite their diversity. The means of achieving aristocratic or near aristocratic status differed from region to region. In the Chesapeake, an individual like George Washington might become a colonial leader through inheritance, marriage, and the ownership of plantations with slaves. South Carolina's leaders also owned slaves but grew rice instead of the tobacco of the Chesapeake. In New England, mercantile enterprise might establish a fortune and allow someone like Thomas Hutchinson or John Hancock to assume an elevated status. In New York, merchants were important, but so, too, were large landowning patroons like the Livingstons and Schuylers. There was more consistency throughout the colonies in the means of achieving competence. In the cities, which held only about 5 percent of the population in 1775, learning a trade and becoming an artisan was the best means to competency. Most colonial Americans, from Georgia to the wilds of the district of Maine, gained competence by working farms just large enough for subsistence plus a small surplus to purchase more land or a few luxuries.

In short, despite differences, there were some crucial similarities between the colonies. There was no separate identity as American colonists—all took pride in being subjects of the British crown. Each colony saw its main bond not with another colony, but to the metropolitan center across the Atlantic—Great Britain. Perhaps most important of all was that the colonists adhered to a value system inherited from Britain that emphasized inequality, hierarchy, corporatism, paternalism, and deference.

Although some individuals saw themselves as Anglo-American aristocrats, or in the case of Franklin, as wanna-be aristocrats, most had more humble aspirations and sought the simple competence of Andrew the Hebridian.

Roots of Rebellion

If competence was the goal of most Americans, that goal became increasing difficult to achieve. If hierarchy, corporatism, paternalism, and deference represented the ideals of eighteenth-century society, they did not always reflect reality. The gap between the ideals of colonial society riveted to a precapitalist world order and a social reality that pushed more and more individuals into a competitive and capitalist market challenged the pre-modern mentality and helps to explain the origins of the American Revolution. Anglo-Americans confronted a series of crises—demographic, social, economic, and intellectual—that brought these problems to the fore.

Population growth created serious difficulties for many colonial Americans by the mid-eighteenth century. Between 1700 and 1750, the number of people in British North America grew from about 200,000 to about one million. While this represented a dramatic increase, in the twenty-five years after 1750, the population doubled again. Part of this population explosion was caused by immigration—many Andrew the Hebridians arriving—and part by natural increase—the Andrews and their wives having many children. Both processes led to difficulties in achieving and maintaining competence.

As Crèvecoeur tells it, Andrew ended up with a one-hundred-acre freehold on newly settled land on the frontier of Pennsylvania. Because of the rich soil of the "best poor man's country," this would be more than enough land to support a family. Moreover, Andrew was lucky: He had only one son to inherit the farm. But what if the other Andrews had five sons and as many daughters? Colonial Americans married younger (age twenty-four for men, age twenty-two for women) than their European cousins. They were also healthier and ate better than Europeans. The result was that pregnancies within marriage came fairly regularly at two-year intervals and most children lived to adulthood. With partible inheritance, in which each child received some land or wealth, the one-hundred-acre competence quickly became insufficient to maintain the same standard of living from generation to generation. The other Andrews would have to do something to increase their holdings to provide for all of their children. Fortunately, rising prices for their produce, the labor from their sons and daughters, and the increased value of their land would help. But even doubling or tripling their wherewithal might not be enough.

One solution to this problem was to move to the frontier, where land was cheaper. Until the mid-eighteenth century, most colonial Americans had clung tenaciously close to the coast; settlement seldom occurred more than one hundred miles from salt water. With this population explosion, however, colonists streamed into the interior. The Great Wagon Road from Pennsylvania, through the Shenandoah Valley in Virginia, and into the backcountry of the Carolinas teemed with people looking for new farms. Others pushed into northern New England, or crossed into the Hudson and Mohawk Valleys of New York. The backcountry of Pennsylvania also gained population. And colonists sought to settle the rich lands of the Ohio River Valley. Benjamin Franklin hoped that his new personal colony, which he lobbied for in London, would be on the banks of the Ohio. George Washington crossed the Appalachians in 1754 and began the French and Indian War in an effort to stake his, and Virginia's, claim to the forks of the Ohio (where Pittsburgh now stands). Daniel Boone, born in Pennsylvania and living in North Carolina, explored the Cumberland Gap in 1767 and began the settlement of Kentucky as a part of this movement.

Migration, however, could cause as many problems as it solved. Conflict erupted repeatedly on the frontier. Recognizing the threat of the more numerous English colonists, many Native Americans joined the French in their wars with the British, especially in the Seven Years' War (known in the colonies as the French and Indian War, 1754–1763). The Indians, however, did not need the French to combat the intrusion of British colonists. After the defeat of the French in Canada, the Ottawa leader Pontiac orchestrated a massive attack on British outposts, capturing every one west of the Appalachians except Forts Detroit and Pitt. On the southern frontier the Cherokee fought an unsuccessful war with the British colonists from 1759 to 1761. And various Native American groups remained restive on the frontier throughout this period. For their part, European settlers also exhibited a great deal of animosity to Indians. In 1763 a group of Scotch-Irish Pennsylvanians called the Paxton Boys engaged in two massacres of peaceful Indians, and then marched on Philadelphia to demand the colonial government take a more bellicose stand against Native Americans.

Migrations of European Americans also created conflict within colonies as leaders in older settled areas were reluctant to give up political power to newly settled regions. The Paxton Boys' uprising in Pennsylvania was as much about strife between Scotch-Irish frontiersmen and the Quaker and German leadership in the colony as it was about hatred of Indians. Tensions broke out into open conflict in the Regulator

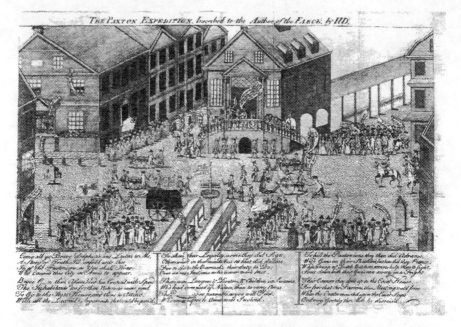

FIGURE 1–3 The Paxton Boys Social tension in the years before the Revolutionary War erupted into violence on a number of occasions. In 1763 a group of Scotch-Irish Pennsylvanians, called the Paxton Boys, massacred peaceful Indians and marched on Philadelphia to demand support from the colonial government.

movements of North and South Carolina. In South Carolina the problem resulted from the lawlessness that seemed to increase in the mid-1760s and the failure of the colonial government in Charleston to provide sufficient legal protection on the frontier. The Regulators were property-owning vigilantes who complained of "large Stocks of Cattel" being "either stollen and destroy'd" and "valuable Horses . . . carried off." They were concerned not only with bandits, but also with the frontier settlers who lived on the fringes of society and seldom paid their debts. As one remonstrance explained,

> No Credit can be given among Us—for no *Writ* can be obtain'd without going to *Charlestown*—No *Attachment* can be su'd out, but in *Charlestown*—and while these are preparing, Your Debtor has taken flight and is quite out of Reach.[11]

To correct these wrongs, the Regulators took the law into their own hands, capturing bandits, and often executing criminals without any court proceedings. They also compelled debtors to pay what they owed and attacked squatters, violators of sexual norms, and hunters and drifters. Only the establishment of a circuit court system in 1769 finally defused the movement. North Carolina Regulators were poor farmers from the back-country who began their activities at about the same time, but more directly opposed the colonial government, which they saw as the cause of their problem. Beginning in 1766, farmers organized to stop abusive legal practices, often interrupting courts and disrupting the normal processes of the law. The movement was an action against placemen—individuals who gained political office through favoritism and then exploited the office for profit—and was a result of regional tensions. The Regulators believed that the backcountry was settled by "good industrious labouring Men" who opposed "Pettyfogging Lawyers, extortionate and griping publicans or Tax gatherers, and such as delighted in building Palaces, at the expence of the honest Farmer, and Tradesman." Regulator Hermon Husbands explained, "all we want is to be Governed by Law, and not by the *Will* of Officers, which to us is perfectly despotick and arbitrary."[12] In September 1770, hundreds of Regulators gathered in Hillsborough, closed the courts, and ransacked the house of lawyer and office holder Edmund Fanning for his ill-gotten gains. Governor William Tryon recruited an army of 1,100 men from coastal North Carolina and fought a pitched battle with about 2,000 Regulators at Alamance Creek on May 17, 1771. Over 150 on both sides were wounded; between seventeen to twenty Regulators and nine militia-men were killed. The governor subsequently executed seven other Regu-lators and thereby put down the rebellion.

Friction appeared between colonies in contests over border disputes as settlers poured into areas previously unoccupied by European Americans. In the Green Mountains between New York and New Hampshire, New Englanders headed by Ethan Allen drove off New York sheriffs and harassed anyone with deeds and papers from a New York court. Although the crown ultimately decided the area belonged to New York, the dispute did not end until after the Revolutionary War and the admission of Vermont as a sepa-rate state in 1791. Connecticut claimed the Wyoming Valley in northeastern Pennsylvania (around modern-day Scranton and Wilkes-Barre), patented a county for the region and sent hundreds of farmers to the upper Susque-hanna River Valley. These Yankees from overcrowded Connecticut stood ready to defend their deeds with force of arms. Several gun battles broke out against Pennamites (those with Pennsylvania deeds) from the beginning of the 1770s through the 1790s. Other colonies, with somewhat less violence, had contests over ill-defined and poorly plotted boundaries.

Migration and population growth were not the only sources of crises in the American colonies in the mid-eighteenth century. Traditional ideas about society sustained attacks from several directions. Corporatism held that every-one shared the same larger interest, but countless interests might be identified along ethnic and religious divisions, and along geographical boundaries within colonies, between colonies, and across the Atlantic. Corporatism depended on everyone being relatively the same in everything but wealth. Colonial society became ever more diverse in the eighteenth century. African American slaves, who numbered a half million by 1775, represented an alien and subjugated people in the midst of the European American population. For those of European descent, there were also growing differences among Germans, Scotch-Irish, and other non-English peoples swarming into the colonies. Greater ethnic divisions brought increased religious differences. The religious revival known as the First Great Awakening furthered these distinctions by splitting even ethnically homogenous communities into New Lights, inspired by evangelical religion, and Old Lights, who adhered to older forms of religious observation. Most colonies had an established church—a community that shared worship was more homogenous and like a corporate society than one with a variety of religious services. But with many different denominations, the corporate ideal became harder to sustain and a de facto religious toleration began to grow.

As much as the colonial elite tried to distinguish itself from the "common herd," and economic distinctions widened during the eighteenth century, the aspiring colonial aristocracy was too new and too open to sustain traditional ideals. Few members of the British nobility settled in the colonies, so the elite generally lacked the hereditary titles of the British aristocracy. As rich as some colonial Americans may have been, and as fancy as some of their homes may have appeared to someone in a one-room cabin, the American would-be aristocrat's wealth paled in comparison to his British counterpart, and his spacious twelve-room house stood in stark contrast with the hundred-room palaces of the British upper crust. North America also remained a fluid place where there were any number of examples of men scrambling up the social ladder, like Honest Ben Franklin, in defiance of their place at birth.

Paternalism represented actions by the elite for the benefit of the lower orders. However, the elite all too often pursued its own aggrandizement at the expense of the rest of society. Crèvecoeur's "princely farmer" was more fiction than reality. In Virginia, the gentry used their political clout to obtain grants of land. A group of planters would petition the colony's council, packed with relatives and friends, and hundreds of thousands of acres would be doled out. George Washington joined with a group of other leading Virginians to petition for over 150,000 acres when he helped form the Great Dismal Swamp Company in 1765. Similar favors were sought by America's would-be aristocrats elsewhere. Sometimes the favor was in land grants, as in Virginia. Sometimes it was in obtaining a profitable provisioning contract or other mercantile advantage. And sometimes it was in the engrossing of office, with all the attendant profits and fees, for family and friends. In the early 1760s Thomas Hutchinson held multiple offices in Massachusetts as a probate judge, chief justice of the colony, councillor, and lieutenant governor. In all of these practices colonial aristocrats merely mirrored the behavior of their well-heeled cousins across the Atlantic.

Such behavior did not go entirely unnoticed by common folk, who began to challenge deference. Some conflict between regions within colonies, including the North Carolina Regulation, had a class component. The North Carolina Regulators typically were small farmers who were repressed by the big planters of the coastal region. Tensions also appeared between landlords and tenants in the Hudson River Valley in the 1750s and 1760s. Farmers from New England and others who were tired of renting farms challenged the property rights of families who had been granted huge parcels of land a generation or two before. This conflict broke out in sporadic rioting in the 1750s and 1760s: The poor farmers tore down houses of leaseholders, refused to pay rent on land, and opposed sheriffs with eviction orders. Within the small colonial cities (Philadelphia was the largest city, with under 30,000 people in 1770), resentment of wealth appeared occasionally in crowd action. The workers and artisans who paraded the streets on Guy Fawkes Day (November 5) to celebrate the Protestant succession loaded their procession with complex symbolism. They marched with effigies of the Pope and the Pretender (the Catholic Stuart claimant to the throne). They had their own street tax assessed on the wealthy to pay for the effigies and to provide drink for the celebration. While asserting loyalty to the Hanoverians, they denigrated the effigies, which were Catholic symbols attired in the clothes of the aristocracy. At the end of the parade, the crowd burned the effigies. Everyone understood the message: The common people remained loyal to the king as long as the king protected the interest of his Protestant subjects. Similarly, Boston mobs on several occasions prevented the export of bread that paternalism, as explained by Crèvecoeur, should have compelled the merchant to sell within the community for a lower price than he could get if he exported it.

Poverty began to spread, especially in the urban centers, and civic leaders created institutions to house the poor and put them to work. During the conflicts with the French the drain on the labor supply as men enlisted, and the demand for goods and services, moderated the long-term economic developments. Overall, however, the wars against the French and Indians at midcentury aggravated the situation, creating a postwar recession during the 1760s. There was an increasing number of widows struggling to support their children. Even intact families were left wanting. Work that was once plentiful along the docks became scarce. One New York artisan lamented in 1762 that, although he was still employed and had cut costs to the bone, " the Expence of living in the most frugal Way has increased so exorbitantly, that I find it beyond my ability to support my Family with my utmost Industry." He complained that he was "growing every Day more and more behind hand, tho' my Family can scarcely appear with Decency, or have necessaries to subsist."[13] Men who had no trouble signing on as sailors on merchantmen and privateers during war, in peace had to settle for lower wages—if they could find a ship that would take them. Farmers who a few years before had no trouble selling grain to army contractors, looked in vain for a market for their year's labor.

Oddly, the economic success of the colonies further contributed to a sense of crisis in the 1760s and 1770s. The West Indies devoured American produce in the 1740s and 1750s, and prices in Great Britain of staples such as tobacco increased. Throughout the eighteenth century the colonies became more and more important economically to Great Britain. In 1700 the colonies absorbed one-twentieth of all British exports; by 1760 the proportion had grown to almost one-quarter. Shipbuilding became a major industry in the colonies, blessed with vast forests and natural resources, and by 1775 one-third of all vessels flying British colors had been constructed in North America. The value of colonial imports from Britain more than doubled between 1747 and 1765. This success, however, came at a steep price. Because most colonial exports were agricultural and most imports were finished and manufactured products, private debt grew significantly. The good news was that a greater number of people seemed affluent enough with property and collateral to be able to borrow extensively. Small farmers and artisans might purchase nicer dishes and even drink tea. Those with great wealth, like George Washington, imported fine china, furniture, and fancy paneling on credit from their British correspondents. The bad news was that year after year, and with order after order, the debt appeared never ending. Within five years of his marriage, and gaining access to his wife's wealth, Washington spent so much on luxury items that he complained that his purchases had been "swallowed up before I well knew where I was, all the money I got by Marriage nay more, brought me in Debt."[14] In the twelve years between 1760 and 1772 personal debt doubled from £2 million to £4 million.

Aggravating all of these developments was the fact that many colonists began behaving in a manner that belied their ideals and thereby created a crisis within themselves. We can see this challenge to colonial ideals in two major areas: a revolt against patriarchy, and an increase in activity we would label as capitalistic. Together, and against the background of the demographic, social, and economic changes transforming the British colonial American world, these developments further threatened hierarchy and sought to do away with the ideal of competence.

The revolt against patriarchy was not a single event; it was a series of ideas and actions that on an individual level did not amount to much, but taken together, paved the way for the new world of equality. On its highest plane this revolt was connected to the great intellectual movement of the eighteenth century—the Enlightenment. The key elements of the Enlightenment lay in a faith in nature and reason; the philosophes (the philosophers) of the Enlightenment held that everything in nature was organized on the principles of reason. All one had to do was study nature and apply reason and the laws of the universe would be revealed. From this premise came a tremendous faith in the perfectability of mankind. John Locke, one of the earliest Enlightened thinkers, believed that knowledge was gained through the senses. If men were neither encumbered by anachronisms inherited from the past, nor ignorant because of the lack of education, then they would be free to fulfill their greatest potential. These ideas, however innocent when bandied about among the elite, had tremendous potential for damage when extended, as they naturally and reasonably should, further down in society. Removing vestiges from the past ultimately questioned hereditary privilege; educating ordinary people, regardless of class, and pushing for perfectability in every man put all mankind on the same level. The danger to the old order in these ideas remained an undercurrent for the first half of the eighteenth century; that danger came surging to the surface after 1750.

The assault on patriarchy had other, less elevated, sources as well. Anglo-American culture had long had a plebeian tradition of antiauthoritarianism. How far back this resentment of place reached remains vague. It was present during the Elizabethan era and can be seen occasionally in the antics of common folk in Shakespeare's plays. Although these characters were intended as buffoons and clowns and were introduced for comic relief, their banter often included some sharp barbs at those further up the social ladder. This antiauthoritarianism appeared with a vengeance among the radical fringes of the English Civil Wars in the 1640s. And it persisted in the notion that Englishmen had a particular irreverence for the elite that seldom appeared among the peasantry of the Continent. This antiauthoritarianism was imported to the English colonies of North America, where social distances were not as great as they were in England.

Some of the revolt against patriarchy also can be attributed to other factors unique to the colonies. Staggering population growth made it more difficult for parents to control their children. With smaller patrimonies at hand, children could more easily ignore their parents by marrying for love rather than money or by moving away from their families. As many as one-third of all New England girls were pregnant when they wed, suggesting a desire to select their life partner, rather than to follow the wishes of their parents. Frequent moves often meant that people were not as rooted in one community and therefore might not be as willing to defer to the local elite, whom they did not know.

Beyond this revolt against patriarchy there was also an increase in individuals behaving in a more capitalist vein. Through thousands of piecemeal decisions, colonial Americans began to pursue profit beyond competence. The process of this change often was subtle and almost impossible to detect in any one person. Sometimes it was a matter of seeking to gain additional resources to help build the patrimony for one's many children. Selling a farm as land prices doubled and tripled helped to put families in motion, both geographically and economically. But there were other pressures for profit as well. The increased desire for consumer goods beyond what could be produced at home led families to encourage women and girls to engage in production of cloth or cheese, or some other item that could be made at home for the market. This surplus, along with foodstuffs in excess of the family's needs, gained the family credits and even cash. Items that had once been deemed luxuries—dishes, fancy textiles, furniture, tea—soon came to be seen as necessities.

With these developments, economic relationships began to shift from the personal to the impersonal. Previously, credit was only one component of a multifaceted relationship between men at different levels of the hierarchy. Increasingly, it became a simple economic arrangement between equal individuals. Farmers in places like Massachusetts clamored for a land bank that would issue them paper money in exchange for a mortgage on their property. Land banks were not the same kind of institution as the banks that emerged in the early republic because they did not have any real deposits, nor did they invest money. Instead, they were simply a mechanism to issue credit to landowners and create a circulation medium that freed individuals from being tied to a specific merchant through debt. The same breaking of ties occurred in the Chesapeake with the emergence of the Scottish factor system. Previously, small planters relied on big planters to act as intermediaries with British merchants. The Scottish factors shattered these ties by dealing directly with the small planters in Virginia and then marketing their tobacco with their own companies in Great Britain.

All of these changes brought a high psychological cost for colonial Americans. Many clung to their traditional ideals and values even as they seemed to practice a different reality. By the 1750s and 1760s the strain must have been incredible. Somehow and in some way, something would have to give—some sort of eruption was bound to take place.

Resistance to Imperial Regulation

All of the accumulated social, economic, and cultural tension did not make the American Revolution inevitable. Yes, some seismic shift in politics was bound to occur. But the cataclysm did not have to render the British Empire asunder. The circumstances that created a new nation in North America were contingent on a host of individuals on both sides of the Atlantic. The course of events that led to American independence operated not only against the turbulent backdrop of mid-eighteenth-century colonial America, but also two crucial developments within Great Britain. The first was the ascension of George III as king of England; the second was the imperial crisis. Together these developments would bring about the unimaginable— resistance that would lead to a rebellion that would become a revolution.

All Britons—whether in England or North America—were excited when the young George III came to the throne. Bostonians held a public celebration on hearing the news of his ascension in 1760. "A vast Concourse of People of all Ranks" listened to a proclamation read from the courthouse attesting the colony's loyalty to the new monarch and responded with three deafening huzzahs to the concluding "God save the king!"[15] George III, grandson of George II, was British to the core. The previous two Georges, who had come from Hanover, had been German in their orientation. This king never set out to usurp anyone's liberty—least of all his colonial subjects. He merely hoped to fulfill his constitutional responsibility as a patriot king. He therefore decided that he should select his own chief minister to run the government. This plan, however, ran afoul of Parliament, which had for fifty years selected the government's ministry. The result was that between 1760 and 1770 there would be seven different ministries and a lack of consistent policy for the colonies and the British empire. Ordinarily, this upheaval would have had a minimal impact on the colonies. However, simultaneously Great Britain engaged in an effort to reorganize its unordered overseas possessions. Given the explosive conditions in the colonies, the result was devastating to the British Empire.

In 1760 the British Empire in North America was in a mess. Anglo-American forces had driven the French out of Canada, but the war had shown serious weaknesses. Individual colonies had been reluctant to pay their share of wartime expenses, and could be persuaded to ante up only when the British government promised to repay the debt incurred by the colonial governments. The colonial militias had often balked at military plans that took them away from their home colonies, and they were usually unreliable in battle. Moreover, smuggling was rampant within the colonies—merchants even traded with the enemy when they could. A survey of the customs collection in 1760 revealed that, regardless of import duties that should have generated revenue, the effort to collect any customs was costing more than what was being brought in. British officers in North America looked around them and recognized that the colonists were the most prosperous people in the world, with lush fields and a light tax burden. Something had to change.

The first thing to be done was to stop violations of the customs laws. Even before the war was over, the British revamped the customs collection, making it more effective. Rather than relying only on customs officials in port to enforce trade regulations, the British authorized the Royal Navy to intercept ships at sea that were suspected of smuggling. Colonial governments used writs of assistance to allow customs collectors to search suspected smuggling vessels more quickly, instead of depending on a specific search warrant that delayed action until the smuggled goods had been unloaded and safely hidden ashore. New regulations protected government officials from civil suit. Previously, merchants might sue customs agents for false seizures, an action that discouraged zealous enforcement of the law because of potential loss through personal liability. The British also reorganized the court system with new vice-admiralty courts, appointing judges with independent salaries to try maritime and customs cases, and reinvigorated the local vice-admiralty courts. In 1764 the British established a vice-admiralty court for all of North America in Halifax, Nova Scotia. In 1768, four district vice-admiralty courts were created in Halifax, Boston, Philadelphia, and Charleston. Before these changes a customs case could be tried before either a local vice-admiralty court or a civil court. Both reflected the interests of the local merchants, most of whom were involved in illicit trade. Under such circumstances, with a vice-admiralty judge partial to the merchants, or a jury in a civil court packed with neighbors and relatives of the smugglers, it was difficult to gain a judgment in favor of the crown. Facing this bias, it was far easier for the customs official to take a bribe and look the other way. Under the new system customs officials and naval officers, who earned money when a vessel was condemned, were encouraged to do their jobs properly. Some colonists, such as James Otis in his famous oration at a trial over writs of assistance, might argue that these measures threatened their liberty, but from a law enforcement point of view they were necessary to protect the sanctity of the law and ensure revenue from customs collection.

With a huge addition of French possessions in North America came new challenges. The colonists wanted the territory west of the Appalachians. But now the Native Americans in that area were also the king's subjects. In an effort to avoid further conflict and to try to guide patterns of settlement the king issued the Proclamation of 1763, which temporarily prevented British colonists from settling west of the Appalachians. The edict made it clear that it was "just and reasonable, and essential to our [the king's] Interests and the Security of our Colonies" that the "Indians with whom We are connected, and who live under our Protection, should not be molested or disturbed" in their own territory. Moreover, since there had been "great Frauds and Abuses" in "purchasing Lands of the Indians, to the great Prejudice of our Interest, and to the great Dissatisfaction of the said Indians" all such purchases were to be halted.[16] The king thereby put a hold on the speculative plans of men like Franklin and Washington who sought title to thousands of acres in the Ohio River Valley. In addition the proclamation set up the colonies of East and West Florida, created the colony of Quebec, and enlarged Nova Scotia. The hope was to encourage settlement of these areas before pushing farther west.

Parliament addressed another set of problems with the Currency Act of 1764. Several colonies had issued paper currency. From the British perspective this action created difficulties because the colonial currencies were highly inflationary. A note printed in Virginia was not the equal to a note printed in Great Britain. But colonists would try to use these notes to pay their debts and thereby defraud British merchants. The solution to the British was obvious—stop printing colonial notes. A similar law prohibiting the New England colonies from printing notes had been passed in 1751. The 1764 law extended the restriction to all the colonies. The problem from the colonial perspective was that there was not enough hard cash—gold and silver—in the colonies. What little hard coin the colonists possessed was usually shipped to Great Britain to service the increasing colonial debt. Without a paper currency the exchange of goods would be difficult if not impossible and the economy would suffer. Complicating matters was the passage of two parliamentary taxes that would have to be paid with hard currency.

The British government also decided to maintain a ten-thousand-man army in North America. This action, like most British measures in the 1760s and 1770s, made sense. The new colony of Quebec had 60,000 French Catholics of dubious loyalty. The French, who maintained a presence in the West Indies, might renew war at any time. Moreover, despite the king's claim of sovereignty over Native Americans west of the Appalachians, Pontiac's rebellion demonstrated how easily an expensive conflict could

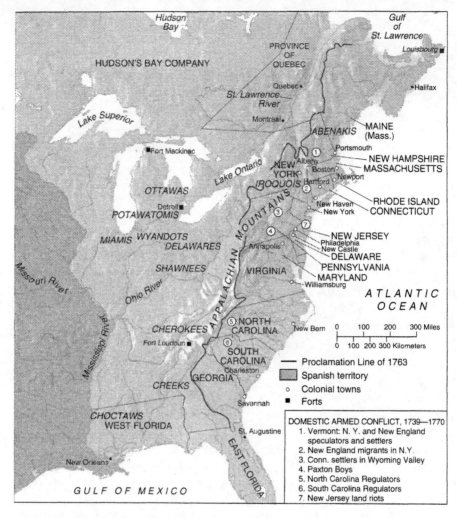

Hudson Bay

Gulf of St. Lawrence

PROVINCE OF QUEBEC

Louisbourg ■

HUDSON'S BAY COMPANY

Quebec •

•Halifax

St. Lawrence River

Lake Superior

Montreal •

MAINE (Mass.)

ABENAKIS

■Fort Mackinac

Portsmouth

Albany

NEW HAMPSHIRE

Lake Ontario

NEW YORK

Boston

MASSACHUSETTS

Hartford

Newport

IROQUOIS

OTTAWAS

Detroit■

New Haven

RHODE ISLAND

POTAWATOMIS

New York

CONNECTICUT

MIAMIS WYANDOTS

NEW JERSEY

DELAWARES

Annapolis

Philadelphia

New Castle

DELAWARE

SHAWNEES

PENNSYLVANIA

VIRGINIA

MARYLAND

Missouri River

Williamsburg

Ohio River

ATLANTIC OCEAN

CHEROKEES

NORTH CAROLINA

New Bern

0   100   200   300 Miles

Fort Loudoun ■

0   100 200 300 Kilometers

SOUTH CAROLINA

Mississippi River

Charleston

GEORGIA

—— Proclamation Line of 1763

CREEKS

Spanish territory

Savannah

o   Colonial towns

CHOCTAWS

■   Forts

WEST FLORIDA

St. Augustine

DOMESTIC ARMED CONFLICT, 1739—1770
1. Vermont: N. Y. and New England
   speculators and settlers
2. New England migrants in N.Y.
3. Conn. settlers in Wyoming Valley
4. Paxton Boys
5. North Carolina Regulators
6. South Carolina Regulators
7. New Jersey land riots

New Orleans •

EAST FLORIDA

GULF OF MEXICO

MAP 1–1   Colonial America in 1763 British North America was divided into a variety of colonies that felt greater allegiance to Great Britain than each other. In order to protect Native American subjects from incursions west of the Appalachian Mountains the king issued the Proclamation of 1763, prohibiting European Americans from settling west of the mountains and encouraging settlement of Florida and Nova Scotia. The colonies also experienced discord over conflicting land claims and issues of law and order on the frontier.

erupt on the frontier. There were thus ample military reasons for this army—which should have been welcomed by colonial Americans needing protection. Moreover, if there were any ungrateful colonists, the presence of the army might persuade them not to step out of line.

The British were concerned with the cost of this army. After all, the nation was saddled with a huge national debt—£135 million. Moreover, after the Seven Years' War, British landowners were screaming for tax relief. The army would cost somewhere between £200,000 and £300,000. The British, under the ministry of George Grenville, therefore decided to have the colonists pay some of the cost for the army. On May 3, 1765, Parliament passed the Quartering Act, which stated that the colony in which troops were stationed had to find billeting for the soldiers in empty buildings or barracks. It also stipulated that the colony had to raise money to support the soldiers. Benjamin Franklin had helped draw up this legislation, which he hoped would not be too offensive as it did not compel anyone to take troops into their own homes and it left the decision on raising of revenue within the colonies themselves. Most colonies complied with the Quartering Act. New York hesitated to do so, but when Parliament threatened to disallow any law passed by the New York assembly, the colony relented and provided some money for the soldiers within its borders.

Grenville believed that more money would be needed to support the army and therefore wanted Parliament to pass legislation to raise about £100,000 within the colonies. These taxes were not intended to pay the British debt. In fact, the total would not put even a dent in the £6 million in interest Great Britain paid each year. Nor were the taxes intended to pay for all of the army; the rest of the money would come from the hard-pressed British treasury. Grenville's ministry passed two colonial taxes. The first was a further reorganizing of the colonial customs collection in the Sugar Act of 1764. It actually lowered the duty on molasses—a huge North American import from the West Indies—from six pence per gallon to three pence per gallon with the idea that more rigorous enforcement and the lower duty would encourage legal trade and therefore increase revenue. Eight colonial assemblies protested the law, claiming that it created economic hardship, but resistance was minimal.

The second piece of legislation, the Stamp Act (1765), incited much greater opposition. In what may have been a cynical effort to placate colonial concerns, Grenville gave the colonists a year to come up with their own tax. He did not expect them to do so: Experience had shown that the colonists were too divided and too selfish to act willingly on their own. Grenville wrote the law to be as innocuous as possible. Britain already had a stamp act, and several colonies had passed such measures in the past. The law created a small fee for every legal document, newspaper, and almanac, and most paper used in the colonies. To make the law more acceptable, the agents who distributed the stamps would be local officials. Benjamin

Franklin, in London at the time and always seeking an opportunity to obtain and dispense patronage, managed to get his political ally John Hughes appointed as stamp agent. He did not do his friend a favor.

The Stamp Act created an uproar. Although the law did not establish a truly burdensome tax, the fact that it had to be paid in specie in the midst of the postwar recession made it appear a hardship. If before the Stamp Act there had been some complaints and protests over new imperial regulations, resistance now erupted from one end of the colonies to the other. The colonial reaction can be examined in three areas: the constitutional argument; boycott and organization; and mob action.

The constitutional argument appeared in pamphlets, resolves, and petitions. These protests always included a strong statement of loyalty to the king and were cast in terms of the British Constitution. The issue at this point—and for much of the next decade—was not independence or a separate American identity. Instead, colonists struggled to understand and define the constitutional arrangement between the North American colonies and Great Britain. Because, like the rest of the British Constitution, there was no one legal document outlining that arrangement, its exact nature remained vague. During the resistance to the imperial measures before 1775, colonial Americans were groping and searching for a clear way to define their relationship with Parliament and Great Britain. It is within this context that distinctions between internal and external taxation and virtual and actual representation need to be understood. Some colonists suggested that Parliament could pass laws to regulate the trade of the empire (external taxation), but they believed that Parliament had no right to pass laws solely for the purposes of raising revenue within the colonies (internal taxation). When Parliament passed the Townshend Duties, this position was quickly abandoned. Writers like Daniel Dulany disputed the validity of Parliament's concept of virtual representation that held that all Britons, whether they voted or not, were represented by a Parliament that guarded the single interest of the British people. Dulany insisted on the idea of actual representation, which held that representatives must be tied to those who voted for them. Virtual representation did not work, Dulany argued, because the legislators could pass laws or taxes that had no impact on them personally. As the resolves passed by the Virginia House of Burgesses on May 30, 1765, explained, the "Taxation of the People by themselves, or by Persons chosen by themselves to represent them" was "the distinguishing Characteristick of *British* Freedom."[17] Parliament remained unconvinced by these arguments, and even when it repealed the Stamp Act in 1766, it passed a Declaratory Act that stated that Parliament had the right to legislate for the colonies "in all cases whatsoever."[18]

It takes more than words, however, to effectively resist a law. Colonists therefore began to organize. On one level, colonists pursued official channels. Several colonial assemblies, as in Virginia, passed resolutions against the Stamp Act. To further coordinate resistance, representatives from nine colonies attended a Stamp Act Congress in New York in October 1765. They agreed on a strongly worded petition that, while duly deferential to the king, also asserted that Parliament did not have a right to raise taxes within the colonies. Echoing the resolutions of the Virginia House of Burgesses, the Stamp Act Congress explained to the king "That it is inseparably essential to the freedom of a people, and the undoubted right of Englishmen, that no taxes should be imposed on them, but with their own consent, given personally, or by their representatives."[19]

There was also a more grassroots movement headed by local committees called the Sons of Liberty. These extralegal associations pushed resistance further by instituting a nonimportation movement in an effort to pressure Great Britain into relenting on the issue of taxation. In community after community the Sons of Liberty, usually composed of leading men but often including some men further down in society, appeared, corresponded with each other to coordinate activities, and held mass meetings. They also contacted the men who had been appointed stamp agents and insisted that they resign. It was in these small groups of determined committees that the resistance movement really coalesced and large numbers of colonial Americans became politicized.

All the petitions and resolutions passed by assemblies and the Stamp Act Congress, and all of the grassroots organization of committee meetings would have been meaningless without some agent of forceful action. Without the mob shouting, screaming, threatening, and intimidating, the resistance movement to the Stamp Act would have gone nowhere. The rioting began in Boston on August 14, 1765, when a crowd paraded outside of stamp distributor Andrew Oliver's house with an effigy and destroyed some of his property along the waterfront. Oliver got the message and resigned his stamp appointment. Twelve days later another mob attacked and gutted the house of Lieutenant Governor Thomas Hutchinson in an action that many colonial leaders found disturbing. The Sons of Liberty—at this time they were called the Loyal Nine in Boston—quickly recognized that although they needed the crowd in the street, they also had to manage a delicate balancing act to prevent excessive mob action. Newspapers attempted to provide guidelines for popular behavior in the streets, urging that "No innocent Person . . . should receive the least Injury" and that crowd leaders needed "to keep an undisciplined irregular Multitude from running into mischievous Extravagancies."[20] People in towns and communities throughout the colonies imitated the popular action in Boston, with the Sons of Liberty sometimes effectively restraining the mob and sometimes losing control. Stamp agents in colony after colony promised not to distribute the stamps. Crowds closed courts and upheld the nonimportation movement. Anyone who stood in the way of these measures found themselves hounded by the people in the street. By the time the Stamp Act was supposed to take effect on November 1, 1765, the tax that the British believed was self-enforceable had become unenforceable.

It is difficult to gauge the effectiveness of this mass movement on the British. Merchants in England who had North American accounts called for some relief. What was particularly galling was that the nonimportation movement allowed merchants within the colonies to empty overstocked warehouses and many colonial Americans used the opportunity of the Stamp Act upheaval to suspend debt payment. Although the hard-pressed British merchant community had some impact on repeal, it was really a change in the ministry of the British government that mattered most. In one of the many shifts in administration during the first ten years of the reign of George III, Grenville lost parliamentary support (not on the basis of issues related to colonial policy) and was replaced by a group of politicians headed by Lord Rockingham, who had all along thought that taxing the colonies was a bad idea. In March 1766, Parliament therefore repealed the Stamp Act, while still asserting its sovereignty in the Declaratory Act. From the colonial point of view the petitions and protests had worked. In June 1766, colonists celebrated both the repeal of the Stamp Act and the king's birthday in an outburst of enthusiasm and British patriotism.

The Rockingham administration did not have much support from George III and was quickly replaced by a new ministry under William Pitt, now Lord Chatham. Chatham, who had led the country during the Seven Years' War, was not well, and the government was left to drift. In these circumstances the Chancellor of the Exchequer, Charles Townshend, decided to again raise revenue from the colonies. Expenses for the North American army had far outpaced earlier estimates, running to as much as £700,000 a year. But Townshend also wanted to use this revenue from additional duties on lead, paint, glass, paper, and tea to support the civil administration in the colonies and thereby limit the influence of the colonial assemblies on the governor and other royal officials. Parliament passed the Townshend Duties in 1767, initiating another round of struggle in the imperial debate. Although colonists followed the same pattern of resistance that had emerged in the Stamp Act controversy with constitutional arguments, organizational efforts by the Sons of Liberty, and by using mob action, the opposition was less effective. Boston remained a hotbed of activity with tarring and feathering of customs agents and several mob confrontations. Elsewhere the result was more mixed. New England and New York initiated a nonimportation agreement in 1768. Most of the rest of the colonies followed with either a nonconsumption or a nonimportation movement in 1769. But the effort was poorly coordinated, with some groups limiting the banned goods to different categories. By 1770, several localities began to defect from the movement, most notably in New York where merchants, with their warehouses finally empty, abandoned nonimportation.

The situation, however, remained explosive. In January there was a large riot in New York City between British soldiers and the local citizenry that capped an animosity that had been building for several years. This conflict was more over local labor conditions and competition for jobs than over larger constitutional issues. Off-duty soldiers obtained employment in the city at the expense of ordinary New Yorkers. Much of this conflict had centered around what was originally a flagpole erected to celebrate the king's birthday and the repeal of the Stamp Act in 1766, but by 1770 the flagstaff had come to be called a liberty pole and had been repeatedly attacked by British soldiers. No one died in this riot. In Boston, similar tensions between soldiers and civilians over jobs that same winter led to a greater tragedy. After several days of intermittent brawling between the two sides, a crowd collected outside the custom's office on King Street on the night of March 5. Words were exchanged between the crowd and a British sentry. A handful of other soldiers arrived and the angry Bostonians started tossing snowballs, some of which may have contained rocks or chunks of ice. In the dark and impassioned moment the soldiers fired into the crowd, killing four and mortally wounding another. This "massacre" has become etched into American popular memory because of a Paul Revere print depicting a group of sinister redcoats, under a building labeled "Butcher's Hall," firing into an innocent-looking crowd. At the time, however, this riot had little impact on the larger imperial controversy.

The British government, unaware of the violence in Boston, defused the situation in 1770. A stable government finally emerged in Great Britain under the leadership of Lord Frederick North. Recognizing the failure of the Townshend Duties, and the damage done to the economy by the imperial crisis, North had the duties repealed, retaining the tax on tea as a symbolic gesture of parliamentary supremacy. The colonists for the most part accepted this concession and did not pursue nonimportation and resistance further.

Although there were some incidents in the colonies between 1770 and 1773, imperial relations followed a less confrontational path during these years. In 1773, however, the British Parliament passed another piece

FIGURE 1–4   Boston Massacre Paul Revere's 1770 print, depicting a group of sinister redcoats firing into an innocent crowd, has come to represent the colonial resistance movement against British imperial measures. But the incident had little immediate impact outside of Boston with the repeal of most of the Townshend Duties and the temporary easing of tensions between the colonies and the British government.

of legislation that would bring the imperial crisis to a head. In 1773 a major financial panic pushed the British East India Company to the brink of bankruptcy. Had this company failed it would have devastated the entire national economy and threatened the British hold on India. Parliament sought a creative means to save the company by passing the Tea Act. This measure would allow the British East India Company to export tea directly to the colonies. Previously, all tea had been sent to Great Britain, where it was taxed, and then reshipped to the colonies where it was taxed again under the Townshend Duties. By not collecting the tax in Great Britain the price of tea would be lowered in the colonies. That lower price would drive smugglers out of business and increase revenues for the East India Company and ensure its continued financial success. Moreover, colonists would eagerly purchase legally imported and taxed tea for the lower price and thus comply with the Townshend Duties and accept, through their actions, supremacy of Parliament.

The plan was too clever by half. Too many colonists had been involved in resisting imperial regulation for too long. Great Britain had seemed willing to bend to this opposition for almost a decade. Many colonists, perhaps encouraged by those merchants who would lose business as a result of the Tea Act, saw this law as another assault on their liberty and another violation of the British constitution. In port after port colonists held mass meetings that convinced officials to turn back the tea before it was unloaded. In Boston, however, Governor Hutchinson refused to allow the tea ships to leave port, insisting that it was his duty as royal governor to uphold the law. On the night of December 16, 1773, a huge public meeting at the Old South Church broke up when Sam Adams proclaimed that there was nothing more to do to save the country. Immediately, a group of Bostonians dressed as "Mohawks" appeared and marched to the docks, where they carefully dumped £10,000 worth of tea into the harbor.

This act of resistance was too much for the British government to bear. In the beginning of 1774 Parliament passed the Coercive Acts to punish Boston and Massachusetts for "dangerous commotions and insurrections."[21] The Boston Port Bill closed Boston to all shipping until the destroyed tea was paid for. The Massachusetts Government Act changed the colony's charter, establishing greater royal control and limiting town meetings to once a year. The Administration of Justice Act allowed the British government to move trials to Great Britain or another colony if officials believed that the local jury was so biased that the suspect was bound to be acquitted regardless of the evidence (which had happened repeatedly). There was also a new Quartering Act that strengthened the earlier law by insisting that troops be billeted close to where they were to be stationed. At about the same time the British government passed the Quebec Act. Although many Americans saw this law as a part of the Coercive Acts, it was not intended to be so. Colonial Americans objected to the measure because it treated the French Catholics in Canada with some leniency, set up a royal colony at Quebec, and ceded much of the Ohio River Valley to that colony.

The people of Massachusetts were not about to back down in this confrontation, and many colonists throughout North America seemed to support them. Again the machinery of resistance was put into motion. In September 1774 a Continental Congress met in Philadelphia to discuss the crisis. This Congress petitioned the king, asking him to intercede, protect

American liberty, and remove the Coercive Acts. It also adopted resolutions, based on the Suffolk Resolves sent from Massachusetts, that set up a timetable for nonimportation of British goods and then nonexportation to Great Britain. Congress created a "Continental Association" to obtain a redress of grievances "which threaten destruction to the lives, liberty, and property of his majesty's subjects, in North-America."[22] Congress also endorsed efforts to prepare some sort of defense of the colonies in case hostilities broke out. To effect these measures many communities organized Committees of Correspondence and Committees of Safety. In Massachusetts and elsewhere the militia began to train and special units appeared, calling themselves minutemen, to respond to emergencies.

The resistance movement had gotten out of hand. All of the pent-up strains within colonial society could no longer be hidden. But the colonists did not blame themselves for their problems. Instead, they projected their anxieties on an external force—the British imperial authorities. If colonial Americans were moving to a new level of resistance, the British were also preparing for a showdown. The new governor of Massachusetts, General Thomas Gage, sent an expeditionary force on the night of April 18 into the countryside to capture opposition leaders and to seize military supplies. On April 19 the British fought with colonial militia at Lexington and Concord. The idea had been to demonstrate the superiority of the British Army and the futility of resistance. Instead, this action began the Revolutionary War.

Endnotes

1. Benjamin Franklin, *Autobiography and Other Writings,* Kenneth Silverman, ed., (New York: Penguin, 1986), 217.
2. Leonard W. Labaree, et al., eds., *The Papers of Benjamin Franklin,* 1– vols. (New Haven: Yale University Press, 1959–), 15: 160–61.
3. Quoted in Gordon S. Wood, *The Radicalism of the American Revolution* (New York: Alfred A. Knopf, 1992), 29.
4. Quoted in Alfred F. Young, *The Shoemaker and The Tea Party: Memory and the American Revolution* (Boston: Beacon, 1999), 3–4.
5. Quoted in Wood, *The Radicalism of the American Revolution,* 21.
6. William Shakespeare, *Troilus and Cressida,* Act I, Sc. 3.
7. J. Hector St. John de Crèvecoeur, *Letters From an American Farmer and Sketches of Eighteenth-Century America,* Albert E. Stone, ed. (New York: Penguin, 1981), 69.
8. Crèvecoeur, *Letters From an American Farmer and Sketches of Eighteenth-Century America,* 411–12. E. P. Thomson was one of the most noted English historians of the twentieth century. He articulated the idea of the moral economy in "The Moral Economy of the English Crowd in the Eighteenth Century," *Past and Present,* 50 (Feb. 1971), 76–136.
9. Crèvecoeur, *Letters From an American Farmer and Sketches of Eighteenth-Century America,* 90–105.

10. Crèvecoeur, *Letters From an American Farmer and Sketches of Eighteenth-Century America,* 67, 80, 89–90.
11. Quoted in Rachel N. Klein, *Unification of a Slave State: The Rise of the Planter Class in the South Carolina Backcountry, 1760–1808* (Chapel Hill: University of North Carolina Press, 1990), 56, 50–51.
12. Hermon Husbands, *A Fan for Fanning, and a Touchstone to Tryon, Containing an Account of the Rise and Progress of the So Much Talked of North-Carolina Regulation . . .* (Boston: [D. Kneeland], 1771), vi, 20.
13. Quoted in Gary B. Nash, *The Urban Crucible: Social Change, Political Consciousness, and the Origins of the American Revolution* (Cambridge: Harvard University Press, 1979), 256.
14. W. W. Abbot and Dorothy Twohig, et al., eds., *The Papers of George Washington: Colonial Series,* 10 vols. (Charlottesville: University of Virginia Press, 1983–1995), 7: 206. See also Charles Royster, *The Fabulous History of the Dismal Swamp Company: A Story of George Washington's Times* (New York: Random House, 1999), 62.
15. Quoted in Richard L. Bushman, *King and People in Provincial Massachusetts* (Chapel Hill: University of North Carolina Press, 1985), 15.
16. The Royal Proclamation, Oct. 7, 1763, The Avalon Project at Yale Law School, www.yale.edu/lawweb/avalon/proc1763.htm.
17. John Pendleton Kennedy, ed., *Journals of the House of Burgesses of Virginia, 1761–1765* (Richmond: Virginia State Library, 1907), 360.
18. The Declaratory Act, Mar. 18, 1766, The Avalon Project at Yale Law School, www.yale.edu/lawweb/avalon/amerrev/parliament/declaratory_act_1766.htm.
19. Resolutions of the Stamp Act Congress, Oct. 19, 1765, The Avalon Project at Yale Law School, www.yale.edu/lawweb/avalon/resolu65.htm.
20. Quoted in Pauline Maier, *From Resistance to Revolution: Colonial Radicals and the Development of American Opposition to Britain, 1765–1776* (New York: Random House, 1972), 66.
21. The Boston Port Act, Mar. 31, 1774, The Avalon Project at Yale Law School, www.yale.edu/lawweb/avalon/amerrev/parliament/boston_port_act.htm.
22. Continental Congress, The Articles of Association, Oct. 20, 1774, The Avalon Project at Yale Law School, www.yale.edu/lawweb/avalon/contcong/10-20-74.htm.

CHAPTER 2

Independence

✪

Virtue and Corruption

No one had wanted war. And throughout the resistance movement (1764–1775) almost no one anticipated independence. From the British perspective, the efforts at imperial regulation had made sense. Neither the king, nor his ministers, nor Parliament, nor the British people had set out to usurp American liberty. From the colonial perspective, all the resistance leaders had done was to defend the British Constitution. Neither the colonial leaders, nor the Sons of Liberty, nor even the howling people in the street, had planned to start a rebellion. Yet somehow the crisis had exploded into a revolution. The key to comprehending these developments resides in understanding how the ideology of republicanism interacted with the imperial crisis and with the social and economic developments of the mid-eighteenth century. Many Americans entered the Revolutionary War with great expectations inspired by republican ideology and the belief that they were defending liberty. The war lasted eight long years and both the British and the revolutionary Americans experienced victories and defeats that pushed them to their limits. The war also divided American society and was more complex than we ordinarily expect, with revolutionaries and loyalists seeking to protect liberty as they understood it. Many Americans fought for ideological reasons, but others were more mercenary. The final peace was a great triumph for the cause of independence even as the war marked an important step away from the hierarchical and single-interest world of the eighteenth century and the dawning of a more egalitarian, multi-interest, and capitalist world of the nineteenth century.

Most Anglo-Americans shared a belief in republicanism—the idea that the government should protect the *res publica* (public thing) or common good. Based in the corporate notion of society that there was a single, clearly identified interest for all members of the polity, republicanism grew out of the seventeenth century's political upheaval in England and the flowering of the Enlightenment in the eighteenth century. The English Civil Wars of the 1640s and the Glorious Revolution of 1688–89 had established a series of compromises between Parliament and the crown that promised to protect the rights of Englishmen and insured against an absolute monarchy. In the eighteenth century these compromises were misunderstood and recast into an Enlightenment mold that emphasized the balance that the philosophes believed inherent in nature and reason. Political thinkers argued that there were three basic elements in the political world: monarchy (the one), aristocracy (the few), and democracy (the many). Left on their own, each could degenerate into a form that did not protect the commonwealth. Monarchy could degenerate into tyranny, aristocracy into oligarchy, and democracy into mobocracy or anarchy. The way to avoid any of these three negative developments, according to Montesquieu's *Spirit of the Laws* (1748), was to balance each of these forms against each other. The English Constitution appeared to do just that with the king, the House of Lords, and the House of Commons. Similarly, the colonial governments had followed the English model with governors, councils, and assemblies. The fact that this perception of the English Constitution and the colonial governments did not reflect reality—one would be hard put to claim that the House of Commons really represented the people—is less important than the fact that all of Enlightened Europe and the Enlightened leaders in the colonies believed that Anglo-Americans had achieved this wonderful balance in their governments.

Whereas the roots of the republicanism of the American Revolution centered on this idealized vision the English Constitution, republicanism also encompassed a critique of the functioning government developed in the eighteenth century by a group of coffeehouse English radicals who are often called the "Real" or "True" Whigs. The Whig political party had emerged in the seventeenth century as defenders of the English Constitution and Protestant succession. (Supporters of the American Revolution would call themselves whigs to identify with this political tradition). The True Whigs believed that under the leadership of men like Sir Robert Walpole, the regular Whig party had been led astray and the balance of the English Constitution had been tipped away from the people and into the hands of a grasping "robinocracy" (named after Walpole). These men believed that the more power government had, the less liberty there was for the people.

As True Whig Thomas Gordon explained in *Cato's Letters*, "Whatever is good for the People"—their liberty—"is bad for their Governors; and what is good for the Governors"—their power—"is pernicious to the People."[1] Under Walpole and the regular Whigs, government had become too strong and the liberty of the people was threatened. The True Whigs argued that the government was corrupt because it put the interests of a few individuals over the interest of the entire people. Those individuals had become enticed by luxury, which they defined as superfluous consumer items that sapped a person's inner strength, and power. The way to counter this corruption was through civic virtue—the willingness to put aside your own personal interest for the common good.

Enlightened thinkers, including the True Whigs, turned to the classics to understand patterns of human behavior and to learn the laws of history. They used pseudonyms from antiquity, like Cato, to warn against the threat to the public welfare. They also cited the example of Cincinnatus to highlight their concept of virtue. Cincinnatus was the early Roman warrior who left his plow to destroy Rome's enemies. After his victories Cincinnatus refused the crown and, in an act of true virtue, returned to his plow. Eighteenth-century philosophes also saw the history of nations as operating in cycles. On the basis of the study of Greece and Rome, all nations followed a predictable path. Nations began as youthful republics and with a virtuous citizenry they energetically expanded. On maturity, the state gained too much power and the republic gave way to monarchy and empire. The empire might thrive for a while, but at the expense of the liberty of the people. Corruption and luxury seeped in, often from the Near East, and the empire began to age and decay. Ultimately, like Athens and like Rome, the empire fell and all that was left of the greatness and splendor were ruins and desolation.

It is against the backdrop of this republicanism that we must understand the resistance to imperial regulation. Colonial Americans opposed imperial regulation less for the burdens it imposed and more because it appeared to be the entering wedge of corruption and the loss of liberty. Having read the True Whig analysis of politics and history, which had a special appeal for a provincial mind that found comfort in the idea that those in the metropolitan center were somehow not as virtuous as those in the countryside, the whole experience of the 1760s and 1770s could be seen as an effort to corrupt American society. The decision to station troops in North America to protect the colonies became an attempt to create a standing army, which from the republican perspective was an instrument of tyranny. Logical efforts to streamline and reform a tainted court system became a mechanism to rob the people of the jury trial and annul an important check on unbridled government power. The Stamp

Act may not have been a heavy burden, but its pervasiveness and its self-enforceable nature made it inimical. The fact that local officials were supposed to serve as stamp agents only demonstrated the effort to corrupt colonial Americans. The Townshend Duties not only represented a tax to raise revenue, they also would free government officials from the representatives of the people, thus upsetting the balance within government. The Tea Act was hateful even if it lowered the price of tea because it granted a monopoly, allowing preference to the merchants with contracts with the East India Company at the expense of all others. The passage of the Coercive Acts, measures that Parliament believed were justified by colonial insolence and destruction of property, seemed to remove the last veil from what had been the hidden British intentions to corrupt American society and destroy liberty through the naked flexing of metropolitan power.

The ideology of republicanism, with its reference to the classics and the writings of the Enlightenment, explains part, but not all of the appeal of the resistance movement. Republicanism worked in tandem and fed on a strain of egalitarianism among common folk that ran throughout Anglo-American history. This egalitarianism emerged during the English Civil Wars in the calls for an equal distribution of wealth that came from such radical groups as the Levellers and the Diggers. It also appeared in the strong tradition of rioting that protected the moral economy and cast the people in the street as the ultimate guardians of the community if the natural leaders of society failed in their paternalistic obligations. It surfaced in the Pope Day processions and in a number of colonial land riots that pitted affluent speculators against poor settlers. Embedded within this egalitarianism were repeated expressions of antiauthoritarianism and a resentment of wealth that helps to explain some of the excesses of the prerevolutionary mob. High-minded attacks on corruption and luxury might strike a responsive chord among the colonial elite educated in the classics; in the street, resistance to imperial measures could be easily translated into a dislike for all distinctions and a reflection of a long-held resentment of wealth.

The nonimportation and nonconsumption agreements drawn up in opposition to various imperial regulations helped to join both the republicanism of the elite and the egalitarianism of the ordinary citizen. As early as 1766, Benjamin Franklin told Parliament that the "greatest part" of colonial imports were "superfluities" that were "mere articles of fashion, purchased and consumed, because the fashion in a respected country [Great Britain], but will now be detested and rejected."[2] From the point of view of elite republicans, "superfluities" and "articles of fashion" were unnecessary luxuries that colonists could do without. Nonimportation thus became an assertion of public virtue as well as a means of putting economic pressure on British merchants. From the point of view of the people in the street, "superfluities" and "articles of fashion" were symbols of wealth and prestige that they were now allowed to attack, giving vent to pent-up animosities. During the height of the Stamp Act opposition in New York, Robert R. Livingston, a resistance leader, confessed that "he that does not appear in Homespun, or at least a Turned Coat, is looked on with an Evil Eye," and liable to the fury of the mob. Nonimportation thus became a means to level society and compel even the most affluent colonial Americans to lay aside "all pride of Dress."[3]

These popular concerns pushed and prodded the republicanism of the elite, refashioning it into a more radical ideology. Republicanism, in other words, was not static. The exact means of achieving the ideal republic shifted over time. Before 1776, it was possible for Americans to envision a republic with a king; after 1776, revolutionary Americans came to believe that the public good could only be achieved without a monarch. A little more than a year after the first gunshots on Lexington Green, many Americans were ready to take an incredible imaginative leap. On July 4, 1776, the Second Continental Congress blamed the entire controversy on the king, overthrew the monarchy, and declared the United States of America an independent republic without a king.

As late as July 1775 most Americans retained faith in the monarchy and were convinced that the king had been led astray by corrupt advisors. Newspapers reporting the battles at Lexington and Concord referred to the "ministerial army" and did not blame the king for hostilities. On July 8, 1775, the Continental Congress, in part to mollify those Americans who still trusted George III, approved the Olive Branch Petition to England proclaiming their loyalty to the king and asking for a redress of grievances. The petition began with the assertion that the colonists were the king's "faithful subjects" and stated that his majesty's minsters had engaged in "delusive pretenses, fruitless terrors, and unavailing severities" in an effort to execute an "impolitic plan" to change the relationship between the colonies and the king. Congress beseeched George III to use his "royal authority and influence" to provide relief from these policies. The petition ended with another statement of loyalty, offering a "sincere and fervent prayer" that "your Majesty may enjoy a long and prosperous reign, and that your descendants may govern your dominions with honor to themselves and happiness to their subjects."[4]

The king refused to accept the petition. Instead, on August 25, 1775, he issued a proclamation declaring the colonies to be in a state of rebellion. If the colonists thought that the king was misled by his ministers, the king believed that his North American subjects were being "misled by dangerous and ill designing men" who convinced many to forget "the allegiance which they owe to the power that has protected and supported them." The result had been "various disorderly acts committed in disturbance of the publick peace, to the obstruction of lawful commerce, and to the oppression of our loyal subjects." In short, the colonies were in "an open and avowed rebellion."[5] The king viewed the colonists as disorderly children who needed a firm hand to be brought back into line. He believed that if he exhibited determination all colonial opposition would crumble.

This reaction stunned many Americans. Yet, it was not until the agile pen of Thomas Paine produced the pamphlet *Common Sense* that large numbers of Americans could turn away from the crown. Paine was an unlikely publicist. A recent arrival from England, where he had been trained as a corset maker, served as a customs officer, and had a failed marriage, Paine wrote his powerful essay in the closing months of 1775. Almost as soon as it was published in January 1776 it galvanized the American people. Within a year, over 100,000 copies of the pamphlet were printed and there were few individuals in the British North American colonies who did not read, or have read to them, its stirring words.

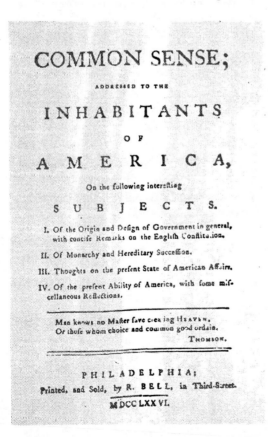

FIGURE 2–1 *Common Sense* Thomas Paine used plain language, Bible references, and the ideas of the Enlightenment to argue for independence in January 1776. This pamphlet sold over 100,000 copies within a year and helped to convince many Americans to renounce King George III.

In plain language, with ample biblical references, and informed by the ideas of the republican Enlightenment, Paine stated the case for American independence. Paine used simple and direct assertions to give the revolution a greater meaning: He proclaimed that "The cause of America is in a great measure the cause of all mankind" and declared that "the sun never shined on a cause of greater worth." For Paine the American rebellion was "not the affair of a city, a country, a province, or a kingdom, but of a continent." Paine, who grew up as a Quaker, used the Bible as a weapon to skewer the notion of the divine right of kings: "Monarchy is ranked in scripture as one of the sins of the Jews." Quoting the Book of Samuel, Paine highlighted God's disapproval of the Jewish monarchy. He concluded: "These portions of scripture are direct and positive. They admit of no equivocal construction. That the Almighty hath here entered his protest against monarchical government is true, or the scripture is false." Paine also simplified the ideas of the Enlightenment and put Locke's theory of the social contract into plain words by asserting that "Society is produced by our wants, and government by our wickedness." Man was a social being; government's only role was to offer protection. Paine wrote, "Society in every state is a blessing, but government even in its best state is but a necessary evil; in its worse state an intolerable one." In short, "Government, like dress, is the badge of lost innocence." Monarchies were a corrupt form of government and "the palaces of kings are built on the ruins of the bowers of paradise."[6]

Paine did more than deal with general principles. He also indicted the English Constitution, the king of England, and even hereditary aristocracy. Paine lambasted the previously vaunted balance of powers that had been the pride of every Anglo-American. Paine recognized that by doling out patronage and pensions the king engrossed an exorbitant amount of power. Paine observed that "the fate of Charles the First," who was executed in 1649 by the English people for abusing power, "hath only made kings more subtle—not more just." He would rather rely on the constitution of the people than the constitution of the government, to ensure liberty. For Paine, "There is something exceedingly ridiculous in the composition of monarchy." Paine wrote that the lineage of the kings of England was not "a very honorable one" as William the Conqueror was nothing more than "a French bastard landing with an armed banditti," who established himself king "against the consent of the natives." This claim to the throne "is in plain terms a very paltry rascally original.—It certainly hath no divinity in it." Building on this logic, Paine attacked all hereditary succession, which he called "an insult and imposition on posterity."[7] Admitting that it was fine to honor a man for rising to distinction in this world, Paine argued that whatever a person's achievements, his children and his children's children might not share the same qualities. By relying on hereditary succession, then, a society guaranteed that at some point in the future, power would fall into the hands of an incompetent, or an imbecile, or someone even worse.

Throughout the spring of 1776 more and more Americans came to the same conclusion—the war had to do more than register protest. It also had to lead to independence. So popular had Paine's pamphlet become that when whig printer Samuel Loudoun in New York announced his intention to print a rebuttal, he was hauled before a local committee to explain himself. When he went ahead and printed the response to Paine, a crowd of artisans broke into his shop, seized the controversial sheets of paper, and burned them in the city's common. By June several states, local committees, juries, and county meetings called for some action by the Continental Congress. In fact, scholars have found at least ninety documents declaring for independence before July 4.[8] In May, Congress opened up American ports to trade with all nations and asked that the colonies form their own governments, in essence acting as an independent country. On June 7, 1776, Richard Henry Lee of Virginia presented a resolution to the Continental Congress stating

> That these United Colonies are, and of right ought to be, free and independent States, that they are absolved from all allegiance to the British Crown, and that all political connection between them and the State of Great Britain is, and ought to be, totally dissolved.[9]

The congress delayed a vote on this drastic step, but appointed a committee of Thomas Jefferson, John Adams, Benjamin Franklin, Roger Sherman, and Robert R. Livingston to draw up a statement asserting independence. Most of the writing was left in the hands of Jefferson. The Continental Congress voted to declare independence on July 2, a day Adams mistakenly believed would be "celebrated by succeeding generations as the great Anniversary Festival" of the nation.[10] After debating and amending the final wording of the document for two days, the Continental Congress approved the document on July 4.

The Declaration of Independence was the consummation of a yearlong transition that redefined the idea of a republic; henceforth, Americans no longer required a king for their commonwealth. After a preamble stating the need to explain their action in breaking with Great Britain, the document asserted the equality of man. The claim that "all men are created equal" counteracted the ideal of hierarchy that had been so central to Anglo-American society and paved the way for a capitalist world of competing individuals on a theoretically level playing field. The Declaration of Independence then described conditions under which it was appropriate for a people to engage in revolution. It asserted that all governments were built on a social contract and that when a ruler broke his part of the bargain by threatening liberty, then the people had little choice but to rebel. Finally, the document applied this principle of revolution to the specific case by stating that "the history of the present King of Great Britain is a history of repeated usurpations, all having in direct object the establishment of an absolute Tyranny over these States" and went on to blame George III for the imperial conflict. The point-by-point charge that George III had purposefully set out to destroy American liberty does not reflect reality. The course of the events of the 1760s and 1770s was not directed by any single individual; it was contingent on a variety of factors and on the decisions of many men on both sides of the Atlantic. Yet the litany of these charges had an important rhetorical effect and helped to focus revolutionary Americans on a specific villain. Demonizing George III offered Americans an easy explanation for what had gone wrong.

Regardless of who Americans blamed, the more basic cause of the revolution lay within themselves. This deeper meaning of the conflict can be seen in the resistance movement and nonimportation of the 1760s and 1770s. Colonial Americans not only sought to put pressure on British merchants, they also sought to combat a corruption that was eating at American society from within. British imports had a nefarious influence on colonial Americans. In 1769 "Brutus" wrote an essay in support of nonimportation in opposition to the Townshend Duties, urging British Americans to "cheerfully resist the temptations of ease and luxury" of goods from Great Britain and argued that they should "consider our oppression as an opportunity given us by indulgent Providence to save ourselves."[11] When the Continental Congress drew up its blueprint for economic sanctions in 1774, it also stated that it would "discountenance and discourage every species of extravagance and dissipation."[12] As one minister explained to his congregation, Americans were being asked "to wash ourselves, to make ourselves clean." This purging was not just a matter of corruption from the outside; more important, it was the need "to put away the evil of our doings" and combat the corruption from within.[13]

Colonial Americans were distressed with the growing disjunction between their ideal vison of society—in which farmers sought competence, the aristocracy protected the single interest of society, and everyone shared the same corporate ideal—and a harsh reality of a competitive and increasingly capitalist world in which individuals pursued their own interest. Everything around them seemed to belie the older values. But rather than blaming themselves, the imperial crisis allowed them to focus on an external threat. If this evil could be stopped now, decay and corruption could be put off and the American people could reassert their old ideal and protect the commonwealth. As Tom Paine pointed out in *Common Sense,* they had to act immediately before it was too late and before Parliament and the king could lure them into the downward spiral that was already enveloping the British Empire.

The irony was that the American Revolution began with an effort to turn back the clock and combat not so much British tyranny as the beginnings of American capitalism. For the internal threat confronted by colonial Americans that they so urgently needed to address was their own consumerism, their own risk taking, and their own entering into the marketplace. However, rather than reestablishing a republic based on public virtue and a disinterested citizenry, the Revolution accelerated change, pushed the hands of the clock to move even faster, and ushered in a new world in which each individual pursued his own interest—a world that would allow the rise of American capitalism.

The Revolutionary War

In the early months of the war the spirit of self-sacrifice among Americans who supported resistance was high. After April 19, 1775, thousands of New England militia left their homes and farms and congregated around Boston, laying siege to the city. The British now knew that they were confronting a serious rebellion. Their casualties on the retreat from Concord stood as stark testimony to the tenacity of the resistance in New England: The British lost 273 men killed, wounded, or missing; the Americans, 95. Neither side made much of a move until mid June, when the British decided to occupy the heights on Charlestown Neck just to the north of Boston. The New England forces, which became the Continental army when the Continental Congress adopted it on June 14, 1775, moved first, setting up positions on Breed's Hill and Bunker Hill. General Thomas Gage hoped to drive what he saw as farmers and amateur soldiers from their positions in a frontal assault on June 17 that was supposed to demonstrate the invincibility of the British army. As General John Burgoyne later explained, "the respect, and control, and subordination of government . . . depends in a great measure upon the idea that trained troops are invincible against any numbers or any position of undisciplined rabble." After April 19, Burgoyne added, "this idea was a little in suspense."[14] In three successive waves British soldiers marched up Breed's Hill, taking devastating casualties. The untrained and entrenched Americans held on until the third assault, when, with the American troops running out of ammunition, the British captured the hill to claim a pyrrhic victory. The British sustained over a thousand casualties (226 dead and 828 wounded) compared to about 400 for the Americans defenders (140 killed and 271 wounded). This battle compelled the British to reevaluate their situation. Until this point the British believed they were confronting a local rebellion in which the army would act as the enforcer of law. This policing approach to the conflict had to be abandoned and a more conventional pattern of warfare followed. When the Continental army, under the newly appointed commander in chief George Washington, occupied Dorchester Heights to the south of Boston, Gage decided to leave Boston and begin a war of maneuver to cut off New England from the rest of the colonies.

At this point many Americans believed that the war was all but over. The great British army had to negotiate its way out of Boston; the British promised not to destroy the city if the Americans would let them embark unmolested. Animated by this success the rebellious Americans sought to export their revolution by invading Canada. Although they were initially successful, the campaign fell apart after a failed assault on Quebec on December 31, 1775, led by Benedict Arnold and Richard Montgomery in a snowstorm. Montgomery died in the attack and Arnold was wounded. Many Americans were captured. The Americans managed to keep enough men in the field to maintain a miserable siege for the rest of the winter. When British reenforcements arrived that spring, the ragtag remnants of the American army were lucky to escape into northern New York. Thousands of young Americans lay dead or imprisoned as a result of this misadventure.

Yet support for the republican revolution remained strong. In colony after colony the revolutionaries seized power and set up provincial governments. In Virginia the revolutionaries compelled Governor John Murray Dunmore to seek refuge in a British ship in the Chesapeake in June 1775, and defeated troops loyal to the governor and king at Great Bridge on December 9, 1775. Dunmore attacked Norfolk in January, but by July he gave up all hope of recapturing his province and returned to England. In North Carolina, Loyalist militia gathered a force of 1,500 men, mostly Scottish highlanders, who intended to rendezvous with British troops in February 1776. Armed mainly with broadswords, they were defeated by about one thousand whig militia with guns at the Battle of Moore's Creek on February 27, 1776. The whigs then raided other Loyalists on their farms, arresting about 800, suppressing opposition to the revolution. The British botched their effort to occupy Charleston when they failed to capture a fort on Sullivan's Island on June 28, 1776. Colonists also imprisoned some Loyalist officials, including William Franklin. In the meantime, Washington gathered a huge army in preparation to meet an invasion of New York from the sea.

The British attack came in the summer of 1776. Far from being defeated, the British had put together the greatest expeditionary force ever launched against North America. As many as thirty thousand British and Hessian troops landed on Staten Island during the summer, supported by scores of warships and over a hundred transports. This British superiority on land and sea made New York City, located on an island and surrounded by water on three sides, indefensible. Urged on by the Continental Congress and not yet fully aware of the limitations of his army and his own general-ship, Washington determined to hold on to New York at all costs. Unfortunately, the costs were very high. In a series of engagements from the end of August to the beginning of December 1776, General William Howe and his British army outmaneuvered and outfought the Continental army under Washington. During the summer Washington had as many as 25,000 men, but after losses at the Battle of Long Island, the Battle of Manhattan, the Battle of White Plains, the Battle of Harlem Heights, and the surrender of Forts Washington and Lee, he had been driven across New Jersey and into Pennsylvania and had under his command a few thousand disgruntled men, many of whose enlistments were about to run out.

Whatever his shortcomings in a set-piece battle, Washington learned important lessons from the campaign in identifying good ground to defend and in the art of slipping away just before disaster struck. He was also fortunate in his opponent. Howe had been sympathetic to the American cause while in Parliament and hoped to negotiate a settlement. He therefore did not press his advantage as hard as he could. In December Howe spread his forces across New Jersey, offered pardons to anyone who signed a loyalty oath, and prepared to await victory in the campaigning season in the spring. As far as Howe was concerned the war was just about over. The Americans would see the folly of their ways and once again become loyal subjects of the crown.

Washington, on the other hand, was not about to surrender. As Tom Paine explained in mid December in his first *American Crisis* essay, these were "the times that try men's souls" when "The summer soldier and the sunshine patriot" shrank "from the service of their country." Whereas "he that stands it *now*, deserves the love and thanks of man and woman." Paine, who had served with the army through its travails in 1776, wielded his mighty pen and reminded his readers that "Tyranny, like hell, is not easily conquered; yet we have this consolation with us, that the harder the conflict, the more glorious the triumph."[15] Washington was no summer soldier nor a sunshine patriot. He knew the situation was bleak and even wrote to his cousin to prepare for the worst. Washington confessed that he apprehended less "danger from Howes Army, as from the disaffection [loyalty to the crown] of

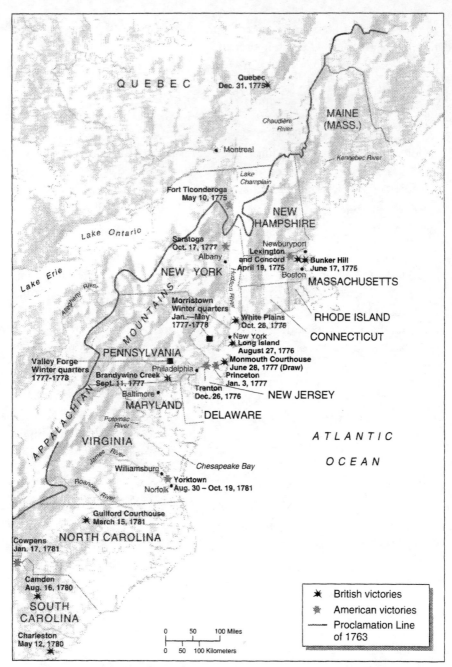

MAP 2–1   Battles of the Revolutionary War Fighting occurred throughout the colonies in the Revolutionary War. The war broke out in New England in 1775. The major action centered on the middle colonies from 1776 to 1778. Although General Washington kept his army near New York City thereafter, much of the war then concentrated in the South, culminating in Lord Cornwallis's surrender at Yorktown in 1781.

the three States of New York, Jersey & Pennsylvania."[16] Somehow he reached down into an inner strength and persisted in the struggle.

We require this behavior from the Washington in history books. We cannot envisage anything less. Our expectations of Washington make him a difficult person to understand. He has become such an icon that he appears more a monument than a man. Americans look on Washington as the father of the country, an individual who not only led the Continental army through trials and tribulations, but who also presided over the writing of the Constitution and served as the first chief executive of the United States. His achievement and his reputation dwarf all of his contemporaries and is matched in the annals of American history only by Abraham Lincoln. Even

FIGURE 2–2 George Washington by Charles Wilson Peale This portrait captures the "father of his country" in his military majesty. During the Revolutionary War Washington emerged as the indispensable leader who became as much a monument as a man. Although not a battlefield genius, he kept the Continental army together by the force of his personality and sustained the cause of independence.

in his own day Washington loomed larger than life and came to embody the cause of independence and the new nation. Such an individual seems etched in stone, with little emotion and less personality. Washington, however, had plenty of emotion, as many of his soldiers who experienced one of his tongue-lashings could attest. He also had a very special, if cultivated, personality as the stoic leader. Washington therefore contributed to our difficulties in understanding him. Deeply imbued with the ideals of republicanism, Washington consciously played the part of the virtuous natural aristocrat putting aside personal interest for the interest of the common good. He may not have been a deep thinker like Thomas Jefferson, nor sparkled with the brilliance of Alexander Hamilton, nor was he as reflective as John Adams, but he was committed to the revolution and understood the role he had to fulfill. He knew he was the American Cincinnatus who had to leave his plow—or at least his plantation where his slaves continued to work the plow—and lead the American people in their moment of danger. Tall (he was at least six foot two), an excellent horseman, and with an air of natural command, he exuded confidence even when he screwed up. Common soldiers would later recount repeatedly the impact he had on the army by just appearing in his uniform amid the chaos of battle. He was not a warm, confiding individual, but he elicited intense loyalty. Regardless of his many battlefield defeats, Washington was the right man at the right place for the cause of American independence.

Late December of 1776 was one of those moments that brought Washington the leader into greater focus. He was desperate to gain a victory to provide some glimmer of encouragement after a miserable campaign. Washington knew that failure might end the revolution and bring ignominy for himself. If captured he would be lucky not to be executed as a traitor. He did not expect a great victory that would compel the British to withdraw from North America; he merely wanted to check the litany of British triumphs and thereby help to sustain the revolution. His biggest concern was to recruit a new army with longer enlistments. He hoped a small victory would convince more men to rally to the cause. To keep his soldiers in the field for just a few more weeks Washington at first appealed to their patriotism. When that failed he offered ten dollars in hard currency for six weeks more service. Interest ruled and enough men agreed to the extension to allow Washington one more chance to confront the British.

Washington gambled and launched a dangerous winter attack on Trenton, an outpost guarded by a brigade of Hessians. Every step of the way was fraught with peril. Washington divided his army into three groups, each to cross an ice-choked Delaware River at different locations on December 25: The main force of about 2,500 men under Washington was to cross north of Trenton, another group of 800 men was to cross near Trenton, and a third contingent of about 2,300 men was to cross south of the town. In a gathering snowstorm only the troops with Washington made it to the other side of the river. Washington planned on attacking before dawn. Once it became clear that the army would not arrive at Trenton until after daylight Washington thought about canceling the assault. Concerned that his men would be "discovered, and harassed on repassing the River," Washington decided to press on.[17] Because he intended to attack the town from two directions, Washington took another risk by dividing his men again as they advanced on Trenton. Despite being slowed by the weather, the Continental troops caught the Hessians by surprise. Popular myth says the Hessians were groggy from celebrating Christmas. Actually, they had experienced enough harassment from small raids that they were on the alert. Only the snowstorm had limited their normal patrolling. The Hessians quickly formed into battle lines; most of the troops had been sleeping in uniform with their weapons beside them, ready to defend their position. However, Washington had brought along enough men and artillery to overwhelm the garrison and captured about one thousand prisoners. Unaware of the full impact of this victory on the enemy, Washington pulled back across the Delaware that evening. When he discovered how disorganized the British reaction was, Washington crossed the Delaware again with even more men. This move was almost a disastrous mistake. Lord Charles Cornwallis had gathered over 8,000 British and Hessian soldiers in Princeton. Washington could have lost the advantage of his stunning victory when Cornwallis moved on Trenton on January 2. Continental troops slowed the British advance, but by late afternoon, the two armies faced one another across Assunpink Creek south of the town. After probing the American positions, Cornwallis delayed his assault for a day, believing he had Washington trapped between the Delaware River and a superior British force. Washington recognized his peril and slipped away that night and marched toward Princeton. On his way he ran into a British regiment under Colonel Charles Mawhood sent to reenforce Cornwallis. Despite being greatly outnumbered, Mawhood attacked before the Americans knew what was happening and briefly gained the advantage. The Continentals rallied under Washington and with greater numbers drove the British from the field. The Americans captured a few hundred more prisoners, and briefly held Princeton before continuing their retreat. By this time both armies were exhausted from the fighting and marching in frigid conditions. Washington headed for winter camp in Morristown, New Jersey. The defeats at Trenton and Princeton convinced the British to abandon most of their outposts in New Jersey and concentrate around New York City. More important, they provided the victory that Washington needed to buoy the cause of independence and contributed immeasurably to his own reputation and the mythology that was beginning to surround him.

Although the campaign in late December allowed the war to continue, and served as a critical check to the British, the revolutionaries still faced great adversity. The soldiers at Morristown suffered terribly that winter. The British, too, had problems in gaining forage from the New Jersey countryside and fought a series of small battles with American militia and Continentals that made life difficult. The next spring the British planned a multipronged campaign. One army under General John Burgoyne moved down from Canada, hoping to capture Albany. Another force, under the command of Colonel Barry St. Leger, invaded through the Mohawk Valley to rendevous with Burgoyne. Howe was supposed to occupy the main Continental army under Washington. Fortunately for the United States, this ambitious plan was not well coordinated. Howe decided to seize Philadelphia, instead of supporting Burgoyne fully. Rather than march the short one hundred miles or so across New Jersey, and possibly engage and defeat Washington, Howe put his army aboard the British fleet and sailed hundreds of miles around the Delmarva peninsula. He landed at the head of the Chesapeake Bay, which was almost as far from Philadelphia as New York. Once ashore, the British moved northward. Washington deployed his army in a strong defensive position behind Brandywine Creek to the south of Philadelphia. The British, however, found a ford further up the stream and outflanked the Americans, compelling them—after a nasty fight—to fall back on September 11, 1777. Howe then outmaneuvered Washington, forcing him to abandon Philadelphia by September 26. Washington sought to dislodge the British with an attack on Germantown on October 4. Victory depended on the simultaneous assault by three separate units on a foggy morning. Although the Americans caught the British by surprise, the discipline of the British army, the disorganized advance, and the fog all contributed to an American defeat. Washington also hoped to hold on to several forts on the Delaware, making it difficult for the British to resupply in Philadelphia, but one by one the outposts fell. Washington pulled back to Valley Forge, where he prepared for a long, hard winter.

If the campaign around Philadelphia ended in defeat, the revolutionaries knew that success in northern New York more than compensated for the loss of the nation's capital. Both prongs of the British invasion from Canada failed. St. Leger had to abort his siege at Fort Stanwix in the Mohawk Valley on August 22, 1777, after his Indian allies abandoned him when word arrived that a large American force was due to relieve the garrison. In the meantime, Burgoyne was running into trouble. The arduous trek through the wilderness and the Americans at Saratoga sealed Burgoyne's fate. Although Burgoyne took Fort Ticonderoga with little trouble on July 6, his efforts to obtain supplies in Vermont ended with the wiping out of a large foraging detachment at the Battle of Bennington on August 16, 1777. Having slogged his way from Canada through the summer and into the fall, and with lines of communications stretched thin, Burgoyne pressed on, hoping to capture Albany before the winter. He ran into trouble when he confronted an American army that swelled to 11,000 men entrenched along Bemis Heights directly in his path down the Hudson River Valley. After failing in two battles to dislodge the Continentals and militia who had gathered under the command of General Horatio Gates, Burgoyne surrendered over 5,000 troops on October 17, 1777.

After Saratoga the British altered their strategy. The American victory convinced the French to sign a formal alliance with the United States on February 6, 1778. The British were now in a struggle for their survival. The conflict assumed global proportions. The colonies in the West Indies had to be protected, as well as possessions in Africa and Asia. An invasion of Britain itself was not beyond possibility. A struggle with contentious colonists had to take a backseat in the face of the more serious challenge from France. The British decided to concentrate their forces on two ports in the North—New York and Newport, Rhode Island—while shifting the main theater of combat to the South, where they expected Loyalist support and where their army would be closer to the British navy stationed in the West Indies. To effect this plan the British had to evacuate Philadelphia. Sir Henry Clinton replaced Howe as commander in chief of the British army in North America. In late June he packed up his army and headed across New Jersey. Washington, who had spent the winter at Valley Forge trying to mold the Continentals into a professional fighting force, decided to pursue Clinton with the possibility of engaging the British before they arrived in New York. An opportunity for an attack opened at Monmouth Courthouse, in central New Jersey, on a sweltering hot June 28, 1778. After some squabbling among his leading officers, Washington placed General Charles Lee in charge of the vanguard. Lee had initially discouraged any attack and refused the command, but wanted it back after Washington selected the Marquis de Lafayette to replace him. Lafayette deferred to Lee as the senior officer. Clinton saw that the Americans wanted a battle and therefore ordered his rear guard under Lord Cornwallis to engage the enemy just enough to allow the rest of the army to continue on its way. Lee, however, had no clear plan of action and quickly decided that the British intended to destroy his entire force and ordered a retreat. As Washington advanced with the main body of the

American army he was outraged by Lee's failure to push the attack. Clinton in the meantime decided that the battle presented an unanticipated opening to defeat the Americans in detail. He committed his main army to the contest. With both armies bringing more and more men into the fray the outcome became more problematical. The heat also took its toll. It was in this battle that Molly Pitcher reportedly replaced her exhausted and wounded husband in working an American artillery piece. In the end both sides claimed victory. Rather than continuing the fight the next day, Clinton moved his army farther along the road to New York that night. In other words, the British accomplished their main goal of getting across New Jersey. Washington's troops held the field, despite heavy losses. Washington encamped his army in the countryside surrounding New York and for the next three years the war in the North settled into a stalemate with countless skirmishes but with few major battles.

The locus of the conflict from 1778 to 1781 was in the South. The British sought to conquer the southern colonies one by one, build on Loyalist strength, and then move northward. At the end of 1778 they seized Savannah and gained control over most of Georgia. In the spring of 1780 they attacked South Carolina. The British captured 5,000 men at Charleston on May 12, and then defeated what was left of the Continental army in the South at the Battle of Camden on August 15, 1780. Despite these victories, full control over South Carolina eluded the British as a bitter internecine conflict erupted between Loyalists and revolutionaries. Frontier militia virtually wiped out about 900 Loyalists at King's Mountain on October 7, 1780. Following this setback, late in 1780 a new Continental force under General Nathanael Greene began to organize. Greene decided he needed to build up his army before directly confronting the British under Cornwallis. To encourage the militia while protecting "the persons and property of the Inhabitants" by checking and restraining "the depredations of the Enemy," Greene divided his men.[18] He retained command of an outpost at Cheraw, South Carolina, to keep in contact with militia under Colonel Frances Marion, and sent half his troops toward the backcountry under General Daniel Morgan. Cornwallis wanted to take advantage of this situation and ordered Colonel Banastre Tarleton's Legion after Morgan. Tarleton plunged headlong into an attack at the Battle of Cowpens on January 17, 1781. Morgan had organized his men in three groups, each one in front of the other. The plan was to have the first two lines fall back after they were attacked by Tarleton. The third line, which had the most disciplined soldiers, would hold steadfast and mow down what Morgan hoped would be a disorganized pursuit by would-be triumphant Britons. The plan worked to perfection and Morgan's Continentals almost annihilated the

British legionnaires. Tarleton was lucky to escape the trap with his life. Morgan proclaimed that the battle was "a devil of a whipping, a more compleat victory never was obtained."[19] The British lost 110 killed and 702 captured; Morgan's casualties were 12 killed and 60 wounded.

To punish the Americans for this defeat, Cornwallis abandoned his heavy baggage and, with added mobility, entered North Carolina in search of Greene and Morgan. Greene wanted to avoid Cornwallis's better-trained troops, but confronted the British at Guilford Courthouse on March 15, 1781. With a battle plan similar to the one Morgan had used at Cowpens, the Americans inflicted heavy losses on the British. But at the end of the day, Cornwallis drove Greene from the field. Despite the British victory—if it could be called that—the North Carolina campaign was a failure. As one American put it, Cornwallis was "like a desolating meteor." He "passed, carrying destruction and distress to individuals—his army walked through the country, daily adding to the number of its enemies, and leaving their few friends exposed to every punishment for ill-timed and ill-placed confidence."[20] Having generated little Loyalist support in North Carolina and antagonized the local population by plundering, Cornwallis decided to take his army to Virginia, join with other British units there, and strike a blow at a state that he believed was vital to the cause of independence. Virginia was already reeling from an invasion led by Benedict Arnold, who had joined the British the year before. The British had captured Richmond and had sent Governor Thomas Jefferson fleeing from his home in Monticello. Once in Virginia, Cornwallis's forces swelled to 8,500—a formidable army. During the summer of 1781, after some indecision, Cornwallis centered his army at a small port on the Chesapeake called Yorktown. He hoped he could be supplied and reenforced by the British navy. This position presented the combined French and American armies with a wonderful opportunity. A French fleet briefly sailed north from the West Indies and beat off a British relief fleet in the Battle of the Capes on September 5. Washington and General Jean-Baptiste Donatien de Vimeur Rochambeau moved their armies from near New York and Rhode Island to Virginia. This maneuver entailed incredible organization and skill and was one of Washington's greatest achievements. Outnumbered at Yorktown by two to one, and cut off from supplies, Cornwallis surrendered on October 19, 1781.

Republicanism on Trial

The Revolutionary War was a bitter civil war that tested American republicanism. Americans today have a roseate understanding of this conflict, believing that the "good" Americans united to defend themselves against the evil Britons who sought to usurp liberty. In this false portrait embattled farmers fought against British redcoats and Hessian mercenaries, outsmarting their enemy by hiding behind trees and rocks. Reality, however, was more complicated and liberty more ambiguous. Americans fought on both sides for a myriad of reasons, ranging from the patriotic to the mundane. Men shifted sides and it was often difficult to tell the good guys from the bad. No one had a monopoly on virtue. Fighting the war had a terrible cost in human lives and material goods.

Liberty could mean many different things depending on the context. The concept of liberty was directly connected to the protection of property. From this perspective, Parliament's taxes were a threat to liberty because they took away colonial property without the colonist's consent. But if executive authority threatened liberty, as described by the Declaration of Independence, many Americans believed that there were other, more serious threats to liberty. Loyalist Samuel Seabury used language similar to the republican rhetoric of the revolutionaries. He asserted that when "the bands of civil society are broken" and "the authority of government weakened . . . Individuals are deprived of their liberty; their property is frequently invaded by violence" through "a flagrant instance of injustice and cruelty committed by a riotous mob." The committees that were the driving force behind the revolution were little more than "half a dozen foolish people" who selected themselves to speak for the people.[21] J. Hector St. John de Crèvecoeur took this analysis a step further by arguing that these committees were controlled by "men who impiously affix to their new, fictitious zeal the sacred name of liberty on purpose to blind the unwary" and yet "they worship no deity but self-interest, and to that idol sacrilegiously sacrifice so many virtues."[22] The same republican emphasis on virtue and pursuing the public good used to defend the revolution could be used to attack it.

As this concern with liberty suggests, although labeled Tories, or the "disaffected," or even "refugees," Loyalists were not nefarious individuals who plotted with the king to destroy American freedom. Nor were they corrupt individuals who allowed themselves to be bribed into supporting the crown. Their motives were complex and differed from individual to individual. Loyalists usually had both ideological and personal reasons for their commitment to George III. Many had opposed the imperial regulations but could not take that final step and make war against the king. They were a diverse group that came from a wide range of society and who were located throughout the colonies. Some were important officeholders like Thomas Hutchinson and William Franklin. Others were Anglican ministers like Seabury. Joseph Galloway of Pennsylvania had even been a member of the First Continental Congress. Included among the Loyalist ranks were rich merchants and landowners, as well as farmers and artisans. Many Hudson River tenants who had rioted against paying rent in the 1760s became Loyalists after their landlords sided with the revolution. In North Carolina, men who were Regulators only a few years before the outbreak of war resented the revolutionary leadership who had joined in suppressing their protest. The Delaware and Maryland countryside swarmed with disaffected farmers who would have been just as happy to see the conflict go away. Southern society was riven between Loyalists and whigs and broke out in bitter internecine conflict after the British turned their attention to the region in 1778. New York, which was occupied by the British from 1776 until 1783, became a magnet for Loyalists from all the colonies. The region around the city often served as a hotly contested no-man's-land fought over by Loyalist and whig militias. Whereas some people on the frontier viewed British restrictions as a hindrance to their freedom to settle west of the Appalachians, others recognized the need for British protection against the Indians. Many Native Americans sided with the British, fearing the colonial settlers clamoring for their land. And thousands of African Americans sought their liberty by heeding the British offer of freedom in exchange for military service.

Those who became whigs—supporters of the revolution—were also a diverse lot. Included among their ranks were some of the richest men in America, such as George Washington and John Hancock, as well as some of the most impoverished. Like their Loyalist brethren, most revolutionaries came from the middle of society and were farmers and artisans. Social and economic status did not dictate how someone chose sides. Many revolutionaries believed the republican rhetoric and saw themselves as defending liberty against encroachments from the king. Some revolutionaries were concerned with the ongoing debt and viewed it as a form of economic bondage. Merchants and city dwellers opposed the imperial regulations that had a direct impact on trade. Those in the countryside might be more disturbed by the Coercive Acts that threatened local government in rural America. Others joined the cause for more personal reasons. Sometimes private connections dictated allegiance and an individual simply followed the lead of a local big shot or member of the family. Often the desire for social advancement came into play. One New Hampshire shoemaker admitted that he joined the army hoping to advance in the ranks. He explained:

> When this Rebellion came on, I saw some of my Neighbors get into a Commission, who were no better than myself. I was very ambitious, & did not like to see those Men above me. I was asked to enlist, as a private Soldier. My Ambition was too great for so low a Rank; I offered to enlist upon having a Lieutenants Commission; which was granted.

This revolutionary soldier went on to explain that if he was killed "there would be an end of me." But if his captain was killed, "I should rise in Rank, & should still have a Chance to rise higher."[23] Just as with the Loyalists who sided with the king, there was a wide range of reasons for joining the revolution.

All too frequently an individual had a mixture of motives that could even pull him in opposite directions. As a result, men also changed sides with uncommon ease. Few men sacrificed more for the revolutionary cause than Benedict Arnold. He led an expeditionary force across the Maine wilderness to invade Canada, headed an ill-fated assault on Quebec in a winter snowstorm, helped delay an invasion by slowing the British advance across Lake Champlain, and contributed to the victory at Saratoga. But his loyalties became more ambiguous in Philadelphia, where he married his second wife, Margaret Shippen, spent extravagantly, ran into debt, and argued with other officers and local officials. In the summer of 1780 he gained command of West Point on the Hudson River and then attempted to surrender the crucial outpost to the British. For this betrayal he became infamous. But he merely did what other, lesser men did many times: He pursued his self-interest even if it meant changing sides. William Lambert was a small-time Boston merchant at the beginning of the war who went to Halifax with the British in early 1776. In Halifax he may have continued an illicit trade with New England. He certainly provided assistance for a profit to several American captains he knew who had been captured by the British. His wife, who had left a daughter from a previous marriage in Massachusetts and who had pro-revolutionary sympathies, hid escaped American prisoners of war in their Halifax house (Lambert claimed he did not know about them). After soldiers searched their house looking for escaped prisoners the Lamberts made plans "with the utmost *secracy*," and surreptitiously left Halifax in the spring of 1778. Once back in Massachusetts, Lambert joined the militia and served in the attack on British-occupied Newport.[24] Many common soldiers followed a similar course. The Continental army had plenty of men who had deserted from the British or who joined in order to avoid confinement as a prisoner of war. British forces had similar recruits—men who once had fought for the United States. Some individuals, such as the common sailor Joseph Bartlett, changed sides repeatedly; between 1778 and 1781 Bartlett switched flags at least ten times. Christopher Stocker, alias William Foster (among other names), deserted the British army in April 1777. He then embarked on a career of "repeated desertion and reenlisting" under different names—each time collecting a bounty. He also served on a privateer for two years.[25] In the last few years of the war, when it became difficult to get anyone to

FIGURE 2–3 Uniforms of the Continental Army American soldiers wore a variety of different uniforms. As the conflict continued year after year, recruits came from lower and lower levels of society. African Americans fought in both the British and the Continental army.

join the Continental army, some communities were willing to pay as much as one hundred dollars as a signing bonus and did not want to ask too many questions on the history of a recruit who would take the place of some local farm boy. Patriotism and ideology did not motivate men like Bartlett and Stocker. Instead, they were more interested in personal gain either from the recruiting bounty or the booty taken from the enemy.

The whig militia, despite sometimes mixing patriotism with profit, were crucial in the contest for allegiance. The militia's significance on the battlefield was limited. Unless they had overwhelming numbers, militia units were usually no match for the British army. But on the local level they were absolutely essential. Militia units from both sides often fought a bitter, nasty, and personal war, raiding each other, burning houses, and committing atrocities. In this process the whig militia were not above gaining economic advantage by purchasing seized Loyalist property on the cheap, or simply helping themselves as they helped the cause of independence. The revolutionary militia had some advantages in this internecine contest because of their connection to the revolutionary committees. These committees had over a decade of organizational experience from the resistance movement, whereas Tory militias were less used to irregular organization and relied on an often absent royal government. Tory militias, which could be just as mercenary, were most effective when they could fight with the British army nearby. Revolutionary militias remained more active throughout the conflict. Attendance at a muster became the acid test of loyalty to the revolutionary regime. If a man did not show up when called by the local whig milita, then he was presumed to be a Loyalist. The militia would hunt him down, arrest him, and requisition supplies for the army from his property.

As pivotal as the militia was to the ultimate success of the revolution, the Continental army was even more important. Washington wanted to have a professional army just like the British, and therefore pushed for longer enlistments and harsh discipline. As the war dragged on the Continental army recruited more poor and propertyless men. Such men fought less for liberty and more to fill their stomachs. With good leadership, provided by Washington and many of the other Continental officers, they were molded into a potent fighting force. But they could also be dangerously mutinous if unpaid and unfed. Connecticut soldiers mutinied in December 1779, Pennsylvania soldiers a year later, and New Jersey troops in January 1781. In 1783, mutinous soldiers demonstrated outside of the Continental Congress, convincing the government to move out of Philadelphia. Whatever the difficulties, the Continental army was essential to victory on the battlefield. Equally important, it provided a focal point for the new United States. Without an army to feed, clothe, and pay (sometimes), there would have been little reason for the Continental Congress to exist. And without a national government, the revolutionary movement might have simply disintegrated under the pressure of the might of the British army.

That national government struggled to provide the material and monetary support for the army. The Continental Congress had initially planned to pay for the war by issuing currency. By the end of 1776, Congress had authorized $25 million to be printed, and the value of a Continental dollar began to slip. In 1777 and 1778 the government printed another $76 million Continentals, creating a depreciation of about 5:1. The release of more paper money pushed the Continental dollar too far. By the end of 1780 the depreciation reached 100:1 and in the spring of 1781 the currency had become worthless and passed out of circulation. Increasingly the United States had to depend on borrowing money. France and the Netherlands extended some credit to the United States. Both national and state governments also borrowed from Americans, sometimes at the point of a gun, either directly or by IOUs for services and goods.

From a republican point of view, the process of funding and supplying the war seemed to be leading some Americans astray. Men such as Robert Morris, who supervised the financial affairs of the young nation for most

FIGURE 2-4 Continental Currency The Continental Congress originally hoped to pay for the Revolutionary War by printing money, but the value of the currency quickly began to fall. By 1780 the Continental dollar had depreciated at a ratio of 100:1. In 1781 the money became worthless.

of the war, saw nothing wrong with combining his own personal interests with the larger interest of the United States. At times this practice adhered to the benefit of the nation: In the later stages of the war Morris used his own credit to underwrite the government's credit. But it could also lead to questionable practices such as assigning naval war vessels to carry private merchandise or the appropriation of Continental funds for his own benefit. Similarly, Morris's sometime business partner Silas Deane charged a commission on every purchase and requisition he made as a diplomat in France. The pursuit of profit, however, was not limited to high government officials and merchants; in an inflationary economy, common farmers squeezed whatever price for produce the market could bear. Farmers often preferred to sell produce to the British and the French because both paid in hard currency rather than with depreciated Continental and state money or IOUs. If the revolution began in an effort to assert an older notion of a republican concern with the common good, as it dragged on, more and more individuals pursued their own interests in an increasingly capitalistic spirit.

Armies from both sides exacted a high price from the countryside. Joseph Plumb Martin, who served in the Continental army for most of the conflict, wrote that one of the few times he had enough to eat as a soldier was when he was part of a foraging detachment in the winter of

1777–1778. He recognized that eliciting supplies from local farmers was a matter of coercion. Martin was concerned that his activities ran

> the *risk* of abuse, if not injury, from the inhabitants when *plundering* them of their property (for I could not, while in the very act of taking their cattle, hay, corn, and grain from them against their wills, consider it a whit better than plundering—sheer privateering.)

A few months later Martin was with the troops pursuing the British across New Jersey after the evacuation of Philadelphia and reported the "devastation" the British "made in their route; cattle killed and lying about the fields and pastures, some in the position they were in when shot down, others with a small spot of skin taken off their hind quarters and a mess of steak taken out." The British also hacked and broke to pieces household furniture, filled wells, destroyed tools of farmers and artisans, and chopped down fruit trees. Having armies marching through a neighborhod was not a good thing regardless of which side the locals supported.[26]

The final cost of the revolution was very high. Over twenty thousand Americans died and countless lives were shattered and people displaced. As many as 100,000 Loyalists left the country. Per capita income actually went down during the war. Towns and cities were mere shells of their former selves. Whole districts of the countryside lay desolate. The frontier, too, had been racked by bitter warfare with Native Americans. Vast tracts of Loyalist property had been seized, thousands of slaves had run away, and huge quantities of property had been destroyed. Hatred ran deep in many areas, especially where the internecine conflict had been most intense. And somewhere along the way, the high ideals of the republican revolution seemed to have been misplaced.

Peace and Independence

The Treaty of Paris that ended the Revolutionary War in 1783 was a great moment for American diplomacy. Not only did Great Britain acknowledge United States independence, but the peace treaty established generous boundaries for the new nation. This success came at some cost—the sacrifice of the idealistic hopes of revolutionary Americans that they could inaugurate a new age in international affairs divorced from the realpolitik of the old world and base all relationships on openness and free trade.

American idealism was best expressed by the "Plan of Treaties of 1776." Written by John Adams, the Continental Congress accepted the document on September 17, 1776, as a model for an agreement with France. The plan reflected the revolutionary fervor of the summer of 1776 and did not ask for a formal military alliance. Instead, it simply sought to establish a relationship based on free trade. The model treaty proclaimed that French subjects and American citizens should "pay no other Duties or Imposts . . . than the Natives" of each respective country.[27] The proposed accord also asserted the notion that free ships made free goods and defined broad neutral rights in times of war. These ideas were truly radical in an age of mercantilism in which trade barriers were viewed as instruments of national power and countries used their navies to limit any trade with their enemies. The treaty also would have fostered the spirit of capitalism through the open exchange of goods. When Benjamin Franklin arrived in France in December he had a copy of the treaty with him.

Although Franklin was greeted as the very embodiment of the Enlightenment and the American resistance movement, a persona that Franklin wisely embraced, the French were not about to abandon old-world diplomacy simply because rustic Americans proclaimed a new millennium in foreign affairs. The French court was interested in the American rebellion because it provided a wonderful opportunity to strike back at Great Britain for its victory in the war that had ended in 1763. In May 1776 the French foreign minister, Charles Gravier, Comte de Vergennes, persuaded the king to allow secret shipments of war materials to the Americans. France also convinced Spain to provide similar aid. It was in response to this assistance that the Continental Congress appointed Franklin and two other commissioners, Silas Deane and Arthur Lee, to arrange a commercial treaty with France. Vergennes played a delicate game of encouraging rebellion while not provoking a costly war with Great Britain. In December, as things went from bad to worse for Washington's army, the Continental Congress decided to put aside its earlier idealism and authorized the commissioners to negotiate a military alliance. France continued its clandestine support, and even allowed American privateers to use its ports, but it was not until after the American victory at Saratoga that the French, fearful of reconciliation between Britain and its colonies, were willing to sign a mutual defense pact and commercial treaty. Both treaties were signed on February 6, 1778, and represented a step away from the ideals embedded in the model treaty. The commercial treaty granted mutual most favored nation status, but not trade equal with the nation's own merchants as the model treaty had stipulated. More important, the formal alliance bound the United States and France militarily. The alliance was critical to the American victory in the war as half the troops at Yorktown were French, and Cornwallis would not have been trapped if Great Britain had controlled the seas uncontested. The treaty stipulated that France and the United States would make "common cause" once war broke out between France and Great Britain, which the treaties made all but inevitable, and pledged not to conclude peace "without the formal consent of the other first obtain'd." The commissioners also agreed to a secret clause concerning the possible entry of Spain into the conflict. In short, the United States made significant concessions to the old world of diplomacy of binding alliances and secret pacts, and retreated from the high-minded ideals of 1776.[28]

As the war in America dragged on, European powers vied for diplomatic advantage. On April 12, 1779, Spain finally agreed to go to war with Great Britain as a French ally, but only after the French guaranteed them British-held Gibraltar. The Spanish made no formal agreement with the United States. Early in 1780 Russia organized the League of Armed Neutrality, joined by Denmark, Sweden, and others, to protect their right to trade with the countries involved with the war. Angered by Dutch aid to the Americans, Great Britain declared war on the Netherlands on December 20, 1780, before that country could join the Russian-sponsored League. Although in 1782 the Dutch recognized the United States, agreed to a commercial treaty, and loaned money to the American government, like the Spanish, they did not sign a formal military alliance. To make the maze of diplomacy more complicated, Austria and Prussia flirted with war with each other, while the Russians threatened the Turks in Crimea. There was also a revolving door within the American delegation in Paris. Franklin remained and was even appointed Minister to France in 1778. Arthur Lee charged Silas Deane with seeking personal opportunities rather than protecting the nation's interests as a commissioner to France. Deane was recalled in 1777 and Lee ordered home in 1779. John Adams replaced Deane in 1777, but he and Franklin did not get along. In June 1781 Congress created a five-man commission—Franklin, Adams, John Jay, Henry Laurens, and Thomas Jefferson—to negotiate with the British if an opportunity arose. By the spring of 1782 the British decided on peace talks. Only Franklin was available when the negotiations began: Jefferson never left for Europe because he had personal affairs to deal with; Laurens had been captured by the British on his way across the Atlantic; Adams was at The Hague; and Jay was in Spain. When the negotiations became serious in the fall, all but Jefferson were on the scene.

The Americans violated their alliance with France by engaging in talks separately with the British. Vergennes acquiesced with this move by the American delegation. The war had almost bankrupted France and the British had won a huge naval victory at the Battle of Saintes on April 12, 1782, in the West Indies. Vergennes wanted peace, but the Spanish were holding out for Gibraltar. If there were an Anglo-American treaty, Vergennes hoped Spain would abandon its insistence on obtaining Gibraltar and a general peace would follow. In this complicated diplomatic dance, the United States gained the advantage. The British and Americans came to a provisional agreement on November 29, 1782. As Vergennes expected, a general armistice was signed on January 20, 1783. The final peace was not confirmed until September 3, 1783, and the last British troops evacuated New York City on November 25, 1783.

While Spain, France, the Netherlands, and Great Britain shuffled territory far and wide in Europe, Africa, Asia, the West Indies, and North America, the United States gained something more tangible and permanent—independence. The terms of the Treaty of Paris were very generous to the United States. Before the war, the colonies had largely been confined to east of the Appalachian Mountains. The treaty established the Mississippi River as the western boundary of the new nation and the Great Lakes as the northern boundary. The southern boundary was more vague because Great Britain ceded East and West Florida to Spain in partial compensation for not surrendering Gibraltar. The enlarged United States boundaries ignored Britain's Indian allies in the region and allowed for the future expansion of American settlement. The Americans were also granted fishing rights off the Grand Banks of Newfoundland and the British were given free navigation on the Mississippi River. Not all articles of the treaty were adhered to by both parties. Because the Americans did not return confiscated Loyalist property, treat Loyalists fairly, or facilitate the collection of debts—the treaty stipulated that Congress would "recommend" to the state legislatures these actions—the British did not fulfill their promise to evacuate forts on the frontier.

As good a deal as the Treaty of Paris was for the Americans, it left some issues untouched. The treaty said nothing about trade. Before the war the British West Indies and the British North American colonies had traded extensively with each other. This commerce was now illegal. Even without a formal agreement the British allowed direct trade between the United States and the British Isles. But throughout the 1780s this trade was dominated by British merchants. Moreover, as John Adams, the first American ambassador to King George III, discovered, independence did not bring respect. American efforts to develop commerce and good relations with the major European powers foundered. Despite the efforts of Jefferson, who served as the ambassador to King Louis XVI, France was unable to replace England as a trading partner for the United States. The Spanish also caused trouble by closing the lower Mississippi River to American traffic. The United States had abandoned its idealism in diplomacy, gained important concessions in the harsh world of realpolitik, but still struggled after independence to revive and extend trade, as well as gain the respect of the international community.

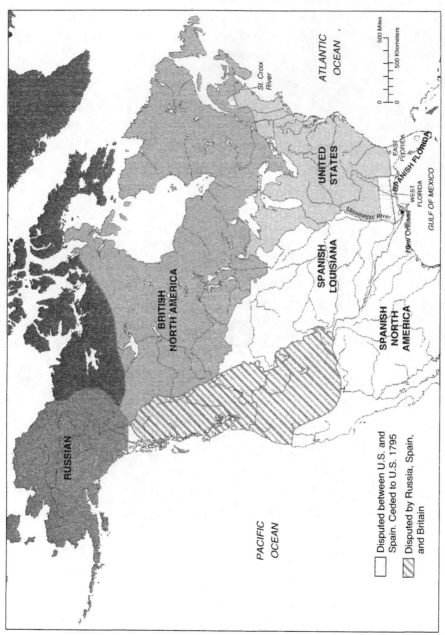

MAP 2–2 The Treaty of Paris of 1783 The final peace agreement provided the new United States with generous borders, reaching to the Mississippi River. In the process, the British ignored the interests of their Native American allies west of the Appalachian Mountains. The seaboard states ceded the western lands to the United States and created a vast public domain that would eventually be integrated into the Union following procedures outlined in the Northwest Ordinance (1787) on an equal basis with the original states.

The treaty also did not address the fundamental causes of the revolution—the stresses and anxieties of Americans that came from a conflict between values that emphasized a corporate, single-interest society and behavior that reflected a rise of individual and aggressive behavior being unleashed in an increasingly competitive market. Despite republican calls for self-sacrifice the war had only compounded the problems by providing new opportunities for individual profit and aggrandizement, and by unleashing the ideal of equality to challenge the hierarchy that had been so central to the old world order. Independence may have created a new nation, but the shape of the society and nature of the economy still needed fuller development and political articulation.

Endnotes

1. Quoted in Gordon S. Wood, *The Creation of the American Republic, 1776–1787* (Chapel Hill: University of North Carolina Press, 1969), 18.
2. "Examination of Benjamin Franklin in the House of Commons (Feb. 13, 1766)," in Leonard W. Labaree, et al., eds., *The Papers of Benjamin Franklin*, 1–vols. (New Haven: Yale University Press, 1959–), 13: 143.
3. Letter from R. R. Livingston to [former Gov. Monckton], Nov. 8, 1765 (Box 3, transcripts), Livingston Family Papers, Manuscripts and Archives Division, The New York Public Library, Astor, Lenox and Tilden Foundations.
4. *Journals of the Continental Congress, 1774–1789,* Worthington C. Ford, et al., eds. (Washington, D.C., 1904–37), 2: 158–61.
5. "A Proclamation, By the King, For the Supressing of Rebellion and Sedition, Aug. 23, 1775," in Peter Force, ed., *American Archives,* ser. 4, vols. 1–6 (Washington, D.C.: M. St. Clair Clarke and Peter Force, 1837–53), 3: 240–41.
6. Thomas Paine, *Common Sense,* Isaac Kramnick, ed. (New York: Penguin, 1976), 63, 65, 73, 76, 82.
7. Paine, *Common Sense,* 69, 71, 76, 78.
8. Pauline Maier, *American Scripture: Making the Declaration of Independence* (New York: Alfred A. Knopf, 1997), 48.
9. Quoted in Maier, *American Scripture,* 41.
10. Quoted in Maier, *American Scripture,* 161.
11. "Restoring Colonial Virtue: Brutus on the Promise of the Nonimportation Associations (June 1, 1769)," in Jack P. Greene, ed., *Colonies to Nation, 1763–1789: A Documentary History of the American Revolution* (New York: Norton, 1975), 157.
12. Continental Congress, The Articles of Association, Oct. 20, 1774, The Avalon Project at Yale Law School, www.yale.edu/lawweb/avalon/contcong/10-20-74.htm.
13. Quoted in Wood, *The Creation of the American Republic,* 116.
14. Quoted in John Shy, "Thomas Gage: Weak Link of Empire," in George Athan Billias, ed., *George Washington's Opponents: British Generals and Admirals in the American Revolution* (New York: William Morrow and Company, 1969), 30. Originally in Burgoyne to Lord George Germain, Aug. 20, 1775, Germain Papers, Clements Library, University of Michigan.

nerican Crisis by Thomas Paine, I, The Avalon Project at Yale Law School,
yale.edu/lawweb/avalon/paine/pframe.htm.

thy Twohig, et al., eds, *The Papers of George Washington: Revolutionary War Series,*
ls. (Charlottesville: University of Virginia Press, 1985–), 7: 291.

hig, et al., eds., *The Papers of George Washington,* 7: 454.

18. Quoted in Don Higginbotham, *The War of American Independence: Military Attitudes, Policies, and Practice, 1763–1789* (New York: Macmillan, 1971), 365.

19. Quoted in Higginbotham, *The War of American Independence,* 367.

20. Quoted in Hugh F. Rankin, "Charles Lord Cornwallis: Study in Frustration," in Billias, ed., *George Washington's Opponents,* 223.

21. Samuel Seabury, *Free Thoughts on the Proceedings of the Continental Congress, Held at Philadelphia, Sept. 5, 1774: Wherein Their Errors Are Exhibited, . . . in a Letter to the Farmers, and Other Inhabitants of North America . . . by a Farmer* (London: Richardson and Urquhart, 1775), 1, 37, 44.

22. J. Hector St. John de Crèvecoeur, *Letters From an American Farmer and Sketches of Eighteenth-Century America,* Albert E. Stone, ed. (New York: Penguin, 1981), 414–15.

23. Quoted in John Shy, *A People Numerous and Armed: Reflections on the Military Struggle for American Independence* (New York: Oxford University Press, 1976), 168.

24. William Lambert, "Letterbook," Massachusetts Historical Society, Boston, Massachusetts.

25. Quoted in Ruth Wallis Herndon, *Unwelcome Americans: Living on the Margins in Early New England* (Philadelphia: University of Pennsylvania Press, 2003), 73.

26. Quoted in James Kirby Martin, ed., *Ordinary Courage: The Revolutionary War Adventures of Joseph Plumb Martin* (St. James, N.Y.: Brandywine, 1993), 69, 74.

27. Plan of the Treaties with France of 1778, Tuesday, Sept. 17, 1776, The Avalon Project at Yale Law School, www.yale.edu/lawweb/avalon/diplomacy/france/fr1778p.htm.

28. Treaty of Alliance Between The United States and France, Feb. 6, 1778, The Avalon Project at Yale Law School, www.yale.edu/lawweb/avalon/diplomacy/france/fr1788-2.htm.

Experimenting with Republican Governments

Creating American Republics

American revolutionaries had utopian hopes of establishing new forms of government after independence. Some revolutionaries wanted to push for greater democracy; others wanted to pursue a more conservative path. Having declared independence in July 1776, revolutionary leaders knew they were embarking on a bold political experiment. The slate had been wiped clean, and the revolutionaries had a unique opportunity to create American governments from scratch. John Adams excitedly proclaimed, "How few of the human race have ever enjoyed an opportunity of making an election of government . . . for themselves or their children!"[1] The focus of this exhilaration was not national; instead, men such as Adams and Thomas Jefferson jumped at the chance to participate in the writing of constitutions of the states. Because of the interest at the state level, most Americans were initially more than happy to have a weak national structure under the Articles of Confederation to protect the liberty of the people from the power of government. However, in the late 1780s many American leaders began to call for a new and stronger national government, one that would foster economic growth and the investment of capital while clinging to the hierarchy of the old order, leading to the writing and ratification of the U.S. Constitution. Antifederalists opposed the Constitution claiming, among other things, that the Federalists who supported the Constitution favored the moneyed elite and wanted to limit the impact of the people on the national scene. Out of the process of writing and ratifying the Constitution a new form of republican government emerged that further accelerated the spread of capitalism and became, to the surprise of the Federalists, increasingly democratic.

In each state, revolutionary leaders sought to devise the right republican formula to guarantee the public good. They began with the classical balance that had been the envy of the Enlightenment—monarchy, aristocracy, and democracy—and sought ways to design a political system that would prevent a crisis similar to the one that engulfed Anglo-Americans in 1775 and 1776. The first impulse in writing state constitutions was to limit the monarchical component of government to prevent its corruption into tyranny and to strengthen the democratic component to reflect the will of the people. Radicals in Pennsylvania wrote the prototype for this approach in their constitution of September 28, 1776. The long shadow of George III hung over the document. The constitution began by echoing the Declaration of Independence and stating the reasons for breaking with the king. Because George III had waged a "most cruel and unjust war against" his North American subjects "for the avowed purpose of reducing them to a total and abject submission . . . all allegiance and fealty to the said king and his successors, are dissolved and at an end, and all power and authority derived from him ceased in these colonies." The "representatives of the freemen of Pennsylvania" continued by asserting that to protect "the welfare and safety of the inhabitants," Pennsylvania needed to be independent with a government that was "derived from and founded on the authority of the people only." To do so the new constitution established "just rules . . . for governing their future society." These "original principles of government" would "promote the general happiness of the people of this State, and their posterity, and provide for future improvements, without partiality for, or prejudice against any particular class, sect, or denomination of men whatever."[2]

Following this preamble there was "A Declaration of the Rights of the Inhabitants of the Commonwealth or State of Pennsylvania" that further demonstrated the desire to guarantee the liberty of the people. Besides protecting individual rights concerning religion, speech, and movement, the Pennsylvania "Declaration of Rights" contained several radical assertions that rearranged the traditional relationship between the rulers and ruled. Article IV stated "That all power being originally inherent in, and consequently derived from, the people; therefore all officers of government, whether legislative or executive, are their trustees and servants, and at all times accountable to them." In other words, each branch of government no longer represented a distinct part of society— monarchy, aristocracy, and democracy. Instead, all branches gained their justification from the people alone. Article V continued along this vein of thought:

> That government is, or ought to be, instituted for the common benefit, protection and security of the people, nation or community; and not for the particular emolument or advantage of any single man, family, or set of men, who are a part only of that community.

In true republican form the government was to be dedicated to the commonweal and not to the needs of an individual—the king—or a group of men—an aristocracy. Moreover, the people reserved "an indubitable, unalienable and indefeasible right to reform, alter, or abolish government" that did not meet their needs.[3]

The provisions of the Pennsylvania Constitution put these ideals into practice. The balance within government tipped away from the executive and toward the people's legislature. The constitution vested executive authority in the hands of a president and a council, with the president elected annually, and the council to be elected on a rotating basis every three years. This executive had limited powers. Pennsylvanians did not create an upper house, thus eliminating a regular role for an aristocracy in government. Real power rested within the assembly that was to reflect the will of the people. The constitution guaranteed popular participation by insisting on annual elections for the assembly, open-door sessions, and the publishing of all laws and the posting of them in public places for popular discussion. No law became permanent until it had been passed by two successive legislatures. Pennsylvania gave the right to vote to every freeman and his adult sons, the broadest franchise in any state. As a further protection for the rights of the people, every seven years there would be a council of censors who would "enquire whether the constitution has been preserved inviolate in every part." They were also to determine if "the legislative and executive branches of government have performed their duty as guardians of the people."[4]

Only Georgia and Vermont followed the model of Pennsylvania. Other states sought different ways to guarantee a republican form of government. Most states relied on a two-house legislature, but struggled to distinguish between the upper and lower houses in the egalitarian atmosphere of the revolution. Some revolutionary leaders believed that radically democratic constitutions such as Pennsylvania's were too open and created an imbalance that threatened anarchy. Critics of the Pennsylvania Constitution ultimately replaced it with a stronger government in the 1780s. In particular, the critics objected to the lack of an upper house, or senate, in the Pennsylvania Constitution. Building on the notion expressed in Article IV of the Pennsylvania "Declaration of Rights" that all elements of government derive their justification from the people, they claimed that an upper house would not represent the aristocracy, but would merely be another forum to represent the people and act as a check on the lower house. Benjamin Rush lamented that in the Pennsylvania Constitution "the supreme, absolute, and uncontrolled power of the State is lodged in the hands of *one body* of men" and that was as bad as, if not worse, than having absolute power in the hands of an individual.[5] Another house of legislature would be a counterweight to this power. The role of the senate became clarified only gradually in the 1770s and 1780s. As early as 1777 the Virginia Senate defined the bicameral legislature as "the representatives of the people, separated into two bodies, and mutually endeavouring to exercise faithfully their delegated power." The critics of the Pennsylvania Constitution in the 1770s and 1780s argued for an upper house so that there would be a "double representation" of the people. As Samuel Chase of Maryland explained in 1787: "Both branches of our legislature derive *all* their power from the people, and *equally* hold their *commissions* to legislate, or make laws, from the *grant* of the people."[6]

The executive, too, remained a point of contention in many states. New York State was in dire straits throughout most of the war. Not only did it experience invasions from the north and the south, but its main city was occupied by the British for much of the war, its eastern counties were in open revolt and wanted their own state (the Green Mountain Boys of Vermont), and its frontier was frequently devastated by raids from Native Americans. To deal with these emergencies New Yorkers wrote a constitution with a strong executive elected by the people for a three-year term. But so as not to lodge too much power in one person, the constitution did not give the governor exclusive veto and appointive power. Instead, it created a Council of Revision, which included the governor and several judges to review laws passed by the legislature and a Council of Appointment, consisting of the governor and four state senators, to dole out state offices. Jefferson, too, sought to limit the power of the governor in his draft of Virginia's constitution. While the Virginia Constitution allowed for a single executive, he was to be elected annually by the two houses of legislature and almost every action he took had to be with the advice of an eight-member Council of State selected by both the assembly and the senate. Another measure of the revolutionary desire to guard against the tyranny of the executive and a powerful government was the effort to spell out the liberties of the people. Virginia, like Pennsylvania, Maryland, Delaware, North Carolina, and Massachusetts, included a bill of rights as a part of its constitution.

The Massachusetts Constitution of 1780, which was written largely by John Adams and became a model for more conservative constitutions, offered a greater balance between the different parts of government.

It had a senate with a property qualification that made it seem aristocratic. The constitution also clearly defined the governor as a strong executive commanding the state's military and wielding a broad range of authority. The governor could veto laws, but this negative could be overridden with a two-thirds majority in both houses. Some critics claimed that the Massachusetts Constitution had turned its back on the demos—the people—by creating a powerful governor. The conservatives who pushed for this stronger executive claimed that he no longer reflected the monarchical element of government. He was to be elected by the people; therefore, he, like the legislature, represented the people. In short, the classical equation of monarchy, aristocracy, and democracy had been abandoned. In the new formulation of American politics a novel balance was achieved by three different elements of government—the executive and two houses of legislature—that represented the people and theoretically ensured that the American republics would be democratic.

The process of writing the state constitutions led to another important innovation in political science—the constitutional convention. Massachusetts again was a model for this development. Most of the state constitutions had been written and ratified by the revolutionary assemblies that assumed control when royal government disintegrated. Regardless of the popular base of these assemblies, this process led to problems. Because any representative body that has the power to create also has the power to change or amend, there was no constitutional guarantee that some future assembly might not simply reconstruct the government at its will for the interest of the representatives but at the expense of the public interest. The solution developed in Massachusetts was a convention that was a special representation of the people called for the sole purpose of writing fundamental law. Once the convention had fulfilled its function it would adjourn, only to be called into being following constitutional provisions for rewriting or amending the constitution. After Massachusetts developed this process, other states followed suit. Ultimately, this idea of a constitutional convention as a special representation of the people became the rationale behind the Philadelphia Convention that produced the U.S. Constitution in the summer of 1787.

Articles of Confederation

A committee of the Continental Congress began to write the Articles of Confederation just as the revolutionaries declared independence. Congress adopted the Articles on November 15, 1777, but they did not become the official form of government until March 1, 1781, after the last state (Maryland) ratified the document. Fear of a strong central government pervaded the deliberations of the committee and informed the way it composed the Articles. Criticizing the Articles, therefore, as an ineffectual structure for a national government misses the point. The Articles were a practical republican solution to the problem of the individual states fighting a revolution against the usurpation of power by a strong central government. The revolutionaries believed that the more power government had, the less liberty the people retained. Limit government and you guarantee liberty. Yet the revolutionaries also knew that somehow the American states had to unite (notice they called themselves the United States, and not the United State) in order to fight the war. Today, the Articles read more like a treaty between sovereign states than a constitution. Article III asserted that "The said states hereby severally enter into a firm league of friendship with each other, for their common defense, the security of their Liberties, and their mutual and general welfare. . . ."[7] The authors of the Articles also recognized that they had a certain affinity for each other and therefore created a bond that went beyond an alliance allowing the people of each state to have "all privileges and immunities" in every state with "free ingress and regress."[8] To further these bonds the Articles created a national legislature and granted management of foreign affairs and the military to the United States. The Articles required the "assent" of nine states to pass most legislation.[9] However, fearful of ceding any power to tax—after all, that was what the resistance movement had been all about—the states retained the right to determine how they would raise revenue for the national govern-ment. Moreover, the union was to be perpetual and the Articles inviolable unless an alteration was "agreed to in a congress of the united states, and be afterwards confirmed by the legislatures of every state."[10]

If the main purpose of the government under the Articles of Confedera-tion was to get allies and win the Revolutionary War, then it was a success. Congress may have muddled through the conflict, but it managed to sustain the war that ended with the Treaty of Paris of 1783. The most difficult task that the Congress confronted was funding the war and supplying the army. Reflecting American hesitance to delegate too much power to any one individual, Congress at first relied on a cumbersome committee system to oversee finances and the functions of government. In 1781 a nationalist movement emerged in Congress that attempted to strengthen the central government without abandoning the Articles of Confederation. Congress dropped the committee system and appointed specific individuals to run departments of the government. Robert Morris, who headed the Depart-ment of Finance, became for all intents and purposes the chief executive of this administration. With the final collapse of the Continental currency, Morris needed some creative financing to keep the government afloat. Foreign loans, credit extended by American citizens, requisitions from the states, commercial dealings in the name of the United States, and even the selling of assets as the army downsized after Yorktown, all helped Morris to try to balance the books. It was not enough. Morris and the nationalists sought to strengthen the government further. Key to this effort was to bring order to national finances. Morris tried to tally the total national debt, which at that point was a hodgepodge of promissary notes handed out by the army and government agents in every state, as well as more regular loans from within the United States and abroad. He believed that once the total figure could be determined he could develop a plan that would enhance the power of the national government. Morris also labored toward having the states meet their quotas of state requisitions—the tax money each state was supposed to raise voluntarily for the expenses of the Confederation. Although not entirely successful, Morris brought in over two million dollars from the states. This total was about half of the amount requested. As a part of this effort to strengthen national finances Congress chartered the Bank of North America to hold government funds, loan money to the United States, and discount all notes. Eventually, so Morris believed, the bank's own notes would become the national currency and nearly every major property owner would invest in bank stock. As Morris explained to John Jay, this plan would "unite the several States more closely together in one general Money Connection," while attaching "many powerful Individuals to the Cause of our Country, by the strong Principle of Self Love, and the immediate Sense of private Interest."[11]

Central to Morris's plan, and the hopes of the nationalists to energize the government under the Articles, was an impost of 5 percent on all imports that would establish an independent source of revenue for the United States and that would be applied to the principal and interest of the national debt. Congress proposed this measure to the states in early 1781, hoping that it would be viewed as a simple revenue act that could be put into place after nine states approved. The states, however, recognized the measure as an amendment to the Articles requiring all thirteen states to agree to it. This decision created what turned out to be an insurmountable barrier. By 1782 all states but Rhode Island had accepted the amendment. Since the Articles called for unanimity, and Rhode Islanders jealously guarded their state autonomy, the measure failed. In March 1783, Congress again attempted to gain the power to tax with a new impost more directly under the control of the states that would expire in twenty-five years. Although Rhode Island eventually accepted this measure in February 1785, New York refused to pass it unless its citizens could use state bills of credit to pay the impost. This situation presented a stumbling block as the tax was supposed to be paid in specie so it could retire the foreign debt. Although some Americans still hoped for a compromise, the situation remained deadlocked in 1786. By that time Congress was having difficulty obtaining a quorum and the Confederation's business had come almost to a standstill. The chance for a stronger national government under the Articles appeared to slip away.

The fact that the national government became increasingly invisible after the Treaty of Paris of 1783 may not have been a bad thing within the context of the original intention of the Articles of Confederation. Many Americans believed that peace made a national government unnecessary. From this perspective the increased independence of the states was just fine. Morris had sought to concentrate the national debt in the hands of Congress. Without an income, Congress could not meet payment on the interest. The states therefore began to assume their share of the national debt and began to pay it back. Over the next couple of years, Pennsylvania, New York, and Maryland made significant inroads in servicing their portion of the national debt. Although the economy stagnated in the first half of the 1780s in a typical postwar recession, in most regions of the country business began to revive after 1785. Even George Washington proclaimed that things were looking better than they had ever had before. He wrote in the summer of 1786 that the "people at large . . . are more industrious than they were before the war" and "the foundation of a great empire is laid" as "our internal governments" acquire strength and the "laws have their fullest energy; justice is well administered; robbery, violence or murder is not heard of from N[e]w Hampshire to Georgia."[12]

Despite these improvements, the United States confronted several problems during this period. Perhaps one of the most difficult of these was guiding the development of Washington's "great empire" and ensuring the United States would not implode under the weight of its own success. This danger appeared in three key areas: expansion to the West; contests between the states; and internal disorder within individual states. In addition, Americans hoped to gain respect overseas and faced financial difficulties. The state and national governments struggled with various degrees of success with each of these issues.

The question of how to settle the western lands, which the British had delayed with the Proclamation line of 1763, remained in 1783. The Treaty of Paris had generously granted the area between the Appalachians and the Mississippi River to the United States. This national domain held out great promises. If administered correctly sale of the public lands could support the government and pay off the national debt. The right type of industrious settlers would help to sustain the "great empire" and strengthen the nation. There were several obstacles, however, to fulfilling this promise. First, the land was already occupied by Native Americans, many of whom had sided with the British in the war. The Confederation government did little to solve this problem, which persisted into the 1790s and beyond. Only the defeat of Native Americans in the War of 1812 and the removal of most tribes to the West in the 1830s finally opened almost all lands east of the Mississippi to European American settlement. Second, there were the settlers themselves. Thousands of Americans streamed across the Appalachians and squatted on land they did not own; critics called them "lawless banditti; and adventurers," creating an eclectic and unordered pattern of settlement.[13] Compounding the situation were land speculators who sought to control vast tracts of acreage. To counter the confusion produced by the squatters and speculators, the government wrote several land ordinances to provide a coherent plan of settlement and a rational integration of the new territories into the United States. The land ordinance of 1785 divided the western territory into neat one-mile squares with thirty-six such sections making one township. The idea was to have a survey to lay out townships before settlement, leading to what was hoped would be an orderly and controlled development of the West. This was an important first step, but Congress needed to provide some mechanism for governing and incorporating new territories into the United States. Congress therefore passed the Northwest Ordinance of 1787, creating a territory north and west of the Ohio River. The territory would be ruled by a congressionally appointed government until it had five thousand "free male inhabitants of full age," after which the territory became self-governing. Once the population of "free inhabitants" reached sixty thousand, the territory could hold a constitutional convention and apply for statehood "on an equal footing with the original States . . . *Provided*, the constitution and government so to be formed, shall be republican" and "consistent with the general interest of the confederacy." The Northwest Ordinance of 1787 allowed new territory to be fully integrated into the union and established a crucial precedent for the expansion of the United States for the next one hundred and eighty years.[14]

During the 1770s and 1780s, jurisdictional disputes between states also held the potential for disrupting the United States. However, the United States through a process of compromise and arbitration successfully dealt with these problems under the confederation government. Maryland refused to ratify the Articles until states like Virginia with large western claims ceded most of them to the national domain. Virginia did so in 1781 and thereby decreased the possibility of conflict over borders. Other states negotiated their disagreements to amicable conclusions. Only in one case, to settle the dispute between Connecticut and Pennsylvania over the Wyoming area of the upper Susquehanna River Valley, did the contesting states turn to the national government and its complicated system of arbitration.

There was also a great deal of tension within the states. Sectional divisions between the coastal regions and backcountry, which had led to popular upheaval in the 1760s and 1770s, continued. One way of alleviating this stress was moving the state capital from the coast to the interior. During the Revolutionary War, Virginians transferred their capital to Richmond. South Carolinians agreed to move their seat of government from Charleston to Columbia in 1786. Other states debated the issue, but delayed any action until the 1790s and early 1800s. Another manifestation of internal divisions within states was popular unrest. Americans had a long tradition of mob activity in the eighteenth century that underpinned much of the revolutionary movement. Independence did not automatically end public faith in rioting. Throughout the 1780s in New England, and occasionally in Virginia and Maryland, mobs disrupted courts and interrupted local government.

This popular unrest reached a crescendo in Massachusetts. Beginning in the summer of 1786, "Regulators" started to close courts to prevent the collection of debts and taxes. There was no single leader of this movement, but opponents quickly dubbed it Shays's Rebellion after Daniel Shays,

FIGURE 3–1   Daniel Shays and Job Shattuck During the 1780s economic hardship led to unrest in the countryside, culminating in Shays's Rebellion in western Massachusetts in the winter of 1786 and 1787.

who commanded one group of insurgents. The rebels hoped to suppress the "tyrannical government in the Massachusetts State." They objected to the state's constitution, which had been the darling of so many conservative revolutionary leaders, because it created a government dominated by aristocratic interests centered in Boston. With high property qualifications for voting, and even higher property qualifications for holding office, the state had increased taxes to pay back the Massachusetts debt from the Revolutionary War. A farmer in western Massachusetts now owed as much as six times in taxes as he had once paid to King George. What was worse, many veterans had been compelled to sell their own government certificates for less than one-fourth their face value. Now those ex-soldiers were being taxed to compensate in full speculators who had "sauntered at home during the war, enjoying the smiles of fortune, wallowing in affluence, and fattening in the sunshine of ease and prosperity."[15] Angered by these inequities the rebels assaulted the government arsenal in Springfield. Massachusetts militia used artillery to beat back the attack, killing at least four Shaysites. Other state militia marched on a rebel stronghold in the dead of winter, breaking up a large force under Shays. By the spring of 1787 the rebellion had collapsed. However, although 4,000 insurgents were temporarily disenfranchised by state law, their cause triumphed at the polls in the next election. A new governor and legislature dramatically reduced taxes and passed measures that would alleviate popular grievances.

The national and state governments under the Articles of Confederation thus dealt with many of the problems they faced within the country itself. Congress passed legislation for the settlement and integration of new territories into the union. Explosive controversies between states had been defused. And a major uprising had been contained by the state militia even as the legitimate concerns of the people were redressed through the electoral process.

The Confederation was less successful in the international arena. European powers did not respect the United States. The British, angered over the failure to compensate Tories and pay prewar debts, refused to evacuate their western forts on American territory. Although trade and commerce between the United States and Great Britain quickly expanded, the British denied American ships access to their West Indies possessions. Despite the goodwill built up during the war, the French were not able to replace the British as America's prime trading partner. Typical of American foreign policy problems was the failed diplomacy with Spain. Secretary for Foreign Affairs John Jay negotiated a treaty with Don Diego Gardoqui of

Spain to open Spanish ports to trade while conceding Spain's right to close the Mississippi River to Americans. The agreement angered many Americans because it did not settle the boundary with Spanish Florida and it would discourage western settlement. In 1786 seven states ratified the treaty, two short of the number required by the Articles of Confederation, leading to its rejection. There were other problems as well. The United States struggled to gain recognition from other nations, and was only able to sign commercial agreements with the Netherlands (1782), Sweden (1783), and Prussia (1785). Despite a treaty with Morocco, Americans suffered from depredations from the Barbary States in the Mediterranean. Although some of these diplomatic difficulties could be attributed to the weaknesses of the Confederation, most of these problems persisted for decades after the creation of the new government under the Constitution.

The Confederation also never successfully confronted its financial predicament. Even if there was some economic improvement after 1785, the fundamental financial problem faced by the Confederation may have been unsolvable. The costs of the war drove every state (except Vermont, which was not recognized by the other states) to increase taxes to levels several times higher than they had ever been under the British. Simultaneously, the ability of Americans to pay taxes decreased. Per capita wealth declined in the 1770s and 1780s and vast amounts of property had been destroyed or lost during the war. The financial equation was simple: Increased taxes combined with decreased wealth equaled fiscal paralysis. To make matters worse, the withdrawal from the United States of the British and French armies after 1783, which had paid for supplies in gold and silver, brought with it a loss of a source of specie. A poor trade balance with Europe, especially with Great Britain, only hurt the economy further. States that attempted to collect taxes in hard money to send to the Confederation had to back off quickly or face political upheaval. By the late 1780s specie had virtually disappeared within the United States, and the states could no longer send any part of their requisitions to the national government. Under these circumstances, even a stronger central government might have failed.

Regardless of its shortcomings, the Articles of Confederation reflected the republican ideology of the revolution and the democratic hopes of the era. No one anticipated a national government, as the war itself had been fought against a strong national government in the guise of Great Britain. In short, the Articles made sense at the time and were a product of the revolution. The critical period was not as critical as we have been led to believe. Certainly there were problems under the Articles of Confederation, but they were not as serious as the textbooks frequently contend.

Perhaps, given a few more years, a stable economic order conducive to the development of capitalism would have emerged.

The real critical period was in the heads of some leading revolutionaries, including James Madison, Alexander Hamilton, and even George Washington, who believed the current government structure neither fostered economic development nor protected the interests of the elite. If independence for the United States was a test of republicanism, then these men feared Americans were failing the test. Washington thought that the current conditions under the Articles threatened "anarchie [and] Confusion" that would ultimately be taken advantage of "by some aspiring demagogue who will not consult the interest of his Country so much as his own ambitious views." He wanted "to have a Government of respectability under which life—liberty, and property" would be secured.[16]

Madison outlined several shortcomings of the Articles in his essay "Vices of the Political System of the United States." Perhaps his most potent arguments concerned the "multiplicity" and "mutability" of laws. Madison believed that the states had passed too many laws; he called it a "luxuriancy of legislation," making it difficult if not impossible to truly master the legal code. Compounding this difficulty was that the legislatures too easily changed their minds. Laws were thereby "repealed or superseded, before any trial can have been made of their merits; and even before

FIGURE 3–2   James Madison
This early portrait shows Madison as he appeared about the time of the writing of the Constitution. Madison's essay "Vices of the Political System of the United States" summarized why some American leaders believed a stronger government was necessary in the 1780s.

a knowledge of them can have reached the remoter districts. . . ." Both problems led to "instability" in "the regulations of trade" that became "a snare not only to our citizens but to foreigners also." Madison believed that the legislatures lacked wisdom because most of their members were motivated by ambition or personal interest instead of the public good. This evil derived from frequent elections and small constituencies. Madison thought that with less frequent elections and larger electoral districts, such as might exist in a powerful national government, it would be possible to "extract from the mass of the Society the purest and noblest characters" who would protect the public interest.[17]

Constitutional Convention

The Constitutional Convention was a great moment in American history when the Founders worked their way through a series of compromises to create a new national framework. Whatever their achievement, the Constitution was also a conservative coup d'etat. The authors of the Constitution did not follow the amendment procedure outlined in the Articles of Confederation and wanted to turn back the tide of a democratic revolution. The best way to enlist "the purest and noblest characters" to serve in the government was to limit the input of a fickle public. The Constitution was also crucial to subsequent American capitalist development. Limiting the multiplicity and mutability of law, while creating a great national umbrella for all business, encouraged investment and economic development.

Nationalists in several states began to look for ways to revise and strengthen the U.S. government in 1785 and 1786. Efforts at passing amendments that required unanimous state approval appeared futile. At the instigation of Madison, Virginia proposed a meeting of states "to consider how far an uniform System in their Commercial regulations may be necessary to their common Interest and their permanent Harmony."[18] Five states sent delegates to the Annapolis Convention, which lasted for only three days in September 1786. This meeting, in turn, issued a call drawn up by Alexander Hamilton for another convention to meet in May 1787 in Philadelphia "to devise such further provisions as shall appear to them necessary to render the constitution of the Federal Government adequate to the exigencies of the Union."[19] This procedure seemed to sidestep the amendment provisions in the Articles. Congress belatedly agreed to the Convention in February 1787, but insisted that it should confine itself to proposing revisions of the Articles.

Fifty-five delegates from twelve states eventually met in the summer of 1787 in Philadelphia. These men included some of the most important political leaders of the nation. The two most famous Americans, George Washington and Benjamin Franklin, attended, although neither took an active role in the debates. Washington served as the presiding officer and Franklin was too old and infirm to participate fully. Younger men, in particular Alexander Hamilton from New York and James Madison from Virginia, set the tone of the meeting. To guarantee an open and free debate, and to limit grandstanding and appeals to the public, they voted to keep all deliberations behind closed doors. They also agreed to go beyond even the broad commission of the Annapolis Convention; they determined to write an entirely new frame of government. Edmund Randolph led the way by submitting the Virginia Plan on May 29. Madison wrote the plan to create a strong national government that would have two houses of legislature, an executive, and a separate judiciary. Although the exact details would be debated, altered, and elaborated, by offering a blueprint for a new government the Virginians dictated the terms of discussion. Madison had wanted a lower house of legislature elected by the people with the other house of legislature and executive elected by the lower house. Representation was to be apportioned by the size of the population of free inhabitants.

The delegates from the smaller states objected to the Virginia Plan and drew up the New Jersey Plan, which would have been merely a revision of the Articles. Even though the Convention quickly rejected the New Jersey Plan, the delegates from smaller states continued to object to representation based on population because they believed it would allow the large states like Virginia to dominate the union. In early July the Convention worked out the Connecticut (or Great) Compromise whereby the states would have equal votes in the upper house (the Senate), and representation in the lower house (the House of Representatives) would be dependent on the population of the states. During the closing days of July and in early August a drafting committee developed many of the details of a new government that had more extensive powers than had even appeared in Madison's original draft.

In August the delegates debated the issue of slavery. Many northerners held that slavery was a moral evil and that the Constitution should at least abolish the importation of slaves, if not take more drastic action. Some southern delegates, like George Mason of Virginia, agreed; Mason believed that the slave trade was especially inimical, calling it an "infernal traffic" that "originated in the avarice of British Merchants." South Carolinians, however, were adamant in the defense of slavery. Charles Pinkney declared that slavery was "justified by the example of all the world" and that "In all ages one half of mankind have been slaves." His older cousin, General

Charles Cotesworth Pinkney, also supported slavery and argued that more slaves would increase the production of export commodities, which would mean "the more of revenue for the common treasury."[20] When delegates like Roger Sherman and Oliver Ellsworth from Connecticut called for a middle ground, another compromise was worked out. The Constitution would say nothing directly about slavery. The United States could not legislate against the importation of "Persons as any of the States now existing shall think proper to admit" (slaves) for twenty years, until 1808.[21] There would be no provision to prevent individual states from passing their own regulations. The Constitution also offered some protection to slaveholders by including a fugitive slave provision. "No Person held to Service or Labour [slavery] in one State . . . escaping into another, shall . . . be discharged from such Service or Labour."[22] Instead, they "shall be delivered up on Claim of the Party to whom such Service or Labour may be due." Similarly, the guarantee to each state "against domestic Violence" was as much to protect against a slave uprising as it was to counter actions such as Shays's Rebellion.[23]

The final document agreed to on September 17, 1787, represented a victory for the conservatives who wished to limit democracy by creating a strong national government. The new office of the president had a tenure of four years with the possibility of unlimited reelection. (The Twenty-second Amendment in 1951 established the two-term limit.) He was made commander in chief of the army and navy, given broad appointive powers, had the biggest voice in international affairs by making treaties and appointing ambassadors with the advice and consent of the Senate. Like a monarch, he would receive foreign emissaries and could pardon any violator of national law. The Constitution set up a complicated procedure for the election of the president. The Founding Fathers intended to filter out the fickle will of the people by having voters in each state select members of the electoral college. The common folk might not know enough to select a national leader, but they could at least recognize the local elite whose judgement could be relied on to select likely candidates for president. Everyone expected that the first president would be George Washington, who would easily gain a majority of the electoral college. After Washington's tenure the decision would not be as clear and the Founding Fathers thought it was unlikely that anyone would gain a majority. The electoral college's main role then would be to provide a slate of the top five candidates for the House of Representatives, voting by state, to choose the president, who had to gain a majority of the state delegation votes. No one anticipated the development of political parties, so the person with the next highest number of votes in the electoral college (each member of the electoral college had two votes), or in the house vote if there had not been a majority for one candidate, would become vice president. The Senate would vote to break any ties for vice president. Congress would thereby identify the two wisest and most disinterested individuals to be president and vice president. (The Twelfth Amendment in 1804 altered the process to have separate ballots for president and vice president.)

The Founding Fathers also sought to ensure that the legislative branch was to be composed of "the purest and noblest characters" by limiting the input of the people. Senators had to be at least thirty years old (the president had to be at least thirty-five) and were elected for a long, six-year term of office. Moreover, the state legislatures determined the election of senators. (In 1913 the Seventeenth Amendment changed this provision, making the senators popularly elected). Because senators would be the wisest and most distinguished individuals from their states, they were given the role of advising and offering their consent to the president's treaties and appointments to the Supreme Court, key administrative offices, and foreign embassies. Although popular election determined membership in the House of Representatives, two-year terms and large electoral districts, the delegates hoped, would guard against overly ambitious and self-interested members of Congress. Because its representation reflected the overall population, and "direct Taxes" were to be apportioned according to the "respective Numbers" of the states, revenue bills originated in the House of Representatives.[24] The delegates, however, had difficulty in defining "respective Numbers." Southerners wanted to count their slaves for representation. Northerners objected. As William Patterson of New Jersey explained: "He could regard negroes slaves in no light but as property. They are no free agents, have no personal liberty, no faculty of acquiring property," and as property they were "entirely at the will of the Master." Patterson then queried "has a man in Virg[ini]a a number of votes in proportion to the number of his slaves?" James Wilson of Pennsylvania pushed these objections further by decrying counting any portion of the slaves for representation, asking "Are they [slaves] admitted as Citizens? then why are they not admitted on an equality with White Citizens? are they admitted as property? then why is not other property admitted into the computation?"[25] Ultimately, both sides agreed to the "three-fifth compromise" whereby representation would be apportioned "by adding to the whole Number of free Persons, including those bound to Service for a Term of Years, and excluding Indians not taxed, three fifths of all other Persons."[26]

The Constitution created a national government with powers that challenged state sovereignty. The Supreme Court served during good behavior and was appointed by the president with the advice and consent of the Senate. Its power extended "to all Cases, in Law and Equity, arising under this Constitution, the Laws of the United States, and Treaties made."[27]

This mandate did not explicitly include judicial review, but was broad enough to allow later courts to claim that right. Unlike the Congress under the Articles of Confederation, the new Congress had "Power To lay and collect Taxes, Duties, Imposts and Excises, to pay the Debts and provide for the common Defense and general Welfare of the United States." If this provision did not strengthen the national government sufficiently, the delegates included an open-ended authority "To make all Laws which shall be necessary and proper for carrying into Execution" the powers "vested by this Constitution in the Government of the United States. . . ."[28]

The "necessary and proper" clause would later be interpreted broadly to foster economic development. The Constitution also included a number of provisions conducive to the rise of American capitalism. First and foremost, the new government guaranteed a national market without trade barriers between states. Congress was empowered to "regulate Commerce with foreign Nations, and among the several States, and with the Indian tribes." The Constitution allowed Congress to create uniform bankruptcy laws that would theoretically encourage investment. The federal government alone could coin money and "fix the Standard of Weights and Measures," assuring consistency throughout the nation. To foster and "promote the Progress of Science and useful Arts" and encourage innovation and invention, Congress could write copyright and patent law. Congress could establish post offices and post roads to facilitate interstate communication. And the Constitution not only allowed the United States to borrow money, but it also assured creditors that all previous debts of the government remained valid. Taken together, these provisions promised a bright economic future under the protective cover of a strong national government.[29]

Federalists and Antifederalists

Had there been a public referendum in 1787 in all likelihood the Constitution would not have been ratified. Large numbers of Americans remained suspicious of a powerful government that might threaten liberty. Nor would the Constitution have passed if the Founding Fathers had followed the amendment procedures of the Articles, which called for all states to agree on any changes to the structure of government. Recognizing that unanimity would be impossible—obstinate Rhode Island had not even sent a delegation to the Convention—the Constitution declared that its new government would be put into effect once nine states had accepted it. The delegates also sought to avoid the state legislatures as the Constitution severely circumscribed their powers. Therefore, the Constitution called for state conventions that would be a special representation of the people to meet to ratify the document. Taken together, this irregular procedure could be interpreted as a coup d'etat.

Of course, few Americans today see the Constitution as an overthrow of the state. In part this position results from the fact that the

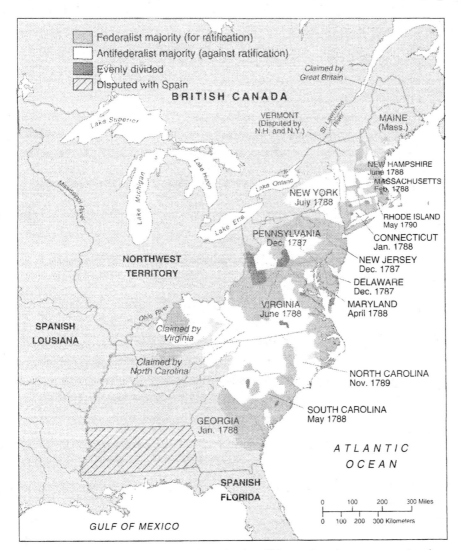

Federalist majority (for ratification)

Antifederalist majority (against ratification)

Evenly divided

Disputed with Spain

BRITISH CANADA

Claimed by Great Britain

Lake Superior

VERMONT
(Disputed by
N.H. and N.Y.)

MAINE
(Mass.)

Lake Huron

Lake Michigan

St. Lawrence River

NEW HAMPSHIRE
June 1788

MASSACHUSETTS
Feb. 1788

Lake Ontario

Lake Erie

NEW YORK
July 1788

RHODE ISLAND
May 1790

Mississippi River

PENNSYLVANIA
Dec. 1787

CONNECTICUT
Jan. 1788

NORTHWEST
TERRITORY

NEW JERSEY
Dec. 1787

DELAWARE
Dec. 1787

SPANISH
LOUSIANA

Ohio River

Claimed by
Virginia

VIRGINIA
June 1788

MARYLAND
April 1788

Claimed by
North Carolina

NORTH CAROLINA
Nov. 1789

GEORGIA
Jan. 1788

SOUTH CAROLINA
May 1788

ATLANTIC
OCEAN

SPANISH
FLORIDA

GULF OF MEXICO

0   100   200   300 Miles

0   100   200   300 Kilometers

MAP 3–1   The Ratification of the Constitution   This map, based on county voting, does not provide a full measure of the opposition to the Constitution. Although coastal and some interior areas tied to the commercial economy tended to support the Constitution, had there been a popular vote on ratification, the Constitution probably would have failed.

Federalists—as the supporters of the Constitution called themselves—won and the frame of government, with a few amendments, has served successfully for over two hundred years. But it is also a result of the debates over the Constitution. Its opponents—the Antifederalists—attacked the Constitution on three interrelated grounds: that it created a too powerful government not subject to the people; that the United States covered too large a geographical area to sustain a republic; and that there was no guarantee of the rights of the people. In the process, they wrangled some important concessions, especially in the guise of the Bill of Rights. The Federalists, in the meantime, struggled to disguise their hierarchical orientation, co-opted some of the democratic rhetoric of their foes, and infused the Constitution with a greater and unplanned democratic meaning.

The Antifederalists feared that the national government had too much power. Patrick Henry argued at the Virginia ratification convention in 1788 that if the president were "a man of ambition, and abilities" he could easily "render himself absolute" and become a king because he not only commanded the army, but could also take control of the militia. Henry believed that granting the rulers so much power might be all right if you could always guarantee that good men would be in office, but history demonstrated that that would not always be the case. The government's "defective, and imperfect construction, puts it in their [the rulers] power to perpetrate the worst of mischiefs, should they be bad men."[30] Henry and other Antifederalists also denounced other aspects of energetic government under the Constitution. Antifederalists thought that the Senate would be an "aristocratic junto" that would probably "continue in office for life." Similarly, because of the large electoral districts, the House of Representatives would be composed of "the *better sort*, the *well born*," and unaccountable to its constituents.[31] Giving Congress control of the time, place, and manner of elections would "totally destroy the end of suffrage" because "The elections may be held at one place, and the most inconvenient in the State."[32] The judiciary, too, was "oppressively constructed" with no provision for jury trial and the judges dependent on Congress.[33] Perhaps the most important item in this Antifederalist list of potential dangers in the Constitution was the concern with the "necessary and proper" clause. Antifederalists imagined that this provision could easily be extended to diminish the state governments by inhibiting the state power to tax. They argued that if a state passed a tax that competed with a federal tax, Congress might "abrogate and repeal" the state tax "upon the allegation that they interfere with the due collection" of U.S. taxes.[34]

The most famous defense of the Constitution appeared in a series of essays written by Alexander Hamilton, James Madison, and John Jay under the pseudonym Publius and collectively called *The Federalist Papers*. They were published individually first in New York newspapers beginning on October 27, 1787, and ran until early April. They were reprinted in newspapers throughout the country and subsequently issued in book form in May 1788. Within a few years *The Federalist Papers* had been reprinted many times and translated into several different languages. Although often written in haste and by three different men, *The Federalist Papers* have come to be viewed as a definitive statement on the thinking of the Founders on the Constitution and have even been cited in decisions by the Supreme Court.

Publius responded to the Antifederalist charges by highlighting the dangers inherent in not forming a stronger union and by emphasizing the checks on unbridled power written into the Constitution. Without a federal government, Alexander Hamilton wrote, the states would quickly divide into little confederacies and would soon be at each other's throats. In this scenario, wars would be inevitable and each confederation would need a standing army and an executive with even stronger powers than those granted under the Constitution. Thus there was more to be feared from not forming a stronger union than from signing on to the Constitution. Hamilton also maintained that any similarity between the president and a king was superficial; the president was elected for a four-year term whereas a king was hereditary and for life. Nor did this executive have complete control over the army and militia. Congress was responsible for raising and supplying the army and the states were responsible for maintaining the militia. The president's role was to have "supreme command and direction of the military and naval forces"; unlike a king he could not declare war or raise and regulate fleets and armies.[35] Moreover, not only was the president subject to the will of the people during reelection, but he could also be impeached for violating the law and the Constitution. Still, Hamilton believed that the United States needed a strong and unitary executive because "A feeble Executive implies a feeble execution of the government. A feeble execution is but another phrase for a bad execution; and a government ill executed, whatever it may be in theory, must be, in practice, a bad government."[36]

The Federalists also defended the other aspects of the Constitution attacked by Antifederalists. *Federalist No. 62* justified the Senate on several accounts. First, the Senate's small size reflected the equality of representation of the states that served as a "constitutional recognition of the portion of sovereignty remaining in the individual States." Second, its very existence was due to the need to have two houses of legislation to double "the security to the people" as it would be twice as hard to corrupt two institutions instead of one. Similarly, the Senate guarded against "the propensity of all single and numerous assemblies to yield to the impulse of sudden and violent passions." Finally, the long terms of office would ensure that the Senators would have "acquaintance with the objects and principles of legislation," preventing the "mutability in the public councils" that Madison believed had so bedeviled the states.[37] Biennial and popular election of the House of Representatives would guarantee that the people at large would have a continual voice in government. *Federalist No. 59* asserted that *"every government ought to contain in itself the means of its own preservation"* as a defense of the provision to set the time and place of its own election.[38] If this power had been granted to the states, the states would control the Congress and each election might be a constitutional crisis. The Federalists also contended that the judiciary was not oppressive. Its members, once appointed and confirmed, had to be independent of the other branches because they were to serve as "an intermediate body between the people and the legislature . . . to keep the latter within the limits assigned to their authority."[39] Nor was there anything in the Constitution to threaten jury trials. The silence on the issue in the Constitution meant that jury trials would continue when appropriate under state law, whereas the Supreme Court, in which knowledge of the law and Constitution were crucial, would act without them when deciding cases on the highest level. Madison addressed the "necessary and proper" clause in *Federalist 44* by stating that without it "the whole Constitution would be a dead letter."[40] Expressly enumerating all of these powers would have involved a complete list of laws under the purview of the federal government. Not only would this list have been cumbersome, but it would be impossible to include every provision that would be needed in the future. To have weakened the statement would have left the new government under the same handicap that the Confederation government had—that the states could dictate what was and was not appropriate for the federal government. In short, the clause had to be constructed broadly to secure the efficacy of government.

Antifederalists also used the best political science of the day to argue against having a republic over so vast an area as the United States. James Winthrop's "Agrippa Letters" spelled out this position. Winthrop wrote: "It is the opinion of the ablest writers on the subject, that no extensive empire can be governed upon republican principles, and that such a government will degenerate to a despotism." The best safeguard for liberty was "a confederacy of smaller states, each having the full powers of internal regulation." Winthrop abandoned the older notion of public virtue as sacrificing for the public good. Instead, he sought ways of identifying the individual's interest with the community. He believed that in a small republic each individual's interest would be identical to the local interest.

In such a situation, "All men having the same view are bound equally to promote the welfare of the whole." A large state would cover so much ground that it would have many different interests competing with one another. Interests of one locality would therefore have to be put aside for the interests of another locality. This disregarding of some local interests was "requiring of one man to do more than another" and subverted "the foundation of a free government."[41]

Madison's *Federalist No. 10* took this argument head-on. Like Winthrop, he abandoned the absolute ideal of public virtue for most people and admitted that society was divided into factions. The purpose of government was "To secure the public good and private rights against the danger" of faction, while preserving "the spirit and the form of popular government." No one community could be totally identified as having a single interest. Each community, no matter how small, either governed as a direct democracy or as a representative republic, would be divided with a majority in a position to act against the interests of the minority. A large republic, however, had distinct advantages. As a republic all issues would be passed "through the medium of a chosen body of citizens, whose wisdom may best discern the true interest of their country, and whose patriotism and love of justice will be least likely to sacrifice it to temporary or partial considerations." And in a large republic you "Extend the sphere," taking in "a greater variety of parties and interests," making "it less probable that a majority of the whole will have a common motive to invade the rights of other citizens."[42] In other words, the Constitution of the United States, covering a huge geographic area, would be a better republic than any one state because its size would help place the right people in government and prevent any one faction from dominating and usurping the liberty of others.

The Antifederalists, however, were not convinced that the Constitution would protect their liberty. In essay after essay they lambasted the document for its failure to include a bill of rights. Several states had included bills of rights in their own constitutions, and it was thought only appropriate for the national government, especially a powerful national government, to include similar guarantees of basic freedoms. Federalists responded by stating that a bill of rights was inappropriate in a general framework of government and that those rights were protected implicitly because there was nothing in the Constitution inhibiting any rights. As Hamilton explained in *Federalist No. 84,* a bill of rights "would contain various exceptions to powers not granted" and, once stipulated, any right not spelled out might be forfeit.[43] The issue came up during the debates in the state conventions, and in key states like Massachusetts and Virginia, Federalists had to promise to add a bill of rights to gain enough votes to secure ratification. To follow through on that promise, shortly after the ratification of the Constitution, Madison drew up a list of rights that became the first ten constitutional amendments. Among these guarantees was the Tenth Amendment—"The powers not delegated to the United States by the Constitution, nor prohibited by it to the States, are reserved to the States respectively, or to the people"—which stood in stark opposition to the "necessary and Proper clause." Although the Antifederalists abandoned any concerted opposition to the federal government after 1789, the debate over state sovereignty persisted in the constitutional space between these two clauses through the American Civil War and beyond.

Federalists and Antifederalist had different perceptions of society. The Federalists clung to a hierarchical worldview and believed that they could speak for the larger public good. They hoped that the new Constitution would place the right type of people in control of the government—men who would be above interest and faction and who would possess "the purest and noblest characters." The Antifederalists saw society divided into different interests and viewed the Federalist elite as just another self-serving faction. Melancton Smith declared at the New York ratification convention that the new government would "fall into the hands of the few and the great." As such it would be "a government of oppression." Because all men were ruled by the same "passions and prejudices" the elite would pursue their own interest at the expense of the middling and the poor. Smith drew a sharp contrast between the elite and the common man. "The great consider themselves above the common people—entitled to more respect—do not associate with them—they fancy themselves to have a right of pre-eminence in every thing." On the other hand "the substantial yeomanry of the country are more temperate, of better morals and less ambition than the great." He called for a government that would include both the yeomanry and the great; one that would be "friendly to liberty and the rights of mankind, which will tend to cherish and cultivate a love of liberty among our citizens."[44] Smith may have seen through the Federalist facade but his speech did not change the outcome of the convention. After much discussion and arm-twisting, one state after another ratified the Constitution.

The Federalists won the day in part by being better organized and in part by stealing Antifederalist thunder. Once several states accepted the Constitution swiftly a momentum had been built up that left states with the choice of joining or of being excluded from the United States. The authors of the Constitution also strove to address the pressing social and economic issues that had led to the revolution. The Founders believed that they had created a political structure that would ensure "the purest and noblest

FIGURE 3–3   The Connecticut Debate over Ratification This Amos Doolittle
illustration demonstrates that even in states like Connecticut, which ratified the Constitution
relatively easily, there was a lively debate over the merits of the new form of government.

characters" would govern, while simultaneously encouraging economic
development. The Federalists miscalculated. They never fully understood
the intimate relationship between equality and capitalism. Despite their best
efforts the Constitution moved in unanticipated directions. Whatever the
intentions of the Federalists in limiting democratic government, they also
used a popular rhetoric to defend their document that emphasized the
sovereignty of the people. The Constitution, after all, began with the assertion "We the people." With the people sovereign, the state governments and
the federal government, as well as the different branches of government,
could be portrayed as merely different expressions of the people's sovereign
will and the Constitution became a much more democratic instrument
than the Federalists ever intended. Fearing that republicanism might fail
without their Constitution, the Federalists had sought to fulfill their image
of a national government in which a disinterested elite would rule for
the public good. The government under the Constitution fell short of these
expectations and gave way to more democratic practices that ultimately
contributed to the growth of equality and the development of a competitive and capitalist nation.

Endnotes

1. Quoted in Gordon S. Wood, *The Creation of the American Republic, 1776–1787* (Chapel Hill: University of North Carolina Press, 1969), 127.

2. Constitution of Pennsylvania, Sept. 28, 1776, The Avalon Project at Yale Law School, www.yale.edu/lawweb/avalon/states/pa08.htm.

3. Constitution of Pennsylvania, Sept. 28, 1776, The Avalon Project at Yale Law School, www.yale.edu/lawweb/avalon/states/pa08.htm.

4. Constitution of Pennsylvania, Sept. 28, 1776, The Avalon Project at Yale Law School, www.yale.edu/lawweb/avalon/states/pa08.htm.

5. Quoted in Wood, *Creation of the American Republic,* 441.

6. Quoted in Wood, *Creation of the American Republic,* 241, 250, 253.

7. Art. III, Articles of Confederation.

8. Art. IV, Articles of Confederation.

9. Art. IX, Articles of Confederation.

10. Art. XIII, Articles of Confederation.

11. E. James Ferguson, ed., *The Papers of Robert Morris, 1781–1784: Vol. I,* 9 vols. (Pittsburgh: University of Pittsburgh Press, 1973–), 1: 287.

12. W. W. Abbot and Dorothy Twohig, et al., eds., *The Papers of George Washington: Confederation Series,* 6 vols. (Charlottesville: University Press of Virginia, 1992–97), 4: 186.

13. Quoted in Peter S. Onuf, *Statehood and Union: A History of the Northwest Ordinance* (Bloomington: Indiana University Press, 1987), 33.

14. Northwest Ordinance, July 13, 1787, The Avalon Project at Yale Law School, www.yale.edu/lawweb/avalon/nworder.htm.

15. Quoted in Leonard L. Richards, *Shays's Rebellion: The American Revolution's Final Battle* (Philadelphia: University of Pennsylvania Press, 2002), 63, 79.

16. Abbot and Twohig, et al., eds., *The Papers of George Washington: Confederation Series,* 5: 222.

17. James Madison, "Vices of the Political System of the United States, April 1787," Robert A. Rutland, et al., eds., *The Papers of James Madison,* 17 vols. (Chicago and Charlottesville: University of Chicago and University of Virginia Press, 1962–1991), 9: 348–58.

18. Resolution Authorizing a Commission to Examine Trade Regulations, Jan. 21, 1786, Robert A. Rutland, et al., eds. *The Papers of James Madison,* 8: 471.

19. Annapolis Convention, Sept. 14, 1786, The Avalon Project at Yale Law School, www.yale.edu/lawweb/avalon/amerdoc/annapoli.htm.

20. The Debates in the Federal Convention of 1787 Reported by James Madison, Aug. 22, The Avalon Project at Yale Law School, www.yale.edu/lawweb/avalon/debates/822.htm.

21. Constitution, Art. I, Sec. 9.

22. Constitution, Art. IV, Sec. 2.

23. Constitution, Art. IV, Sec. 2, and 4.

24. Constitution, Art. I, Sec. 2.

25. The Debates in the Federal Convention of 1787 Reported by James Madison, July 9 and July 11, The Avalon Project at Yale Law School, www.yale.edu/lawweb/avalon/debates/709.htm and www.yale.edu/lawweb/avalon/debates/711.htm.

26. Constitution, Art. I, Sec. 2.

27. Constitution, Art. III, Sec. 2.

28. Constitution, Art. I, Sec. 8.

29. Constitution, Art. I, Sec. 8.

30. Ralph Ketchum, ed., *The Anti-Federalist Papers and the Constitutional Convention Debates* (New York: New American Library, 1986), 214.
31. Ketchum, ed., *The Anti-Federalist Papers,* 235, 334.
32. Ketchum, ed., *The Anti-Federalist Papers,* 215.
33. Ketchum, ed., *The Anti-Federalist Papers,* 212.
34. Ketchum, ed., *The Anti-Federalist Papers,* 243.
35. "The Federalist Papers: No. 69," The Avalon Project at Yale Law School, www.yale.edu/lawweb/avalon/federal/fed69.htm.
36. "The Federalist Papers: No. 70," The Avalon Project at Yale Law School, www.yale.edu/lawweb/avalon/federal/fed70.htm.
37. "The Federalist Papers: No. 62," The Avalon Project at Yale Law School, www.yale.edu/lawweb/avalon/federal/fed62.htm.
38. "The Federalist Papers: No. 59," The Avalon Project at Yale Law School, www.yale.edu/lawweb/avalon/federal/fed59.htm.
39. "The Federalist Papers: No. 78," The Avalon Project at Yale Law School, www.yale.edu/lawweb/avalon/federal/fed78.htm.
40. "The Federalist Papers: No. 44," The Avalon Project at Yale Law School, www.yale.edu/lawweb/avalon/federal/fed44.htm.
41. James Winthrop, Agrippa Letters, www.constitution.org/afp/agrippa.htm.
42. "The Federalist Papers: No. 10," The Avalon Project at Yale Law School, www.yale.edu/lawweb/avalon/federal/fed10.htm.
43. "The Federalist Papers: No. 83," The Avalon Project at Yale Law School, www.yale.edu/lawweb/avalon/federal/fed84.htm.
44. Ketchum, ed., *The Anti-Federalist Papers,* 344, 347.

Revolutionary Visions Unfulfilled

Native Americans

African Americans

Women

✪ American Culture

Native Americans

Other Americans saw new possibilities born out of the circumstances created by the Revolutionary War, only to discover their revolutionary visions unfulfilled. Native Americans may not have been inspired by the European American rhetoric of liberty, but many saw in the conflict between the British and their American colonists an opportunity to protect their way of life and their own notions of liberty. Despite some military triumphs, by the mid-1790s most Native Americans east of the Mississippi remained hard-pressed by the influx of European American speculators and settlers scrambling to claim their lands. African Americans reacted to the revolution. Some eagerly fought for liberty wearing the king's or the Continental army's uniform. Others took the revolutionary language to heart and pushed for emancipation. Most remained in bondage and would provide the labor for the expansion of the cotton production that helped to fuel the burgeoning American economy of the early republic. Women, too, were inspired by the revolution, joining in the resistance movement, and pushing for a new role in society. Despite gaining some ground in education and developing the ideal of republican motherhood, women continued to be denied political rights and even legal identity. Women's work, although often unacknowledged by men, frequently added cash to the household and represented the cutting edge in the development of American capitalism. Even the great white men found some of their dreams for the revolution unfulfilled. Their hope to create a new age of classicism and high culture foundered on the rock of crass realities of the market and the leveling effects of equality.

Indians were the big losers of the Revolutionary War. Whether they fought for or against the revolution, or remained neutral, Native Americans lost. The Treaty of Paris of 1783 did not even mention them by name. Yet the peace agreement ceded their vast domain between the Appalachians and the Mississippi River, hitherto land occupied largely by Indians, to the United States. Native Americans, however, did not simply accept this decision by diplomats a continent away. They had their own vision of a revolutionary America that excluded white settlers and that would sustain their culture, even as it incorporated elements of the European-American world they opposed. To uphold that vision Indians fought either as individual groups or in larger confederacies. This resistance was not a rearguard action by a doomed people facing the onslaught of white civilization. It was a decades-long effort that saw many victories in the 1780s and early 1790s. Even in defeat, in the South among the Cherokees and Creeks and in the North at the Battle of Fallen Timbers in 1794, Native Americans compelled a reluctant United States to at least come to the treaty table.

To understand the reaction of Native Americans to the Revolutionary War we need to take a closer look at the way Indians lived. From the moment of the first contact between Europeans and Indians, the Europeans misunderstood Indian society. Europeans identified nations or tribes among the Indians while minimizing the permanence of settlement patterns. Because men hunted and women farmed, Europeans underestimated the agricultural base of most eastern North American natives. Because settlements—towns really—moved frequently, adjusting to the seasons or to be close to new fertile fields for their corn, beans, and squash, European Americans refused to recognize the sense of permanence and attachment to the land among Indians. Because natives did not build fences or covet the ideal of private property, European Americans refused to respect the Indian claim to the countryside. Recently, historians have labored to provide a more complex picture of Native Americans.

Certainly there were groups of Indians we can call tribes who spoke distinct languages, shared cultural traits, and who might even be affiliated in confederations or identify themselves as belonging to a particular people and sharing a kinship system. But native cultures were never static and unchanging. Even before European contact there were migrations, mergers, and wars that made for dynamic societies. After contact, and with the onslaught of new diseases, the introduction of different trade patterns, and the increased presence of European Americans, the situation became more agitated. By the late eighteenth century, through adoption and combination, many native towns became an ever changing kaleidoscope of peoples. The Iroquoian town of Oquaga on the upper Susquehanna River contained not only members of some of the tribes of the Six Nations—Oneida, Cayuga, Mohawks, and Tuscarora—but also Shawnees, Mahicans, and Nanticokes. Similar conglomerations appeared elsewhere in Indian country. Contact also altered native material culture as Indians incorporated European textiles, metal, weaponry, and alcohol into their daily lives. Native men did not gain their sense of identity from possessions; rather, their status depended on their skill as a hunter, a warrior, or even as an orator. Native women tilled the field, had some political voice, and, with a matrilineal society, were the main conduit of the kinship system. Mutuality and respect were more important than property and possessions. Loss of hunting territory—land Europeans saw as empty— threatened these societies and challenged the independence of native culture.

It is against this cultural backdrop that we must look at the Native American reaction to the Revolutionary War. The conflict posed the same problem for Indians as it did for other inhabitants of the British North American empire: Should they support or oppose the rebellion? Indians would have been happiest just to be left alone. But as the war dragged on, that became less and less of an option. Most Native Americans, like many of their European American counterparts, therefore followed an uneven course between loyalty to the crown and loyalty to the revolutionary cause. Like European Americans they sometimes shifted sides as their interests seemed to dictate. The polyglot nature of many of their communities contributed to this mixed reaction to the revolution, sometimes dividing communities in a bitter civil war, and sometimes allowing a town to play both sides simultaneously. A few Indian groups, including the Stockbridge Indians of western Massachusetts, the Oneidas of New York, and the Catawbas in the Carolinas, eagerly joined the revolutionary cause. Choosing the winning side did not help. The Stockbridge Indians fighting with the Continental army suffered devastating military casualties during the war. Many of the remaining natives sold their small property holdings to pay debts, a practice that began before the war, and moved to land offered by the Oneidas in New York. For their part, the Oneidas suffered from the general assault on all the Iroquois despite their loyalty to the United States, and, in a series of postwar treaties, gave up much of their own land to white settlers. The Catawbas fared somewhat better, holding on to many elements of their culture and clinging to a dwindling territory that became increasingly surrounded by a sea of white farmers.

By the end of the war, especially on the frontier, more and more Indians sided with the power that could best protect their liberty—the British. Even during the war European American settlers continued to stream across the mountains to stake claims in Indian country. To protect their way of life and their own ideal of freedom, large numbers of Indians fought against the United States. They suffered for this decision. American troops marched into Cherokee territory in 1776, 1779, 1780, and 1781, destroying towns and torching cornfields. General John Sullivan followed a similar scorched earth policy during his invasion of Iroquoia in 1779, crushing the power of the Six Nations in New York. George Rogers Clark invaded Shawnee territory in 1780 and 1782, razing a few towns and burning fields of corn, leaving desolation in his wake.

Native Americans, however, were resilient in the face of these offensives and wreaked havoc on white settlements. In many cases, soon after the American forces withdrew, Indians rebuilt their towns on a site nearby—this type of residential mobility was a part of their cultural landscape. The loss of agricultural produce was more difficult to replace and many natives died as a result of dwindling food supplies. Others became refugees, moving to unmolested towns or concentrating in encampments near British outposts such as Fort Niagara. Indian men took the war to the Americans as well in murderous raids on frontier settlements. In July 1778 a combined Indian and British force struck the Wyoming Valley in northeastern Pennsylvania, annihilating settlements, torturing captives, and leading to the death of hundreds. In November, many of the same Indians struck again at Cherry Valley in New York, killing more than fifty men, women, and children. Natives repeatedly raided Kentucky, destroying farms and settlements as well as defeating local militia. By 1782, many natives in the Ohio country began to think that they were winning the war, especially after the victory over some of Clark's troops near the Ohio River in late 1781 and the routing of Kentucky militia at the Battle of Blue Licks and Pennsylvania troops at Sandusky in 1782.

The Treaty of Paris in 1783 therefore came as a complete shock to Native Americans. The Iroquois were distraught with the peace and told the British commander at Fort Niagara "that if it was really true that the English had basely betrayed them by pretending to give up their Country to the Americans without their Consent, or Consulting them, it was an Act of Cruelty and injustice that Christians only were capable of doing."[1] As the Cherokee Little Turkey explained, "The peacemaker and our Enemies have talked away our Lands at a Rum Drinking."[2] Similarly, Alexander McGillivray, a Creek leader, believed that the Indians had not done anything to permit the king to give away their lands "unless . . . Spilling our blood in the Service of his Nation can be deemed so." Having fought so hard, and suffered so much, Native Americans felt they had been "most Shamefully deserted."[3]

The United States had little sympathy for their old enemies among the Indians—nor did it seem to care much for the few Indians who had fought

MAP 4–1   Native American Wars For Native Americans and European Americans on the
frontier the Revolutionary War lasted almost twenty years. After 1783 Native Americans
continued to oppose the United States and the European American settlers who began
to stream across the mountains. Only with the United States victory at Fallen Timbers
(August 20, 1794), after a series of previous defeats, was land north of the Ohio River opened
for European American settlement and the near continuous warfare in the region ended.

with them. From the American perspective the territory west of the
Appalachians was theirs by right of conquest and the Indians had to pay for
choosing the wrong side. At the end of the war there was a veritable orgy of
land cessions often made with whatever Indian who was willing to sign an
agreement, whether the individual represented his tribe or not. Both the
states and the national government got into the act. In 1783 the Congress
declared it preferred "clemency to rigor" and that "with a less generous

people than Americans," Indians "might be compelled to retire beyond the lakes." However, as Congress was "disposed to be kind to them [Indians]" and, "from motives of compassion," the government would "draw a veil over what is passed" and "establish a boundary line between them and us."[4] In other words, the United States would obtain what land it wanted, and the Indians should feel lucky that the generous Americans did not seize immediate possession of all the land east of the Mississippi. Unlike the British and other European powers, Congress refused to negotiate with the Indians or provide gifts; instead, the Americans as the victors claimed that they could dictate all terms concerning the western domain.

Native Americans resisted this idea. Having never signed a peace treaty, and believing that the king "had no right Whatever to grant away to the States of America, their Rights or properties," many Indians continued to fight to protect their land and their liberty.[5] In the South, tribes such as the Creeks and Cherokees were divided into factions, with some individuals seeking to appease the Americans, and others seeking further resistance. Elements of the Creeks under John McGillivray found support with the Spanish in Florida. Although many Cherokees ceded lands to the Americans, another group under Dragging Canoe persisted in its opposition and continued along the path of war. North of the Ohio, several native groups formed a pan-Indian confederacy. In 1786 in Detroit the Iroquois Joseph Brant spoke to an intertribal council urging unanimity: "The Interests of Any One Nation Should be the Interests of us all, the Welfare of the one Should be the Welfare of all the others."[6] As one Indian orator put it a few years later: "We are one people, of one color, on this island [North America] and ought to be of one mind, and . . . become as one people in peace and friendship."[7] Containing many towns and over a dozen tribal groups, the confederation never achieved full unity and was hampered by some of the same divisiveness that infected the American government under the Articles of Confederation. But like the American government it also achieved some successes.

The constant warfare of the 1780s compelled the United States to abandon its more bellicose policy and pursue agreements with the Indians. As early as the mid-1780s Secretary of War Henry Knox began to urge a more balanced approach to Indian affairs. It was in the spirit of this new way of thinking that the Northwest Ordinance included a provision that guaranteed "the utmost good faith" in dealing with the Indians and promised that "their lands and property shall never be taken from them without their consent."[8] In August 1787, Congress supported the abandonment of "a language of superiority and command" and wanted to deal "with the Indians more on a footing of equality."[9] Knox elaborated on this "conciliatory system" in 1789.

"The Indians being the prior occupants, possess the right of the soil." To dispossess them of their land, other than with their own agreement or in a "just war," would be "a gross violation of the fundamental laws of nature, and that distributive justice which is the glory of the nation." Knox argued "both policy and justice" dictated this approach. Continuing the previous "system of coercion and oppression" in the long run would "amount to a much greater sum of money," and "the blood and injustice which would stain the character of the nation, would be beyond all pecuniary calculation."[10]

Although the United States and various Indian groups negotiated land cessions that included payments to Indians, the native confederation north of the Ohio River persisted in its resistance to American incursions. British agents stationed in forts on American soil encouraged this conflict. The Northwest Ordinance had promised that Indians would remain secure "in their property, rights, and liberty" unless Congress authorized "just and lawful wars."[11] The United States decided that a "just and lawful" war was necessary in 1790 to subdue the native confederation that opposed the selling of land at the Fort Harmar Council in 1789. The federal government underestimated the power of the native opponents. In 1790 Indians surprised and routed a force under General Josiah Harmar and in 1791 they inflicted another dramatic defeat to an American army under General Arthur St. Clair, the governor of the Northwest Territory. Embarrassed by these debacles, President Washington ordered a new army to be organized—the Legion of the United States—under General Anthony Wayne. This force took over two years to prepare for its invasion of Indian country. On August 20, 1794, Wayne's 3,000 men encountered an Indian force of half that number at the Battle of Fallen Timbers close to present-day Toledo, Ohio. When the outnumbered Indians finally retreated they sought shelter at the nearby British outpost of Fort Miami. The British, wanting to avoid a direct clash with the Americans, did not protect their Indian allies.

After the defeat, the Indian confederation began to splinter. Not only had the British refused to come to their aid in battle, but, following the provisions of the Jay Treaty (1794), the British soon withdrew from their forts south of the Great Lakes. Simultaneously, the Spanish signed an agreement with the Americans in 1795 that saw them withdraw their claims for much of the area of the old southwest (north of present Florida). In 1795 the northwest Indians agreed to the Treaty of Greenville, granting about half of the future state of Ohio to American settlement. Although this move represented a major setback for the Indians, at least they had forced Wayne to the bargaining table. Moreover, Wayne had pledged that the lands still in Indian control would remain inviolable and that any squatters would be subject to Indian justice. However empty this promise turned out, it did represent a rhetorical concession and reflected the new American policy of negotiation.

The American Revolution had held out several possibilities for Native Americans. Most Indians simply hoped that they could survive the conflict unmolested, or somehow play one side against the other. As the war raged on, this position became more and more untenable. A few Indians envisioned a world in which they could fight for liberty by siding with the revolutionaries. Despite "winning" the war they continued to lose ground to their European American neighbors. By the end of the conflict most Indians had decided that the British offered them the best opportunity to protect their way of life. These Indians clung to their traditional culture even as it was changing around them. For these Indians the war against the Long Knives (as they called the Americans) continued after 1783. Although ultimately defeated, they compelled the United States to adopt a less belligerent policy. In the face of the American encroachment Native Americans even turned to a pan-Indian vision. This unity was ephemeral. It led to some spectacular victories, but was difficult to sustain in the face of defeat. More and more lands were opened for European American speculation and settlement, encouraging investment and the expansion of a capitalist economy.

African Americans

The American Revolution transformed slavery in North America. Few people questioned slavery before the conflict. Once European Americans complained that the British were out to enslave them, logic led inevitably to the condition of African American slaves. The war itself provided opportunities for freedom as first the British and then the Americans offered to emancipate African Americans if they fought on their side. As a result of the contest thousands of African Americans became free. Many more remained in bondage.

Slavery existed almost unchallenged in all of the colonies before 1750. About 90 percent of colonial slaves lived south of Pennsylvania. Although there were not many slaves in New England or the middle colonies, the economies of both regions depended heavily on trade with the plantation economy of the West Indies and its brutal slave system. In the Chesapeake and in the Carolinas, with staple crops such as tobacco and rice, slaves represented an important factor of production and a crucial symbol of wealth. Few people, north or south, questioned the right to own slaves— a slave merely occupied the lowest level within the larger hierarchy. There were isolated antislavery rumblings before the revolution. As early as the seventeenth century Samuel Sewell attacked the biblical defense of slavery. Quakers in the eighteenth century led by John Woolman argued that slavery was a violation of the golden rule: to treat others as you yourself would be treated. By the 1750s the Philadelphia Yearly Meeting had ordered its members to free their slaves. Evangelical groups like the Methodists and Baptists also began to attack slavery. Simultaneously, the Enlightenment ideal of natural rights emphasizing liberty and equality of all men created a secular argument against slavery.

After 1765 the rhetoric of liberty became contagious. No sooner had revolutionary leaders called for the defense of liberty against the Stamp Act, and labeled the British tax policy an effort to enslave the American people, then some men—both black and white—made the connection between the bondage of one-fifth of the inhabitants of British North America and the cause of liberty. The first fruit of this movement was an attempt to end the Atlantic slave trade. The Massachusetts assembly passed such a measure in 1771 only to have it disallowed by the royal governor, Thomas Hutchinson. Pennsylvania, Rhode Island, and Connecticut each passed prohibitions against the slave trade before the outbreak of the Revolutionary War, and the Continental Congress included an agreement to stop slave importations as a part of the Continental Association of 1774. Other states debated the issue.

The various currents of antislavery thought in the revolutionary era can be seen in "Address on Slavery," written by Arthur Lee, scion of a Virginia slave-owning family. Lee, who was exposed to a strong dose of the Enlightenment while at medical school at the University of Edinburgh, published his essay in the *Virginia Gazette* in 1767 in an unsuccessful effort to persuade the House of Burgesses to abolish the slave trade. For Lee, slavery was "a Violation both of Justice and Religion," and a danger "to the safety of the Community." It destroyed "the growth of arts & Sciences," and produced "a numerous & very fatal train of Vices, both in the Slave, and in his Master." Lee also asserted that "freedom is unquestionably the birth-right of all mankind, of Africans as well as Europeans," and declared that owning Africans slaves was "a constant violation of that right." Lee's argument included a religious dimension. He believed Christianity dictated that all men, who after all were made in the image of God, should be treated equitably. To do otherwise would lead to damnation and the destruction of one's "eternal welfare." From a more pragmatic perspective, sooner or later slavery would lead to rebellion by the slaves—a rebellion whites would have a difficult time suppressing as slavery created "indolence, which debillitating our minds, and enervating our bodies, will render us an easy conquest to the feeblest foe."[12]

The Revolutionary War itself provided a more direct challenge to slavery. Confronted by rebellious slaveholding planters, the royal governor of Virginia, Lord John Murray Dunmore, did the unthinkable: On November 7, 1775, he offered freedom to all servants and slaves who fought under the king's banner. Hundreds of African Americans rallied to his support. During the course of the war thousands of blacks fought for their liberty by joining the British army. Some were placed in military units, many more were simply used as auxiliary labor. Although most runaways were young males, older slaves and whole families sought sanctuary behind British lines. Like other groups in North America, the decision to fight in the war was never clear-cut. African Americans, especially in the northern states, might also obtain freedom by joining the Continental army. Whatever the decision, it was not always easy for a slave to turn his back on everything he knew. Slaves recognized that they could be exploited by British masters just as they could by their American masters. Most slaves simply used the opportunity of a passing British army to run from their masters. About thirty slaves escaped from Thomas Jefferson when Cornwallis's army approached his plantations in 1781. Somewhere between 80,000 and 100,000—or one-fifth of the entire slave population—may have left their owners during the war.[13] This represented a staggering loss to the American economy. It also reflected an impressive clarion for freedom.

The final result of this movement was mixed. Many slaves were recaptured and returned to slavery. Lord Cornwallis, for instance, ordered all of the African Americans who had followed him to Yorktown out of the encampment to save dwindling food supplies. Because the British were surrounded, this action delivered the ex-slaves into bondage again. Others died from the diseases that followed eighteenth-century armies. Smallpox in particular took a heavy toll. British soldiers were either inoculated or had experienced the disease earlier in life; African Americans had no such protection. According to the Treaty of Paris, the British were supposed to turn all runaways back to their masters at the end of the war. Instead, the British took many freed African Americans with them as they evacuated their last outposts. The fate of these black Loyalists, however, was not always enviable as they were spread across the British Atlantic world. They were sent to the West Indies and the Bahamas, where some were even reenslaved. They went to Canada, Nova Scotia, and Great Britain, where they often encountered race prejudice and economic hardship. A few eventually found refuge in Sierra Leone, the British African colony established as a haven for ex-slaves.

Some of the runaways remained in the United States, blending into a growing free population of blacks in a country where, in the 1780s and

1790s, the revolutionary vision of liberty for all men still seemed a possibility. Although the Constitution had included a provision preventing Congress from ending the slave trade for twenty years, every state passed its own law to stop the international trafficking in human flesh. More important, several states provided for emancipation of slaves and loosened restrictions on manumissions. These developments were most pronounced in the North, but also appeared in the Chesapeake. South Carolina and Georgia remained more committed to slavery. South Carolina passed its ban on slave importations to limit the slave population and avoid slave revolts. It rescinded the anti-slave trade law in 1803.

Emancipation took different forms in different states. Vermont, which would not be recognized as a state until 1791, led the way with its 1777 constitution, which abolished slavery completely. Given Vermont had only about twenty-five slaves in 1770, the law did not affect many lives. Massachusetts had more slaves, amounting to about 2 percent of its population. During the 1780s there were several court cases that ended slavery based on the argument that the state constitution declared that all men were "born free and equal."[14] New Hampshire followed a similar course and ended slavery by 1790. The Northwest Ordinance of 1787 prohibited slavery from entering the territory north of the Ohio River. Pennsylvania came up with a different solution. By passing a gradual emancipation bill in 1780, Pennsylvanians dealt with two problems: the loss of property held in slaves and the integration of blacks into free society. Gradual emancipation compensated the slave owner by providing him with years of servitude before emancipation, and it offered a period of transition to prepare the slave for his own freedom. Similar measures were passed in Connecticut and Rhode Island in 1784, New York in 1799, and New Jersey in 1804. Over the next thirty to forty years the northern states pursued their legal termination of slavery. By 1830 there remained only a few slaves above the Mason–Dixon Line.

Manumission laws also had an impact on the development of a free black population. In a state such as New York, with about 20,000 slaves in 1790, the growth of the free black population accelerated as masters negotiated deals with slaves to allow them their freedom in exchange for money or additional work. Virginia in 1782 and Maryland in 1783 each passed laws allowing masters the option of freeing their slaves. In Virginia this led to the freeing of 10,000 slaves, whereas in Maryland as much as 20 percent of the African American population was free by 1810. Delaware's manumission laws significantly decreased the proportion of enslaved African Americans. In all of these states some of these manumissions were the result of the benevolence of the slave owner, but many came at the instigation of the slaves seeking ways to earn and purchase their own freedom and the freedom of members of their family.

Before the Revolutionary War, there had been only a handful of free African Americans in the colonies. By 1790 there were about 60,000 in the United States, and by 1810 there were over 180,000.[15] Surprisingly, the majority of these free blacks lived in the South. A small number of these freed people, especially in the Deep South, turned their backs on their enslaved brethren and hoped to melt into the white population. In Charleston, South Carolina, a group of mulattos formed the Brown Fellowship Society in the 1790s to distinguish themselves from darker skinned and unfree African Americans. Most free people, however, embraced their African American identity, created their own institutions, and sought ways to oppose slavery.

Central to these developments was religion. During the first half of the eighteenth century there had been little effort to bring Christianity to black slaves. Starting with the First Great Awakening, and then accelerating during the early republic, evangelicals looked for converts among free and slave African Americans. These efforts gained success among blacks who were increasingly removed from their African roots as the war had interrupted slave imports and the state regulations against the international slave trade had significantly decreased the introduction of new slaves from Africa. Although many evangelical groups had allowed interracial worship, by the 1790s blacks began to complain of unequal treatment in white churches. In reaction, African Americans organized their own religious institutions. Blacks formed their own Baptist church in Williamsburg, Virginia, during the 1780s, but only received official recognition in 1793. In Philadelphia, Absalom Jones and Richard Allen helped to establish the Free African Society—a religious and mutual aid association for African Americans—in 1787. Both men played a central role in later founding local Episcopal and Methodist churches. Peter Williams and other African Americans in New York City organized a Methodist church in 1796. In the next few decades other churches followed, often proudly asserting their racial identity by including the words *African, Abyssinian, Ethiopian,* or *Negro* into their names.

Free African Americans gravitated toward cities and towns. In urban areas they were more likely to interact with other free blacks, increasing the chances of marrying and finding employment. Within cities, African Americans often congregated in specific neighborhoods, although there were few exclusively black areas. Wherever they resided they confronted an intensifying racism during the early republic. Skilled artisans sometimes discovered that they had to take more menial jobs when white tradesmen refused to work with them. Many black men found employment as sailors. One-fourth of Philadelphia's young black males went to sea in the early years of the American republic. Others worked along the docks or as day laborers. African Americans found employment in the most disagreeable of tasks, picking up the "night soil" (emptying privies) or cleaning chimneys. Black men and women also worked in the service sector, selling oysters and other food, operating tobacco and barber shops, performing household duties, and waiting tables. Pushed to the periphery of society, some African Americans engaged in illicit activities, including prostitution and thievery.

A few African Americans earned a degree of respectability and property. Men such as scientist Benjamin Banneker, and ministers Absalom Jones and Richard Allen became symbols and spokesmen for their race. Banneker was a free black from Maryland who was one of three men on the team assigned to survey the Federal District (later Washington, D.C.) in 1791. Known for his astronomical and mathematical abilities, he published a popular almanac annually from 1792 to 1797. He is most famous

FIGURE 4–1   Benjamin Banneker This free African American published his own almanac, was an amateur astronomer, and helped survey Washington D.C. in the 1790s. He also directly challenged Thomas Jefferson's belief that blacks were incapable of complex thought. Banneker wrote to Jefferson, cited the Declaration of Independence, and asserted the equality of all mankind.

for sending a letter in 1791, and a copy of his first almanac, to Thomas Jefferson to demonstrate to the slaveholding Sage of Monticello that black men were capable of complex thought and calculations. Banneker reminded Jefferson that the "one universal Father . . . hath not only made us all of one flesh, but that he hath also, without partiality, afforded us all the same sensations and endowed us all with the same faculties." Regardless of an individual's position in society, religion, or color "we are all of the same family, and stand in the same relation to him [God]." Banneker also used Jefferson's own words against him, quoting the Declaration of Independence and the assertion that all men were created equal. He wrote that it was "pitiable" to think that Jefferson had once been "fully convinced of the benevolence of the Father of Mankind, and of his equal and impartial distribution of these rights and privileges," but continued "in detaining by fraud and violence so numerous a part of my brethren, under groaning captivity and cruel oppression." He charged Jefferson with being "guilty of that most criminal act" (slavery) that Jefferson had "professedly detested in others."[16]

Both Absalom Jones and Richard Allen were born into slavery and achieved their freedom in the tumultuous years surrounding the Revolutionary War. After selling Jones's mother and siblings, Absalom's master moved from Delaware to Philadelphia in 1762. Only fifteen at the time, and with some elements of literacy, Jones went with his master and was put to work in his store. During the next twenty-two years Jones labored long hours, married, and even bought property as a slave. He accumulated enough money to purchase his slave wife's freedom, and then, after some reluctance on the part of his master, he bought his own freedom as well. Jones continued to work diligently and became an entrepreneur and a religious leader in Philadelphia's black community. Richard Allen was also a Delaware slave. He experienced a conversion to Methodism in 1777. In 1780, inspired by the same Methodism, his master allowed Allen and his brother to purchase their freedom. For the next six years Allen worked intermittently as a sawyer, shoemaker, wagon driver, and as a Methodist circuit rider. In 1786 he moved to Philadelphia to minister to the religious needs of the black community.

Jones and Allen wrote an important pamphlet defending Philadelphia's black community from racial slander after the yellow fever outbreak in 1793. During that epidemic, in which 4,000 Philadelphians died, Jones and Allen had organized the city's African Americans to nurse the sick and collect and bury the dead in the mistaken belief that Africans were immune to yellow fever. Although many blacks died during the epidemic, they hoped to gain the goodwill of the white community. Once the yellow fever ended with the onset of cold weather, some whites claimed that blacks extorted large sums from the sick and robbed the dead. The Jones and Allen pamphlet denied these charges and asserted the equality of all men in the eyes of God. They wrote that blacks, "although reduced to the most abject state human nature is capable of," were able to "think, reflect, and feel injuries." They pointed out that if African American children had the same educational opportunities as whites, they would "not be inferior in mental endowments" to anyone. And they declared that slavery was hateful "in the sight of . . . God" and implored, "If you love your children, if you love your country, if you love the God of love, clear your hands from slaves, burden not your children or country with them."[17]

By the mid-1790s there were some disturbing signs suggesting that it would be a long time before the revolutionary vision of equality and the end of slavery would be fulfilled. Some states, such as North Carolina, were so resistant to manumission that they passed laws compelling freed slaves to leave the state or face reenslavement. Many white Americans became transfixed by events in St. Domingue, where a rebellion that began in 1791 spread to a race war between slaves and their masters. This upheaval became of even greater concern to Americans in 1793 when thousands of refugees from the West Indies arrived with tales of massacre and atrocity. In February 1793 Congress passed a fugitive slave law that provided federal support for the recapturing of runaway slaves who left their home state. During the 1790s the upper South planters supported the end of the international slave trade in part to increase the value of their own slaves as they began to ship their excess slaves across the Appalachian Mountains. Cotton production only enhanced this process and helped to further entrench slavery south of the Ohio River. However, in the mid-1790s the full implications of these developments for American politics and economy lay in the future. Although most African Americans in the United States remained in bondage and those who were freed confronted a deepening racism, an African American leadership had emerged that articulated a breathtaking ideal: a revolutionary vision of liberty for all mankind.

Women

Abigail Adams admonished her husband on March 31, 1776, to "Remember the Ladies" as Congress considered independence and drew up a new "Code of Laws." Abigail explained:

> Do not put such unlimited power into the hands of the Husbands. Remember all Men would be tyrants if they could. If perticuliar care and attention is not paid to the Ladies we are determined to foment a Rebelion, and will not hold ourselves bound by any Laws in which we have no voice or Representation.

She went on to assert "That your Sex are Naturally Tyrannical" and reminded her husband that men who would be happy "willingly give up the harsh title of Master for the more tender and endearing one of Friend."[18] John Adams did not take Abigail seriously. He laughed at the idea of a code of laws that would remember the ladies. John noted that the revolutionary leaders had been told their "Struggle has loosened the bands of Government every where" and that children, apprentices, students, Indians, and slaves all challenged their betters. Abigail's letter was the first he had heard of "another Tribe more numerous and powerfull than all the rest were grown discontented." He jokingly continued by declaring, "We know better than to repeal our Masculine systems," as women were the real rulers. Giving up the name of master would "compleatly subject Us to the Despotism of the Peticoat."[19] Abigail, certainly the intellectual equal of her husband, thought that this response was ungenerous and soon dropped the subject in her correspondence. But her often quoted letter expressed an unfulfilled vision of the revolutionary era: that there would be a fundamental transformation in gender relationships, shifting from inequality to equality.

The economic, political, and legal status of women did not change as a result of the Revolutionary War. Although before and after the Revolutionary War, only female black slaves and the poorest of white women ordinarily worked in the fields with men, both in the preparation of food and the making of clothing, no household could function efficiently without female labor. Therefore both men and women assumed that the normal condition was marriage. Household production went beyond subsistence and often contributed significantly to the family income as women spun cloth, made cheese, and produced items for the market. Examination of account books, however, often hide this vital economic activity because women remained legally invisible. Transactions were usually in the husband's name. The concept of *femme covert*—a woman's identity was covered by her father or husband—predominated in the early republic. A few women escaped this all-encompassing doctrine either because they inherited some property as a widow or a wily father did not trust his future son-in-law and insisted on a prenuptial agreement to protect the property that the father intended for his daughter. In the vast majority of cases any property belonging to a woman became her husband's once they were married. Because women were dependent beings economically, they were also denied a political voice. Women, except for a small number in New Jersey, could not vote. They could not serve in public office, nor did they sit on juries. Husbands retained unlimited power and women had no voice or representation in the law. Women, however, had participated in the revolution and out of that involvement came both a call for rights and some small changes.

The revolution touched all Americans regardless of gender. During the 1760s and early 1770s women may not have joined in the committees of correspondence or actively participated in the crowd, but they were instrumental in the nonimportation movements and boycotts in opposition to imperial regulation. If Americans were to wear homespun instead of imported cloth, then women had to do the spinning at home. Any effort to stop the drinking of tea also depended on women, who prepared the beverage and who drank tea at social functions. When a 1770 Boston broadside identified a violator of a nonimportation agreement, it asked "the Sons and Daughters of LIBERTY" to not buy anything from him "for in so doing they will bring Disgrace upon *themselves,* and their *Posterity,* for *ever* and *ever.*"[20] Spinning, not drinking tea, and purchasing goods thus became political activities. In recognition of this development, fifty-one North Carolina women on October 25, 1774, formed an

FIGURE 4–2 The Edenton Ladies On October 25, 1774, a group of women from Edenton, North Carolina, held a meeting in support of the opposition to the Coercive Acts. As demonstrated by this cartoon lampooning the meeting, the British criticized the involvement of women in politics.

association to do the "duty that we owe not only to our near and dear relations and connexions, but to ourselves, who are essentially interested in
their welfare," to support the North Carolina legislature in opposition to
the Coercive Acts.[21] What is striking is that these Edenton ladies, who
were subsequently lampooned in a British cartoon, took this stand for the
"publick good" in part because of their position within their families, and
in part for themselves as political beings.

If the resistance movement began to awaken a political identity among
some women, then the war itself both furthered and tested that identity. As
with other groups in American society, the war pushed and pulled women
in a variety of directions. Many women would have been just as happy to
see the war go away, as it took men from the household and could threaten
women directly as armies marched nearby. Some women simply followed
their husbands, silently and obediently accepting their fate even if it meant
suffering and loss as a result of that choice. Others became ardent supporters of one side or the other. Benedict Arnold may have turned traitor in
part because of the Loyalist sympathies of Margaret Shippen, his second
wife. The Edenton ladies and Abigail Adams demonstrated their commitment to the revolutionary cause in writing. Poorer women also chose sides.
Both the British and the Continental armies had camp followers as a paid
component to their military force. These women, often married to a soldier
in the regiment to which they were attached, performed crucial services in
cooking, cleaning, and nursing. At least one woman, Deborah Sampson,
even donned a military uniform and served in the army in disguise.

Regardless of a woman's decision to be a Loyalist, revolutionary, or
somehow stay neutral, the war created hardship. Even affluent women like
Abigail Adams struggled to keep the family farm together, raise children,
and manage business affairs as her husband was off making a revolution.
Connecticut's Mary Silliman had a similar experience when her husband
Sellick fought with the militia and was captured by Loyalists in retaliation
for his actions as state's attorney. Mary saw her farm burned by a British
raiding party and petitioned Connecticut's governor to negotiate an
exchange. Inflation wreaked havoc on many households. On over thirty
occasions women rioted in an effort to regulate markets when the price of
scarce supplies was too high. Women extended this crowd activity to other
areas: Believing that their community had sacrificed enough and fearing
the loss of men needed to work their farms in 1781, about one hundred
women prevented a draft occurring in Virginia. Besides the daily struggle
to survive in a nation divided by war, women remained vulnerable to
Indian attack, marauding militias, and the depredations of armies from
both sides.

This experience brought new expectations on the highest levels of society in the notion of republican womanhood. Combining the traditional domestic ideal with the new sense of civic responsibility and virtue, elite women began to believe that they had a special role in society to maintain the home as a refuge for the family and to devote themselves to their husbands and to raising their children in true republican spirit. Ideally the home became a sanctuary to provide a moral compass for the entire family. A husband could retreat to the fireside and be comforted and come under the virtuous influence of a wife. Sons were to be prepared for their future role as independent citizens, and girls were to be taught to become republican women. On one level this concept was confining because it relegated women to a separate domestic sphere; on another level, it elevated women as the special repositories of virtue and provided a political purpose that opened the door to a more public role for women in the 1780s and 1790s.

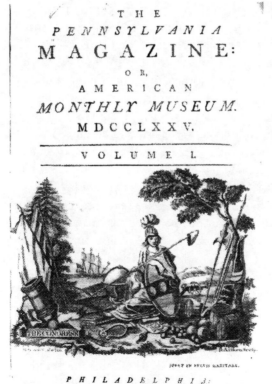

THE
PENNSYLVANIA
MAGAZINE:
OR,
AMERICAN
MONTHLY MUSEUM.
MDCCLXXV.

VOLUME I.

PHILADELPHIA:
Printed and sold by R. Aitken, printer and bookseller,
opposite the London Coffee-House, Front-Street.

FIGURE 4–3 *The Pennsylvania Magazine, 1775* Revolutionaries borrowed iconography from the British and used the female figure to represent North America and the cause of independence. This female Columbia/Miss Liberty came to represent the United States and was often surrounded by warlike emblems as well as symbols of trade and prosperity.

During the first two decades of the early republic women gained a more visible role in society as symbols of republicanism, through involvement in partisan politics, calls for education, and the development of print culture. The female figure had a prominent role in eighteenth-century iconography. Partially clad women had been used to represent the continents, with a Native American signifying North America. The English embraced a similar symbol to embody their national identity in Britannia. Naturally, Americans combined the two in the form of Columbia and Miss Liberty. This representation appeared as early as 1775 on the front page of the *Pennsylvania Magazine* and continued throughout the early republic. Often the female Columbia/Miss Liberty stands on the shore with ships and symbols of economic prosperity surrounding her, emphasizing how virtue and a bustling economy went hand in hand. Americans also relied on real females to symbolize the purity of their actions. When New York officials imprisoned Alexander McDougall in 1770 because of his opposition to the colony's compliance with the Quartering Act, forty-five young maidens, described as virgins, visited him in jail. When George Washington undertook his

FIGURE 4–4 Women and Girls Greet Washington at Trenton, 1789 As George Washington headed to New York to accept the presidency in 1789, crowds greeted him with enthusiasm. Women were often featured in these public spectacles, as can be seen in this illustration of Washington's arrival in Trenton, location of his surprising victory in 1776. With Trenton bridge bedecked with flowers, and surrounded by female celebrants, a canopy welcomed Washington by proclaiming him "The Hero Who Defended the Mothers Will Protect the Daughters."

triumphant progression to New York in 1789 to accept the presidency, he was often greeted in ceremonies that featured women. Celebrants bedecked a bridge in Trenton in flowers and a canopy that proclaimed "The Hero Who Defended the Mothers Will Protect the Daughters."[22] He was surrounded by young women and girls who threw flowers in his path.

Recognizing their own symbolic importance, some women seized the initiative and claimed a political identity. During the political partisanship of the 1790s, women asserted their allegiance by wearing either the tricolor (Republican) or black (Federalist) cockades. They eagerly participated in public demonstrations of support for and against the French Revolution. Francophile women called themselves citizeness, or citi for short, and joined in processions singing French patriotic songs such as "Ça Ira." In Boston in 1793 fifty women met to celebrate the French victory at Valmy "to contribute their part in the late frequent celebrations of liberty and equality."[23] Federalist women were less likely to appear in the streets in the early 1790s, but expressed themselves in writing. Annis Boudinot Stockton wrote a poem attacking French ambassador Edmond Genêt in 1793 and declared that "Columbias *daughters*" would defend Washington and "soon would put your San Culottes to flight."[24] Federalist women appeared in the street to support the military during the Quasi War crisis in 1798–1800 and one group of Philadelphia women even pledged to take up arms in the event of a French invasion. Women also assumed a political role in setting up salons during the 1790s, creating a forum for political discussion for both sexes. Martha Washington established the first political salon in 1789 when she set aside each Friday evening to entertain a republican court composed of local dignitaries and foreign officials. She also hosted a few special events such as a Christmas Eve celebration, a New Year's reception, and a birthday party for her husband. Other women, such as Anne Bingham, hosted their own salons at which politics was never far beneath the surface.

Female education became increasingly important in the early republic to ensure the proper training of elite women to fulfill their roles as republican women and cultured hostesses. Although this education could be traced to the Enlightenment ideal that learning was the key to the realization of human potential, only after the Revolutionary War was there a concerted effort to establish institutions devoted to teaching young women. Benjamin Rush argued that education was crucial to allow women to help their husbands in business, to run a household, to add to social conversation, and to improve the well-being of women and their families. He still expected women to be subordinate because he believed "that the female temper can only be governed by reason," but he also held, in the spirit of the Enlightenment, "that the cultivation of reason in women, is alike friendly to the order of nature, and to private as well as public happiness."[25] Inspired by such ideas, John Poor opened the Young Ladies' Academy in Philadelphia during the 1780s. The curriculum included reading, writing, arithmetic, grammar, composition, rhetoric, and geography. The idea was to allow women to enrich their minds and promote virtue. Education thus had a personal application in the simple pleasure to be derived from learning and participating in "an age of light and refinement" while simultaneously developing practical skills that would benefit both the family and nation.[26]

Educating women, however, opened up the possibility of new demands for equality. A few of the students at the Young Ladies' Academy saw this connection and argued that education made women the equal of man. One student, Priscilla Mason, pushed this idea to extremes and argued that public speaking was "part of the rights of woman," and believed that "despotic man" had shut women out of "The Church, the Bar, and the Senate."[27] Perhaps the most famous American woman advocating women's rights in the 1780s and 1790s was Judith Sargent Murray. Murray published several essays on a variety of subjects, including women, in magazines and in her book *The Gleaner* (1798). Murray advocated education as a vehicle for female independence, believing that "THE SEX [women] should be taught to depend on their own efforts, for the procurement of an establishment in life." She asserted that women were the intellectual peers of men and that only inferior education created inequalities. Although she did not push for complete political equality, she believed that women could exert sound judgement on political issues and that women were "equally concerned with men in the public weal. . . ."[28] Murray and other women readers had access to more radical feminist ideas from Europe, especially Mary Wollstonecraft's *Vindication of the Rights of Women,* first published in London in 1792. Printers immediately reissued Wollstonecraft's book in Boston and Philadelphia, and writers summarized and discussed it at length in American newspapers and magazines. Wollstonecraft called on men to recognize the intellectual equality of women and asked that women be allowed "to participate in the inherent rights of mankind." She entreated men "to emancipate their companion" and "generously snap our chains." If men were "content with rational fellowship instead of slavish obedience" they would have "more observant daughters, more affectionate sisters, more faithful wives, more reasonable mothers—in a word, better citizens."[29] These ideas attracted a great deal of attention in the mid-1790s, but by the end of the decade Wollstonecraft's own unconventional lifestyle (she had a child out of wedlock) and the innate conservatism of American society made her views less attractive.

The fact that Murray and Wollstonecraft were able to express their ideas as published authors reflected another crucial development: the expansion of a print culture by, for, and about women. During the 1780s and 1790s, women became increasingly engaged in writing and reading about women. The best-selling American book during the early Republic was *Charlotte Temple,* by Susannah Rowson. This sentimental tale related the story of a young woman seduced with promises of marriage by a British officer and abandoned during the Revolutionary War in New York City. Although the plot is neither original nor liberating (Charlotte's downfall comes from not listening to her parents), it is a book that was written by a woman, with a female as the lead character, that appealed to a feminine audience. This same trend can be seen in other books, magazines, and the theater. Hannah Foster published *Coquette* in 1797 and Sally Wood's *Julia and the Illuminated Barron* and *Amelia, or the Influence of Virtue, an Old Man's Story* appeared anonymously in 1800 and 1802. During the 1790s, magazines devoted especially to women were produced in Philadelphia and New York. Even more general magazines sought the female reader. Conservative Noah Webster, editor of the *American Magazine,* hoped "that many of the Ladies, who are favorites of Minerva and the Muses, will be found in the number of his correspondents."[30] Women were also playwrights: Susannah Rowson's *Slaves in Algiers* and Anne Kemble Hatton's *Tammany, or the Indian Chief* were performed on the Philadelphia stage in 1794.

The final result of all of the rhetoric for women's rights and the emergence of a woman's literature was limited. In postrevolutionary America women from the upper levels of society assumed a new political identity—republican womanhood—and played a larger role in the public realm. There were also some slight legal changes. Briefly, until 1808, New Jersey allowed propertied women to vote. By 1799, twelve states and the Northwest Territory had made it legal to divorce and it was even possible in some states for an individual to divorce on the grounds of the loss of affection.[31] But the basic elements limiting a woman's political and legal identity remained in place. If anything, coverture became more deeply embedded in the legal system. In the words of a 1791 South Carolina court ruling, prenuptial agreements separating the husband and wife's property were "deviations from the fixed laws of the land" that would create unhappiness in marriage and "relaxes the great bond of family union"—property.[32] In a society that emphasized the importance of the independent man, the dependence of women had profound implications, especially for nonelite women.

Women in the general population may have been losing status before 1776. This trend persisted into the early republic. In the seventeenth century unequal sex ratios meant a guaranteed marriage for every woman. With nearly equal sex ratios by the mid-eighteenth century, marriage seemed less assured and widowhood, increased by casualties of war, often led to a life on the margins. Changes in the economy also had an effect. The spread of wage labor often left women poorly paid for their services and without the compensation of room and board. Expansion of manufacturing and mass production of household items might decrease the value of items previously made at home. Young women became less likely to have land as their portion of a family estate. Instead, they were given personal wealth in household items that was more easily controlled by the husband. Fewer women were provided with dower rights on the death of a husband or were named the executor in their husband's wills. A cash economy increased the need to obtain credit; without the control of land, or even a legal identity, women found it difficult, if not impossible, to borrow. On the other hand, women's work that produced domestic items such as cloth or cheese added capital to a household and provided an important entree into a market economy. These changes affected all women, but those on the bottom of society experienced the most difficulties. For such women, any talk of republican womanhood seemed irrelevant and obscure. Caught in a cycle striving for survival, their dependent status left women vulnerable to exploitation and far removed from republican ideals.

And yet somehow the new ideas about equality reached even the poorest of women. As one early nineteenth-century hotel maid explained to an Englishman, "In this country there is no mistresses nor masters; I guess I am a woman citizen."[33] Both the extent and the limit of these ideas can be seen in the story of Lanah Sawyer of New York. We do not know if as a seventeen-year-old girl Lanah read novels or if she had any notion that "all men were created equal." We do know that as the daughter of a seafaring man she came from a humble background and worked as a seamstress. She also held a sentimental notion of romance that appeared in many eighteenth-century novels that allowed her to believe it was possible for a rich man to fall for a poor girl. One night during the summer of 1793 she met the affluent Henry Bedlow, who introduced himself simply as "lawyer Smith." Bedlow treated Lanah to ice cream and walked her around the Battery and won her heart. The night ended in a brothel where, so Lanah claimed, Bedlow raped her. The court case that followed became a cause celebre. Bedlow's lawyers argued that the sex was consensual. As proof of this position they asserted that a girl like Lanah—from obscure origins—had to know that the only reason a well-dressed gentleman would pay any attention to her would be to gratify his carnal desires. One of the defense lawyers asked rhetorically: "Considering the difference of their situations," from what motive "Could she imagine that a man of [Bedlow's] situation would pay her any attention, take her a walking, carry her to Coore's and treat her with ice cream, unless with a view of promoting illicit commerce?"[34] Lanah had not seen it that way and had believed Bedlow's protestations of love. The jury agreed with Bedlow and acquitted him. There was no hope for equality for women like Lanah. A handful of elite women may have pushed the edges of revolutionary ideology and imagined a world in which women would be treated differently, but that vision could not be sustained in the face of glaring inequalities.

American Culture

It should come as no surprise that the visions conjured by Native Americans, blacks, and women remained unfulfilled in the years after 1776. More unexpected was the failure of the revolution to realize the fondest aspiration of the Founding Fathers; that the revolution would bring the dawning of a new age in culture based on Enlightenment ideals that would equal the glories of classical antiquity. Even before independence there was a growing belief that North America was bound for greatness. In 1771 Philip Freneau and Hugh Henry Brackenridge wrote a commencement poem for their Princeton graduation called "The Rising Glory of America" in which they proclaimed that America would soon have poets like "a Homer and a Milton rise" and "Nations shall grow and states" emerge "not less in fame Than Greece and Rome of old."[35] Independence only seemed to enhance this promise. Even a European philosophe like the Abbé Raynal, who only a few years before had dismissed the American wilderness as inferior to the Old World, proclaimed in 1778 that the United States would be "a new Olympus, a new Arcady, a new Athens, a new Greece."[36] Thomas Jefferson argued for American greatness in his *Notes on the State of Virginia* (1787), pointing out that although a young nation with a small population, America had already a pantheon of heroes. America had "produced a Washington, whose memory will be adored while liberty shall have votaries, whose name will triumph over time, and will in future ages assume its just station among the most celebrated worthies of the world." In physics, Jefferson wrote "we have produced a Franklin," and proclaimed that "no one of the present age has made more important discoveries, nor has enriched philosophy with more, or more ingenious solutions of the phænomena of nature." Jefferson also asserted that David Rittenhouse was "second to no astronomer living: that in genius he must be the first, because he is self-taught."[37] Taken together these were high expectations that Americans in the new republic were only partially to fulfill in architecture, art, literature, science, and republican reform.

In few areas were the classical hopes for the American republic more transparent than in architecture. In direct imitation of classical forms, Americans planned to build the next Athens and the next Rome. Jefferson took up this mantle, directly drawing his plans for the Virginia statehouse in 1785 based on the Roman temple Maison Carrée in Nîmes, France. The problem was that it would be decades before the muddy streets of the new state capital in Richmond would become a city where such a building did not look out of place. The District of Columbia faced similar problems. During the 1790s, Pierre L'Enfant drew up an elaborate plan of intersecting streets and monumental buildings. Auctions to sell lots in the future city, however, attracted hardly any buyers. When the government moved there from Philadelphia in 1800, much of the city remained unbuilt and open spaces that were not swamp were used to graze cows. Despite being the seat of national power, with a Senate, a Capitol (the names were taken from the Romans), and some classical architecture, no one in the first half of the nineteenth century would confuse the Potomac with the Tiber, nor Washington with Rome. On a less grand scale, this pattern was repeated elsewhere. No sooner had some dreamer planned a new

FIGURE 4–5 The State Capitol in Richmond, Virginia The revolutionary generation expected the United States to be a new Rome or Athens. To fulfill this promise, architects designed public buildings after classical structures. Thomas Jefferson modeled the Virginia state capitol on the Maison Carrée in Nîmes, France. Amid mud-strewn streets and American rustic simplicity, such buildings appeared out of place.

"metropolis," than there would be an effort to erect a public building based on classical models. Even the names of many of the towns reflected an interest in the ancients. Upstate New York, settled during the 1790s and early 1800s, is sprinkled with placenames such as Rome, Ithaca, and Syracuse. The architecture in more established cities, as evidenced by the monument-like building that housed the First Bank of the United States in Philadelphia, reflected classical interests, as did the homes of the most affluent Americans.

Artists also confronted problems in the new republic. In the late colonial period there developed a handful of successful portrait painters, the most skilled of whom trained in Europe. The revolution divided the artist community, much as it divided the rest of American society. The most talented American artist, Benjamin West, became a Loyalist and worked under the patronage of George III in England. John Trumbull and Charles Willson Peale were ardent supporters of independence. However, in the new republic of the United States they had to redefine their role as artists. Many people questioned the need for art in a republican society; as John Adams explained to Thomas Jefferson, "Every one of the fine Arts from the earliest times" had been "inlisted on the service of Superstition and Despotism."[38] Trumbull's solution to this problem was to use the historical style popularized by the Loyalist West, which portrayed great moments in British history in classical poses and modern dress, to visually chronicle the signal events of the revolution. The idea was to create for the American public a record of self-sacrifice and triumph in over 250 paintings. Although Trumbull succeeded in molding popular images of the revolution, so much so that it is his depiction of the signing of the Declaration of Independence that remains with us today, financial security eluded him in a democratic marketplace. Peale focused his efforts on portraits. He decided to create a gallery of heroes and set out to paint every leading revolutionary he could find and place their portraits in a museum for all to see. In 1788 he opened his museum in Philadelphia, including natural curiosities such as rattlesnake skins and a stuffed buffalo. The audiences, however, seemed to like the curiosities more than the hall of heroes. To keep the public interested Peale added more and more bizarre items and even included stage shows. Neither art for art's sake, as many elite imagined had been the case in antiquity, nor art as a celebration of republican values, attracted the democratic crowd, which simply sought vulgar entertainment.

Certainly if there were any art form in which Americans might capture the spirit of classical antiquity it would be in literature. Skilled pens had been turned to great effect during the 1760s and 1770s to articulate colonial grievances. Newspapers abounded and printing presses ran in almost every town. Moreover, Americans had the highest literacy rate in the world. Despite expectations, no Homer and no Milton appeared. Americans eagerly read newspapers, but efforts to establish literary magazines usually faltered. Would-be Augustan poets in New England—the so-called Connecticut Wits—ineptly copied the style of Alexander Pope. At first they embraced the promise of the revolution, then they soured and wrote scathing satire about the egalitarian impulses of their poorer neighbors in almost undetectable rhymes. A few poets, such as Philip Freneau, fared better by writing democratic verse. Freneau, however, also gained employment as a Jeffersonian placeman and newspaper editor. Novelists struggled. Charles Brockden Brown wrote six novels in a two-year period (1798–1799) in rushed prose and with awkward plots that placed characters in a gothic American setting that often hinged on implausible gimmicks such as ventriloquism. Even with editing a short-lived magazine Brown found it difficult to earn a living from his literary efforts. Hugh Henry Brackenridge, although a Jeffersonian, expressed his disappointment in the egalitarianism of American society in *Modern Chivalry,* a rambling novel modeled after *Don Quixote.* Brackenridge's hero, Captain Farrago, travels across the countryside with an imbecilic Irish sidekick who is improbably elevated by a fickle society to a variety of important positions including congressman, philosopher, and excise man. This saga had a limited appeal. What sold were sentimental tales like *Charlotte Temple* or fabricated biographies like the work of Parson Mason Weems. There was little chance to fulfill the promise of the Enlightenment and to match the glories of ancient Greece here.

Despite the claims of Jefferson for the greatness of American scientists, the American republic again fell short of expectations. Franklin's work on electricity was significant, but was completed long before independence. He added little to his scientific reputation before his death in 1790. Rittenhouse was an important astronomer both before and after the Revolutionary War, building an orrery—a working model of the solar system—and discovering a comet in 1763. Like Franklin and Rittenhouse, most American scientists were more known for observation than theory. William Bartram, for example, published in 1791 a book on his travels in the southern United States, which became the most important naturalist study in late eighteenth-century America, with detailed illustrations of plants, birds, and wildlife. In fact, the greatest American scientific breakthroughs were more technological and practical rather than in the realm of either observation or theory. In 1787 and 1791 John Fitch developed prototypes of a steamboat but was denied sole patent authority because he did not have good political connections with the Washington administration.

It would be over a decade before a working steamboat could be put into operation. Samuel Slater was not an innovator. He merely memorized the blueprints of English textile machinery and built the first American textile factory in 1791. Major scientific achievements were in short supply, unless money could be made.

The Founding Fathers also hoped that the early republic would epitomize a new sense of benevolence and lead to the reform of society on the basis of reason and nature so that man's potential could finally be fulfilled. In 1786, Pennsylvania changed its criminal code to eliminate corporal punishment and minimize capital punishment. Men like Benjamin Rush argued for further reform and insisted that a prison should be a "house of repentance" where criminals would be kept in isolation and learn to change their behavior.[39] Inspired by these ideas, in 1790, Philadelphia's Walnut Street Prison became an institution of private punishment and labor. Other states followed this prototype, including Virginia, where Thomas Jefferson designed the Richmond Penitentiary based on the Philadelphia model. These prisons never quite matched the ideal and often were dirty and overcrowded. Rather than changing behavior, the brutal and austere life in prison became a breeding ground for further vice and crime. Reformers also wanted to make sure that the general population received enough education to become a virtuous citizenry and guarantee the future of the republic. As Jefferson explained, "the most effectual means of preventing" the perversion of power into tyranny was "to illuminate . . . the minds of the people."[40] Repeated efforts in Virginia to pass an education bill authored by Jefferson failed in the 1780s. When the legislature enacted the elementary school portion of the bill in 1796, it remained a dead letter because implementation was left in the hands of local authorities. Common schools fared better in Massachusetts because the 1789 statute merely wrote into law what most towns had already been practicing. Still, inspired by the ideals of the revolution, somewhere between 100 and 200 new academies, the equivalent of high schools, were established between 1775 and 1800. There was also an expansion of colleges: Six had been founded before 1776; over twenty more were created by 1800. This education, however, had become democratized. With students from a greater variety of social and economic backgrounds, including young men in their twenties, colleges were more often the scene of raucous behavior and challenges to authority than institutions of reason and nature demonstrating the perfectability of mankind.

The American Revolution raised expectations for many Americans. Revolutionary leaders thought that they could somehow put into place the ideals of the Enlightenment and create a new golden age similar to classical antiquity. Despite modeling buildings on ancient temples, trying to create a republican art and literature, or applying ideas from nature and reason to the world around them, they came up short. In this failure to realize their highest vision, the elite's experience paralleled the experience of people less close to the mainstream. Many Native Americans saw in the Revolutionary War, whether they sided with the British or the Americans, an opportunity to sustain their culture in the face of sweeping change. African Americans grasped onto the idea of liberty yearning to break the shackles that held them in bondage. Women sought to redefine their role in society, with some even advocating equality. Each group used the revolution to gain some concessions. Each group, whatever the promise, did not have its fondest revolutionary visions fulfilled.

Endnotes

1. Quoted in Colin G. Calloway, *Crown and Calumet: British–Indian Relations, 1783–1815* (Norman: University of Oklahoma Press, 1987), 10–11. Originally in Brigadier General Allan Maclean to Haldimand, 18 May 1782\3Haldimand Papers, Correspondence and papers of General Sir Frederick Haldimand, 1758–1791, 21756: 138–40, British Museum, London.
2. Quoted in Colin G. Calloway, *The American Revolution in Indian Country: Crisis and Diversity in Native American Communities* (Cambridge: Cambridge University Press, 1995), 273.
3. Quoted in Calloway, *The American Revolution in Indian Country*, 276.
4. *Journals of the Continental Congress, 1774–1789,* Worthington C. Ford, et al., ed. (Washington, D.C.: 1904–37), 25: 686.
5. Quoted in James H. Merrell, "Declarations of Independence: Indian–White Relations in the New Nation," in Jack P. Greene, ed., *The American Revolution: Its Character and Limits* (New York: New York University Press, 1987), 202.
6. Quoted in Merrell, "Declarations of Independence," in Greene, ed., *The American Revolution,* 202–03.
7. Quoted in Alan Taylor, "Land and Liberty on the Post-Revolutionary Frontier," in David Thomas Konig, ed., *Devising Liberty: Preserving and Creating Freedom in the New American Republic* (Stanford, Cal.: Stanford University Press, 1995), 94.
8. Northwest Ordinance, July 13, 1787, The Avalon Project at Yale Law School, www.yale.edu/lawweb/avalon/nworder.htm.
9. *Journals of the Continental Congress, 1774–1789* (1787), 33: 479.
10. *American State Papers: Indian Affairs* (Washington, D.C.: Gales and Seaton, 1832), Pt. 2, Vol. 1, 13.
11. Northwest Ordinance, July 13, 1787, The Avalon Project at Yale Law School, www.yale.edu/lawweb/avalon/nworder.htm.
12. Arthur Lee, "Address on Slavery," Rind's *Virginia Gazette,* March 19, 1767, reprinted in Gary B. Nash, *Race and Revolution* (Madison, Wis.: Madison House, 1990), 92, 94, 95.
13. This number is taken from Sylvia R. Frey, *Water From the Rock: Black Resistance in a Revolutionary Age* (Princeton: Princeton University Press, 1991), 211.
14. Quoted in Nash, *Race and Revolution,* 19.

15. For these statistics, and the numbers of free slaves in the previous paragraph, see the tables in Ira Berlin, *Many Thousands Gone: The First Two Centuries of Slavery in North America* (Cambridge: Harvard University Press, 1998), 369–75.

16. Benjamin Banneker, *Copy of a Letter from Benjamin Banneker to the Secretary of State, with His Answer* (Philadelphia: Daniel Lawrence, 1792), 4–5, 8.

17. [Absalom Jones and Richard Allen], *A Narrative of the Proceedings of the Black People, During the Late Awful Calamity in Philadelphia, in the Year 1793: And a Refutation of Some Censures, Thrown upon Them in Some Late Publications* (Philadelphia: William W. Woodward, 1794), 23–25.

18. Letter from Abigail to John Adams, 31 March–5 April 1776, Adams Family Papers: An Electronic Archive, www.masshist.org/exhibitions/aea2.cfm.

19. Letter from John Adams to Abigail Adams, 14 April 1776, Adams Family Papers: An Electronic Archive, www.masshist.org/exhibitions/aea2.cfm.

20. Mary Beth Norton, *Liberty's Daughters: The Revolutionary Experience of American Women, 1750–1800* (Boston: Little, Brown, 1980), 158.

21. Peter Force, ed., *American Archives: Consisting of a Collection of Authentick Records, State Papers, Debates, and Letters and Other Notices of Publick Affairs . . .* 4th ser. [Washington: U.S. Government, 1837–53] 1: 891–2.

22. Linda K. Kerber, *Women of the Republic: Intellect and Ideology in Revolutionary America* (Chapel Hill: University of North Carolina Press, 1980), 108–09.

23. Quoted in Susan Branson, *These Fiery Frenchified Dames: Women and Political Culture in Early National Philadelphia* (Philadelphia: University of Pennsylvania Press, 2001), 78.

24. Quoted in Branson, *These Fiery Frenchified Dames,* 80.

25. Benjamin Rush, *Thoughts upon Female Education, Accommodated to the Present State of Society, Manners, and Government, . . .* (Philadelphia: Prichard & Hall, 1787), 25.

26. Quoted in Margaret Nash, "Rethinking Republican Motherhood: Benjamin Rush and the Young Ladies' Academy of Philadelphia," *Journal of the Early Republic,* 17, 182.

27. *The Rise and Progress of the Young-Ladies' Academy of Philadelphia . . .* (Philadelphia: Stewart & Cochran, [1794]), 91, 93.

28. Quoted in Kerber, *Women of the Republic,* 205; and Branson, *These Fiery Frenchified Dames,* 34.

29. Quoted in Branson, *These Fiery Frenchified Dames,* 36–37.

30. Quoted in Branson, *These Fiery Frenchified Dames,* 26.

31. Norma Basch, "From the Bonds of Empire to the Bonds of Matrimony," in Konig, *Devising Liberty,* 222.

32. Quoted in Kerber, *Women of the Republic,* 141.

33. Paul A. Gilje and Howard B. Rock, eds., *Keepers of the Revolution: New Yorkers at Work in the Early Republic* (Ithaca, N.Y.: Cornell University Press), 254.

34. William Wyche, *Report of the Trial of Henry Bedlow for Committing a Rape on Lanah Sawyer . . .* (New York: no pub., 1793), 40.

35. The poem was published only under Freneau's name. Philip Morin Freneau, *A Poem, on the Rising Glory of America: Being an Exercise Delivered at the Public Commencement at Nassau-hall, September 25, 1771* (Philadelphia: Joseph Crukshank, for R. Aitken, 1772), 21, 24.

36. Quoted in Joseph J. Ellis, *After the Revolution: Profiles of American Culture* (New York: Norton, 1970), x.

37. Merrill D. Peterson, ed., *The Portable Thomas Jefferson* (New York: Viking, 1975), 102.

38. Lester J. Cappon, ed., *The Complete Adams–Jefferson Letters: The Complete Correspondence Between Thomas Jefferson and Abigail and John Adams*, 2 vols. (Chapel Hill: University of North Carolina Press, 1959), 2: 502–03.

39. Quoted in Michael Meranze, *Laboratories of Virtue: Punishment, Revolution, and Authority in Philadelphia, 1760–1835* (Chapel Hill: University of North Carolina Press, 1996), 132.

40. The quotation is from the preamble in Jefferson's *A Bill for the More General Diffusion of Knowledge (1779)* in *Thomas Jefferson: Public Papers, 1775–1825,* Jefferson Digital Archive, University of Virginia, http://etext.lib.virginia.edu/jefferson/texts/.

Contested Republic

Hamilton's Program

Jeffersonian Response

The French Revolution and the Party System

The Problem with Commerce

✪

Hamilton's Program

Everything was new in 1789 when George Washington became the first president. Even though the Constitution had provided for elections for an executive and a two-house legislature, no one was entirely sure what shape the government would take. Vice President John Adams, who "presided" over the Senate, even wanted to debate how to address the president. Was the president an elected king who should be called "His Majesty" or "His Highness," or was he merely the first among equal republicans? Adams's concern brought derision. He was charged with "nobilimania" and referred to as the "Duke of Braintree"; some wags, noting the vice president's ample waistline, called Adams "His Rotundity."[1]

With so much that was new and yet to be decided, every piece of legislation and every public act was pregnant with meaning. Washington settled the title issue—he was "Mr. President." Mimicking European courts, Washington established formal state occasions, called levees, where he received foreign dignitaries, government officials, office seekers, and others hoping for favor. Empowered by the Constitution to set up federal courts in addition to the Supreme Court, Congress passed the Judiciary Act of 1789 organizing district and circuit courts to hear cases concerning federal law between parties of different states. Both the Senate and House of Representatives had to create rules and committees to facilitate procedures. Congress also legislated into existence a federal bureaucracy, including the Treasury and State Departments. In turn, Washington had to appoint "secretaries" to run these departments, with the advice and consent of the Senate.

Determined to have the best men for the job, Washington appointed Alexander Hamilton to the Treasury and Thomas Jefferson as secretary of state. Washington knew Hamilton well. Everyone acknowledged Hamilton's brilliance. Although his parents were not married and he was born in the West Indies, Hamilton had come to North America as a young man, excelled in his studies, and ingratiated himself with several powerful men in New York. An ardent supporter of the revolution, he served as an aide to Washington for most of the war. During the 1780s he practiced law and married Elizabeth Schuyler, a member of one of the richest and most influential families in New York. Hamilton also supported the movement to strengthen the national government, attended the Annapolis and Philadelphia Conventions, and authored many of the *Federalist Papers.* Given his personal connection to the president, his keen intellect, and prominent role in supporting the ratification of the Constitution, he seemed the perfect individual to control the Treasury and give direction to the new government. Jefferson, too, had sterling credentials. A Virginian like Washington, Jefferson had served in the Continental Congress, written the Declaration of Independence, governed Virginia for several years during the war, and had diplomatic experience as ambassador to France for much of the 1780s. Putting two such qualified men in the cabinet together was what the Constitution was all about—bringing talented, natural aristocrats into the national government to ensure the public good. The two had very different ideas about the public good, however, and their disagreements had profound implications for the development of American capitalism. Hamilton hoped to foster economic development from the top down. Jefferson pushed for a greater freedom for the individual that, whether he realized it or not, would ultimately encourage an aggressive and competitive market tied to the ideal of equality for the common man. This debate would tear the Washington administration apart, lead to the formation of political parties, and almost foment a civil war.

Alexander Hamilton seized the initiative. Believing that the weak confederation of the 1780s had jeopardized the revolution, Hamilton wished to mold the U.S. government under the Constitution into a strong national entity that would guarantee the public good. In the spirit of the Philadelphia Convention, Hamilton had little faith in the virtue and independence of the common man. He concluded that the best way to ensure the future of the republic was to tie the interests of each individual to the national state. As secretary of treasury, a position he envisioned as something akin to the British prime minister, Hamilton wrote a series of reports in 1790 and 1791 that offered a sweeping plan to extend the power of the central government. This program, which mirrored many of the elements of Robert Morris's effort to strengthen the Confederation in the early 1780s, consisted of five parts: the full funding of the national debt, the assumption of state debts, the creation of a national bank, encouragement of manufacturing, and a system of taxation to pay for everything.

The full funding of the national debt was a bold stroke. Put simply, America's finances were a mess. The Revolutionary War cost somewhere between $158 million and $168 million in real money—gold and silver. No one, not even Hamilton, probably fully understood the complicated and convoluted way the war had been funded. At the beginning of the conflict the Continental Congress had optimistically hoped that its printed currency could absorb the cost of the war. Congress thought that the Continental dollar would be used to pay state taxes and returned to the federal government and retired. That didn't work. Almost $250 million worth of currency had been printed by 1781, which proved so inflationary that it brought a real value of goods and services of about $45 million. When Congress gave up on paper money in 1781, all bills in circulation became worthless. Benjamin Franklin approached this turn of events with aplomb, viewing the currency emission simply as a form of taxation that had fallen heaviest on the wealthy. He saw the paper money emissions as "a *gradual Tax*" on money that "has fallen more equally than many other Taxes, as those People paid most who being the richest had most Money passing thro' their Hands."[2] The United States also received about $10 million in foreign loans and gifts, 80 percent of which came from France. During the 1780s, Congress failed to meet its payments on the French loans, but managed to make its interest payments on $2 million in Dutch loans, barely keeping American international credit afloat. Congress also had a domestic debt of about $28 million in principal with another $12 million in accrued interest. This debt came in three basic forms: loan certificates issued to individuals who had lent Congress money directly; impressment certificates issued by government officials for goods rendered, often under compunction, during the war; and military certificates given to solders in lieu of payment for military service. Although Congress strove to at least keep up with the interest on the loan certificates, by the mid-1780s this became impossible. At the insistence of local merchants, several states, such as Pennsylvania and New York, assumed these debts and began making payments, further weakening the national government. The value of these notes varied widely during the 1780s, but in general, even the most highly regarded of these notes (loan certificates) sold well below par. The final form and largest portion—perhaps as much as $65 million plus interest—of expenditures from the revolution was by the states and included many different forms ranging from printed currency to various types of certificates. The price of state notes also ranged greatly, depending on the type and the state involved.[3]

Rather than viewing the debt as a drain on the nation, Hamilton embraced the debt as a positive force to bind the republic together. Whereas the Confederation and the state governments during the 1780s had been at pains to raise hard money to erase the debt, thereby helping to precipitate a political crisis, Hamilton viewed an ongoing debt as a source of political stability. Hamilton planned to fully underwrite the $40 million domestic debt. A creditor could demand specie payment if he wanted, but Hamilton provided encouragements to limit this drain on real wealth in the hands of the government. Instead, creditors could exchange their current notes for new government securities, two-thirds of which would pay 6 percent interest immediately, and one-third would pay 6 percent deferred interest after 1800. Certificates of interest issued during the 1780s, called indents, brought 3 percent interest. In addition, old paper money issued by Congress during the war would be valued at 100:1 and be considered part of the public debt. Speculators made a killing. Many original holders of the certificates—farmers who had been compelled to sell livestock or grain, and soldiers who fought for years without receiving any pay—had sold their notes for pennies on the dollar. Within a few years, 6 percent certificates were selling at $1.20 and someone who had purchased a $100 worth of securities in 1786 for $15, which probably carried $25 in accrued unpaid interest, could sell the note for $121.50 in 1792. This type of windfall did not bother Hamilton at all. In fact, it was part of his plan. He wanted to tie merchants and moneyed men to the United States through the national debt to ensure the future of the republic. He assumed that there was a chain of dependence running from the merchants to the rest of society. If the merchants were vested in the well-being of the nation, then the farmers, artisans, laborers, and sailors would follow suit.

The same thinking lay behind the assumption of state debts. Hamilton recognized that every creditor wanted his debtor to be powerful and economically viable to ensure continued interest payments and eventual repayment. When New York, Pennsylvania, and other states began to take over the national debt in the mid-1780s, Congress became weaker and the states became stronger. Hamilton intended to reverse this process. Assuming the remaining state debts would enhance the need to create federal taxes and to have an activist government. Under Hamilton's plan the creditors could hand in state notes for U.S. certificates at slightly less interest than the regular domestic debt. Almost $20 million was added to the debt by this process. Hamilton also set up a commission to determine how much of the cost of the revolution, including the debt, each state had already paid. Any state that had paid more than its share, based on its proportion of the total national population, would be issued government notes for the excess amount.

Crucial to Hamilton's plan for strengthening national finances was the creation of the Bank of the United States (BUS). Even more than Morris's Bank of North America, the BUS would be a quasi-public institution. Capitalized at $10 million, the charter of incorporation issued by Congress in 1791 stipulated that the United States would own one-quarter of all its stock and appoint five of twenty-five directors. The rest of the bank would be privately owned, with three-quarters of all stock purchased with government bonds. In other words, with only $2 million in specie from investors, the BUS would issue $10 million in notes, creating out of thin air millions of dollars' worth of capital to help develop the national economy. The BUS would also be the principal depository of U.S. funds and act as the fiscal agent for the Treasury in foreign and domestic transactions. The bank notes would provide a stable currency in lieu of a direct paper currency printed by the United States. Because the BUS would be such a powerful financial engine, it could also control and regulate any smaller banks chartered by state governments (only three such banks had been chartered by 1791, but more were to come). Perhaps most important of all, the BUS would further tie business interests to the federal government. Every individual with money of any consequence would purchase BUS stock, use BUS notes, and transact business with the BUS.

Hamilton extended his vision for a dynamic American economy with a "Report on the Subject of Manufactures" submitted to Congress on December 3, 1791. Although the United States sought free markets in Europe and elsewhere in the 1780s and 1790s, Hamilton feared the mercantilist policies of the Old World that might restrict the import of American agricultural products. Moreover, Hamilton believed that the United States would never truly be independent as long as it relied on manufactured goods from Great Britain. The solution was simple: Develop American manufacturing and build an urban base that would consume the farmer's excess production. As Hamilton explained, "Not only the wealth but the independence and security of a country appear to be materially connected with the prosperity of manufactures."[4] Because the British could provide manufactured items cheaper than any nascent American business, Hamilton hoped to establish a protective tariff and create bounties for building factories. To go beyond the copyright provision in the Constitution, he wanted to have the government offer premiums for improvements in quality and special awards for labor-saving devices. Congress, however, was unreceptive to this part of the Hamiltonian program. Private enterprise stepped into the breach with the creation of the Society for Establishing Useful Manufactures (SEUM) chartered by the State of New Jersey in late 1791 for $1 million in stock. The SEUM planned to build an industrial city on the shores of the Passaic River. These dreams, however, came to naught in a financial panic in 1792 and Americans would have to take a private and eclectic path toward industrialization.

Hamilton was more successful with full funding, assumption, and the BUS. But he still had to pay for this ambitious program. The United States owned an incredible asset. During the Revolutionary War several states had relinquished their claims to land west of the Appalachians, creating a huge national domain. The Treaty of Paris in 1783 ceded this territory to the United States, much to the distress of the Native Americans who lived there. Despite the effort to organize the territories through surveys in accordance with the Land Ordinance of 1785, and the plan to integrate new territories as equal partners into the United States with the Northwest Ordinance of 1787, Indian opposition meant delays in cashing in on the bonanza of western land. Eventually, land sales might fill the Treasury's coffers, but Hamilton needed revenue starting immediately to carry his program forward. The Constitution provided Congress with a power denied under the Articles of Confederation—an independent source of national revenue based on Congressional legislative action. Almost as soon as the government came into being in 1789 Congress passed a 5 percent tariff on most imports, with a few luxury items, such as coaches, taxed at a higher rate. In January 1791 Congress also passed an excise tax on all domestic and foreign spiritous liquor.

Taken together, Hamilton's agenda was pro-capitalist and forward looking in that it envisioned an integrated economy with agriculture, commerce, and manufacturing. It welcomed the growth of industry and cities. However, rather than allowing an entrepreneur free rein as an individual, Hamilton hoped to guide the economy along a specified path, rewarding the rich, talented, and well-born. His vision was therefore also backward looking because it emphasized hierarchy and sought to bind every citizen's personal interest to the U.S. government.

Jeffersonian Response

Thomas Jefferson and James Madison opposed Hamilton's program and came to see it as a concerted effort to corrupt and destroy the American Republic. Rather than believing that all men were dependent creatures who would blindly follow their interests, they still had faith in the virtue of the common man. The ideal republic was a nation of small agricultural producers—yeoman farmers—who lived independently. As Madison explained, "The class of citizens who provide at once their own food and their own raiment, may be viewed as the most truly independent and happy." They were at the same time "the best basis of public liberty, and the strongest bulwark of public safety."[5] For Jefferson, "Those who labour in the earth are the chosen people of God . . . whose breasts he has made his peculiar deposit for substantial and genuine virtue."[6] Properly educated and not connected by interest to anyone above or below him (and by definition the citizen-farmer was male) this individual would exercise his judgement and vote for representatives who would be from a natural aristocracy—men like Jefferson and Madison.

Although both Jefferson and Hamilton served in the cabinet, there developed an ideological and eventually a personal antipathy between the two men. Hamilton believed that men were innately dependent; Jefferson wanted to keep citizens independent. Hamilton wanted to develop an integrated economy that included manufacturing; Jefferson wanted to sustain an agrarian republic. Hamilton advocated a strong activist government; Jefferson believed in a weak, almost invisible, government. Personally, the two men competed for Washington's attention. Hamilton's Treasury Department had over one thousand employees and all of the government's money flowed through his office. His reports to Congress set the terms of debate. His policy guided the national government. Jefferson had a mere six clerks at the State Department and a few ambassadors serving in a handful of European countries. He wrote reports, too, on international trade and the fisheries, but they garnered little attention. All too often his agenda was shunted aside and his influence ineffectual. Personally, the men were a study in contrasts. Hamilton was flamboyant and aggressive, Jefferson retiring and plotting.

James Madison, as a member of the House of Representatives, initiated the political controversy in debates over the first revenue measure passed by Congress in 1789—the tariff. Madison argued for a policy of discrimination against Great Britain, which controlled so much of American commerce. Passing a heavier duty on the British would compel them to open their markets in the British Isles and the West Indies to the United States. Until the British relented, Madison believed, American commerce would develop other markets and trade with our ally France would increase. Madison held that the United States produced food that the British needed desperately, and that Great Britain merely exported "superfluities" such as manufactured luxuries. Any "necessaries" the United States obtained from Great Britain could probably be manufactured by Americans.[7] Therefore, punishing the British with a discriminatory tariff would sooner or later convince them to open their markets on the basis of free trade. Hamilton wanted no part of discrimination. He needed the tariff revenue to restore the credit of the

United States and, from his perspective, it was useless to ruin American trade in the hope of forcing almighty Britain to change its ways. Economic independence could come only with the development of a manufacturing sphere within the United States. Much to Madison's chagrin, and to Jefferson's, whose report on commerce advocated discrimination a few years later, Hamilton won out with Congress.

The bigger battle emerged over the funding program. Madison agreed that establishing American credit was crucial. As he explained from the floor of Congress, "No logic, . . . no magic . . . can diminish the force of the obligation." This position was consistent with his efforts during the 1780s to strengthen Congress and his support of the Constitution. But Madison was also outraged by the speculation that had driven up the price of government securities. A few thousand moneyed men seemed to control vast quantities of debt. Whereas Hamilton saw this development as positive, Madison thought it inimical. Worse, it appeared that there was some insider trading. Men such as William Duer, who worked at the Treasury Department, were actively involved in the securities markets. And friends of Hamilton, including merchant Andrew Craigie, seemed to have known the contents of Hamilton's report, no doubt passed on in a social conversation, before it was released. Madison believed that rewarding these moneymen by seven or eight times their investment was unfair. He wanted to compensate the original holders of the government notes as "a tribute due to their merits" as they were the ones who sacrificed during the revolution. Rather than leaving the speculators totally without profit, Madison suggested that the funding of the debt be divided, with the speculators being paid "the highest price which has prevailed in the market; and let the residue belong to the original sufferers."[8] This position was not popular with many members of Congress, who pointed out that identifying and paying the original holders would be cumbersome and expensive. Madison's opponents also argued that his plan would be a repudiation of a public contract and hurt the credit of the United States as no one could ever be sure if a security would be honored at face value or not. Madison's proposal failed in the House, and Congress passed the measure to fully fund the national debt in February 1790.

If Madison lost the first skirmishes over the Hamiltonian program, he fared better in the contest over assumption of the state debts. Madison opposed assumption for several reasons. First, speculation in state notes had the potential to reap even more profits for moneyed men than speculation in U.S. notes. Fearing the corrupting influence of rewarding moneyed men out of all proportion to their investment made opposition to assumption Act Two in Madison's effort to protect the virtue of the republic. But there were also some important state issues involved as well. Allowing the Treasury

Department to take over the remaining debt would be conceding too much power to the federal government. Madison may have wanted a stronger national government, but he did not want to see his Virginia entirely disappear. His original proposal for the Constitution had included proportional representation in both houses of legislature, knowing that Virginia had the largest population and therefore would have the greatest voice in the government. Assumption would lead to the consolidation of power controlled by the Secretary of Treasury and his northern minions—the speculators who had bought up both state and federal notes after the writing and ratification of the Constitution. In addition, Madison's Virginia had shrunk much of its debt during the 1780s. Assumption would mean that Virginia, and other states in a similar situation, would be taxed to pay for the arrears of states such as South Carolina and Massachusetts, which had large outstanding debts. Virginians also believed that they had already paid for more than their share of the Revolutionary War. They therefore wanted to tie any assumption of state debts to a final accounting of the cost of the war. If the final accounting determined that Virginians were correct, then the federal government would compensate the state with U.S. securities, allowing the state to ease if not eliminate taxation.

Madison, who was a master at parliamentary maneuver, did not attack assumption outright. Instead he amended the bill to insist that a final accounting of state expenditures during the revolution must occur before the assumption of state debts. Because this process would be time-consuming, the final accounting was not complete until 1796, in essence, this ploy would put off assumption for several years. With the support of his fellow Virginians and representatives of states who thought the final accounting would be to their advantage, Madison eked out a narrow majority in favor of assumption with the accounting amendment in April 1790.

This outcome did not hold, and in late July 1790 Madison acquiesced in the passage of the assumption bill. The reason for this shift was a compromise worked out between Hamilton and Madison. Jefferson, who came to rue the bargain, claimed that the agreement was struck at a dinner party he hosted in late June 1790 at which Madison agreed to withdraw his opposition to assumption and Hamilton agreed to have the permanent capital placed on the banks of the Potomac. The resolution was not quite so simple. No doubt the dinner reported by Jefferson occurred, but it was only one of a series of meetings in June whereby not only was a deal negotiated for establishing the capital on the Potomac, but there was also a deal to balance Virginia's accounts with the U.S. government. Madison had feared that the Treasury would assume the $3 million debt that Virginia still owed, and then tax the state $5 million. Instead, Hamilton agreed to assume about $3.5 million in state debt, while setting Virginia's federal taxes at the same amount. As Jefferson explained, "Being therefore to receive exactly what she is to pay" Virginia "will neither win nor lose by the measure."[9]

In December 1791 Congress began consideration of the bill to incorporate the BUS. By this time Madison and Jefferson had begun working in tandem on a regular basis to oppose Hamilton, his moneyed supporters, and their pro-British policies. Jefferson and Madison again planned to push discrimination against British trade until Great Britain signed a commercial agreement with the United States. They were overwhelmed by the steamroller of Hamilton's fiscal agenda. With their efforts stymied in Congress, and Hamilton undercutting Jefferson's diplomacy through secret backdoor contacts with the British, both Jefferson and Madison began to worry over the direction of the nation under Hamilton's leadership. The BUS became just another building block in the Hamiltonian edifice of corruption, dependence, and moneyed interest. Madison spoke out against the BUS in Congress, arguing that the Constitution did not allow for its incorporation. Here was the man who in *Federalist Paper No. 44* had defended "the necessary and proper clause" and the importance of a broad interpretation of the Constitution, declaring the need for strict construction. Despite Madison's objections, Congress passed the bill.

Madison's concerns, however, had raised doubts with President Washington. Before signing the bill he asked for written advice from three members of his cabinet. Attorney General Edmund Randolph, from Virginia, and Jefferson thought the bill unconstitutional and urged Washington to veto the measure. Jefferson quoted the Tenth Amendment in his brief—"all powers not delegated to the United States, by the Constitution, nor prohibited by it to the States, are reserved to the States or to the people"—to demonstrate the limited ability of Congress to pass laws based on implied powers. Jefferson believed that to "take a single step beyond the boundaries thus specially drawn around the powers of Congress, is to take possession of a boundless field of power, no longer susceptible of any definition."[10] Jefferson continued by indicating that there was nothing in the Constitution to explicitly permit the BUS and that the necessary and proper clause did not apply. He agreed that it might be convenient to have a bank, but convenience was not the same as a necessity. Hamilton wrote the third opinion, with the other two in hand, and tore the arguments of the two Virginians to shreds. Without implied powers, "the United States would furnish the singular spectacle of a *political society* without *sovereignty*, or of a *people governed*, without *government*." Hamilton then went on to assert that "it is unquestionably incident to *sovereign power* to erect corporations" that are relative "to the *objects* intrusted to the management of the government."[11] With lawyerlike precision Hamilton pointed to other corporate entities created by the United States—territorial governments—and demonstrated how the BUS was necessary to fulfill a variety of functions of government. The BUS would help with the collection of taxes by providing a single repository, simplifying accounting. Whenever the government needed a short-term loan as it awaited final collection of taxes, the BUS would be there to extend credit. By providing a unitary paper currency that held its value the BUS would help to regulate trade. And in case of war, when expenditures would quickly exceed the Treasury's ability to pay, the bank would have millions available for the United States and thereby ensure the common defense. Convinced by his friend Hamilton, Washington signed the bill.

For Jefferson and Madison each piece of the Hamiltonian program seemed to move the United States closer to an aristocracy and monarchy dominated by a handful of moneyed men. When Hamilton submitted his Report on Manufactures in December 1791 the two Virginians were determined to make sure it would go nowhere. Although he would change his mind when president, in the 1780s and 1790s Jefferson believed the development of manufacturing inimical to the virtue of the people. In 1785 Jefferson wrote that he considered "the class of artificers [men who worked in manufacturing] as the panders of vice and the instruments by which the liberties of a country are generally overturned" and in his *Notes on the State of Virginia* he proclaimed that "While we have land to labour . . . let us never wish to see our citizens occupied at a work-bench, or twirling a distaff." As for the "general operations of manufacture," Jefferson maintained "let our workshops remain in Europe." He also railed against cities: "The mobs of great cities add just so much to the support of pure government, as sores do to the strength of the human body." Preservation of a republic depended on the vigor in the "manners and spirit of a people." Any "degeneracy in these," such as occurred with workmen from the city, "is a canker which soon eats to the heart of its laws and constitution."[12] From this perspective, men who worked in factories or lived in cities could never be independent because their livings depended on someone else. They would vote for their "masters" and further strengthen the hand of the speculators and moneyed pseudoaristocracy. Hamilton's desire for an integrated economy that included the development of cities, commerce, manufacturing, and agriculture was therefore unacceptable.

With this ideological background, and with a sense of having already lost much ground to forces destroying the republic, Madison orchestrated resistance to the Report on Manufactures in Congress. In February 1792 he defeated the principle of bounties. The Senate initiated a bill to provide a "bounty" for the cod fishery to offset the taxes paid by fishermen for salt. The bill appeared to follow suggestions in Jefferson's earlier Report on the Fisheries, but several congressmen objected to the word *bounty* because it would set a precedent for manufacturing. Hugh Williamson of North Carolina declared that the measure would establish a doctrine that might be applied by "people of every trade and occupation . . . until they have eaten up the bread of our children," and William B. Giles of Virginia called the measure as leading "to a complete system of tyranny." Madison replaced the word *bounty* with *allowance*. Madison argued that allowance was merely a modification of existing laws to ensure their fairness, whereas a bounty was beyond the constitutional power of Congress that, if passed, "would subvert the very foundation, and transmute the very nature of the limited Government established by the people of America." Having destroyed bounties as an option, Madison focused his attention in March on protective tariffs. The United States needed additional revenue to pay for the Indian war in Ohio country after the defeat of Arthur St. Clair. Hamilton proposed an increase in tariffs that also was a first step toward encouraging manufacturing. His opponents rose to the challenge, lecturing Hamilton that he was supposed to offer "a provision to defend the frontier" and was not authorized to create a "system for the encouragement of manufactures."[13] Because the situation on the frontier was something of a crisis the measure finally passed. But the message was clear: Congress would be loathe to accept any additional legislation in support of Hamilton's Report on Manufacturing.

Whatever the previous working relationship in the cabinet between Jefferson and Hamilton, things began to sour in 1791. Some of the civility in the exchanges between the two secretaries decreased. Madison and Jefferson began to lay the foundation for an organized opposition to the government both men served. They contacted leaders with similar sentiments throughout the country and prepared for the next round in what seemed an ongoing battle for the soul of the new nation. Distressed with the pro-government fulminations in John Fenno's newspaper, *Gazette of the United States,* they looked for an editor for a newspaper that would represent their views. They found their man in Philip Freneau. A poet and gifted writer, Freneau began publishing his *National Gazette* in October 1791. Jefferson had moved heaven and earth to convince Freneau to edit the paper. He provided him with a position in the State Department as a translator (with a salary of $250 a year), funneled government printing contracts to Freneau, guaranteed he would not personally lose any money in the operation, and both Jefferson and Madison actively recruited subscribers for the paper. At first Freneau was relatively measured in his political commentary. In March 1792, however, he published a barrage of attacks on Hamilton. Freneau claimed that the finance system had "given rise to scenes of speculation calculated to aggrandize the few and the wealthy" transferring "the best resources of the country forever into the hands of the speculators."[14] This assault coincided with a run of speculation triggered by William Duer that led to a financial panic that spring. But even after that bubble burst and the economy recovered by the summer, Freneau persisted in his attacks, joined in several essays written by Madison. In July, Hamilton struck back in the pages of Fenno's *Gazette*, pointing to the salary Freneau collected from the State Department. This war of ink persisted through the fall elections. By the end of the year, after all the debate over the Hamiltonian program and the public charge and countercharge in the newspapers, there began to emerge the first party system. Jefferson and Madison called their supporters "Republicans." These Republicans shared the Jeffersonian vision of an agrarian world of independent yeoman farmers. They used a democratic rhetoric that attacked their opponents as stockjobbers and would-be aristocrats. They emphasized the equality of man. On the one hand their resistance to the Hamiltonian program can be seen as antidevelopment and hostile to capital investment; on the other, their concern with the independence of men and the absence of a controlled economy would eventually unleash the unprecedented and unfettered American capitalism of the nineteenth century.

The French Revolution and the Party System

The French Revolution transformed American politics. Most Americans greeted the effort to change the French government in 1789 with enthusiasm. When the National Assembly abolished feudal privileges (August 4, 1789), and issued the Declaration of the Rights of Man (August 26, 1789), it appeared to be the dawning of a new republican age. As reform gave way to radicalism in 1792, some Americans began to wonder where the French Revolution was going. When the Jacobins executed the royal family in January 1793, many in the United States believed the revolution in France had gone too far. The next month, France and Great Britain went to war. This conflict changed everything. Interest in the French swept through the country and polarized politics. The Jeffersonian rhetoric attacking aristocracy and asserting equality took on a new meaning. Hamilton's supporters were aghast at these developments and called for order in society as well as the economy.

The French Revolution thus accelerated the development of the first American two-party system. But this nascent party system was unlike other party systems in U.S. history. Partisans on both sides decried the idea of party politics. Parties were evil because men devoted to them put the interests of their party above the larger interest of the public good. Jefferson wrote that if the only way he could go to heaven was by supporting a party, he would rather not go. Washington and Hamilton were equally adamant in their denunciation of party. If these men acquiesced in the development of parties it was only because they thought that their opponents were out to destroy the republic. Jefferson and Madison really believed that Hamilton intended to create an aristocracy and advocate a policy that was in the interest of stockjobbers and moneyed men at the expense of everyone else. Hamilton and his followers were equally convinced that Jefferson and Madison were pursuing a path of wide-eyed democracy opening the floodgates to the masses. The end result would be mobocracy, anarchy, and the destruction of the republic.

More than an antiparty ideology separated the first party system from later party development. The American Revolution may have meant the end of a world of deference and paternalism, but that change did not occur overnight. Nor was the direction of future change obvious to those who lived through this upheaval. The Constitution was written to stem the tide of democracy and to ensure that the right people would lead the republic. During the 1790s the debate between Jefferson and Hamilton was initially as much about which aristocrats would rule—landed gentry or a moneyed aristocracy—as it was over policy. On the local scene, however, politics operated on a personal level. The key to local power was to develop an "interest," a series of personal, social, and economic connections that bound together a leader and his followers. An interest in the 1790s and early 1800s was not simply a matter of political patronage, which became the hallmark of later American politics. Jobs and money were not exchanged for votes. Instead, there was supposed to be an ongoing relationship between a member of the local social elite and his "friends"—those beneath him, those on his level, and those above him—that lead to support in an election. An individual did not put himself up for office. His friends organized a nominating committee that, speaking for the community in a public meeting, selected the individual as the candidate. In the ideal world, which was seldom met in full, a candidate did not "run" for election; instead, he "stood" for office. The friends would canvass their own interests, write in the newspapers, station themselves at the polls, and even hand out printed ballots to voters. Candidates, of course, sometimes practiced electioneering, claiming that they did so to counter the efforts of opponents. Within this world, we should not assume that an "interest" was a matter of coercion. A well-developed interest could bring surprising majorities that no amount of compulsion could have created. The founder of Cooperstown, New York, William Cooper, sold most settlers their land on generous terms and controlled local business, but was on such cordial terms with his neighbors that in congressional elections he garnered 97 percent in 1796 and 95 percent in 1798 of the vote in his home township.[15]

Compounding the difficulty in understanding the first party system was the role of honor. For leaders, honor was essential. But like local politics, this honor was extremely personal. Honor meant having integrity, self-possession, and bravery. Each of these terms was ambiguous in the volatile politics of the early republic. Integrity meant you were a man of your word. Yet alliances could change as each individual politician struggled to understand the new political world that surrounded him and sought the best avenue to maintain his reputation. George Washington was like a rock, with his integrity unassailable. James Madison seemed to do a complete about-face from the 1780s, when he was a strong nationalist, to the 1790s when he became an ardent supporter of states' rights. Aaron Burr appeared to pursue whatever policy would advance his career. Yet each man would claim to have integrity. Self-possession was one of the distinguishing characteristics of being a gentleman in an increasingly democratic world. Again, Washington was the ultimate example of a man self-possessed, appearing unflappable, dignified, and awe-inspiring. William Cooper, who worked his way from being a wheelwright to affluent land speculator and businessman on the frontier, never quite had enough self-possession. He may have appeared the gentleman to his farmer neighbors in Cooperstown, but his willingness to wrestle in the street and mix with the common man, his poor spelling and lack of classical education, meant that he never quite measured up as a true gentleman in the eyes of the great families of New York. Bravery was very personal. It transcended bravery on the battlefield, and included a need to defend one's honor following an elaborate code. If another gentleman traduced your integrity this ritual could lead to a duel. If a person beneath your status questioned your word you could beat the individual with a cane—if he let you. In either case you had to demonstrate your personal honor through an act of bravery. The politician's reputation as a gentleman was crucial to maintaining his "interest."

The personal nature of politics and the role of honor meant that each state was a conglomeration of shifting interests, usually centered around an individual, group of individuals, or families, that defies easy categorization into one political party or another. Ideology was not entirely absent, and almost all candidates used some version of republican rhetoric claiming to safeguard the public good. It took the outside stimulus of the French Revolution to strengthen the connection between ideology, national politics, and the local scene.

Popular enthusiasm for the French Revolution appeared throughout the country. Americans celebrated French military victories with public festivities marked with parades and songs. The people of Boston paraded through the streets displaying a roasted ox on January 24, 1793, to commemorate the French victory at Valmy, where revolutionary armies turned back a combined Austrian and German force. Draping the ox were French and American flags, tricolor ribbons, and a sign proclaiming "PEACE OFFERING TO LIBERTY AND EQUALITY." The procession attracted a huge crowd eager to demonstrate their support for the French, and to partake in the ox, bread, and punch that would be distributed during the ceremony. The procession marched passed the French Consul's residence, the remnant of the old liberty tree from the 1760s and 1770s, and Oliver's Dock, sight of an anti–Stamp Act riot in 1765, rechristening the location "Liberty Square." At the State House butchers distributed the food while a band played the "Ça Ira," a French revolutionary tune. The festivities ended at Faneuil Hall, where officials drank toasts to the American and French revolutions, and "the fraternity of Freemen."[16] As can be seen in the Boston example, Americans adopted many of the emblems of the French Revolution. Some taverns even displayed little models of the guillotine to demonstrate support for the French cause. The Phrygian, or liberty, cap also became an important insignia of this revolutionary spirit. In June 1793 in New York City, "*friends* to *Liberty, Equality,* and the *Rights* of *Man*" placed a liberty cap "in defiance of all despotic tyrants" in the Tontine Coffee House. One newspaper described it as "a beautiful crimson adorned with a white tassel, and supported by a staff."[17] The liberty pole had been taken up by the French and was revived by Americans in a show of republican solidarity. After the January celebration in Boston a waterfront crowd placed the horns from the barbecued ox on a liberty pole they erected in Liberty Square.

Not all Americans shared in this enthusiasm. Within a few months of the January celebration, another Boston crowd organized by the friends of order gathered at Liberty Square and took down the liberty pole. They then interred the pole, and the horns of the ox that had been affixed to the pole, as an expression of their grief over the execution of Louis XVI. On June 11, 1793, apprentice Alexander Anderson in New York reported that "last night there was an affray at the Tontine Coffee-House between Whig and Tory, or to modernize it, Aristocrat and Democrat" over the liberty cap.[18] The friends of order also were outraged that anyone would celebrate an instrument of violence and destruction like the guillotine. For the time being, however, they avoided direct confrontations with the Francophile republicans in public, and usually limited themselves to comments decrying

FIGURE 5–1   Raising the Liberty Pole This nineteenth-century roman-
ticized depiction of a liberty pole by F. A. Chapman ignores how controversial these symbols of resistance were in 1776, and again in the 1790s
when Jeffersonian Republicans used the poles to signify their support
for the French Revolution and opposition to the Hamiltonian Program. For
their part, Federalists in the 1790s labeled liberty poles "sedition poles."

the radical bent of the French Revolution, while they commemorated
holidays closer to their interests, such as Washington's birthday.

Into this maelstrom entered Citizen Edmond Genêt. Sent to the
United States in early 1793 by the revolutionary government of France,
Genêt sought to build on the French alliance of 1778. He did not neces-
sarily want to bring the United States directly into the war with Great
Britain. Instead, he hoped to use the United States as a base to recruit
privateers and launch expeditions against British Canada and Spanish
North American colonies. Genêt arrived in Charleston, South Carolina, on
April 9, 1793, and was greeted by an immense public celebration. He then

continued overland to Philadelphia, with jubilant and supportive crowds in every village and town on the way. By the time he reached Philadelphia the city was abuzz with excitement. After having deposited Genêt in Charleston, the French frigate *L'Embuscade* had sailed for Philadelphia, arriving before the French ambassador. With banners flying from each masthead, the French warship proclaimed its support for liberty by declaring "Enemies of equality, reform or tremble!" "Freemen, behold we are your friends and brothers!" and "We are armed for the defense of the rights of man!"[19] French sailors streamed into the waterfront grog shops, telling all who would listen about the glorious fight for liberty and the money that could be won from rich British prizes. Despite popular support for the French, by the time Genêt arrived in Philadelphia in May, Washington had issued a proclamation on April 23 asserting American neutrality. This document, written by Edmund Randolph, and supported by both Jefferson and Hamilton, made it clear the United States would not honor its 1778 treaty with France and would pursue "a conduct friendly and impartial toward the belligerent Powers."[20] The administration advised all Americans to avoid any acts that might be seen as helping one side or the other and stated clearly that anyone who committed such an act would not be protected by the U.S. government.

Genêt, buoyed by his popularity and all of the festivities in his honor, had a hard time believing Washington would ignore public opinion. In Charleston he had already issued letters of marque to four ships and began recruiting men for his larger projects. Genêt continued to press his case, proclaiming that France had opened its ports to American trade and that the Treaty of 1778 allowed him to recruit men and arm privateers. The crisis came to a head in the summer of 1793 when Genêt issued papers for a privateer called *Le Petit Democrat*. Throughout June and July there were a series of meetings between Secretary of State Jefferson and Ambassador Genêt at which Jefferson tried to persuade Genêt to stop his military activities. Genêt ignored Jefferson's entreaties, threatened to appeal to the people as an authority above the president, and ordered *Le Petit Democrat* to sea. This action sealed his fate and in August the Washington administration demanded Genêt be recalled. (Genêt, however, did not leave the United States. A change in French politics would have meant the guillotine for Genêt had he returned. He married the daughter of New York's George Clinton and lived to a ripe old age as a gentlemen farmer in the United States).

Jefferson may have preferred a policy more partial to France, but he recognized the political reality that whatever the hoopla that accompanied Genêt, most Americans were content to not get directly involved with the war. In the aftermath of the Genêt controversy he asked Madison, who had written several essays against neutrality, to back off. Jefferson also determined to step down from his position in government. He hoped that retirement to Monticello would allow him to get his personal affairs in order. It would also place him in a better position as an outsider to the administration in the 1796 presidential election. Government came to a halt in the fall of 1793 as yellow fever devastated Philadelphia and in December Jefferson resigned as secretary of state.

Although the United States articulated a policy of neutrality supported by the entire cabinet, the Genêt imbroglio and the radicalization of the French Revolution intensified political divisions. During the height of the pro-French excitement of the spring of 1793 a new form of associational activity appeared—the Democratic–Republican Societies modeled after the Jacobin clubs of the French Revolution. Ostensibly a forum for political debate, these organizations quickly became pro-French and pro-Jeffersonian cells of local partisan activity. Philadelphians had one society in place by May. As the members of the society explained a year later, they were determined to "preserve and disseminate their principles, undaunted by the frowns of power, uncontaminated by the luxury of aristocracy, until the Rights of Man shall become the supreme law of every land." Their vision was almost messianic as they foresaw the day when "their separate fraternities" would be "absorbed in one great democratic society comprehending the human race."[21] By the end of 1794 there were about fifty-five of these Democratic–Republican clubs. Membership included merchants, lawyers, and artisans. Meetings were often at night to allow working men to attend. Debate came to mean a careful examination of government policies and assertions of support for the French. These societies represented an important step away from the personal politics of the elite by delving into electoral politics and helping to bring discussion of national issues to the local level.

Democratic–Republican clubs also became important in the frontier uprising known as the Whiskey Rebellion. Hamilton's excise on spiritous liquor was never popular on the frontier. Many farmers living on the far side of the Appalachians distilled alcohol for their own consumption and as a means to change bulky grains—corn and wheat—to whiskey that could be transported across mountains more economically. Opposition to the tax made the excise law a dead letter in the backcountry of South Carolina, North Carolina, Kentucky, and Virginia. Perhaps the most concerted resistance took place in western Pennsylvania. In 1791 and 1792 settlers around Pittsburgh held public meetings decrying the excise and connecting it to Hamilton's larger fiscal program. The 1791 meeting passed resolutions

FIGURE 5–2 The Whiskey Rebellion In opposition to an excise tax on liquor, western Pennsylvanians held massive demonstrations and tarred and feathered several government officers in 1794.

attacking the "exorbitant salaries of officers" in the federal government and against the funding and assumption scheme they were now being asked to pay for. The 1792 meeting agreed: The law was "unjust in itself, and oppressive upon the poor" because the average person paid proportionally more than a wealthy person.[22]

Frontiersmen, many of whom were Revolutionary War veterans, viewed the excise as similar to the British imperial taxes of the 1760s and 1770s—exactions placed on them by a distant government controlled by men who were not protecting the interest of the common man. Resistance therefore went beyond public meetings, petitions, and even the formation of committees of correspondence. Efforts to enforce the excise were met with mob action. Crowds tarred and feathered several would-be excise collectors. On at least one occasion the men donned women's dress, an action that harked back to European practices of disguise to hide the identity of the mob and to enhance the humiliation of the victim. "Tom the Tinker"—a mythical name for the leader of the anti-excise movement—led his followers in threatening distillers who were willing to comply with the law. When the threats did not work, "Tom" and his men destroyed the offending stills and pulled down barns of those who paid the tax. "Whiskey Boys" also raised liberty poles, reflecting the influence of both the American and French Revolutions, as a symbol of the popular resistance to tyranny.[23] Within this context, opponents of government policies formed Democratic–Republican Societies in Washington County and Mingo Creek in early 1794. Although there is no evidence of direct involvement in antigovernment activities, the societies' rhetoric contributed to the intensifying controversy that reached a crisis in mid July 1794. Mingo Creek settlers became incensed when John Neville, who had been appointed Supervisor of Collection, issued writs to western Pennsylvanians for noncompliance with the excise that ordered excise violators to appear in court in far-off Philadelphia. Gun battles between Mingo Creek rebels and government officials broke out at Neville's house on July 16 and 17, leaving three Whiskey Boys dead and several wounded. On July 23, opponents of the excise held a large public meeting outside of Pittsburgh and threatened to march on the town. They also seized some U.S. mail.

From the point of view of Hamilton and Washington, things had gotten out of hand. Attacks on government officials, massive resistance to federal law, robbing the mail, and threatened military action against a town all suggested that rebellion might lead to anarchy. The federal government needed to demonstrate that it could suppress this challenge to its authority. In August, Washington therefore called up over 12,000 militia and, donning a uniform himself, led these troops on their way to western Pennsylvania. Before the army reached its objective that autumn, the rebellion fell apart and Washington allowed General Henry Lee to take command of the expedition. Once in western Pennsylvania the army arrested 150 "rebels." Twenty of these men were tried in federal court. Only two were found guilty and they were pardoned by Washington. Not only had the majesty of the law been upheld, but Washington also seized the opportunity to denounce "self-created societies" like the Democratic–Republican clubs, which had been so effective in organizing opposition to his administration. For Washington the idea that "self-created bodies" would form themselves into "*permanent censors*" and "under the shade of night" question the policies of the government was "absurd," "arrogant" and "pernicious to the peace of society."[24]

The Problem with Commerce

Against this backdrop of political developments there emerged a dynamic economy in the late 1780s and early 1790s that is difficult to quantify. One measure of this energy can be seen in the various processions celebrating the ratifying of the Constitution. In several port cities the new form of government seemed to promise an unending prosperity. Artisans marching in these parades demonstrated their optimism with exhibitions of their trades and banners wedding commerce and work. In the New York parade the ship-joiners marched under a banner that trumpeted both the federal state and the mock ship *Hamilton,* which they had a hand in building, that was the centerpiece of the procession. They proudly proclaimed "This federal ship [the Constitution and the *Hamilton*] will our commerce revive." Artisans from other trades less directly connected to shipping expressed the same sentiments. The butchers' flag proclaimed: "Skin me well, dress me neat, And send me aboard the federal fleet." The cartmen's banner declared that "the federal ship of fame" would find employment for all trades and that the cartmen, with more business, would "have their share of joy." Even the pewterers saw a silver lining in the new Constitution. Their standard announced:

The Federal Plan Most Solid & Secure

Americans Their Freedom will Endure

All Arts Shall Flourish in Columbia's Land

And All her Sons Join as One Social Band.[25]

FIGURE 5–3   The Pewterers Banner Reflecting the optimism that many master craftsmen had for the strengthened federal government under the Constitution, New York pewterers marched under this banner in July 1788 in a parade celebrating ratification.

Another measure of this optimism was the effort of entrepreneurs to find new ways of making money. William Cooper managed to gain control of tens of thousands of acres around Lake Otsego in upstate New York in 1786. He rapidly sold much of this property to New England farmers pouring into the state eager to occupy the land once held by the Iroquois. By offering generous terms, often issuing a mortgage without a down payment, Cooper attracted hundreds of settlers, earning a national reputation for himself as a champion land promoter. Cooper's ambitions went beyond land speculation. In 1789 and 1790 he developed a plan that, had it been successful, could have transformed the world economy. Northern New York had an excess of trees, especially maple trees. Eager for a quick profit, Cooper decided to tap this natural resource and produce enough maple sugar to replace the sugar cane of the West Indies. This may seem like a hare-brained idea, but it captured the imagination of many Americans. Two of Philadelphia's leading citizens, Benjamin Rush and Tench Coxe, wrote pamphlets and newspaper articles in support of the plan, extolling the virtues of maple sugar. Thomas Jefferson and George Washington were both interested in the project and planted maple trees on their Virginia plantations. Cooper gave a lecture on maple sugar in 1791 before the New York Society for the Promotion of Agriculture, Arts, and Manufactures. Word of the potential of this enterprise even reached Europe. Not only would maple sugar make settlement on the frontier profitable, but it would have liberated the American economy from its connection with the West Indies, and possibly led to the end of slavery. Despite the hoopla, the final product did not meet expectations. The weather did not cooperate, and only a fifth of the projected sugar went to market. By the time it could be brought overland to the Hudson River and then shipped to Philadelphia, much of the sugar was ruined. After two years of experimentation, maple sugar as a marketable product came to naught. But the dream and enthusiasm it inspired suggest the kind of entrepreneurial energy that swirled through the United States in the early 1790s.

William Duer generated a different kind of economic excitement in the spring of 1792 by speculating in the stock of the BUS. Duer was a prominent businessmen in New York, who previously worked for Hamilton in the Treasury Department. In 1790 and 1791 Duer had his hand in several projects, including a Pennsylvania canal company, a Boston bridge company, and new banks in Providence, Boston, New Hampshire, Albany, and New York. He also became governor of Hamilton's pet project, the Society for Establishing Useful Manufactures (SEUM). He had invested in United States securities before full funding and state notes before assumption. The consummate insider, he was also a great salesman. Convinced that the

BUS stock was about to skyrocket, he leveraged himself to the maximum, borrowing money from rich and poor alike at high interest rates. He managed to get Walter Livingston to advance him $800,000 and William G. Smith loaned him $100,000. He applied $10,000 from the SEUM to his speculations and borrowed another $50,000 from that institution. Strapped for money, Duer's agents obtained small loans from "shopkeepers, widows, orphans, butchers, cartmen, Gardners, market women, & even the noted Bawd Mrs. McCarty."[26] His optimism became infectious and he sucked hundreds into his scheme. Duer engaged in exactly the type of moneyed manipulation that Jefferson and Madison feared—an effort to create paper wealth without any real backing. It was at the height of this speculative frenzy in early March 1792 that Philip Freneau began his sustained attacks on Hamilton. When the BUS stock price showed a little weakness, and when the federal government sued Duer for $250,000 in unsettled accounts from when he worked at the Treasury Department, Duer's financial scheme began to unravel. Duer stopped payment on all of his obligations on March 9. Two weeks later he was in debtor's jail. Panic seized New York City and all the financial markets contracted. People were so angry that a crowd of 300 to 500 gathered outside the jail on April 18, 1792, pelted stones at the building, and shouted "*We will have Mr. Duer, he has gotten our money.*"[27]

While Cooper and Duer pursued ephemeral dreams of wealth, Samuel Slater and Eli Whitney put their energies to more pragmatic purposes— machinery. These efforts, however, also represent the sense of expectation and opportunity that marked the earliest years of the American republic. Born in England in 1768, Slater served an apprenticeship in a textile factory where he learned to construct machinery and to manage production. As he neared the end of his apprenticeship in 1789, Slater decided to seek his fortune in the United States. To leave Great Britain, Slater disguised himself as an agricultural worker because there were laws against the immigration of individuals who understood industrial technology. Once in the United States, Slater met Moses Brown, a merchant from Rhode Island who was attempting to start his own textile mill. Slater took over the management of these efforts and then, in partnership with Brown and William Almy, he built a new textile factory in Pawtucket, Rhode Island, in 1793. Organizing labor around families, employing parents and children, Slater developed a formula for successful factory operation that gradually spread through much of rural New England. Hamilton's SEUM may have failed, in part because of the financial manipulations of Duer and in part because of the lack of technical know-how, but at the same time the American industrial revolution began modestly with Samuel Slater.

Eli Whitney was born in Massachusetts and set out for Georgia as a tutor in 1792. Before he took over his duties as a teacher he visited with Catherine Greene, widow of Revolutionary War hero, Nathanael Greene. Over the course of the winter of 1792–93 Whitney worked on creating a machine that would separate the sticky seeds from the cotton lint in green-seed, short-staple cotton. By April he had built a working model of the cotton gin that could perform the labor of fifty men. Supported by Phineas Miller, Catherine Greene's plantation manager, Whitney headed back north to register a patent for his invention. Although he obtained a patent in 1794, the machine was easily copied. Whitney and Miller did not reap the great rewards they had anticipated from their efforts. But the cotton gin in its many variations allowed the spread of the growth of cotton production over the next several decades.

The economic energy of the late eighteenth century went beyond individuals and also included the development of two key and interrelated institutions—the corporation and the bank. Both had been around the Anglo-American world for centuries. Americans released from the inhibitions of the British Empire could now experiment with these institutions on their own. Previously, the corporation had been a special grant of privilege by the government to a group of individuals who would pool their resources to pursue some end for the public good. In the colonial period Parliament, local assemblies, and governors had parceled these grants out carefully to establish colonies, city governments, colleges, and other quasi-official bodies. During the 1780s and 1790s, aggressive entrepreneurs sought charters of incorporation with state governments for a variety of projects such as building roads and bridges and Hamilton's SEUM. In each instance the would-be incorporators had to present their charter to the state legislature, make a case for how the particular activity would benefit the public, and have the legislature vote yea or nay on the charter. By 1800, over 300 such charters had been granted for a host of enterprises. One area of active incorporation was the bank. Colonial Americans knew about banks in England and used land banks to lend farmers money and create a paper currency. But the first real American bank that sold stock and had deposits was the Bank of North America. This was followed in 1784 by the Bank of New York and the Massachusetts Bank. The new federal government chartered the BUS in 1791. Several states chartered banks during the 1790s, and by 1800 there were a total of twenty-nine banks in the United States.[28] These banks became incredible instruments of capitalism. Ordinarily, their capitalization was spelled out in the charter. But because they did not have to have gold and silver deposits equal to the notes they issued, they could in essence create their own money to be loaned out and invested. The full impact of the innovative nature of the American corporation and bank would not be felt until the early nineteenth century, but during the 1790s, Americans were well on their way to using these institutions to expand and drive their economy.

Entrepreneurs seeking new ways to make fortunes and the development of new institutions for capital concentration were important to American economic growth. But the most immediate spur to the U.S. economy was growth in international commerce. The wars in Europe generated an American economic boom in the 1790s and early 1800s. Trade had, by hook and sometimes by crook, begun to expand before 1793. Americans found new markets, while also relying on older trading patterns. The most ambitious merchants reached across the globe. In 1784 the *Empress of China* sailed from New York to begin direct U.S. trade to the Far East. The voyage netted a 30 percent profit. Vessels from Boston and Salem soon followed. To gain the goods necessary for this trade, these ships obtained furs and seal skins in the Pacific, including the northwest coast of North America. Other American merchants stretched the boundaries of law, trading with the British and Spanish in the West Indies regardless of regulations. Local officials, often needing American produce and a market for their own goods, either looked the other way or simply ordered a temporary suspension of rules. Although the French did not generate a significant trade with the United States, some exchange of goods continued in this period, and thanks to the commercial treaties with the Netherlands, Sweden, and Prussia, new markets opened in Europe as well. Even without a commercial treaty, the British remained the biggest trade partner of the United States.

The Franco-British war that began in 1793 dramatically altered the situation, settling the old problem of the balance of trade while making new difficulties. With the outbreak of the war, American merchants had an unprecedented opportunity; the United States could become the greatest neutral carrier in the world. In 1790 the United States exported about $20 million worth of goods. That level of exports increased slightly over the next couple of years and then took off after 1792, reaching over $70 million by 1800. Much of this export was agricultural produce, especially wheat. This commerce, in turn, increased the value of farmland and helped to push more settlers to frontier settlements like Cooperstown in New York, and eventually encouraged settlement of the Ohio River Valley further west. Ports such as New York, Philadelphia, and Baltimore hummed with activity, with soaring populations, new construction, and an expansion of production by artisans like those who had marched in the Constitutional processions of 1788. Americans also entered the reexport trade by shipping goods from the West Indies to the United States, and then reshipping the goods to France and Great Britain. This trade hardly existed in

1790, but reached almost $50 million by 1800. American vessels gained a bigger share of international trade. In 1790 less than 60 percent of the ships entering American ports from overseas belonged to the United States. By 1797, the total tonnage had almost doubled and American vessels carried over 90 percent of the foreign trade.[29]

Maintaining this success was not easy. For most of the next twenty years American diplomacy veered first one way, then another, in an effort to keep this economic miracle afloat. The controversy surrounding the mission of Citizen Genêt was only the first episode in this complex diplomatic saga. The British presented the United States with a second crisis in 1794 by asserting the Rule of 1756, which stated that all trade denied to a country in peacetime should also be denied to the country in wartime. In other words, a mercantilist power like France that kept its colonies closed before a war could not open those colonies during war simply to allow a neutral country to carry on its trade. The British pounced on American shipping early in 1794, seizing over 250 ships in the West Indies because they were trading with the French. Most Americans believed war was imminent and Congress passed an embargo shutting down all trade. Just as the United States braced itself for a war with the British, news arrived in April indicating a moderation in the British position; they promised that they would capture only vessels that carried war contraband. This shift in the British position opened a window of diplomatic opportunity. The embargo ended after two months and Washington sent Chief Justice John Jay to Great Britain to negotiate.

Jay confronted a difficult situation in Great Britain when he arrived on June 8, 1794. The British had little reason to take the Americans seriously; they had no respect for the American military and could continue to seize American shipping at will. Without many bargaining chips, Jay wrangled few concessions from the British, but managed to piece together a treaty by November 19, 1794, that would at least avoid war. The most important provision allowed for "a reciprocal and entirely perfect Liberty of Navigation and Commerce" between Great Britain and the United States whereby each country gave most favored nation trading status to the other.[30] Although, like the treaties with other nations, this agreement ignored the model treaty of 1776, it established direct commercial relations. However, although the British opened their European ports to the Americans and even permitted trade with India, they insisted on limiting the size of U.S. vessels sailing to the West Indies colonies to under 70 tons. The treaty left several other issues—compensation for illegally seized American shipping, prewar debts owed the British, and some boundary issues—to future commissions. Jay did manage to convince the British to abandon all forts on American territory and thereby withdraw crucial support for Indians hostile to the United States.

Jay's Treaty was controversial in the United States. On seeing the final accord in January 1795, Washington decided to keep its details secret until the Senate convened in June. In turn, the Senate discussed the treaty behind closed doors, deleted the article that limited trade with the West Indies, and ratified the rest of the agreement by a twenty to ten margin. Once news of the treaty became public in early July, there was a popular outcry. From the Jeffersonian point of view, Jay had abdicated American sovereignty with a commercial treaty that prevented the government from ever compelling the British to concede the outstanding issues of neutral rights and free trade in the West Indies. To compound matters, the whole affair had been done in secret and demonstrated how, in Madison's words, "a British party, systematically aiming at an exclusive connection with the British Governt." could sacrifice "the dearest interests of our Commerce as the most sacred dictates of national honor."[31] Demonstrations broke out up and down the Atlantic seaboard with crowds burning effigies of Jay and his treaty. When Hamilton attempted to address one outdoor meeting in New York City, the crowd shouted him down and even pelted a few stones at him. Taken aback by the uproar, Washington hesitated for two months before signing the treaty and then confronted a heated debate in the House of Representatives over funding the measure.

Within a year, however, the treaty proved a success on several fronts. Trade grew at a heady pace as Great Britain remained America's major commercial partner. Ships still sailed to the Carribean as governors desperate for American goods set aside restrictions. Even the carrying trade continued to thrive. The British abandoned their posts and their Native American allies, helping to set the stage for the Treaty of Greenville and the opening of half of Ohio to American settlers. Concerned that the British and the Americans might join forces, the Spanish signed the Treaty of San Lorenzo (also known as Pinckney's Treaty) on October 27, 1795, allowing Americans to navigate the Mississippi River to its mouth and permitting the United States to ship goods through New Orleans without paying duties. Spain also recognized neutral rights and set the boundary of Florida at the 31st parallel, leaving the southwest Indians without the support the Spanish had previously provided.

Whatever positive good the Jay Treaty may have brought the United States diplomatically and economically, it marked a watershed in the development of party politics. The division between Hamilton, supported by the "friends of government," and Jefferson, supported by the "friends of the people," that had emerged in the debate over the fiscal program, intensified with the radicalization of the French Revolution and hardened with the Jay Treaty. The Federalists (as Hamilton's supporters came to be known) feared disorder and anarchy from self-created democratic societies. The Republicans feared self-created, stockjobbing aristocrats. In 1796 both sides geared up for the first contested presidential election in the United States. All the retiring Washington could do was to issue a final farewell, oddly authored in part by Madison and Hamilton, in which he warned "against the baneful effects of the spirit of party" and urged Americans to avoid "passionate attachments" to foreign powers.[32]

Endnotes

1. Quoted in Joseph P. Ellis, *Founding Brothers: The Revolutionary Generation* (New York: Random House, 2000), 168.
2. "Of Paper Money of America," ca. 1780, Leonard W. Labaree, et al., eds., *The Papers of Benjamin Franklin,* 1– vols. (New Haven: Yale University Press, 1959–), 34: 231–32.
3. The best account of the debt remains E. James Ferguson, *The Power of the Purse: A History of American Public Finance, 1776–1790* (Chapel Hill: University of North Carolina Press, 1961), 329–35.
4. Henry Cabot Lodge, ed., *The Works of Alexander Hamilton,* 12 vols. (New York: G. P. Putnam's Sons, 1904), 4: 135.
5. Quoted in Drew R. McCoy, *The Elusive Republic: Political Economy in Jeffersonian America* (Chapel Hill: University of North Carolina Press, 1980), 156–57.
6. Merrill D. Peterson, ed., *The Portable Thomas Jefferson* (New York: Viking, 1975), 217.
7. Quoted in McCoy, *The Elusive Republic,* 140–41.
8. Quoted in Stanley Elkins and Eric McKitrick, *The Age of Federalism* (New York: Oxford University Press, 1993), 143–44.
9. Thomas Jefferson to Albert Gallatin, Oct. 11, 1809, Thomas Jefferson Papers Series 1, General Correspondence,1651–1827, Digital Archives, Library of Congress, Image 304.
10. Jefferson's Opinion on the Constitutionality of a National Bank, 1791, The Avalon Project at Yale Law School, www.yale.edu/lawweb/avalon/amerdoc/bank-tj.htm.
11. Lodge, ed., *The Works of Alexander Hamilton,* 3: 447–48.
12. Peterson, *The Portable Thomas Jefferson,* 384, 217.
13. Quoted in Elkins and McKitrick, *The Age of Federalism,* 276–79.
14. Quoted in Elkins and McKitrick, *The Age of Federalism,* 283.
15. Alan Taylor, *William Cooper's Town: Power and Persuasion on the Frontier of the Early American Republic* (New York: Alfred A. Knopf, 1995), 253, 255.
16. Quoted in Simon P. Newman, *Parades and the Politics of the Street: Festive Culture in the Early American Republic* (Philadelphia: University of Pennsylvania Press, 1997), 122–24.
17. *New York Journal,* June 15, 1793.
18. Alexander Anderson, "Diarium," June 1, 1793, microfilm, Columbia University, New York City. Original is in the Rare Book and Manuscript Library, Columbia University, New York City.
19. (Philadelphia) *General Advertiser,* May 17, 18, 1793.
20. The Proclamation of Neutrality 1793, The Avalon Project at Yale Law School, www.yale.edu/lawweb/avalon/neutra93.htm.

21. Quoted in Eugene Perry Link, *The Democratic-Republican Societies, 1790–1800* (New York: Columbia University Press, 1942), 109.

22. Quoted in Thomas P. Slaughter, *The Whiskey Rebellion: Frontier Epilogue to the American Revolution* (New York: Oxford University Press, 1986), 112, 116.

23. For "Tom the Tinkerer" see Slaughter, *The Whiskey Rebellion,* 184–85.

24. Quoted in James Thomas Flexner, *George Washington: Anguish and Farewell (1793–1799)* (Boston: Little, Brown and Company, 1969), 190.

25. (New York) *Independent Journal,* Aug. 2, 6, 1788.

26. Quoted in Robert F. Jones, *"The King of the Alley": William Duer, Politician, Entrepreneur, and Speculator, 1768–1799* (Philadelphia: American Philosophical Society, 1992), 176.

27. Quoted in Paul A. Gilje, *The Road to Mobocracy: Popular Disorder in New York City, 1764–1834* (Chapel Hill: University of North Carolina Press, 1987), 84.

28. Bray Hammond, *Banks and Politics in America: From the Revolution to the Civil War* (Princeton: Princeton University Press, 1957), 144–45.

29. Douglass C. North, *The Economic Growth of the United States, 1790–1860* (New York: Prentice-Hall, 1966), 17–58.

30. The Jay Treaty, Nov. 19, 1794, The Avalon Project at Yale Law School, www.yale.edu/lawweb/avalon/diplomacy/britian/jay.htm.

31. Robert A. Rutland, et al., eds., *The Papers of James Madison,* 17 vols. (Chicago and Charlottesville: University of Chicago and University Press of Virginia, 1962–1991), 16: 47. See also Lance Banning, *The Sacred Fire of Liberty: James Madison and the Founding of the Federal Republic* (Ithaca, N.Y.: Cornell University Press, 1995), 381.

32. Washington's Farewell Address, 1796, The Avalon Project at Yale Law School, www.yale.edu/lawweb/avalon/washing.htm.

CHAPTER 6

The Revolution of 1800

The Triumph of Federalism

John Adams won the election of 1796. In the volatile politics of the late 1790s the Federalists appeared, momentarily, to triumph. After the Jay Treaty the French began to capture American ships. Amid the clamor for war with the French, the passage of laws to suppress dissent, and the expansion of the army, the nation stood on the brink of a new order. Then, with the war crisis defused, the election of 1800 reversed everything. Americans experienced, as Thomas Jefferson explained in 1819, "as real a revolution in the principles of our government as that of 1776 was in its form." This revolution ultimately went beyond politics and marked the triumph of a new society of common men. Given the intensity of the emotions on both sides—federal troops intimidated opponents while at least one Republican governor was prepared to call out the militia to ensure that the voice of the people would be heard—Jefferson was amazed that this revolution was "not effected indeed by the sword, . . . but by the rational and peaceable instrument of reform, the suffrage of the people."[1]

Party politics remained rudimentary in the 1790s. Most men involved in government knew where they stood and where their opponents stood on the issues. Men caucused together, corresponded, read partisan newspapers, and might even join politically oriented organizations like the Democratic–Republican Societies. But there was no official national organization called the Federalist or Republican Party. Politicians often refused to even acknowledge they were up for an election. Throughout the fall of 1796 Jefferson stayed at Monticello pretending he was not running for president as James Madison, without directly informing his friend Jefferson, managed the campaign a few miles away on his plantation at Montpelier. John Adams was more honest, having written Abigail early in 1796 acknowledging that he was heir apparent to Washington. He, too, stayed at home through the summer and fall of 1796, quietly working his farm in Quincy, Massachusetts, eagerly watching the developments.

The campaign was nasty. Newspapers charged that Adams was a monocrat, a "champion of kings, ranks, and titles."[2] Federalist editors struck out as well, calling Jefferson a coward because he fled before British armies as governor in 1781. They labeled him a Jacobin and an atheist. Alexander Hamilton sought to manipulate the Federalists to exclude Adams and elect Thomas Pinckney in his place. In some states political leaders sought to sway the mass of voters with pamphlets, handbills, and newspaper articles. Pennsylvania Republicans distributed 30,000 hand-written ballots, although only 24,420 people voted. Personal loyalties and the weakness of the party structure created a patchwork quilt pattern of electoral votes. Only eight of sixteen states voted straight party tickets. Thirteen different men received votes. Some Virginian Republican electors so distrusted Aaron Burr that they cast one of their votes for Jefferson, and the other for Sam Adams. In South Carolina the electors voted for Jefferson, a Republican candidate, and favorite son Pinckney, a Federalist candidate. When all was said and done, Adams's strength in New England and the middle Atlantic states eked out a narrow victory: Adams had seventy-one electoral votes and Jefferson (each elector voted twice and the person with the second-highest votes became vice president) had sixty-eight electoral votes.

The result was not as bizarre as it may seem. We might assume that it is strange for men from different political parties to serve in the same administration, and the Twelfth Amendment in 1804 would change the system to make this less likely, but the Founders had not anticipated a two-party system and therefore planned for the two best men to fill the office of president and vice president. Arguably, Adams and Jefferson were the best men in terms of experience and ability and neither saw themselves as representing a party. Before the election was final, Jefferson had expressed the hope that in the event of a tie, the nod would go to Adams; as Jefferson put it, "He has always been my senior, from the commencement of my public life."[3] Adams even suggested to Jefferson that he might want to serve in the cabinet rather than wasting his time presiding over the Senate in an office that Adams knew was nearly invisible and unimportant. Jefferson declined. A long-standing friendship, strained but not broken by the events of the Washington administration, also held out the possibility of a fruitful collaboration. Adams and Jefferson, however, did not work together in the waning years of the eighteenth century. Instead, events drove them apart. The pro-British policy articulated in the Jay Treaty brought on another diplomatic crisis—this time with the French—that prevented the two old friends from forming a political partnership.

The French were not happy about the Jay Treaty. It was one thing to not follow the letter of the alliance of 1778; it was another to pursue a policy that seemed to put the British above the French. A few French privateers began capturing American shipping in the West Indies in the spring of 1796. The French government provided some official support for these seizures with a decree on July 2, 1796. Soon there were French cruisers off the coast of the United States. Over the next two years the French captured more than 330 American merchant vessels, driving insurance rates from 6 percent to over 40 percent. These captures, and the insurance rates that came with them, threatened to destroy America's burgeoning overseas trade.

Adams confronted this diplomatic crisis when he became president in March 1797. He called a special session of Congress for May and condemned the French for their depredations and for dividing Americans. But he was not eager for war even though the French had not recognized the new American ambassador and had issued new orders on March 2, 1797, denying that free ships made free goods and threatening that any American taken aboard a British man-of-war would be treated as a pirate. At the special session Adams asked Congress to strengthen American defenses. As luck would have it, three superfrigates that had been commissioned in 1794 were just being completed. These vessels—the *Constellation,* the *United States,* and the *Constitution*—became the centerpieces of a revitalized navy. Adams also pursued diplomatic channels by sending a delegation—Charles Coatsworth Pinckney, John Marshall, and Elbridge Gerry—to France. When they arrived in October 1797 they found a new government in power under the Directory. After a brief meeting with French Foreign Minister Tallyrand, three French agents, referred to in official correspondence as "X, Y, and Z," approached the American delegation stating that before negotiations could proceed the United States had to pay a bribe of $250,000 to Tallyrand and loan $10 million to the French government. In addition, the French agents insisted that Adams repudiate his comment that the French had sought to alienate the American people from the U.S. government. The American diplomats refused to make these concessions, not only came through unofficial channels, but were also insulting and asked the diplomats to go beyond the authority and instructions. After several months of backdoor exchanges, Tallyrand ordered Marshall and Pinckney, both ardent Federalists, to leave France in April 1798. Gerry, who had Republican leanings, stayed in Europe. Tallyrand thought that he might be able to manipulate Gerry if he were on his own. Gerry merely hoped the French would have a change of heart.

News of the XYZ affair galvanized American public opinion. Diplomatic dispatches describing the state of negotiations arrived in the United States in early March 1798, but were kept secret by the executive department. Congress, reluctant to take any more measures against France, requested the dispatches on April 2. Once word of the insults and demands for a bribe became general knowledge, war fever swept through the nation. Reflecting the tenuous state of party politics, Republican opposition melted in Congress. The Federalist government pushed into action, buying more ships and converting them to military purposes. The Federalists also expanded the army, which had about 3,000 men, by 12,000, with a provisional force of 10,000 to be called in case of emergency. To pay for this military expansion Congress levied new taxes, including an assessment on every house in the country.

The Federalists did not stop with these preparations and seized the opportunity to pass the Alien and Sedition Acts. The three Alien Acts sounded imposing, but had only a limited impact. The Federalists believed that many of the thousands of immigrants who had come to the United States during the 1790s were tainted with republicanism and opposed their policies. At one point Federalist Harrison Grey Otis gave a speech in Congress in which he decried the "hordes of wild Irishmen" and "the turbulent and disorderly of all parts of the world" who had come to disturb American tranquility.[4] The Naturalization Act, passed June 18, extended the period an immigrant had to wait before he could become a citizen from five to fourteen years. Federalists hoped that the legislation would limit the impact of immigrant voting in upcoming elections. This ploy backfired because many immigrants applied for citizenship before the new regulations took effect. Congress passed the Alien Act on June 25, empowering the president to deport any foreigner he deemed a threat to the nation. Set to expire in two years, President Adams never used the law. The third of these measures, the Alien Enemies Act, Congress enacted on July 6, 1798. The law stated that citizens of a country at war with the United States could be "apprehended, restrained, secured and removed, as alien enemies." Because France and the United States never declared war officially, the law was not used at this time.[5]

If the Alien Acts were mostly bluster, the Sedition Act of July 14 was more serious. The act stipulated that "if any person shall write, print, utter, or publish . . . any false, scandalous and malicious writing or writings against the government of the United States . . . with intent to defame the said government," federal courts could prosecute the offender and he could be assessed up to two thousand dollars in fines and serve up to two years in prison. The law did not violate the First Amendment right of free speech as it was then understood because it did not invoke prior restraint. Following both English and American precedents, an individual could only be prosecuted after, and not before, he published the sedition. In addition, the law actually protected some rights because it allowed "the truth of the matter contained in the publication" to be used as a defense.[6] The Federalists, however, wielded the measure in an effort to stifle dissent. At least fourteen Republican editors spent time in jail because of convictions under the provisions of the Sedition Act. The Federalists turned to the law to prosecute Congressman Matthew Lyon from Vermont. Lyon was an immigrant who had come to North America as an indentured servant. He was also a former artisan and printer resented by the Federalists who saw Congress as the exclusive province of natural aristocrats like themselves. In early 1798 Lyon spit in the face of Congressmen Roger Griswold for insulting him. Griswold retaliated by attacking Lyon with a hickory cane on the floor of the House of Representatives, while Lyon tried to defend himself with fireplace tongs. The Federalists then attempted to censure

FIGURE 6–1 Griswold fighting Lyon in Congress, 1798 Federalists detested Matthew Lyon as an immigrant upstart Republican. When Lyon spit in Federalist Roger Griswold's face on the floor of House of Representatives, Griswold attacked Lyon with a hickory cane. Lyon defended himself with a nearby set of fireplace tongs.

Lyon, but failed to get the necessary two-thirds vote. The Sedition Act provided a new opportunity to put the upstart Lyon in his place. The Federalists charged Lyon with sedition because he had lambasted the president's efforts to prepare for war by associating it with "a continual grasp for power, in an unbounded thirst for ridiculous pomp, foolish adulation, or selfish avarice" in an essay he wrote for a Vermont newspaper. They also accused Lyon of slanderous speeches in which he quoted a Republican friend in Europe who thought that the president ought to be in a madhouse for telling Congress that the French "had turned pirates and plunderers." The court found Lyon guilty, fined him one thousand dollars, and sent him to jail for four months.[7]

Federalist repression did not stop with official channels. With a newfound popularity, Federalists sought to intimidate their opposition any way they could. William Duane, who edited the leading Republican newspaper, the Philadelphia *Aurora,* became a special target of Federalist wrath. Not only was he indicted for sedition, sued for libel by several Federalists, and forced into hiding for breaching legislative privilege, but he was also the victim of personal violence. Thirty soldiers barged into his office on May 15, 1799, dragged Duane into the street, and brutally beat him. Extralegal activity occurred elsewhere. During the summer of 1798 crowds of Federalists—a Republican journal identified the rowdies as "a number of *'unjudged would be soldiers'* "—paraded through the streets of New York singing "Hail Columbia" and other patriotic tunes. Often they would stop outside the house of Republican congressman Edward Livingston and regale him with a late-night serenade.[8] Throughout the United States, Republicans rallied to liberty poles, only to find them labeled as "sedition" poles and attacked by Federalists. On August 13, 1799, twenty-three men wearing black cockades—a Federalist symbol—rode on horseback into Mendham, New Jersey, chopped down a liberty pole, fired pistols into the air, and intimidated the local populace. Federalists also used strong-arm tactics during elections, threatening workers with loss of employment if they did not vote with them, handing out ballots at the polls, and otherwise coercing voters. During the summer of 1799 recruits to the newly expanded military swaggered through the streets of Baltimore, Philadelphia, and New York looking for Republicans to harass. In New York a group of navy petty officers, including the son of William Duer, formed an organization called the Knights of the Dagger. These men bumped into civilians in the street, hoping to start a row.[9]

All of this behavior may not have been really necessary—the war scare did bring the Federalists some genuine popularity. Probably for the only time in his long career of government service, John Adams could relish true public acclaim. He even at times donned a uniform and sword to greet well-wishers. When he headed for Quincy in July 1798 a huge crowd greeted him in New York "under the display of our flags, and the thunder of our cannons, amidst the glitter of our swords, a forest of bristling bayonets, and the shouts and acclamations of assembled thousands."[10] The president became the subject of a popular sailor song, "Adams and Liberty," which trumpeted his efforts to protect commerce by declaring "That ne'er shall the Sons of COLUMBIA be slaves, While the earth bears a plant or the sea roles its waves."[11] Even without intimidation the Federalists would have made electoral gains in 1798 and 1799. After the 1798 congressional election the Federalists held 64 of 106 seats in the House of Representatives and 19 of 32 seats in the Senate.

The Republicans, of course, did not surrender in the face of the Federalist onslaught. They practiced the popular politics that had worked so well before the war scare by erecting their liberty poles, wearing the tricolor cockade, and singing French Revolutionary songs. Often, they met the Federalists head-on in the street. Secretary of State Timothy Pickering and Attorney General Charles Lee, along with a group of city magistrates, broke up a pro-French Philadelphia crowd one night in early May 1798. After the celebration of John Adams's arrival in New York, his secretary Samuel Malcolm, Peter Jay (John Jay's son), and a few companions merrily cruised along the Battery singing Federalists tunes until they ran into a large group of Republican artisans and waterfront workers who objected to the young gentlemen's music. A scuffle broke out in which both Malcolm and Jay were injured. Similar street battles erupted over liberty/sedition poles or wherever Federalist and Republican crowds came face-to-face.

The Sedition Act also did not stifle the Republican press. If anything, it strengthened the resolve of the opposition newspapers. Before the Sedition Act there were about 50 Republican-leaning newspapers out of 185 across the country. Only ten of these were blatantly partisan like the Philadelphia *Aurora*. The rest of the papers supported the administration. Repression compelled many of the moderately Republican papers, which previously had attempted to present both sides of a debate, to take a more strident tone. It also led to the creation of over forty more Republican papers. Editors now posed as defenders of sacred liberties. Charles Holt, a Connecticut editor prosecuted under the Sedition Act, warned that the sedition law contravened "one of the most essential articles in the code of freedom, and as clearly defined as any other clause in the bill of rights, namely, *liberty of speech, printing and writing.*"[12] Throughout 1798 and 1799 Republican editors relentlessly assailed Federalist policies and Federalist high-handed practices. The atrocious antics of soldiers and sailors in the cities and their efforts at political intimidation became, through the lens of Republican criticism, examples of the evils of standing armies.

Opposition to government taxation led to open rebellion. Many German Americans in rural eastern Pennsylvania believed that the new tax on property, which depended on the number of windows and size of a house, was unfair because it did not affect wealthy land speculators as much as middling farmers. When tax collectors in the summer and fall of 1798 attempted to measure houses and count windows in the disaffected region, they were greeted with buckets of boiling water and were driven off. The federal government could not tolerate this type of resistance and arrested twenty-three men. On March 12, 1799, John Fries led a rescue of these prisoners from jail in Bethlehem, Pennsylvania. President Adams ordered the military into the region, capturing Fries and about sixty others. Fries was tried for treason, convicted, and sentenced to death. Fortunately for Fries, Adams ignored the more ardent Federalists and later pardoned him.

Republicans also raised serious constitutional issues in the Virginia and Kentucky Resolutions, asserting states' rights over federal authority. Thomas Jefferson anonymously authored the Kentucky Resolutions passed on November 16, 1798. The document began with the assertion that "the several States composing the United States of America, are not united on the principle of unlimited submission to their General Government." Seizing on the Tenth Amendment that "the powers not delegated to the United States by the Constitution . . . are reserved to the States repectively, or to the people," Jefferson argued that each state had "the residuary mass of right to their own self-government." He held that the federal government should not be "the exclusive or final judge of the extent of the powers delegated to itself." Instead, "*each party has an equal right to judge for itself*" the limits of federal authority. Based on these assumptions, Jefferson declared that the Alien and Sedition Acts were "altogether void, and of no force."[13] Madison authored the Virginia Resolutions of December 24, 1798, and was more moderate in tone. He asserted Virginia's continued commitment to the Constitution, but protested that the alien and sedition laws were a violation of that Constitution. Jefferson and Madison hoped that other states would follow their lead. But the implications of the resolutions were so outrageous and threatening to the republic that no other states adopted them. Here was the vice president of the United States and one of the country's leading congressmen writing what amounted to sedition: resolutions that urged that entire states ignore federal law.

All of this activity formed a backdrop for the Quasi War. President Adams pushed for the creation of a cabinet-level navy department in 1798. Under the able leadership of Secretary of Navy Benjamin Stoddert, not only were the superfrigates quickly completed and launched, but within two years the navy expanded to fifty-five ships. As early as July 7, 1798, the U.S. *Delaware* captured a French privateer, *Le Croyable,* off the coast of New Jersey. Soon the North American waters were safe for American shipping and the navy took the war to the Caribbean. Two frigate-size battles were fought by the *Constellation.* On February 9, 1799, the American frigate pounded the slightly smaller *L'Insurgente* into surrender, and a year later the *Constellation* engaged the larger *La Vengeance.* In the second contest the Americans claimed that only nightfall, which allowed the French to veer off under the cover of darkness, saved the French from capture. Both battles were touted as victories and became symbols of American naval prowess. Perhaps more important was the fact that the American navy patrolled the West Indies, making it much more difficult for the French to continue their depredations.

In the meantime there was not much, besides harassing Republicans, for the army to do on land. In the spring of 1798 wild rumors of an invasion swept through the United States. There was even some talk of a French army recruited from freed blacks from St. Domingue attacking the South and starting a rebellion among American slaves. By the summer and fall most people no longer believed those rumors, especially after news of the destruction of the French fleet by the British at the Battle of the Nile. But the Federalists continued building their army. Adams appointed Washington as commander in chief. No one expected the old general to take much of an active role in military affairs. Instead, the real head of the army would be his second in command. Much to Adams's discomfort, Washington insisted that Hamilton be given that position. Hamilton poured his energy into organizing this force and dreamed of worlds to conquer. There was talk that he might take the army to the West Indies or seek to capture Spanish colonies to the south. Who knew what else Hamilton might do with an army?

Adams, however, was moving in the opposite direction. Gerry, who was an old friend of Adams, returned to the United States in October 1798 with word that Tallyrand was now ready to negotiate in earnest. William Vans Murray, American ambassador at The Hague, reported that Tallyrand had contacted him with the news that the French would now officially acknowledge a new mission. Armed with these diplomatic signals, Adams surprised the more bellicose Federalists by announcing in February 1799 that he planned to send a new delegation to France. Many delays followed, in part because most of Adams's cabinet procrastinated; more loyal to Hamilton than to the president, they were aghast at the idea of peace. But Adams, too, was indecisive. In October a three-man commission—Murray, Oliver Ellsworth, and William R. Davie—was dispatched to France where they confronted a government now dominated by Napoleon Bonaparte. Almost a year later they had an agreement of sorts. The Convention of 1800 was far from a diplomatic triumph. It ended the unofficial hostilities, but France refused to pay any reparations for seizing American shipping. The French did agree to respect American neutrality and they accepted the fact that the French alliance of 1778 was null and void. The Senate initially balked at these terms; however, it eventually ratified the convention. Napoleon was glad to have this little conflict behind him and kept his real motives hidden. Within days of signing the Convention of 1800 he secretly compelled Spain to retrocede Louisiana, hoping some day to extend his control into North America.

Election of 1800

On the surface the election of 1800 appears straightforward enough. John Adams put politics aside and acted as a statesman. He avoided war, experienced diplomatic triumph, alienated his supporters, and guaranteed his own political failure as the nation rejected the aristocratic policies of the Federalist Party. The will of the majority prevailed through the "peaceable instrument of reform, the suffrage of the people." The election, however, was a complicated affair that defies such an easy description. Any number of different scenarios could have developed. A few hundred votes here, or a change of heart there, and the "suffrage of the people" would have left the United States with another president.

Most Americans—and here we are talking about only those who had the right of franchise (mainly white, male property owners)—never had the opportunity to vote for the electors who would chose the president. In ten of the sixteen states the state legislatures determined the electors. In these states it was local assembly and state senate elections that really counted. Moreover, the election process took almost the entire year to unfold. One of the most important contests occurred in New York, which held its election the first few days in May. New York Republicans, organized largely by Aaron Burr, swept key contests in New York City and won in a few Federalist strongholds upstate by nominating an impressive slate of candidates and carefully working the polls. Once the outcome of the election became known, the Federalists could still have stolen the day. Both Alexander Hamilton and Philip Schuyler urged Governor John Jay to call a special session of the old Federalist-dominated legislature to select electors. Jay thought this action inappropriate and designed for "party purposes" that, as he explained, "I think it would not become me to adopt."[14] Burr's labors garnered him the nod of a Republican caucus as the candidate for vice president. New York's twelve electors voted for Jefferson and Burr.

The Federalists did their best to sabotage their chances elsewhere as Hamilton again plotted to snare the election away from Adams. In early May the Federalists caucused and agreed to support Adams and Charles Cotesworth Pinckney equally. Hamilton hoped that this decision would help Pinckney in those areas where Adams was strongest, New England and the middle Atlantic states. Once those electors were committed he thought that the South Carolina legislature would do what it did in 1796, select electors who would vote for both Jefferson and a Federalist favorite son—only this time it was Thomas Pinkney's brother, Charles Cotesworth. Pinckney, however, would have none of this subterfuge and asserted that he would accept no electors from South Carolina but those who also voted for Adams. Hamilton's efforts wreaked more immediate havoc. As soon as Adams heard of the caucus he suspected something was up. He summoned James McHenry, the secretary of war and Hamilton's minion, to discuss some minor issues. At the end of the conversation Adams had one of his infamous fits of private temper. He turned on McHenry and lambasted him for his role in getting Hamilton appointed major general of the army and for trying to undermine the mission to France. Adams told McHenry what he thought of Hamilton, whom he blamed for the New York disaster. He declared that Hamilton led a "British Faction," and that he was an intriguer, "a man devoid of every moral principle," a foreigner and a bastard. McHenry had little choice but to resign.[15] A few days later, Adams requested Secretary of State Timothy Pickering's resignation. When Pickering, who was also close to Hamilton, refused to comply Adams fired him.

The Federalists were in complete disarray. But at last Adams, who had kept most of Washington's cabinet, could make some of his own appointments. John Marshall became his secretary of state, and Senator Samuel Dexter of Massachusetts took over the war department. With a peace agreement with France looming on the horizon, Adams began to dismantle Hamilton's army.

Hamilton, however, was not finished with Adams. His honor had been violated. He could not fight a duel with the president, although he would later fight a duel with a vice president, so he turned to pen and paper. Against the advice of his friends he wrote *Letter from Alexander Hamilton, Concerning the Public Conduct and Character of John Adams, Esq., President of the United States,* which he published privately in October. Hamilton argued that the presidency was beyond Adams's talents and that he had "great and intrinsic defects in his character, which unfit him for the office of Chief Magistrate." Those defects included a lack of sound judgment, inconsistency, vanity, and "a jealousy capable of discoloring every object." Hamilton went on to attack the recent peace mission to France, the pardon of Fries, and the abuse and firing of cabinet ministers. Hamilton also defended himself, declaring that he always had the interests of the republic at heart and was not the leader of any faction, British or otherwise.[16]

The Republicans soon had a copy of the letter of their own, and made much of the Federalist infighting. Madison was convinced that the letter guaranteed the complete triumph of the Republicans in the election. The *Aurora* proclaimed that "*Hamilton's* precious letter" was felt "from one end of the union to the other." It revealed the "treachery, not only of the *writer*, but of his *adherents* in the public counsels," and, the *Aurora* asserted, "it has thrown a blaze of light on the real character and designs of the writer and his partizans."[17]

Even with the loss of New York, and the Adams and Hamilton schism, the Federalists still almost won the election. District elections in Maryland and North Carolina allowed those states to split their electoral votes between Federalists and Republicans. The legislature in Pennsylvania was also divided. In 1799 the Republicans had won the lower house, but the Senate remained in the hands of the Federalists. The two houses compromised by giving eight electors to Republicans and seven electors to Federalists. Had there been a popular vote in New Jersey, the Republicans probably would have won. Instead, the Federalists controlled the legislature and voted their party ticket. The election boiled down to which way South Carolina would turn: support Adams and favorite son Pinckney, or Jefferson and Burr, allowing the recently elected weak Republican majority in the legislature to hold sway. It was a near thing because party loyalties of some of the South Carolina Republicans were not very strong. In the end, with Charles Pinckney insisting that any elector who supported him must also support Adams, and with the political maneuvers of another Pinckney, a Republican distant cousin also named Charles, the legislature picked eight Republican electors.

The final tally of electoral votes—seventy-three each for Jefferson and Burr and sixty-five for Adams—created one more problem. Because all of the Republican electors cast both of their votes for the two Republicans, there was no clear winner. With no single candidate getting a majority, the election went to the House of Representatives, in which each state delegation had one vote. This might not have been an issue if the newly elected Congress, which swept in sixty-five Republicans to forty-one Federalists, made the decision. But the election was placed in the hands of the old Federalist-dominated Congress. Here was yet another opening for a different outcome for the election of 1800.

And why shouldn't the Federalists seize the moment? Everything they had worked for was at risk. Their army was already disbanding. A Jefferson victory might lead to the reversal of their entire legislative program. In 1800 the Federalists had passed a bankruptcy bill that would allow big-time speculators such as Robert Morris to get out of debtor's prison, liquidate their assets, and start over with a clean slate. The Republicans detested that law. More serious was the threat to the Bank of the United States, the tax code support, the navy, the expanded bureaucracy, and the elaborate funding scheme that had propped up the nation's credit. Even the development of the new capital at Washington, where the government had moved only a few months before, was in jeopardy. Federalists were also concerned about Jefferson's diplomacy. They expected that he would ally himself with France and lead the nation into a disastrous war with Great Britain. Moreover, a decentralized government would return the nation to the drift, weakness, and, from the Federalist perspective, near anarchy of the 1780s. Burr might just be their last hope to save the republic.

Most Federalists viewed Burr as an unprincipled individual more concerned with personal acclaim than party. If they could maneuver so as to elect Burr president, some Federalists hoped, then he would be their creature and support their policies. It was a vain hope. Burr apparently thought about this unholy alliance, but hesitated to declare his willingness to any deal. He also did not step aside and proclaim for Jefferson. With Burr neither in nor out of the game, Congress became deadlocked. Several Federalists, including Hamilton, thought there was more wrong with an unprincipled Burr than there was with a wrongly principled Jefferson. The first ballot in mid February failed to give Jefferson a majority: Eight states went for Jefferson, six for Burr, and three divided. After six days and thirty-five ballots, the vote remained the same. A change occurred on the thirty-sixth ballot when Delaware's lone representative, James A. Bayard, decided to switch his vote. Once Bayard stated his willingness to support Jefferson, the Federalists in two of the split delegations agreed to not vote either way, allowing their states to shift to Jefferson. Bayard did not even have to fill in his ballot.

The Federalists had one last gambit to stem the Republican tide: They sought to ensure their control of the judicial branch. Adams had taken the first step in this direction on January 20, 1801, when he nominated John Marshall to be Chief Justice of the Supreme Court. The Federalist Senate confirmed the appointment. Federalist legislators also passed a new Judiciary Act on February 13, 1801. This law abolished the circuit court obligation for the justices of the Supreme Court and organized six new circuit courts with sixteen newly appointed federal judges. The law also expanded additional judicial officers such as marshals, clerks, and attorneys. In the last days of his administration Adams busied himself with filling these officers with Federalist appointees, the so-called midnight judges. These final measures distressed Jefferson, who wrote that the Federalists "have retired into the Judiciary as a strong hold," in which "the remains of federalism are to be preserved & fed from the treasury, and from that battery all the works of republicanism are to be beaten down & erased."[18]

The twists and turns of the election of 1800 muddle the outcome. Had there been a popular vote, Jefferson would have won. In that sense, Jefferson could lay claim to a democratic legacy of "the suffrage of the people." But there was no popular vote, and the peculiarities of an electoral college system intended to filter out the will of the people made the outcome almost serendipitous. To complicate matters even further, the Federalists were quick to point out that Jefferson owed his election to the Constitution's three-fifths clause. Counting three-fifths of each slave for representation added twelve electoral votes to the southern states that voted for Jefferson—more than the eight margin by which he beat Adams. Had representation been based solely on white inhabitants (or the actual population eligible to vote), the result of the election of 1800 would have been different. From this perspective, as Federalists exclaimed, Jefferson was the "Negro President" who rode "into the temple of Liberty on the shoulders of slaves."[19]

Of course Jefferson did not see it that way. He did not consider himself a "Negro President." Instead, he believed that the election expressed the will of the people and justified his opposition to Federalist policies. He was now armed with a new mandate to create a smaller government that adhered more closely to the delegated powers in the Constitution. In his first inaugural address he admitted that "the contest of opinion through which we have passed" might leave the impression that Americans had sharp differences. However, the issue had been "decided by the voice of the nation" following the rules of the Constitution. Therefore "all will . . . arrange themselves under the will of the law, and unite in common efforts for the common good." The majority would rule, respecting the rights of the minority. He called on his fellow citizens to "unite with one heart and one mind" and most famously proclaimed "We are all republicans—we are all federalists." Yet he also articulated a vision of the government and the economy that would have profound implications for the development of American capitalism. Gone would be the government of privilege and the active management from above. Jefferson advocated "a wise and frugal

FIGURE 6–2   Thomas Jefferson The Sage of Monticello came to symbolize the Republican Party. Elected president in 1800, Jefferson reversed the course of the federal government by shrinking its size and role in American lives. Jefferson as a politician and a man, however, was full of contradictions.

government, which shall restrain men from injuring one another, which shall leave them otherwise free to regulate their own pursuit of industry and improvement, and shall not take from the mouth of labor the bread it has earned."[20]

Jeffersonian Conundrum

Regardless of President Jefferson's assurances of putting aside party, the Federalists had every right to be concerned with what he would do to their program. As he promised in his inaugural address, Jefferson quickly sought to change the course of the nation and simplify government. He repudiated the Alien and Sedition Acts. The Sedition Act had conveniently been set to expire on March 3, 1801, just as the new president took office. The Republicans let the law lapse without any effort at reinstituting it to wield against the Federalists. The two Alien Acts empowering the government to deport enemies or undesirables had never been invoked and remained dead letters. Congress revised the Naturalization

Act to once again allow immigrants to become citizens after five years. The army and navy were more or less dismantled. The army shrank to 3,000 men and was stationed mainly on the frontier. Jefferson reduced the navy from thirteen frigates to six, more than halving the budget. In 1802 the government spent only $915,000 on the navy; during the Adams administration as much as $3.5 million had been spent in a year. Jefferson also did not pursue the building of any of the larger ships that had been planned. Instead, he advocated the construction of smaller gunboats to protect coastal waters. Jefferson sought to cut the rest of the bureaucracy that, although relatively tiny, he saw as "too complicated, too expensive," and "multiplied unnecessarily."[21] By doing away with internal taxes (the excise and house taxes) all of the collectors of those revenues could be dismissed. He cut the diplomatic corp to only three foreign missions— Great Britain, France, and Spain.

The Republicans also repealed the Judiciary Act of 1801, thereby killing two birds with one stone. They shrank the size of government and removed the positions held by many of the last-minute appointments—the midnight judges—of the Federalists. However successful the Republicans were in reducing the judiciary, they received a check on controlling the power of the Supreme Court with John Marshall's *Marbury v. Madison* (1803) decision. In this case one of the new court officials under the Judiciary Act of 1801, William Marbury, sued for a writ of mandamas (an order from the court dictating executive action) because Madison had not delivered Marbury's commission, signed by Marshall while he was still secretary of state. Marshall, knowing it might be difficult for the court to order the executive office under Jefferson to do anything, came up with a brilliant way of asserting the independence of the court without confronting the Republicans directly. He admitted that under the Judiciary Act of 1789 the writ should have been issued. However, he also declared that the Judiciary Act of 1789 was unconstitutional in providing the Supreme Court the power to issue such writs. Thus, in one ruling Marshall established the principle of judicial review while simultaneously giving the Republicans the ability to diminish the number of federal court officers.

Jefferson and his secretary of the treasury, Albert Gallitan, also wanted to erase the national debt. This policy grew out of a basic Republican premise that debt was bad because it fostered dependent men and not independent citizens. Jefferson believed that if the United States did not extinguish the debt "we shall be committed to the English career of debt, corruption and rotteness, closing with revolution. The discharge of the debt, therefore, is vital to the destinies of our government."[22] The Federalists had been mainly concerned with paying the interest on the debt, and thereby sustaining the credit of the nation. They had also allowed it to grow to $82 million. With the reduction of government expenditures, and continued revenue from customs duties, Jefferson and Gallitan planned on wiping out the debt within fifteen years. (At the end of Jefferson's second term, the United States had reduced the debt by one-third.)

Jefferson's administration marked not only a change in the substance of policy, it also signified an alteration in the style of government. Jefferson did little to foster the building of the new capital in Washington, D.C. A backwater national capital would reflect an invisible government. The Republicans had repeatedly charged that both Washington and Adams had made the office of the presidency too much like a monarchy, emphasizing pomp and ceremony in formal levees, processions, and procedures. Jefferson sought to simplify the ceremonial aspects of the office. Rather than read his addresses to Congress "from the throne" like British monarchs and Federalist presidents, Jefferson preferred to submit his messages in writing. He would often greet foreign dignitaries in his slippers and less formal dress. Instead of holding larger, courtlike receptions, Jefferson became famous for his more intimate dinners. Usually the guest list included congressmen and cabinet members, along with their wives. But there were also times when diplomats were invited as well.

The informality of these occasions triggered a diplomatic flap in the winter of 1803–04. The new British minister to the United States, Anthony Merry, and his wife had expected to be the guests of honor at what they thought was a state dinner. Instead, they were just one of several equal guests. Attending the dinner was the French chargé d'affaires, who was not at the same diplomatic rank and represented a nation antagonistic to Britain. The situation violated European diplomatic protocol. Worse, when the guests were called to dinner, Jefferson took the hand of Dolley Madison, wife of Secretary of State James Madison, and escorted her to his right side at dinner. Merry believed that this distinction should have been reserved for his wife. Instead, Mrs. Merry had to settle for a seat two places from Jefferson, and Merry had to scramble to get a seat at all. The controversy festered for months, exacerbated by further social affronts, with notes exchanged and a series of newspaper articles on the brouhaha. Jefferson at last sought to end the discussion by anonymously writing a letter published in the *Aurora* that explained his position. First, Jefferson proclaimed that March 4, 1801—the day of his inauguration—ended any pretensions to an American "court." "That day buried levees, birthdays, royal parades, and the arrogation of precedence in society by certain self-stiled friends of order, but truly stiled friends of privileged orders." Jefferson went on to explain the practice at his own dinners by declaring that in American "social circles all are equal, whether in, or out, of office, foreign or domestic; & the same equality exists among ladies as among gentlemen." In this egalitarian setting, "No precedence therefore, of any one over another, exists either in right or practice, at dinners, assemblies, or any other occasions. 'Pell-mell' and 'next the door' form the basis of etiquette in the societies of this country."[23]

If Jefferson set the American government on a clear and different course from the Federalists, as a man he was full of personal contradictions. Whatever his pronouncements concerning simplicity and frugality in government, he remained a natural aristocrat who could never live within his own means. He had to have a French chef to cook his White House dinners and his annual wine bill during his first term as president was about $2,400— a princely sum at the time. Wine had long been important to Jefferson. When he returned from France in 1789, hoping to finally find a way out of his perpetual debt, he spent a small fortune on French vintages. His aristocratic taste can also be seen in his home, Monticello. Jefferson rejected the more provincial Georgian style of most of his fellow Virginia planters and modeled his mansion on the work of Andrea Palladio. This Renaissance Italian architect designed buildings inspired by the villas of ancient Roman aristocrats. Jefferson was forever building and rebuilding Monticello, reworking every detail. The house was packed with clever inventions and expensive furniture that typified Jefferson's taste for the finer things in life. These private expenditures stand in stark contrast to his public economy and contributed to his near bankruptcy at the end of his life. Nor did he entirely reject the idea of aristocracy. As he later explained to John Adams, what he wanted was an aristocracy of talent based on "Worth and genius" rather than "wealth and birth." [24]

Jefferson pursued a political course that often conflicted with his stated ideals. He may have proclaimed that he was antiparty, but as president Jefferson often acted in a highly partisan manner. The dinner parties revealed this partisanship. Jefferson entertained both Federalist and Republican legislators at the executive mansion, although he invited them on different evenings. These events were more than social or intellectual; they were also an opportunity for Jefferson to use his personal charm to exert political influence. Direct political conversation was avoided. But as Jefferson confessed, he cultivated "personal intercourse with the members of the legislature . . . that we may know one another," avoid misunderstanding, and promote "harmony and mutual confidence." One Federalist, recognizing the effectiveness of this strategy, admitted "No one can know Mr. Jefferson and be his personal enemy."[25] However, Jefferson did not invite Federalists whom he believed had publicly insulted him. During the course of his administration the list of Federalists excluded grew larger and larger, and even some Republicans who opposed him were no longer invited.

Jefferson was also very political in the way he approached doling out government offices. He claimed that he would not play favorites when making appointments, but he decided that he could only make politically neutral selections after there was an equal number of Federalists and Republicans in government. He later reconsidered this position and determined it would be only fair to have the total number of Republican office holders in proportion to the Republican population in general—which he figured as somewhere between two-thirds and three-fourths of all Americans. In short, Jefferson never quite returned "with joy to that state of things when the only questions concerning a candidate shall be: is he honest, is he capable, is he faithful to the Constitution?"[26] Jefferson rewarded several of the individuals who had been instrumental in his election. Charles Pinckney, who had helped guide South Carolina's electoral vote to the Republican column, became minister to Spain. Edward Livingston, once a Burr ally, had played a crucial role in the congressional deliberations in February 1801. He became the federal district attorney for the state of New York and his brother became secretary of the navy. Even the army was not immune from politics: As Jefferson reduced the size of the army, he dismissed many of the Federalist officers who had dominated the force in the 1790s, opening a path for junior Republican officers to advance. The creation of West Point in 1802 to train officers was also a means of cutting out would-be aristocrats from military appointment.

Political opponents did not fare well. From the House floor Federalist James Bayard denounced the practice of rewarding "by Presidential favor" every politician who had helped Jefferson to the executive office.[27] Stung by this criticism, Jefferson convinced Caesar A. Rodney to run against Bayard. Rodney won by fifteen votes. Jefferson could also not quite forgive Burr for not quickly renouncing any claim to the presidency in 1801. That silence brought Burr, who after all was as much responsible for Republican success in the election as anyone, very little patronage. Jefferson reversed himself in 1804, doling out offices to several Burr supporters because he hoped to influence Burr as he presided over the impeachment trial of Justice Samuel Chase in the Senate. However, when the government later charged Burr with conspiracy, Jefferson did everything he could to encourage a conviction and the death penalty.

Jefferson could also be equivocal in his politics, as can be seen in the Republican attack on Federalist judges. There can be little doubt that Jefferson wanted to destroy the Federalists who clung to their position on the federal bench. He may even have hoped to get at John Marshall.

Ultimately, however, Jefferson pulled back and pursued a middle course that antagonized more-radical Republicans like fellow Virginian, Congressman John Randolph.

The assault on the courts began with a weak link in the Federalist-dominated judiciary. Thomas Pickering was a federal district judge from New Hampshire who had a distinguished earlier career, but who had become an alcoholic and was also probably insane. He had been relieved of duties under the Judiciary Act of 1801, which permitted circuit judges to appoint one of their own to replace an incapacitated district judge. Repeal of the law, however, forced Pickering back to the bench, where he acted arbitrarily, shouted obscenities, and misbehaved. As he was not exactly rational, Pickering refused to resign. Jefferson decided to have him impeached in 1803. The problem was that the Constitution stipulated that only "Treason, Bribery or other high Crimes and Misdemeanors" were cause for impeachment. The document was silent about insanity, drunkenness, and outrageous behavior. Regardless, the House of Representatives voted impeachment and the Senate, following a strictly party-line vote, agreed to dismiss Pickering from office in 1804.

Almost immediately the Republicans moved to the next level, targeting Justice Samuel Chase of the Supreme Court. Chase was an ardent Federalist who had been stridently political from the bench. He had been outspoken in the sedition trials and had virtually dictated the conviction of Fries. In 1803 he issued a charge to a federal grand jury in Baltimore that lambasted the repeal of the Judiciary Act of 1801 and berated the Republican legislature in Maryland. He maintained that "The independence of the national judiciary is already shaken to its foundation" and that without some change "Our Republican Constitution will sink into a mobocracy." On hearing of the charge, Jefferson wondered, "Ought the seditious and official attack on the principles of our Constitution and of a State to go unpunished."[28] Spurred on by this kind of presidential support, the House voted to impeach. However, the case was not particularly strong: Chase was charged with criminal behavior and judicial indiscretion. Jefferson had second thoughts about such blatant use of political clout and advised more moderate Republicans to vote against dismissal from office.

Besides politics there were personal and intellectual issues, such as Jefferson's ideas on race and slavery, which were also a bundle of contradictions. The Sage of Monticello believed slavery was bad for both whites and blacks. It was bad for whites because it corrupted "manners and morals" with absolute power over others. It was bad for blacks because it kept them in bondage. "The whole commerce between master and slave is a perpetual exercise of the most boisterous passions, the most unremitting despotism on the one part, and degrading submissions on the other." In this formulation, however, Jefferson was almost more concerned with the impact of slavery on the masters than on the slaves. Slavery not only corrupted the master, it made him lazy and unindustrious: "in a warm climate, no man will labour for himself who can make another labour for him." Slavery posed a danger because, as an immoral institution, it removed the only "firm basis" of "the liberties of the nation"—"a conviction in the minds of the people that these liberties are of the gift of God." As a slaveholder, Jefferson feared God's wrath, exclaiming, "Indeed I tremble for my country when I reflect that God is just: that his justice cannot sleep for ever." He foresaw the possibility of a turn of the "wheel of fortune" that could lead to "an exchange of situation."[29] Jefferson therefore hoped for a peaceful emancipation. Whatever his hopes, Jefferson did little to liberate most of his own slaves. As a planter struggling with debt, he could not simply liquidate such a valuable asset. His inaction also came from his conviction that blacks and whites could not live together as a free people, and his fundamental assumption that blacks were an inferior race.

Jefferson held that blacks and whites were in a natural state of war. Only the subjugation of blacks as slaves prevented wholesale violence by both blacks and whites. Liberating slaves was therefore impossible without also removing them from the United States. As Jefferson explained, "if a slave can have a country in this world, it must be any other in preference to that in which he is born to live and labour for another." After emancipation, whites and blacks would quickly be at each other's throats. "Deep rooted prejudices entertained by the whites; ten thousand recollections, by the blacks, of the injuries they have sustained" would combine with "new provocations" and "real distinctions which nature has made" to "produce convulsions which will probably never end but in the extermination of the one or the other race."[30] Although Jefferson argued that "nothing is more certainly written in the book of fate than that these people [black slaves] are to be free," he wanted to delay emancipation until blacks could be sent to their own country and bitter racial warfare avoided. Toward the end of his life Jefferson wrote that "our happiness and safety" depended on establishing "an asylum to which we can, by degrees, send the whole of that population from among us," where, under American "patronage and protection," blacks could be "a separate free, and independent people, in some country and climate friendly to human life and happiness."[31]

Underpinning Jefferson's ideas on the difficulty of freeing the slaves was his belief in the inferiority of blacks. Jefferson argued that "the difference is fixed in nature, and is as real as if its seat and cause were better known to us." Whites, in Jefferson's eyes, had "superior beauty" with "flowing hair" and "a more elegant symmetry." Africans also had "less hair on the face and body." Being a man of science in the age of Enlightenment, Jefferson traced differences that went beyond the skin. "They secrete less by the kidnies, and more by the glands of the skin, which gives them a very strong and disagreeable odour." Because of this "greater degree of transpiration," blacks were rendered "more tolerant of heat, and less so of cold, than the whites." Intellectually, blacks were no match for whites.

> Comparing them by their faculties of memory, reason, and imagination, it appears to me, that in memory they are equal to the whites; in reason much inferior, as I think one could scarcely be found capable of tracing and comprehending the investigations of Euclid; and that in imagination they are dull, tasteless, and anomalous.

Jefferson believed blacks were incapable of complex thought or appreciation of art: "But never yet could I find that a black had uttered a thought above the level of plain narration; never see even an elementary trait of painting or sculpture." So different did Jefferson view blacks as a race, that he declared the idea of interracial sex was unacceptable: "amalgamation with the other color produces a degradation to which no lover of his country, no lover of excellence in the human character can innocently consent."[32]

Jefferson's ideas, however, did not always match his practice. In September 1802 James Callender, a newspaper editor whom Jefferson had previously supported with intermittent payments of cash, published a scurrilous account of Jefferson's sexual liaisons with Sally Hemmings. Callender, disappointed when Jefferson did not make him postmaster of Richmond, wrote that "It is well known" that the president "keeps, and for many years past has kept, as his concubine, one of his own slaves." This "African Venus" had, according to Callender, several children with Jefferson, and was "said to officiate as housekeeper at Monticello."[33] Most white historians in the twentieth century dismissed the charge as simply personal and political invective that was out of character for the high-minded Jefferson. The Hemmings family claimed Jefferson's paternity since the early nineteenth century. More recently, scholars generally agree that Jefferson, despite his ideas on race, had a long-term relationship with Hemmings. (Hemmings was also probably Jefferson's dead wife's half-sister and was fair-skinned). In 1998, DNA evidence demonstrated a genetic match between the Jefferson and Hemmings families. Moreover, Jefferson was at Monticello approximately nine months before the birth of each of Sally's children. Finally, the only slaves Jefferson freed were members of the Hemmings family, including his five children with Sally Hemmings.

These contradictions and shifts in policy and ideas have led many historians to portray Jefferson as something of a conundrum. This Jeffersonian enigma is most evident in the area of race. The man who wrote that all men were created equal, owned slaves and proclaimed the racial inferiority of blacks. Committed to racial separation, Jefferson fathered children with a black slave. More than any other area, Jefferson's ideas on race and slavery have puzzled scholars, leaving many to admire him for his intellect, and, especially in light of the Sally Hemmings connection, to vilify him as a hypocrite.

In his politics and in his life Jefferson seemed to twist and turn in all sorts of directions simultaneously. Whatever his own personal contortions, and however we might want to criticize him, his achievement is unmistakable. Not only did he eloquently articulate the ideal of equality in the Declaration of Independence, and thereby set the terms of debate for much of the subsequent history of the United States, but his election in 1800 redirected the course of events in the early republic. The Federalist ideal of a hierarchical world controlling the economy from the top down was defeated. In its place there would emerge an egalitarian ethos of nearly invisible government standing aside as unfettered individuals scrambled in the economic free-for-all that came to be the hallmark of American capitalism.

Endnotes

1. Thomas Jefferson to Spencer Roane, Sept. 6, 1819, Thomas Jefferson Papers Series I, General Correspondence, 1651–1827, Digital Archives, Library of Congress, Image 836.
2. Quoted in David McCullough, *John Adams* (New York: Simon & Schuster, 2001), 462.
3. Thomas Jefferson to James Madison, Dec. 17, 1796, Thomas Jefferson Papers Series I, General Correspondence, 1651–1827, Digital Archives, Library of Congress, Image 1053.
4. Quoted in Stanley Elkins and Eric McKitrick, *The Age of Federalism: The Early American Republic, 1788–1800* (New York: Oxford University Press, 1993), 694.
5. An Act Respecting Alien Enemies, July 6, 1798, The Avalon Project at Yale Law School, www.yale.edu/lawweb/avalon/statutes/alien.htm.
6. An Act in Addition to the Act, Entitled "An Act for the Punishment of Certain Crimes Against the United States," The Avalon Project at Yale Law School, July 14, 1798, www.yale.edu/lawweb/avalon/statutes/sedact.htm.
7. Quoted in Elkins and McKitrick, *The Age of Federalism,* 710.
8. New York *Argus,* July 26, 1798.
9. Quoted in Paul A. Gilje, *The Road to Mobocracy: Popular Disorder in New York City, 1763–1834* (Chapel Hill: University of North Carolina Press, 1987), 110–11.
10. New York *Daily Advertiser,* July 30, 1798.
11. Robert Treat Paine, *Adams and Liberty; Together with Hail Columbia, and the American Sailor* ([Boston?]: no pub., 1798?), broadside.
12. Quoted in Jeffrey L. Pasely, *"The Tyranny of Printers": Newspaper Politics in the Early Republic* (Charlottesville: University Press of Virginia, 2001), 136.
13. Draft of the Kentucky Resolutions, Oct., 1798, The Avalon Project at Yale Law School, www.yale.edu/lawweb/avalon/jeffken.htm.

14. Quoted in Dixon Ryan Fox, *The Decline of Aristocracy in the Politics of New York,*
    1801–1840 (New York: Columbia University Press, 1919), 3.
15. Quoted in Elkins and McKitrick, *The Age of Federalism,* 736.
16. Alexander Hamilton, *Letter from Alexander Hamilton, Concerning the Public Conduct and*
    Character of John Adams, Esq. President of the United States (New-York: Printed for John
    Lang, by George F. Hopkins, 1800), 4, 7.
17. Quoted in Elkins and McKitrick, *The Age of Federalism,* 739.
18. Thomas Jefferson to John Dickinson, Dec. 19, 1801, Thomas Jefferson Papers Series I,
    General Correspondence, 1651–1827, Digital Archives, Library of Congress, Image 291.
19. Quoted in Garry Wills, *"Negro President": Jefferson and the Slave Power* (Boston:
    Houghton Mifflin, 2003), 2.
20. Thomas Jefferson, First Inaugural Address, Mar. 4, 1801, The Avalon Project at Yale Law
    School, www.yale.edu/lawweb/avalon/presiden/inaug/jefinau1.htm.
21. Thomas Jefferson, First Annual Message to Congress, Dec. 8, 1801, The Avalon Project
    at Yale Law School, www.yale.edu/lawweb/avalon/presiden/sou/jeffmes1.htm.
22. Thomas Jefferson to George Gilmer, July 25, 1790, Thomas Jefferson Papers Series I,
    General Correspondence, 1651–1827, Digital Archives, Library of Congress, Image 952.
23. Quoted in Dumas Malone, *Jefferson the President: First Term, 1801–1805 (Volume Four of*
    Jefferson and His Time (Boston: Little, Brown, 1970), 388.
24. Merrill D. Peterson, ed., *The Portable Thomas Jefferson* (New York: Viking, 1975), 537.
25. Quoted in Merrill D. Peterson, *Thomas Jefferson and the New Nation: A Biography*
    (New York: Oxford University Press, 1970), 725, 727.
26. Quoted in Wills, *"Negro President,"* 99–100.
27. *Annals of Congress,* 7th Congress, 1st sess., 640–41.
28. Quoted in Richard E. Ellis, *The Jeffersonian Crisis: Courts and Politics in the Young*
    Republic (New York: Oxford University Press), 79–80.
29. Peterson, ed., *The Portable Thomas Jefferson,* 214–15.
30. Peterson, ed., *The Portable Thomas Jefferson,* 215, 186.
31. Thomas Jefferson, July 27, 1821, Autobiography Draft Fragment, Jan. 6 through July 27,
    Thomas Jefferson Papers Series I, General Correspondence, 1651–1827, Digital Archives,
    Library of Congress, Image 517; and Thomas Jefferson to Jared Sparks, Feb. 4, 1824,
    Thomas Jefferson Papers Series I, General Correspondence, 1651–1827, Digital Archives,
    Library of Congress, Image 267. See also Peter S. Onuf, *Jefferson's Empire: The Language of*
    American Nationhood (Charlottesville: University Press of Virginia, 2000), 151.
32. Peterson, ed., *The Portable Thomas Jefferson,* 186–89, 546.
33. Quoted in Peterson, *Thomas Jefferson,* 706–07.

The New Society

Myth of the Yeoman Farmer

Thomas Jefferson's election marked the triumph of the common man. No longer would the government identify itself with the aristocratic pretensions of the Federalists and dependent men. A new society emerged that appeared to fulfill the promise of the American Revolution. Trumpeting the common man seemed to ease some of the tensions and anxieties that had surfaced in the turmoil of the 1760s and 1770s. Individuals no longer saw themselves tied to a hierarchy and a corporate society. Instead, they were released, for good or evil, to act on their own as equals. By no means was this transition complete nor was it developed evenly in all parts of the country. But by 1800 the direction was unmistakable—the ideal of the independent man was becoming central to the American national identity.

Who were these independent common men? Jefferson scanned the working population and divided it into three components: agriculture, commerce, and manufacturing. There can be little doubt that he viewed those who worked in agriculture—cultivators of the earth—as "the most valuable citizens" as "they are the most vigorous, the most independent, the most virtuous, and they are tied to their country and wedded to its liberty and interests by the most lasting bands."[1] At first he denigrated the other two groups, especially those who worked in manufacturing, but by the opening decade of the nineteenth century he had come to appreciate their economic and political contributions. As Jefferson explained to James Jay in 1809, "an equilibrium of agriculture, manufactures and commerce, is certainly become essential to our independence."[2] This triad, however, missed many other Americans. Day laborers, the underemployed, and the impoverished did not fit easily into Jefferson's categories. He saw women and dependents as mere auxiliaries to independent males. And although Jefferson took the labor of slaves for granted, he viewed African Americans as misplaced beings who did not really fit in his republic. Even the common men Jefferson trumpeted—farmers and mechanics—often behaved in ways he could not comprehend. Jefferson espoused a rational religion of the Enlightenment just as many common men turned to emotional evangelicalism. It is hard to imagine that Jefferson, this aristocratic man of the Age of Reason, ever understood what life was like for the common men he came to represent.

Few Americans resided in a Monticello, or even one of the Federalist-style houses we dub "colonial" that can be visited as museums on the East Coast. Most Americans lived in one- or two-room shacks with a modest amount of comfort. "Yeoman" Thomas Springer of Mill Creek, Delaware, had a log home, 19-by-23-feet, with single rooms on top of one another.[3] His kitchen was in a separate building, which was typical of houses in the warmer South. This log construction probably reflected the Swedish and German influence in the Delaware Valley. Ordinarily, poor people built these structures in the Pennsylvania–Delaware area, the backcountry of the South, or on the western side of the Appalachians. As soon as families could afford a timber-frame construction with clapboard sides, they would replace the log cabin.[4] The two stories made Springer's house a relatively

FIGURE 7–1   View from Bushongo Tavern 5 miles from York Town on the Baltimore Road, 1788 During the early republic most Americans lived in the countryside in simple houses 18 by 20 feet, similar to the buildings depicted in this engraving.

spacious abode of unusual size for log construction. Thanks to the Federalist house tax in 1798 we know that only one-third of the houses in Worcester County in Massachusetts had more than one floor. In 1798 almost half of the housing in the United States had a valuation of under $100 and ordinarily had single-floor dimensions similar to Springer's (usually either 20-by-24-feet or 18-by-20-feet). Most of these houses had a fireplace in the structure itself, especially in the North, both for cooking and for warmth. The poorest houses had dirt floors, but most had wooden boards.[5] Frontier conditions were even more primitive; log cabins, like the one in which Abraham Lincoln was born in Kentucky in 1809, usually measured 16-by-18-feet. The housing of the yeoman farmer, in other words, was not particularly impressive. Whether the walls were made of logs or clapboard, they were usually unpainted and the yard was littered with debris. The privy, if there was one, was a short walk away.

Jefferson took pains at Monticello to ensure that his guests at dinner would not have to see many of the slaves serving the courses of the meal. Privacy was impossible for the yeoman farmer. The Springers may have used their second story as a bedroom, but it is not clear who slept where. Their household included their own children, several white dependents—either servants or relatives—and, in 1798, four slaves. Smaller houses were even more tightly packed. Anything that occurred in one part of the home, whether an intimate sexual moment, an idle comment, or the passing of gas, was sure to be heard by everyone else in the household.

Space in such buildings had to be used for many purposes. At night, beds and bedding would be shared and spread all over the confined floor space. The best bedding was made of feathers; many of the poor had to rely on scratchy straw. During the day some of the sleeping furniture would be stowed, sometimes even tied up against the walls to make room for food preparation and other household work. The fine featherbed, however, would remain in sight as a symbol of wealth and as a comfortable place to sit. Furniture was spartan. Usually there would be a table, some stools, and a bench. Chairs were a sign of growing affluence, and by 1800 many families had six or more for sitting during meals and for entertaining guests. The walls had little adornment. The floor might be strewn with sand, which the most particular housekeepers swept into patterns. Light streamed in from an open doorway or the two or three small windows during the day. Candles and the fireplace hearth provided limited light at night. Most yeoman families would have only two or three candles for artificial illumination. More effective whale oil lamps would not become widespread until the 1820s and 1830s. At night people groped around in the near dark and went to bed early. In the summer the open door and windows provided the only ventilation, allowing flies and bugs to swarm indoors and offering little relief from heat that was often increased by the need for a fire to cook meals. In the winter, uninsulated walls allowed chilly air to pour in. The family would huddle around the fireplace, toasting the half of the body closest to the embers, while the cold besieged the half turned away from the fire.

Jefferson believed that a manufacturing worker would quickly abandon his trade and seek to earn money in any way possible so "that he can soon lay up money enough to buy fifty acres of land, to the culture of which he is irresistibly tempted by the independence in which that places him."[6] This assertion demonstrated how little Jefferson knew either the world of the common man in agriculture or manufacturing. Except for the most fertile of lands, fifty acres was not enough to sustain a farm. Thomas Springer owned 129 acres in Delaware. He planted only about forty-five acres of that land with a crop, leaving the rest of his property either as fallow pasture (another forty-five acres), unimproved woodland for timber and fire wood (twenty-five acres), grassy marshland for feed for cattle (ten acres), and the rest in orchards, gardens, outbuildings and his home.[7] Springer's estate fit into the 80–150 acre category that a Massachusetts agricultural magazine indicated was a reasonably sized farm. Many farms in more developed areas, however, were smaller. Approximately half the farms in two western Massachusetts towns at the turn of the century were undersized at fewer than fifty acres and reflected poverty rather than independence.[8] Farms on the frontier might be larger, but had a smaller percentage of land under cultivation.

A farmer's existence followed a course dictated by the natural rhythms of the seasons. For most crops, especially those grown by northern and western white farmers, sowing began in the spring and harvesting took place in the late summer and fall. Corn, which was one of the most important food sources in the North and South, entailed weeding and reworking the furrows. Grains such as wheat and rye demanded less persistent attention, but required intensive labor for short periods of time, especially when the crop had to be harvested before the weather turned bad. Work was regulated by the sun and the task regardless of the hands on a clock. Long days in the summer meant more hours for labor; short days in the winter left less time to maintain equipment, repair outbuildings and barns, and perhaps work a trade. The seasons also had an impact on the farmer's private life. Marriages were grouped in March and April before planting and in November and December after harvest as the darkest part of winter approached. Conception of children followed a similar pattern and generally occurred in late spring and early summer, leading to many babies being born in late winter and early spring. Although disease and fatal illness occurred throughout the year, the winter was the cruelest season. More deaths occurred when the weather was frigid, work was scarce, and there was less fresh food.

A farmer's life also followed a cycle that had a certain timelessness. A man would usually not establish his own farm and household until he married sometime in his mid-twenties. Thomas Springer waited until his late twenties to get married. But he was a youngest son whose father may have wanted him to help support the family farm for as long as possible. That dependency paid off when his father gave him land that created Thomas's relative affluence. Most young men were supposed to bring land to a marriage. Women were usually a few years younger than their husbands and contributed to the marriage a variety of household goods that represented their share of their parents' estate. If a young woman was not already pregnant when she got married, she soon became pregnant and would have children every two to three years until she either died—constant pregnancy took its toll on women—or reached menopause. Families began to practice some reproductive planning in the late eighteenth century; there was a slight decline in fertility when compared to the seventeenth century. A woman who married before 1800, but who continued to have children after that date, had an average of 6.4 children compared to 7.4 children in the seventeenth century. Fertility rates dropped to 4.9 children for women married between 1800 and 1849. This pattern emerged first in urban areas and the northeast, then spread to the countryside and into the South and West.[9] Although almost every family experienced the loss of some children, most grew to adulthood. Parents usually sent their children to a district school for a few years to learn the rudiments of reading and arithmetic. Teachers were poorly paid and were often harsh disciplinarians who had to struggle to control and teach students ranging in age from three or four to eighteen. Children were an important source of labor for the yeoman farmer. More children attended school during winter sessions, when there was less farm work to be done, than in the summer months. By the time they were seven or eight, both boys and girls could contribute to the family's well-being by caring for younger siblings, and by doing chores and minor jobs around the house. As they became teenagers the amount of work increased, and the time with schoolbooks decreased. Boys could help with the planting and harvesting. Girls could provide additional income by spinning, sewing, producing cheese or butter, or creating any number of handcrafts that could be sold to a merchant. A family was at its greatest economic viability when the oldest children reached adulthood and before they married. The parents would be relatively strong in their forties, and could still rely on the labor of their sons and daughters. Once those sons and daughters began to marry and leave the house they took wealth—either land or goods—and their labor with them. Aging parents, if they managed to stay alive, had to get on with less material wealth, until the last child was ready to break away. Then the old couple, or more likely a single widow or widower, might well become a dependent of one of their own children.

Women were instrumental to the success of the yeoman farmer. Few white women labored in the fields with their husbands; instead, they did crucial work around the house. Ordinarily, they were responsible for the garden that grew the vegetables that added variety to the diet. They also took care of the barnyard animals and preserved meats, fruits, and vegetables. Women cooked and prepared three meals a day. Women also made the homespun clothing for the family. These activities were crucial for the household economy because they conserved scarce cash resources that would have been expended if the items produced had to be purchased in the market. Women's labor also generated income. Martha Ballard in Maine was a midwife who earned cash delivering babies and who, during her most productive years, supervised the spinning and weaving of cloth by her daughters and other dependents. Margaret Springer, wife of Thomas, was responsible for the butter production that was such an important component of their farm. Other women participated in a variety of work activities that earned money.

Jefferson praised the farmer because of his supposed independence. But the farmer was not as independent as Jefferson believed. Not only did the farmer depend on his wife and family, but by 1800 he was increasingly involved in an intricate web of connections in his community that eventually extended into a larger market economy. On the most fundamental level, neighbors exchanged labor. Working together to raise barns or husk corn even became communal events. Such activity was sporadic or seasonal. More regular was the day or two of labor that one farmer might provide for another, keeping either a mental note or even a comment in a ledger against the day when accounts were balanced through similar services, goods, or cash. In this way a man with small children might be able to get his crop in, knowing that he could make some sort of payment later. Ultimately, however, the yeoman farmer sought a surplus for cash from a more distant market. The actual farm commodity to be sold varied from region to region—sometimes it was in the form of grains, livestock, and even timber —but the end was the same: profit. In 1802 Jefferson relished the "mammoth cheese" (it weighed 1,235 pounds) sent to him as the product of independent Massachusetts farmers. It might best be seen as the symbol of a new form of commercial farming.

FIGURE 7–2   Venerate the Plough, 1786 Jefferson wrote "Those who labour in the earth are the chosen people of God . . . whose breasts he has made his peculiar deposit for substantial and genuine virtue." This illustration depicts a farmer, his plow, and a female representation of liberty and prosperity (she carries a sheaf of wheat in her hands and has a halo of stars to represent the United States). But the farmer was not as independent as Jefferson believed, as he was dependent on his wife and family for labor, and external markets for his produce.

Manufacturing

Initially, Jefferson expressed nothing but contempt for tradesmen. In private correspondence and in his *Notes on the State of Virginia,* Jefferson belittled the labor of artisans and manufacturers.[10] During his presidency he changed his mind. Mechanics had embraced the Republican Party and helped to put Jefferson in the White House. They also became more necessary when Jefferson attempted to limit trade as a diplomatic tool during his administration. In 1805, when there was a discussion of reissuing his *Notes on the State of Virginia,* he backpedaled on his attack on artisans and said that he had been misunderstood. He wrote that he had "been quoted as if meant for the present time here." That wasn't the case. He was looking toward a possible future when he warned against manufacturing. Jefferson believed that "as yet our manufacturers are as much at their ease, as independent and moral as our agricultural inhabitants, and they will continue so as long as there are vacant lands for them to resort to."[11]

Workers in manufacturing—artisans—lived modestly. Rural artisans lived much like their farmer counterparts, with perhaps a shop attached to their home where they could practice their trade. Urban artisans were in a period of transition in housing during the 1790s and early 1800s. For much of the eighteenth century, most urban master craftsmen occupied buildings that served as both their place of work and place of abode. Moreover, their household would usually include apprentices, and sometimes even journeymen (young adult workers skilled in the trade) who had agreed to a long-term contract. This arrangement began to break down at the end of the eighteenth century with master craftsmen setting up shop in a different building, and even a different neighborhood, from their residence. Successful masters might live in a multiroom structure made of brick. Their workers, both apprentices and journeymen, were left to find housing for themselves. Real estate was at a premium, so older houses were either torn down for the construction of multifamily dwellings and tenements, or were partitioned with paper-thin walls to the same effect. Young single workers—male or female—might simply board with a family in an already crowded apartment. By the early 1800s, the most densely populated cities such as New York, Boston, and Philadelphia even had extra buildings erected in the backyards of established tenements. Sanitation suffered with overflowing "necessary houses" only occasionally emptied by the night-soil men. Many of the buildings were made of wood and became firetraps any time a conflagration might erupt. Public spaces were piled with garbage, cleaned only by the pigs and dogs allowed to roam the streets. In Charleston, vultures performed the same service.

Life for urban artisans followed patterns similar to their country cousins. The seasons mattered. There was more work in the springtime and summer, when business and construction picked up, and less opportunity for employment in the inclement weather of late fall and winter. Like farmers, most city mechanics married sometime in their mid-twenties and would have a large number of children. However, within the urban environment it was easier for both men and women to be independent outside of their parents' households as boarding houses provided a housing option. Women were an important part of the city workforce. Their household chores may not have been as comprehensive as farm women's, as there was less land available for gardening and raising livestock, but they included many of the same cash-saving activities in addition to scavenging for firewood, clothing, and even food. Women also contributed more directly to the market economy, sometimes helping in the artisan's shop, but more often taking in laundry or sewing. Children, too, were seen as an economic asset. Both males and females helped in any number of small tasks when very young. Adolescents could earn cash: Young men worked as apprentices, day laborers, or even seamen; young women entered domestic service or became seamstresses.

From one perspective the early years of the American republic were a golden age for artisans. Both in the countryside and the city, thousands of new positions for craftsmen opened up. The growing shipping industry meant employment for shipwrights, coopers, blockmakers, ropemakers, and a host of other maritime trades. The demand for urban housing brought more work for carpenters, plasterers, and painters. A rising interest in consumer goods increased jobs for all kinds of tradesmen. The new trumpeting of the common man changed the status of the hardworking artisan who now came to see himself, along with the farmer, as the epitome of republican virtue. In 1809 John Treat Irving declared that mechanics compose "the sinews and muscles of our country." They were "men who form[ed] . . . the very axis of society."[12] Fashion reflected the rising status of laboring men. Knee breeches, long-tailed coats, buckled shoes, cocked hats, and wigs of the old aristocracy increasingly "became objects of curiosity, almost derision to the boys in the street." The epitome of style for men became full-legged pants, waist coats, brimmed hats, and trimmed hair typical of men who worked for a living.[13] Even the word *mechanic* changed its meaning. Used to describe anyone who earned his living by skilled work with his hands before the American Revolution, the term was considered an insult. In the 1790s and early 1800s it became a label laboring men identified with virtue and proudly seized on. People inserted the word into the names of their communities; new towns appeared called Mechanicsville and Mechanicsberg in states such as Pennsylvania and Ohio.

In the dynamic economy of the early republic, artisans could follow a Franklinesque path to success. Stephen Allen served as an apprentice sailmaker during the Revolutionary War in British-occupied New York City. When his Tory master departed the city at the end of the war he was left to his own devices and hired himself out as an underaged journeyman. Although he was driven from some sail lofts because of his youth— journeymen were expected to be at least twenty-one—he had enough skill and determination to find near constant employment. In 1793 he entered into a partnership with a master sailmaker, and a few years later he established his own independent loft. Allen was fortunate because "the belligerent state of all Europe had called into action the whole commercial resources of our country," but especially in his business of sail-making.[14] He often labored for fourteen hours a day and earned great profits not only by finishing the work on time, but also by turning into a wholesaler of sailcloth for other sailmakers. In 1788, when he married, he had a scant $25 to his name; eight years later he was worth $4,000 and on his way to a successful business and political career and would eventually become mayor of the City of New York. Both his industry and his willingness to expand to wholesaling had paved the way for his fortune. Paul Revere, one of the period's most famous artisans, showed even more flexibility and business acumen. Apprenticed in Boston as a silversmith with his father before the Revolutionary War, Revere focused mainly on skilled production and some engraving in the 1760s and 1770s. During the war he saw new opportunities and began operating a foundry to make brass cannon. After the war he continued as a silversmith, but made cheaper, more basic, items for a larger market, while continuing manufacturing and learning the complicated process of smelting copper. In the 1790s and early 1800s he was awarded a series of lucrative government brass and copper contracts. Like Allen, he profited from the expansion of maritime trade by making copper bolts that were essential to shipbuilding. He also rolled copper for ship bottoms. He ended up worth over $40,000.

What the revolutionary economics and politics gave with one hand, they took away with the other. During the colonial period the artisanal workforce was divided into unpaid apprentices seeking training in the trade, skilled journeymen who worked for others, and master craftsmen who owned their own shops. Although tradesmen retained this craft structure well into the nineteenth century, it came under increasing strain from market forces. Aggressive and entrepreneurial masters like Allen and Revere searched for ways to increase profits and minimize costs. The impact of these efforts differed from trade to trade and varied in timing, but the overall trend was for the master to become less a worker in his shop and more a businessman in an office, for the journeyman to become a hired hand who had diminished opportunity to own his own shop, and for apprentices to become only half-trained and a source of cheap, partially skilled labor. Complicating these developments were changes in the means of production; laborers began to manufacture individual parts rather than using their skill to complete a work of craftsmanship and owners introduced machinery to cut costs. Successful masters, of course, were excited about these changes. Young men, too, might eagerly sign on for a wage, even if it were lower than the going rate for journeymen, rather than endure an unpaid bondage as apprentices.

Journeymen were caught in the middle and began to protest these developments through labor organizations and strikes. During the colonial period there may have been an occasional strike or two. In New York City there was a tailors' strike in 1768 and a printers' strike in 1778, and Philadelphia sailors refused to work in 1779 and 1781 in opposition to payment in depreciated currency. But the turnout, as the strike was called, was a relatively novel tool of labor negotiation that developed more fully in the 1790s and early 1800s. Before this period journeymen and masters tended to share a sense of identity in their trade that fostered relatively benign labor relations. Both master and journeyman worked in the shop together and the economic distance between the two did not appear that great. Opportunity for some masters, however, began to create vast economic differences, especially in certain conflict-prone trades such as shoemaking, printing, tailoring, cabinetmaking, and construction. Masters became entrepreneurs whose main activities were marketing and raising capital, rather than physical labor.

These developments became evident in Philadelphia's shoemaking industry when the masters shifted from bespoke work in which journeymen

FIGURE 7-3   Shoemakers at Work Artisans took pride in their labor and viewed themselves as the "axis of society." But changes in manufacturing in competitive trades like shoemaking made it increasingly difficult for journeymen to earn a living. This development led to some the first strikes by laborers in the United States.

made shoes for specific customers, to shop work in which journeymen made shoes for a customer to buy off the rack in the master's shop, to order work in which the master made a contract to deliver shoes to another location and had his journeymen produce large numbers of generic shoes for export elsewhere. In the process, masters reduced wages and increased their profits, arguing that they needed to be compensated for the capital they invested in materials, time, and marketing. The Philadelphia master who signed a contract to sell $4,000 worth of shoes in New Orleans, in other words, operated on a much different level than the master who simply took an order for a specific pair of shoes for a couple of dollars. If the entrepreneurial risks were greater, so were the profits. In 1800, a Philadelphia journeyman shoemaker might be able to earn $600 a year if he worked every day but Sunday for long hours. Less diligent workers would be lucky to clear $300 a year. A master who hired twenty-five journeymen might make a princely $6,000 a year. Recognizing this disparity, the journeymen shoemakers in Philadelphia organized an association in 1792, agreeing not to labor in a shop or lodge in a house with anyone who "scabbed"—at this time a scab was someone who accepted work below the association's agreed-on wage. A series of turnouts followed in 1798, 1799, 1804, and 1805 as wages rose, encouraged by the general economic prosperity. The masters also had an organization and persistently pursued ways to lower wages. In 1806 the masters persuaded the State of Pennsylvania to indict the Philadelphia cordwainers for conspiracy because, as the charge stipulated, "no man is at liberty to combine, conspire, confederate, and unlawfully agree to regulate the whole body of workmen in the city."[15]

The journeymen's case became a cause celebre taken up by the Republican Party. William Duane in the *Aurora* wrote that "the case of the shoemakers is only another proof of the tendency of *lazy luxury* to enslave the men of industry who acquire their bread by labor."[16] Lawyer Caesar Rodney argued for the defense that the masters themselves had an organization and that there was no real difference between the journeymen cordwainers' organization and any other civic society such as merchants forming partnerships, students organizing college clubs, or even farmers attending a country dance. Rodney called the masters greedy and grasping: "They are not satisfied, with the rapid rate at which they are at present amassing wealth. They wish to make their fortunes by a single turn of the wheel." He claimed that if the masters won, then they would be allowed not only to determine wages, but they might even begin to dictate where the journeymen could live or what they ate. He posed the case as a battle between the powerful masters and the weak journeymen. Perhaps most important, Rodney saw the contest as crucial to the future of liberty in the republic. Allowing the masters to win would reverse the outcome of the American Revolution by denigrating labor. The United States was "the last retreat of freedom and liberty." Following English common law in the conspiracy case (there was not a Pennsylvania statute that addressed the issue) would be a "return to servitude."[17]

The defense fell on unsympathetic ears. At the end of the trial, Judge Moses Levy reminded the jury that the journeymen's combination injured the public welfare by ignoring the forces of the market. "The usual means by which the prices of work are regulated, are the demand for the article and the excellence of its fabric," Levy declared. "Where the work is well done, and the demand is considerable, the prices will necessarily be high. Where the work is ill done, and the demand is inconsiderable, they will unquestionably be low." He concluded that

> To make an artificial regulation, is not to regard the excellence of the work or quality of the material, but to fix a positive and arbitrary price, governed by no standard, controuled by no impartial person, but dependant on the will of the few who are interested; this is the unnatural way of raising the price of goods or work.

As in similar cases elsewhere, the jury found the shoemakers guilty and ruled their organization illegal.[18]

Not all journeymen objected to entrepreneurship. Many hoped to follow the path of the masters and break out of the grind of wage labor. These men wanted to use the new economy to their own benefit. As printer James Carey explained to his more successful brother, Mathew, should his efforts at establishing his own shop and becoming a publisher in Savannah fail, "I may possibly fall into the more humble and obscure walks of life—still contenting myself with the solacing idea, that although unsuccessful, I have made the necessary efforts to obtain consequence—I meant to say *competence*—however let them both stand."[19]

This shift from the common man's concern with "competence" to a concern with "consequence" represented a crucial development in the rise of capitalism in the early republic for both the artisan and farmer. Jefferson, no doubt, never fully appreciated it. But his revolution in 1800 grew out of this shift and reflected an important milestone in its evolution. By extolling the virtues of everyday farmers—and even artisans—Jefferson helped to unleash the forces of individualism and entrepreneurship that would transform the United States. Not every common man succeeded in his search for consequence. But his striving became the hallmark of the early republic. Men like William Manning of Massachusetts were not content with being simple farmers. During the 1790s he railed against a Federalist elite as a leisured aristocracy, but he extended economic activities beyond small-scale farming, opening a tavern, running a saltpeter works for gunpowder, helping to build a canal, while selling and buying land, borrowing money, and supporting the creation of state banks. This interest in the market by the common man would have powerful implications for American expansion and government policy.

The Lower Sort

Jefferson considered only one group of the "lower sort" as productive members of society. Jefferson's work as a diplomat and as secretary of state compelled him to think about the needs of sailors. He viewed fishermen as farmers of the sea and merchant seamen as valuable because their labor allowed commerce to thrive. The mass of other laborers was less important to him. The countryside swarmed with day laborers struggling to survive, and the cities were packed with workers searching for employment wherever they could find it. There was also an ever increasing number of poor people who needed public assistance.

Farmers depended on commerce, as Jefferson recognized, to get their products to market. During the 1790s and early 1800s a war-plagued Europe clamored for American grain. Sailors therefore were instrumental to the development of the American economy. Tens of thousands of Americans worked on ships during these years. Most men who went to sea were young. Their career as a sailor would begin in their late teens and would probably end, if they survived, by their early thirties. There were many reasons for young men to become sailors: wanderlust, lack of prospects at home, a maritime tradition within the family, seeking one's fortune, or a desire to earn enough to establish oneself in some land-based occupation. We have no statistics on the age of marriage for seamen. Younger sailors would not be married. Many of the men who did marry, probably in their mid to latetwenties, soon looked for ways to earn a living ashore. Mari-time culture was often a trap. Although a sailor might earn twelve dollars a month and come ashore with several months' wages in his pocket, he would frequently spend it binge drinking and carousing. Once his pockets were emptied, an obliging boardinghouse-keeper would lend him some money against future wages. After a few more days, the boardinghouse-keeper would sign the young tar for another voyage, taking a month's wages paid in advance for his troubles. Some sailors avoided temptation and used their earnings to buy a farm or start a trade. Others worked their way through the ranks to become a captain and gain some affluence. Whether the money was spent on a spree or saved for the future, sailors worked for a wage and participated in a market economy.

Housing for sailors was even more limited in space than for artisans or farmers. At sea, sailors slept in a crowded forecastle in the front of the ship.

Regardless of the type of vessels or the size of the crew, these accommodations were always cramped. A ship's crew of ten would be squeezed into bunks stacked by twos in a space that might be 12-feet-long and at most 10-feet-wide, tapering off toward the bow. The only furniture would be the sailors' chests, which stowed their belongings and served as table and chairs. Ashore, most sailors lodged in a boardinghouse near the waterfront. These establishments varied from buildings devoted entirely to boarding, with a bar on the first floor and scores of sailors sleeping six or more to a room, to apartments with limited space to lodge a sailor or two. Sailors in their home port stayed with their relatives, usually in tenements with only one or two rooms available for the entire family. Under any of these circumstances privacy was all but impossible.

Sailors were aware of their particular place in the new American republic. Considering themselves "Brave Republicans of the Ocean," seamen believed that they made a special sacrifice to sustain American commerce, confronting danger from the elements as well as threats from the Barbary States and depredations by the French and English. Despite their marginal existence they participated in the politics of the street of the 1790s and early 1800s. They were also able to take collective action when their own interests were directly involved. In 1800, Baltimore sailors struck over wages, marching along the wharves with "drums and fife, and colours flying," assaulting a vessel manned by underpaid seamen.[20] There was a similar turnout in New York in October 1802 that lasted several days. The mixed crowd had European American seamen following two white "commodores" and African American seamen following two black "commodores." Both sets of leaders were "decorated with ribbons and feathers." The crowd of strikers "traversed the docks with drums and colors, encouraging all seamen to work for no less than fourteen dollars a month." The men even attacked a schooner with underpaid sailors aboard, and "with great coolness and order . . . proceeded to dismantle her of her sails and rigging, which they very carefully stowed away in the hold."[21]

Working as a sailor was often just one phase of a laborer's life. Men might go to sea for a voyage or two and then work ashore either on the waterfront or even in the interior. Sometimes seamen would settle down to a trade. More often, they joined an undifferentiated mass of laborers who took any type of work that was available. Men all too easily flitted from one low-paying, menial job to another. Both the cities and the countryside teemed with workers seeking employment. They often lodged with their employer, sleeping in any space available, including outbuildings and barns. These individuals are hard to trace because they left little permanent record in any one place. But they were an important part of the early republic's landscape. Hiring themselves out by the day, week, season, or year, casual laborers seldom had long-term job security and could be dismissed at any time. As agricultural workers they might help with the planting or harvest, clear fields, build fences, or assist with the livestock. In seaports they would unload vessels, move goods, or perform the most basic chores requiring a strong back and a willingness to work. As urban day laborers they might sweep or clean up a shop, unpack a delivery, or even chop some local firewood. Transient labor also would be hired to help construct roads or build canals. Even on job sites that demanded a core skilled labor force—an iron forge in southern New Jersey or a shipyard in Philadelphia, for example—there were also tasks for casual laborers. Mark Noble, who lived a part of his life in Providence, Rhode Island, had been trained as a youth in "the farming business," but toiled mainly in "the business of a laborer," which he described as "chopping wood, butchering, &c."[22]

Not all casual laborers served time at sea. Many were simply part of the excess population born to large families unable to provide a legacy for children. Sometimes the families were poor to begin with. Other times the family farm of under one hundred acres was not productive enough to sustain a family with a half-dozen children or more. The capriciousness of the market could also drive families into poverty. If an individual was not nimble enough, he could easily find himself scrambling just to get by. Grant Thorburn could earn a good living making nails by hand in the 1790s; when factory-produced cut nails were introduced around 1800, he lost his trade. Thorburn survived and even thrived by setting up a grocery and eventually selling potted plants and seeds. Other workers were not so adroit and, facing similar circumstances, worked wherever and whenever they could. Injury and illness could also come into play, forcing someone out of regular employment.

Many laborers were immigrants. The great waves of immigrants that swept into the United States later in the nineteenth century dwarf the earlier immigration of the 1790s and early 1800s. But we should not let this comparison minimize the impact of foreigners in the early republic. At least 250,000 immigrants arrived in what became the United States from 1783 to 1819. In a population of a little over 5 million in 1800 these foreigners could have a significant affect on society, especially when they congregated in specific neighborhoods and communities. Many of these people came as political refugees either from the French West Indies during the racial upheaval that followed the French Revolution or Ireland after the failed rebellion of 1798 and 1799. Others arrived simply looking for economic opportunity. The Federalists were obviously chagrined at the influx of pro–Republican immigrants and passed the Alien Acts to hold these newcomers in check. Animosity to immigrant groups reached beyond the politicians, especially against Irish Catholics. Beginning in the 1790s, xenophobic Americans borrowed an English practice and paraded on St. Patrick's Day with effigies filled with straw to insult the Irish. On several occasions such demonstrations led to street brawls. In 1806 nativist Americans harassed the Christmas Eve services at a Catholic church in New York City. When they followed this insult with an intrusion into the Irish neighborhood of the Sixth Ward a riot broke out. In the ensuing melee one police officer was killed and several people on both sides of the conflict were wounded.

Other groups also became casual laborers. Manumitted African Americans often found regular employment difficult. Even when they had a skill they sometimes discovered their trade was closed to them by whites who refused to work by their side. Many young African American males signed on as sailors because that was an occupation that was open to them in the early years of the republic. Others simply hired on as day laborers as best they could. Native Americans, especially in areas long conquered by European Americans, like New England, worked on the margins of mainstream society, going to sea, hiring themselves out during harvest, or simply filling some immediate labor need.

There was also a large number of women who entered this casual workforce. Phoebe Perkins was an agricultural worker in rural Rhode Island during the 1780s, doing a variety of odd jobs from picking "greens for sauce" and strawberries to general household labor. Moving from position to position, sometimes she stayed with one family for a few weeks as hired help, and sometimes she was employed an entire season.[23] Women also toiled in the towns and cities as domestic help, washerwomen, and seamstresses. They took in lodgers, even if all they had was a small, two-room apartment. Often it was enough just to rent a space for someone to sleep on the floor. In the cities women were hucksters, street vendors for fruit and vegetables, or found work in the food service industry. A few turned to prostitution either as a permanent occupation, or as an occasional supplement to a meager living. As resourceful as their male counterparts, women would often shift occupation as opportunity and the seasons allowed. Unlike their male counterparts, however, women had a significant disadvantage. Men and women engaged in sexual encounters with each other. If a pregnancy resulted, a male could walk away from any permanent obligation, whereas a woman was left holding an infant. Phoebe Perkins had managed to get by until she got pregnant—suddenly, she became a liability to the community she had lived in for years.

These laborers truly were the "mobs of great cities" (or the country-side for that matter) that Jefferson believed were like "a canker which soon eats to the heart of its laws and constitution." Faced with few options, some of these individuals turned to criminal activity, stealing what they could not earn. Others found solace in alcohol and rowdy behavior, joining in affrays and general disorder. New York police magistrate Charles Christian commented in 1812 that the divisions within society, derived from "the obvious inequalities of fortune," along with "the insatiable appetite for animal gratification . . . in weak and depraved minds," led to a "wretchedness" among "a heterogenous mass."[24] Men like Christian sought ways to deal with the "lower sort" who could not find employment or who turned criminal. Communities in southern New England relied on the traditional warning-out system whereby an individual and his or her family would be forced to leave the community as an indigent to return to the place of his or her birth for public assistance. Faced with unemployment during the slack winter season, Mark Noble found himself hauled before Providence officials in December 1787 and compelled to leave Providence with his family. Pregnant Phoebe Perkins was "warned out" of the town where she had labored for years after officials discovered her swelling belly. Other communities created new institutions to deal with both the poor and the criminal. Almshouses became "bettering houses" where the indigent were compelled to work for their keep and thereby learn the value of labor. Prisons were also built with the idea that they would not just punish, but reform the criminal. Both institutions quickly became overcrowded and did little to change the behavior of the "heterogenous mass."

Americans in the city and in the countryside, especially the "lower sort," were assaulted by debilitating disease and their health remained marginal. Dirt and germs abounded. Common hygiene practices of today were almost unheard of. Few people took baths on a regular basis and splashing water on one's face and hands was considered washing. Americans ate more meat, usually pork, and better food than almost any other people on the globe. But drinking water was frequently contaminated, and spoiled or poorly prepared foods contributed to intestinal disorders. Alcoholic beverages were so popular in part because they may have been the safest way to quench one's thirst. Fevers or agues erupted everywhere. Malaria, sometimes called intermittent fever, persisted throughout the South. Victims experienced high temperature, chills, weakness, and shakes. Although malaria did not usually kill, it left an individual weak and vulnerable to other diseases. Tuberculosis, or consumption, was a more urban illness and spread when a sick person coughed or sneezed. It killed its victims slowly, and often infected whole families. More dramatic were the smallpox and yellow fever epidemics. Smallpox was most virulent during the 1770s and 1780s and had become less widespread by 1800. Outbreaks continued to occur, however, especially among populations previously unexposed to the disease. Even more lethal were the bouts of yellow fever that struck American cities in the 1790s and early 1800s. Philadelphia lost 10 percent of its population in 1793. Every summer urban dwellers watched for the first signs of sudden fever, black vomit, and the telltale jaundice-yellow skin color. As soon as a case was reported, those who could afford to leave the city headed for the safer clime of the country, leaving the poor to suffer and hope for a quick frost that miraculously ended the pestilence.

Bound Labor

Even if Jefferson did not include them in his discussion of useful citizens, unfree workers were an important part of the early American labor force during the early republic. In the colonial period, bound labor included European Americans who had agreed to a term of service in exchange for transportation to North America as well as apprenticeship to train youths for life as an artisan. Enslaved Africans were also a form of bound labor, except that their servitude lasted for life and passed from one generation to the next. Revolutionary rhetoric proclaimed all men were equal, and by implication they should be free. Despite such language, indentured workers did not entirely disappear among European Americans in the expanding economy of the new republic and, of course, African American slavery remained deeply embedded in the fabric of much of the United States.

Indentured servitude, although it still existed, was in decline for European Americans after the Revolutionary War. Many Americans came to believe that this form of labor no longer fit their image of what life should be like for any white American. The British government also passed legislation that made it more difficult for immigrants to bind themselves as labor to pay for passage to the United States. Moreover, with the outbreak of the French Revolution, and the wars that followed, it became increasingly difficult to recruit indentured servants from Continental Europe, especially Germany (a major source of bound labor in the mid-eighteenth century). Still, throughout the late eighteenth and into the early nineteenth century, a few hundred immigrants arrived annually having signed away their freedom for a term of years to pay their way to North America. There were approximately two hundred servants listed each year in the Philadelphia registry for redemptioners (a redemptioner was a type of indentured servant) throughout the 1790s and there appeared occasional advertisements for indentured servants, such as the notice in a New York paper in 1786 for two Germans and an Irishman who had run away from their masters.[25]

In contrast, youths were bound out in large numbers. Apprenticeship may have been challenged by the changing modes of artisan production, yet thousands of young people signed these contracts that bound them to a master for a specified number of years or until they reached age twenty-one. Bill Otter in New York City wanted to become an apprentice in a trade in 1805. He tried shoemaking, venetian-blind making, and carpentry on probation for a week or two, but found in each case, as his father put it, "hard work" and young Bill "had had a falling out." Confronted with "fooling away" his time "to no purpose" and leaving one trade after another, Bill and his father were afraid that, as Bill explained in his reminiscences, "my name would become so notorious that I could not get a master." They therefore determined to sign indentures immediately for Bill's next effort as an apprentice, binding Bill to a plasterer for four years. Fortunately Bill liked this work and stayed with his master for three years before running off only partially trained to earn his living in Pennsylvania. Bill did not mind his shortcomings as a skilled tradesmen and the fact that he could not execute the finer detailed plastering. Instead, he bragged about his speed in working on straight walls and simple jobs. Nor did he object to the fact his master had hired eight other apprentices as a cheap labor source and did not supervise his time after work. Such arrangements were fine with young men like Bill Otter, who used evenings to contract work on his own to earn money to spend on sprees in taverns and dram shops and eventually to pay for his escape.[26]

Indentures bound the children of the very poor to service as a means of public relief for those unable to support a family. In the late 1790s, Exeter, Rhode Island, officials found the unmarried "black woman" Roseanna Brown "not capable of taking care of herself" or her four children. To avoid paying for the children's support, the officials bound out three of Brown's children as servants. (The fourth child was placed under the guardianship of a town resident, suggesting that the boy may have had some legacy left him by a relative.) In 1797, eleven-year-old Susannah was indentured as a servant to one family, who were obligated only to teach her to read. In 1800, officials also bound out twelve-year-old John and six-year-old Isabel. The new master agreed to teach John and Isabel to read and write. He also pledged to provide "sufficient meat, drink and lodging, and comfortable wearing clothes for everyday wear and a decent suit of clothes at the end of said term of time"—age twenty one for John and age eighteen for Isabel. There was no specific trade mentioned in any of these indentures. The assumption was that the children would do the daily labor needed by their masters to sustain a household and a farm. Similar indentures were signed for many other children—African American, Native American, and European American— some as young as four years old.[27] In Philadelphia the Committee of Guardians of the Pennsylvania Abolition Society helped to find indentures to teach African American youths in newly freed families a trade. The committee not only identified a "suitable place" for such youths, thus smoothing over the transition from slavery to freedom, but they also monitored the treatment of these bond servants, ensuring they received the education promised and that they eventually found their way to complete freedom.[28]

By far the greatest number of bound workers were African American slaves. The American Revolution had triggered an emancipation movement that brought freedom to thousands of slaves in both the North and the South. However, the total number of African Americans liberated from bondage was limited. In fact, the enslaved population grew in the South from 676,601 to 1,165,405 between 1790 and 1810. Some of this growth came from additional imports, but most of this growth came from natural increase.[29] Recent studies concerning slave life have emphasized the diversity of the experience over time and space—what it meant to be a slave differed depending on the location and the era. Two factors, however, persisted: Slavery was a repressive institution and slaves were human beings who acted with their own agency. During the years of the early republic, there were four distinct areas of slavery: the North; the Upper South, which included the Chesapeake Bay region; the Lower South, consisting of South Carolina and Georgia; and the frontier, which would include the backcountry and the Mississippi Valley.

Slavery may have been dying in the North, but in 1810 there were almost 30,000 slaves in the region, largely in New York and New Jersey. During the early republic, northern slaves generally resided in the countryside, where African Americans worked as agricultural labor. In the area surrounding New York City in 1800, half of the households in Kings County held slaves, whereas in nearby Richmond a third of the households had slaves, and in Queens County a fifth of the households contained slaves. Almost all of the 800 slaves in Pennsylvania in 1810 lived in the countryside near the border with Maryland.[30] There were few large slaveholdings in the North, leaving the enslaved population relatively dispersed. It was therefore hard for rural African Americans to interact with one another and form lasting relationships. This labor force either resided within the master's household or in an outbuilding on the farm. Few slaves developed into skilled artisans. As soon as a slave gained freedom, which under the various gradual emancipation laws usually occurred after a slave reached a certain age, he or she was likely to move to an urban area where more elaborate African American communities were developing. Northern slavery could be harsh. In 1809, upholsterer Amos Broad was convicted of excessive cruelty to his slave Betty for beating her and forcing her to strip in the winter and wash herself outside in the snow. He also poured hot water into her hand, asking her "Am not I a good doctor to doctor negroes?" when he was displeased with her serving him. Betty, for her part, managed to get the New York Manumission Society to take up her cause and gained freedom for herself and her daughter as part of the legal settlement that came out the case.[31]

The largest number of slaves lived in the Upper South during the early republic. In Virginia alone the slave population grew from about 300,000 to close to 400,000 between 1790 and 1810. By the mid-eighteenth century many slaves in the Upper South had been able to enter relatively stable, long-term relationships—marriages were not technically legal for slaves—with members of the opposite sex. The development of slave families meant procreation, increasing significantly the number of slaves without having to import slaves from overseas. Even during the upheaval of the Revolutionary War the slave population increased at an annual rate of 2 percent a year in the Chesapeake. George Washington saw this demographic growth as a burden, complaining that it was "demonstrably clear" that he had "more working Negros by a full moiety, than can be employed to any advantage in the farming system."[32] Most planters believed the increased numbers were an asset they could turn into a profit by sending the excess slaves where they were needed in the Lower South and the frontier. As many as 115,000 slaves left tidewater Virginia and Maryland between 1790 and 1810. Notwithstanding this forced exodus, the number of slaves still increased. Oddly, if the natural increase derived from the development of slave families, it also led to the breakup of those families as children were sent to distant parts and husband and wife were sometimes separated. Almost every slave family felt the impact of the interstate slave trade. Once a family member was moved (and sometimes the migration would cover hundreds of miles) in all likelihood the family members would never hear from each other again.

Other factors also affected the world of the slave in the Upper South. Although tobacco remained an important crop, it no longer reigned supreme. Instead, owners of slaves diversified their holdings, growing more grain, hiring out slaves to others, and using slave labor to work in the iron foundries. This new economic variety enhanced the geographic mobility of even those slaves who stayed in the region. Whereas in the mid-eighteenth century most male and female slaves in the Chesapeake worked

FIGURE 7–4   Life of George Washington—The Farmer This idyllic illustration shows Washington supervising his slaves during a wheat harvest. The slaves do not appear overworked and seem content. Life for slaves, including those at Mt. Vernon, was much harsher than appears in this picture. Work was often unrelenting, and treatment severe and marked by brutality.

in gangs in the labor-intensive hoeing, weeding, and processing of tobacco, men and women were increasingly separated in the workplace. Slave labor was used in all aspects of the economy, so male slaves could find themselves employed as ploughmen, watermen, skilled artisans, even iron workers at the furnaces that sprang up in the Virginia countryside. Women labored in the fields or were relegated to service within the household. Despite this development, a vibrant and independent African American community developed in the region. Although many slaves lived in outbuildings, or even in the same house as their master, more and more slaves lived in family units, either in single dwellings or duplexes that provided anywhere from 150 to 250 square feet of living space. Few lived in barracklike quarters. Some slaves had beds, but often with little more than "straw and old rags thrown down in the corners and boxed in with boards" with one blanket for covering.[33] Masters provided slaves with minimal food and clothing. Corn was the crucial nutritional source and most meals were some sort of single pot, slow-simmering stew. Masters did not give slaves much meat, although slaves supplemented their fare by hunting and occasionally pilfering domestic animals. Adult slaves were generally provided a suit of clothes each year consisting of a jacket, a pair of pants, two shirts, and a pair of shoes and stockings for men. Women would be furnished with shoes and stockings as well as two shifts and a petticoat. However, it was not unusual to see slaves only partially clad and barefoot. Children often wore little more than a long shirt with no bottoms at all.

Slaves in the Lower South did not live that differently from the slaves in the Upper South. They resided in similar housing, ate much the same food, and wore as little, if not less, clothing. However, there were some significant differences in the composition of the labor force, the work experience, and the lives of slaves. The Revolutionary War had devastated the Lower South and threatened to destroy its slavery. Lower South masters proved themselves resilient in the face of this adversity. They cruelly crushed many of the maroon communities (runaway slave settlements in the backcountry), either reenslaving their inhabitants or pushing them further into the swamps or to Spanish Florida. The masters also reasserted control over their plantations with brute force and heavy use of the lash. Simultaneously they increased slave numbers by imports from the Upper South and from overseas. Although South Carolina banned the international slave trade from 1787 to 1803, between 1782 and 1787, and again between 1803 and 1807, South Carolina imported 90,000 slaves. Many of these newcomers were from Africa. Combined with natural increase, South Carolina's slave population in 1810 stood at 196,365 and Georgia's a staggering 105,218 in 1810.[34] With this labor force masters resuscitated the rice trade, expanding exports even beyond prerevolutionary highs, and began to grow cotton in greater quantities.

This demographic growth had profound implications for the daily life and work of slaves in the Lower South. Coastal regions of South Carolina and Georgia became more heavily African American with three-quarters of the population enslaved. Although whites ruled supreme, they could not closely supervise their slaves on a daily basis. In the low country, work was organized on the task system. Each slave performed a certain amount of labor each day. Once he or she finished, the slave could use the time as he or she pleased. As one observer explained in the 1790s, after slaves completed the assigned labor they were "at liberty to cultivate for themselves as much land as they choose."[35] Slaves not only tended a garden and raised cash crops for themselves, they also hunted and fished. Taken together these activities allowed low country slaves to add food to their meals and to obtain some money to purchase a few goods. The lack of supervision also allowed slaves to develop a certain degree of autonomy in their personal lives, enhancing the opportunity to develop a unique African American culture. The fact that tens of thousands of African slaves joined the labor force only enhanced the African content of that culture.

The expansion of slavery in South Carolina and Georgia included movement to the backcountry. In 1760, only about 10 percent of South Carolina's slaves lived out of the low country; in 1810, about half of the state's slaves had been moved beyond the coastal regions. This migration was a part of a larger shift of slaves to the West and across the Appalachians. Many of the backcountry slaves in South Carolina and Georgia were put to work to grow the short staple cotton that Eli Whitney's cotton gin had made more profitable. Although the upcountry plantations were smaller than the low country plantations, they found the gang labor system more conducive to cotton agriculture. This form of labor organization and the primitive nature of these new plantations left slaves with less control over their daily lives. The dispersed slave population meant less interaction with large numbers of other African Americans. Slaves who were moved farther west were more isolated. Kentucky went from having 12,430 slaves in 1790 to 80,561 in 1810. The number of Tennessee slaves grew in the same period from 3,417 to 44,528. Slaves, many of them recent African imports, came up the Mississippi from New Orleans or overland from Florida, settling in the Mississippi Territory. The frontier slaves spent their first years in a new settlement in the backbreaking labor of clearing land and beginning commercial agriculture. However, they also spent time herding cattle and working more closely with their masters. Their lives might not have been as enriched by an autonomous African American culture as the slaves on the Atlantic Coast, but they were not yet so strictly confined to the cotton field.

Slaves found means to oppose the institution that bound them. Just by molding some aspects of their own lives, whether it be in building a house or how they buried their dead, African Americans asserted an identity in opposition to their masters. Slaves also committed more overt acts of resistance, including sabotage of work and running away. Some African Americans, armed in part by the revolutionary rhetoric of the age, plotted to overthrow the system that oppressed them. In 1800 a skilled blacksmith and Virginia slave named Gabriel, who often hired out his own time, planned to march an army of supporters on Richmond, seize Governor James Monroe, and demand liberty for the slaves. A late August thunderstorm and the loose tongues of some informants foiled the conspiracy. Gabriel and twenty-six others were executed. As one insurgent explained at his trial: "I have nothing more to offer than what General Washington would have had to offer, had he been taken by the British and put to trial."

He continued: "I have adventured my life in endeavouring to obtain the liberty of my countrymen, and am a willing sacrifice in their cause."[36]

Religion

Much to Jefferson's chagrin, many common Americans—farmers, mechanics, laborers, and even slaves—increasingly began to turn to evangelical religion during the early republic. This development was ironic because Jefferson believed that one of the greatest achievements of the American Revolution was the guarantee of freedom of religion. He viewed the Virginia Statute for Religious Freedom in 1785, which he wrote, as crucial in this development and hailed it as the authoritative statement on the separation of church and state. Jefferson was a gentleman deist born out of an Enlightenment that emphasized a rational approach to religion. The evangelicals were common folk diehard Christians born out of a religious revival that emphasized emotion and one's personal experience with God. Jefferson hoped that disestablishing the Anglican or, as it came to be known in the United States, the Episcopal Church would create a marketplace of religious ideas that would lead inevitably to the spread of deism—a belief in the deity unattached to the "superstitions" of the Bible. The evangelicals assumed that without the shackles of a state-supported church, the "will of God" would prevail and their revival could sweep through American society unabated.

The Virginia Statute for Religious Freedom reflected Jefferson's deism. The law asserted free will by beginning "that Almighty God hath created the mind free," and implied, following the standard notions of deism, that once God created man that He did not intrude in worldly affairs. Any effort to influence religion using "temporal punishments or burthens, or by civil incapacitations, tend only to beget habits of hypocrisy and meanness" and was "a departure from the plan of the Holy author of our religion." Jefferson wrote into the law his belief "that our civil rights have no dependance on our religious opinions, any more than our opinions in physics or geometry." Further emphasizing the connection between religious freedom and the Enlightenment, the law expressed faith "that truth is great and will prevail if left to herself." Jefferson hoped, in other words, that free enquiry concerning religion would lead to the widespread acceptance of reason. Confident of the rational outcome, Jefferson wrote into the law a total disengagement between church and state by declaring

> that no man shall be compelled to frequent or support any religious worship, place, or ministry whatsoever, nor shall be enforced, restrained, molested, or burthened in his body or goods, nor shall otherwise suffer, on account of his religious opinions

or belief; but that all men shall be free to profess, and by argument to maintain, their opinions in matters of religion, and that the same shall in no wise diminish, enlarge, or affect their civil capacities.[37]

Passage of the law depended on religious dissenters, mainly Presbyterians, Lutherans, and Baptists. As early as 1776 the majority of Virginians no longer belonged to the Anglican Church. Madison explained in 1788 that most people knew "that a religious establishment wd. have taken place in that State, if the legislative majority had found as they expected, a majority of the people in favor of the measure." Instead, dissenters argued for a release from "a long night of ecclesiastical bondage" and wished that "all church establishments might be pulled down, and every tax upon conscience and private judgement abolished." Echoing Jefferson to some extent, these groups held to the idea that "each individual" would be "left to rise or sink by his own merit and the general laws of the land." Some groups went so far as to decry any establishment of the "Christian religion," claiming that there was no justification for establishing Christianity that could not "be pleaded, with equal propriety, for establishing the tenets of Mohammed by those who believe the Alcoran." Concern with preference of one religion over another would be impossible "without erecting a chair of infallibility, which would lead us back to the Church of Rome."[38]

Not all Americans bought into this idea of religious freedom. Opponents to complete separation of church and state delayed Virginia's law for almost a decade; Jefferson penned the legislation in 1777 and it did not become law until 1786. Although they accepted the idea of religious toleration, several New England states retained official support for a religious establishment for the Congregational church. New Hampshire did not abolish tax-supported churches until 1818; Connecticut kept its established church until 1819. Maine embraced religious freedom in 1820 when it separated as a state from Massachusetts. Massachusetts, in turn, provided state support for the Congregational church until 1833. Other states retained a connection between the state and religion. South Carolina established "the Christian Protestant religion" and then offered a set of criteria defining acceptable Protestant doctrine. Several New England states, North Carolina, Maryland, and Delaware, had a "declaration of a belief in the Christian religion" required for state officials. North Carolina's constitution insisted:

> That no person, who shall deny the being of God or the truth of the Protestant religion, or the divine authority of either of the Old or New Testaments, or who shall hold religious principles incompatible with the freedom and safety of the State, shall be capable of holding any office or place of trust or profit in the civil department within this State.[39]

Established churches historically had been seen as a means of tying together a corporate society. In the more egalitarian world created by the American Revolution, however, religion became a divisive force. The authors of the Constitution, despite their otherwise aristocratic pretensions, therefore avoided religion in the document that emerged from the Philadelphia Convention. They included one reference to religion that stated "no religious test or qualification shall ever be annexed to any oath of office under the authority of the United States." Some Antifederalists attacked the Constitution as antireligious and chided the Founding Fathers for failing to ensure that the United States would be a Christian republic. Most Antifederalists took the opposite tack and believed that the document did not go far enough and wanted a constitutional separation of church and state. The First Amendment attempted to reassure this larger criticism by declaring "Congress shall make no law respecting an establishment of religion, or prohibiting the free exercise thereof."

By the 1790s and early 1800s, as new states avoided any hint of establishing religion, Jefferson's marketplace of ideas on religion came to predominate. Historians usually emphasize the religious revivals that occurred in the 1740s—the First Great Awakening—and the early nineteenth century—the Second Great Awakening. Closer examination of religion in the years in between reveals a persistent spread of evangelicalism that makes it difficult to distinguish between the two awakenings. Although some common people became deists, many more turned to this evangelical revival. If ideas about religion were being sold in the marketplace, apparently the evangelicals had the more attractive product.

The two biggest popularizers of deism were Ethan Allen and Tom Paine. One came from the frontier; the other was a mechanic turned international revolutionary. Leader of the Green Mountain Boys, Revolutionary War leader, and Vermont speculator and settler, Allen published *Reason the Only Oracle of God* in 1784. He denied the divine origin of the scriptures and argued that the Bible was little more than a compendium of scattered documents collected together without divine inspiration. Allen, like all good deists, asserted that there was a God, but that He could only be known through nature and reason. Morality did "not derive its nature from books, but from the fitness of things." Any book that teaches morality, even if it was the "Alkoran," was acceptable. In other words, "The knowledge" of morality and religion "as well as all other sciences, is acquired from reason and experience." Ultimately truth, reason, and nature were the best ways to understand God and all Creation.[40] Tom Paine published his thoughts on religion in the *Age of Reason* in 1794. Paine declared in his own succinct style: "I believe in one God, and no more." He went on to assert his commitment to "the equality of man" and exclaimed "that religious duties consist in doing justice, loving mercy, and endeavoring to make our fellow-creatures happy." Paine declared that all organized religion was balderdash. He proclaimed that he did "not believe in the creed professed by the Jewish Church, by the Roman Church, by the Greek Church, by the Turkish Church, by the Protestant Church, nor by any church that I know of" and boldly avowed "My own mind is my own church." He viewed "All national institutions of churches, whether Jewish, Christian or Turkish" as "no other than human inventions, set up to terrify and enslave mankind, and monopolize power and profit."[41] Both Paine and Allen were widely read. Some embraced their ideas. Many more rejected and condemned them.

The great wave of popular religion that had begun in the mid-eighteenth century continued to swell in the years after the Revolutionary War. The shouts and hollers—and those inspired by revival often cried out at the top of their lungs—of evangelical religion drowned out the rational discourse of deism. Democracy and Christianity combined to form a powerful movement that swept all before it. This religion was optimistic. There was no sense of limitations. Rather, religious enthusiasts dreamed of a new social and political order that promised at least a secular millennium if not the actual second coming of Christ. Both deism and evangelicalism tore down the old church authority; both centered on the individual; both were egalitarian. But the revival offered a sense of inspiration and emotional satisfaction with which deism could not compete.

Like deism, evangelicalism was antiauthoritarian. This movement attacked church hierarchies and refused to accept the authority of the clergy based simply on training and education. At times these attacks became so shrill that they reflected class antagonism. One evangelical layman in 1799 mocked "these great MEN OF RENOWN" who put a "D. D." or a "REV." by their name and felt that they "must be maintained like Princes and addressed as gods." Defenders of the traditional church recognized the source of this antagonism. During the 1790s Episcopalian Devereux Jarratt complained of "our high republican times" and lamented a revivalism "under the supreme control of tinkers and tailors, weavers, shoemakers, and country mechanics of all kinds." A few years later another religious conservative groused about the "unrestrained freedom" that had swept the Ohio Valley, making it a "hot-bed of every extravagance of opinion and practice." Untrained itinerants and others "think themselves called to God to preach the gospel, and to go on, relying on their inward call, and neglecting almost every ministerial qualification required in the sacred Scriptures." Evangelicals rejected the past as the fountain of wisdom and turned inward, empowering the ordinary person to open his or her own direct communication with God.[42]

Free will became central to this new sense of faith, and, just as with Jefferson's more rational approach, included a commitment to the separation of the church and state. The hymn "Freedom of the Human Will," published in 1805, had elements that any deist might accept. "Know then that every soul is free/ To choose his life and what he'll be" and the assertion that "Freedom and reason make us men." But if man had freedom to choose, and here deists would disagree, he needed to choose God and evangelical religion:

> Those that despise grow harder still;
> Those that adhere he turns their will;
> and thus despisers sink to hell,
> While those that hear, in glory dwell.[43]

Deists and evangelicals also shared a commitment to equality. Indeed, revivalists often drew on the Enlightenment's language to express their egalitarianism. Lorenzo Dow, an itinerant and colorful Methodist preacher known for his long, flowing hair and emotional sermons, wrote that "if all men are 'BORN EQUAL,' and endowed with unalienable RIGHTS by their CREATOR, in the blessings of life, liberty, and the pursuit of happiness"— words borrowed from Jefferson—"then there can be no just reason, as a cause, why he may or should not think, and judge, and act for himself in matters of religion, opinion, and private judgement." If Dow could sometimes sound like a product of the "Age of Inquiry," however, he was also convinced that it was an "Age of Wonders" in which God worked in mysterious and even magical ways. When push came to shove, man's rationality and equal freedom of choice led to a greater dedication to the word of God.[44]

Evangelical religion in the early republic had four important assets with which deism could not compete: a basis in popular culture; emotional content; entertainment value; and organization. First, the revival built on the Bible and popular beliefs deeply imbedded in Anglo-American culture. Almost every family owned a Bible. In fact, the Bible continued as the best-selling book throughout the period and was the basis of most people's literacy. Deists like Allen and Paine denied the divine origin of the Bible. This position may have seemed rational to a philosophe of the Enlightenment, but it ran counter to every "truth" ingrained in Protestant Americans from infancy to death. Armed with the Bible and the belief that anyone could and should read and interpret the Bible on his own, evangelicals preached a gospel of hope and equality. Evangelicals also had an interest in the magical and supernatural. Seers and visionaries had long been a part of Anglo-American culture, surfacing during the English Civil Wars and in the Salem witch trials of 1692. Evangelical religion allowed similar practices to appear in the name of religion. At the most extreme fringes of the revival were a group of prophets who claimed divine revelation and who spoke of visions and apparitions. Eliza Thomas from Connecticut published a chapbook in 1800 describing a visit from the ghost of an old friend who told her about "the dreadful and lamentable situation of many of the people of this Country;—they are deluded;—believing that God is not a being who will punish the transgressions of their children."[45] Self-created prophets like Thomas may have been on the periphery of the evangelical movement, but an element of their ideas crept into the activities of many itinerants. Methodist Freeborn Garrettson knew "that both sleeping and waking, things of a divine nature have been revealed to" him.[46] Lorenzo Dow, as one commentator put it, included in his "weapons against Beelzebub . . . providential interpositions, wondrous disasters, touching sentiments, miraculous escapes." Even more mainstream Methodists and Baptists, if there was such a thing as mainstream in this period, used faith healing and miracles to garner notoriety.[47]

Such extravagant behavior reminds us that evangelical religion played to the emotions, something that deism could not do. By definition, deism was the result of rational thought. The revival allowed common folk a release of pent-up psychological energy. Itinerant evangelical Henry Alline was overwhelmed by God's love, "ravished with a divine ecstasy beyond any doubts or fears, or thoughts of being then deceived."[48] Dow at times would be "flung" into "spasms like convulsions," shaking "his constitution to the centre." One commentator in Tennessee in 1810 described "an exercise called the *jirks*" in which an individual overcome by the power of religion was "deprived of his own power, and sometimes his speech." The subject was "thus taken with an irresistible force, altogether off his feet and dashed to the ground or floor, and from one place to another, sometimes hours together." People struck with the "*jirks*" would laugh uncontrollably or screech, holler, shout, and dance.[49]

Revivals also became a form of popular amusement. As Methodist leader James Snowden admitted, the "expectation of being entertained with something new, together with the novelty of the scene" had "drawn forth the multitude."[50] Some evangelicals traveled incredible distances bringing the word of God to community after community. Their visits became special occasions for neighbors to gather and feel the spirit of the Lord. A part of the attraction was to watch famous itinerants like Dow, who spoke at over five hundred meetings in 1804 and even toured the

British Isles in 1807, and whose wild eyes and gravelly voice could be riveting. But even local evangelicals had their appeal. For over two decades Johnny Edwards, a Welsh immigrant and artisan (not to be confused with the famous eighteenth-century minister, Jonathan Edwards), would take to the street corners of early nineteenth-century New York City to decry vice, sin, drinking, worldly possessions, and "all manner of wickedness." Occasionally the crowds that gathered to hear him would grow rowdy, but most of the time he was allowed to rant as he pleased to the mild amusement of the onlookers.[51] Itinerants worked both the city and the countryside. By 1800 New York had five Methodist chapels and the city experienced an outdoor revival led by English evangelical Dorothy Ripley and Edwards in 1810. But revivals had their biggest impact in the countryside where there developed a peculiar American tradition—the camp meeting. Country folk would travel many miles to congregate for several days of preaching and religious experience in the open or under huge tents. Some scholars point to the great Cane Ridge meeting in Kentucky in August 1801 as the beginning of this movement. But the camp meeting was merely an extended form of the outdoor preaching practiced by revivalists since the 1740s. The camp meetings often had special sections for those whose souls were ready to be transformed by religious experience, a preplanned program of preachers, and even appointed guards to control any who misbehaved. These guards were unconcerned with the shouts and screams of converts, or the lamentations of self-professed sinners whose divinely inspired clamor created a "roar of Niagara" or whose bodily contortions and frenzied histrionics made them fall "as if a battery of a thousand guns had been opened upon them."[52] The guards were after rowdy interlopers or people drinking, gambling, or possibly engaging in sexual activity. Revivalists used a plain language, sarcasm, and biting humor to appeal to the common people. Combined with a developing folk religious music and extensive religious publications, evangelicals provided a winning formula.

As can be seen in the camp meetings and the publishing of religious tracts, evangelicals were well organized despite denominational variety. This organization was another advantage they had over deists. Methodists like Francis Asbury prided themselves in having a "REGULAR" system with circuits, districts, and conferences, with appointed preachers, presiding elders, and bishops. This organizational framework allowed all Methodists across North America to have something in common. As Snowden exclaimed, "If we search the continent at large where shall we find a people so widely extended whose laws, whose regulations are so universally the same, and which bear so equally upon all."[53] As a result, between

1770 and 1820, American Methodism grew from fewer than 1,000 members to over 250,000. The Baptists grew tenfold in the decades after the Revolutionary War. At first they were loosely organized, but gradually they developed local associations, state conventions, and missionary societies. By 1814, when the first national Baptist Convention met in Philadelphia, the Baptists had two thousand churches, sixteen hundred ministers, and one hundred associations.[54]

Evangelical groups spread the gospel across social, economic, ethnic, and even racial lines. In particular, the Baptists and Methodists initially included an appeal to African Americans, both slave and free. This effort had profound ramifications as African Americans turned to Christianity in great numbers, becoming more American than African in the process. In the nineteenth century both denominations would turn their backs to racial equality and African Americans would create their own separate Baptist and Methodist churches. However, in the early years of the American republic evangelical religion became a centerpiece for the call of racial equality and even abolition.

The new society that emerged by 1800 was a far different place than the rational yeoman republic imagined by Jefferson. Farmers, mechanics, laborers, and slaves moved in unexpected directions. Armed with Jeffersonian republican rhetoric they were creating a new world of their own. Expansion to the West became crucial to this development.

Endnotes

1. Thomas Jefferson to John Jay, Aug. 23, 1785, Thomas Jefferson Papers Series I, General Correspondence, 1651–1827, Digital Archives, Library of Congress, Image 193.
2. Thomas Jefferson to James Jay, Apr. 7, 1809, Thomas Jefferson Papers Series I, General Correspondence, 1651–1827, Digital Archives, Library of Congress, Image 1055.
3. The reference to Thomas Springer, and his wife, Elizabeth, here and below comes from Barbara Clarke Smith, *After the Revolution: The Smithsonian History of Everyday Life in the Eighteenth Century* (New York: Random House, 1985), 43–86.
4. Christopher Clark, *The Roots of Rural Capitalism: Western Massachusetts, 1780–1860* (Ithaca, N.Y.: Cornell University Press, 1990), 50–51.
5. Jack Larkin, *The Reshaping of Everyday Life: 1790–1840* (New York: Harper and Row, 1988), 105–48.
6. Thomas Jefferson to Thomas Digges, June 19, 1788, Thomas Jefferson Papers Series I, General Correspondence, 1651–1827, Digital Archives, Library of Congress, Image 570.
7. Clark, *The Roots of Rural Capitalism*, 51–53.
8. Clark, *The Roots of Rural Capitalism*, 61–62.
9. Robert V. Wells, *Revolutions in American's Lives: A Demographic Perspective on the History of Americans, Their Families, and Their Society* (Westport, Conn.: Greenwood, 1982), 92.

10. For these comments see Chapter 4. Thomas Jefferson to John Jay, Aug. 23, 1785, Thomas Jefferson Papers Series 1, General Correspondence, 1651–1827, Digital Archives, Library of Congress, Image 193; and Merrill D. Peterson, ed., *The Portable Thomas Jefferson* (New York: Penguin, 1975), 217.

11. Thomas Jefferson to John Lithgow, Jan. 4, 1805, Thomas Jefferson Papers Series 1, General Correspondence, 1651–1827, Digital Archives, Library of Congress, Image 154.

12. John Treat Irving, *Oration Delivered on the 4th of July, 1809, before the Tammany Society* (New York: 1809).

13. Quoted in Larkin, *The Reshaping of Everyday Life,* 182–83.

14. Paul A. Gilje and Howard B. Rock, eds., *Keepers of the Revolution: New Yorkers at Work* (Ithaca, N.Y.: Cornell University Press, 1992), 127. Originally in Stephen Allen, "The Memoirs of Stephen Allen," typescript, BV Allen, Stephen, New-York Historical Society.

15. John R. Commons, et al., eds., *A Documentary History of American Industrial Society,* 10 vols. (Cleveland, Ohio: Arthur H. Clark, 1910), 3: 68.

16. Quoted in Ronald Schultz, *The Republic of Labor: Philadelphia Artisans and the Politics of Class, 1720–1830* (New York: Oxford University Press, 1993), 162.

17. Commons, et al., eds., *A Documentary History of American Industrial Society,* 3: 68, 202, 205.

18. Commons, et al., eds., *A Documentary History of American Industrial Society,* 3: 228.

19. Quoted in Rosalind Remer, *Printers and Men of Capital: Philadelphia Book Publishers in the New Republic* (Philadelphia: University of Pennsylvania Press, 1996), 49. Originally in James Carey to Mathew Carey, Dec. 1, 1792, Incoming Correspondence, Lea and Febiger Collection (Coll 227B), Historical Society of Pennsylvania.

20. David J. Saposs, "Colonial and Federal Beginnings (to 1827)," in John R. Commons, et al., *History of Labour in the United States,* 4 vols. (New York: Macmillan, 1918), 1: 110–11.

21. *New York Spectator,* Oct. 23, 1802; *New York Evening Post,* Oct. 21, 1802. See also Paul A. Gilje, *The Road to Mobocracy: Popular Disorder in New York City, 1763–1834* (Chapel Hill: University of North Carolina Press, 1987), 182–83.

22. Quoted in Ruth Wallis Herndon, *Unwelcome Americans: Living on the Margin in Early New England* (Philadelphia: University of Pennsylvania Press, 2001), 105.

23. Herndon, *Unwelcome Americans,* 185–86.

24. Charles Christian, *A Brief Treatise on the Police of the City of New York* (New York: Southwick & Pelsue, 1812), 28–29.

25. Sharon V. Salinger, *"To Serve Well and Faithfully": Labor and Indentured Servants in Pennsylvania, 1682–1800* (Cambridge: Cambridge University Press, 1987), 180–81; *New York Daily Advertiser,* Sept. 1, 1786.

26. William Otter, *History of My Own Times,* Richard B. Stott, ed. (Ithaca, N.Y.: Cornell University Press), 36–38.

27. Quoted in Herndon, *Unwelcome Americans,* 44–47.

28. Quoted in Gary B. Nash, *Forging Freedom: The Formation of Philadelphia's Black Community, 1720–1840* (Cambridge: Harvard University Press, 1988), 158–61.

29. Ira Berlin, *Many Thousands Gone: The First Two Centuries of Slavery in America* (Cambridge: Harvard University Press, 1998), 369–70.

30. Berlin, *Many Thousands Gone,* 237.

31. Amos Broad, *The Trial of Amos Broad and His Wife on Three Several Indictments for Assaulting and Beating Betty, a Slave, and . . . Sarah, Aged Three Years: to Which Is Added,*

the Motion of Counsel in Mr. Broad's Behalf . . . and the Reply of Mr. Sampson . . . (New York: Henry C. Southwick, 1809).

32. Quoted in Berlin, *Many Thousands Gone,* 264.

33. Quoted in Philip D. Morgan, *Slave Counterpoint: Black Culture in the Eighteenth-Century Chesapeake and Low Country* (Chapel Hill: University of North Carolina Press, 1998), 114.

34. Berlin, *Many Thousands Gone,* 303–10, 370.

35. Quoted in Morgan, *Slave Counterpoint,* 186.

36. Quoted in Douglas R. Egerton, *Gabriel's Rebellion: The Virginia Slave Conspiracies of 1800 and 1802* (Chapel Hill: University of North Carolina Press, 1993), 102.

37. Peterson, ed., *The Portable Thomas Jefferson,* 251–53.

38. Robert A. Rutland, et al., eds., *The Papers of James Madison,* 17 vols. (Chicago and Charlottesville: University of Chicago and University Press of Virginia, 1962–1991), 11: 298. Also quoted in Frank Lambert, *The Founding Fathers and the Place of Religion in America* (Princeton: Princeton University Press, 2003), 209–10, 227–28.

39. Quoted in Lambert, *The Founding Fathers,* 249–51.

40. Ethan Allen, *Reason the Only Oracle of Man, or a Compenduous System of Natural Religion . . .* (Bennington, Vt.: Haswell and Russell, 1784).

41. Thomas Paine, *The Age of Reason, Being An Investigation of True and Fabulous Theology* (Paris: Barrois, 1794), 2–3.

42. Quoted in Nathan O. Hatch, *The Democratization of American Christianity* (New Haven: Yale University Press, 1989), 44, 21.

43. Quoted in Hatch, *The Democratization of American Christianity,* 231–32.

44. Quoted in Hatch, *The Democratization of American Christianity,* 37.

45. Quoted in Susan Juster, *Doomsayers: Anglo-American Prophecy in the Age of Revolution* (Philadelphia: University of Pennsylvania Press, 2003), 61.

46. Quoted in Hatch, *The Democratization of American Christianity,* 10.

47. Quoted in Hatch, *The Democratization of American Christianity,* 40.

48. Quoted in Hatch, *The Democratization of American Christianity,* 10.

49. Quoted in Juster, *Doomsayers,* 108, 105.

50. Quoted in Dee E. Andrews, *The Methodists and Revolutionary America: The Shaping of an Evangelical Culture* (Princeton: Princeton University Press, 2000), 238–39.

51. Quoted in Gilje, *The Road to Mobocracy,* 214.

52. Quoted in Stephen Aron, *How the West Was Lost: The Transformation of Kentucky from Daniel Boone to Henry Clay* (Baltimore: Johns Hopkins University Press, 1996), 176.

53. Quoted in Andrews, *The Methodists,* 238.

54. Hatch, *The Democratization of American Christianity,* 94.

Frontier Expansion

Speculation and Land Development

Louisiana

"Civilizing" Native Americans

Speculation and Land Development

Thomas Jefferson believed that the future of America lay in the West. As long as there was land on the frontier his republic would be safe. European Americans would continue to move to new lands and guarantee the expansion of an independent yeomanry for generations. Seizing a unique opportunity in 1803, Jefferson purchased the Louisiana Territory, doubling the size of the republic and ensuring, from Jefferson's perspective, that the United States would remain an agrarian nation for one thousand years. Most Americans viewed the Native Americans who stood in the path of this expansion as a dying race who would be best served by removal beyond the frontier. There the Indians could either gain time to adjust to "civilization" or somehow fade away.

Jefferson misunderstood the West. The frontier was not simply a verdant paradise where farmers could easily establish their independence. Instead, it was a contested ground that helped establish the peculiar nature of American capitalism. Federalists and Republicans argued over how to guide settlement. Speculators sought to engross millions of acres. Poor people sought to settle the land any way they could—sometimes with a title from the government or a speculator, and sometimes by squatting and claiming the land as their own. Nor did the land itself easily conform to the will of pioneers. Parts of the Louisiana Territory would become farmland in less than one hundred years; much of it is sparsely settled to this day. Native Americans also contested Jefferson's vision for the frontier. Some Indians surrendered to the assault on their world and lived on the margins of European American society. Others, like Handsome Lake among the Seneca and Tenskwatawa (also known as the Prophet) among the Shawnee, reenergized their culture through religion. Military resistance continued as well: In the opening decade of the nineteenth century, Native Americans threatened to unite under the leadership of Tecumseh and drive whites back across the Appalachians.

Native American ownership and occupation of the land was only the most visible obstacle to frontier expansion. Before European Americans settled any new land there was a debate over the very nature of frontier society. Federalists hoped to regulate growth, whereas the Jeffersonians wanted to allow the individual greater freedom to determine where and how he would establish his own farm. Underpinning Federalist ideas was a negative view of the first pioneers, who seemed more savage than civilized. Benjamin Rush in 1786 wrote that "the *first* settler in the woods is generally a man who has outlived his credit or fortune in the cultivated parts of the State." He was more Indian than white, planting small fields of corn and depending on hunting and fishing. "He loves spirituous liquors, and he eats, drinks and sleeps in dirt and rags in his little cabin." As the settlement expanded around him, he grew discontented. Wild animals began to disappear and the pioneer was forced to raise domestic animals for subsistence. But this settler did not build fences and his cattle trampled on his neighbors' grain, creating conflict. He opposed civil order because "Above all, he revolts against the operation of laws" and "He cannot bear to surrender up a single natural right for all the benefits of government." Soon enough he retreated to the woods, starting the process over again. Federalists hoped to skip this first stage of development and any intermediary stages, and go straight to a "species of settler" who was "a man of property and good character" with well-mended fences, grew a variety of crops, and "in proportion as he encreases in wealth, he values the protection of laws: hence he punctually pays his taxes towards the support of government."[1]

The Federalist hope for the West can best be seen by the effort to bring order and regularity to the Ohio country. The Northwest Ordinances of the 1780s set up a framework to survey the land in grids, starting from the east and moving gradually west, with a local government organized from the top down. Federalist investors formed the Ohio Company of Associates in 1786, which purchased with Continental certificates earned through military service over fifteen million acres from Congress in 1787 and established Marietta, the first legal town in Ohio, in 1788. Their plan was to model "the western country" after the "morrals, religion, and policy" of the "eastern states" and see "the whole territory of the United States settled by an enlightened people, and continued under one extended government."

FIGURE 8–1 **Marietta Courthouse** The Federalist hopes of bringing an orderly settlement to the West can be seen in the courthouse they built in frontier Marietta, Ohio in 1789. In a world of shacks and log cabins, this balanced and massive structure was to symbolize the importance of government. These hopes, however, were shattered by the helter-skelter scramble for land by speculators and squatters, and the absence of government control supported by Republicans.

They hoped to create an urbane West that would become "the garden of the universe, the center of wealth, a place destined to be the heart of a great Empire," where each person would know their place in a set hierarchy.[2] During the 1790s the Ohio Company, led by men who had served as Continental officers during the Revolutionary War, combined with Federalist office holders like Governor Arthur St. Clair, to use their economic clout and political leverage to create their vision of a well-ordered community in the region immediately surrounding Marietta.

Jeffersonian Republicans challenged this vision by insisting on local control and pursuit of self-interest. Embracing the market, men like Nathaniel Massie centered their activities in the fertile Scioto Valley, which Congress had designated in 1791 as the Virginia Military Tract. Land here could be obtained with a warrant that had been issued by the State of Virginia in lieu of pay for serving in the army during the Revolutionary War. Massie purchased, either directly or through agents, warrants for over 75,000 acres. He then resold the land in small parcels to settlers, creating a more helter-skelter frontier. Other Republicans did the same, sometimes even selling land to which they did not have legal title. As John Cleves Symmes, who repeatedly sold land he did not own, explained, "As an

American" he had "the right of Adam to the soil . . . founded in prior occupancy." Like Jefferson, these men believed that the common farmer could be trusted to do the right thing—choose Massie and his cronies as the natural leaders of their society. Republicans vehemently denounced the Federalist territorial administration. One Ohio Jeffersonian, Michael Baldwin, declared in 1802 that the territorial government was "aristocratic in its principles, and oppressive and partial in its administration." Advocating statehood, Baldwin proclaimed that "all power" should be derived "from the people" because they were "fully competent to govern themselves." The people, after all, were "the only proper judges of their own interests and their own concerns."[3] Ohio statehood in 1803 marked a defeat for the Federalist dreams for an ordered frontier and a political triumph for the Republicans. This victory, however, was somewhat hollow. The frontier as a land of individuals scrambling to get ahead did not really fit either the Federalist model of ordered settlement from the top down nor the Jeffersonian paradigm of natural aristocrats selected by the voice of the people.

The activities of the Ohio Company of Associates, and individuals like Massie and Symmes, suggests how important land speculation was to the development of the American West in the early republic. Many Americans during the 1790s and early 1800s viewed this land speculation as the perfect investment. Control of thousands, even millions, of acres could be a ticket to life as a landed gentleman. Expectations of easy wealth and elevated status, however, were often mere pipe dreams that led to some spectacular financial implosions. No one soared as high, nor fell as low, as the great financier of the American Revolution, Robert Morris. In the early 1780s Morris's personal credit kept the finances of the United States afloat. A decade later Morris was on the edge of financial ruin after failing to corner the French tobacco market. By 1800 Morris was languishing in debtor's prison. After the tobacco fiasco, Morris might have turned his energies to the world of trade where his experience and connections would work to his advantage. Morris had bigger aspirations and hoped to restore his fortune through land speculation on a grand scale. During the 1790s Morris bought millions of acres in New York, hundreds of thousands of acres in Pennsylvania and large holdings in several other states. He also invested heavily, and poorly, in city lots in the new capital of the District of Columbia and formed, with two other partners, the North American Land Company in 1795 that claimed to control six million acres spread across Pennsylvania, Virginia, North Carolina, South Carolina, Kentucky, and Georgia (over two million acres in this state alone). All of this land could have made Morris fabulously wealthy. Instead, it bankrupted him. The trick to land speculation was to buy land and then sell it quickly for a profit. Although this operation sounds simple enough, the intricate web of detail of Morris's wheeling and dealing boggles the mind. Complicating the process were multiple partnerships, countersigned notes, obtaining title from Native Americans, state and federal requirements, surveying costs, legal and commission fees, installment payments, interest, overlapping claims, and a host of other difficulties impossible to foresee. Not even the form of payment was stable. Contracts often stipulated the price of land in specific currencies, bonds, stocks, and bank notes—all of which could fluctuate between the time when a deal was made and final payment was due. Morris would purchase land from speculators, as well as state and federal governments, then sell it to other speculators, who in turn would sell it to yet other speculators in a dizzying spiral of obligations and debt. Most of the purchasers would not have cash in hand. They hoped to pay off their installments with the profits from the resale. When things went right, and amazingly they sometimes did go right, huge profits could be reaped. Morris made $116,128 by selling a million acres in upstate New York to English investors. But disaster always loomed on the horizon. In 1792 Morris mortgaged some of his New York land to raise capital. He then sold some of the mortgaged land in what he called an "innocent transaction," setting off a series of legal suits in 1795. Simultaneously, creditors began to press him for payment on notes he signed for partners, for payment on land in contracts, and for failure to adequately develop the city lots in the District of Columbia. The house of cards began to tumble. In 1797 Morris had to lock himself in his own home to escape the sheriff—the law prevented the sheriff from entering a private abode to seize a bankrupt—before surrendering himself to debtor's prison. With his financial situation hopelessly beyond repair, Morris took advantage of the Federalist bankruptcy law of 1801 to get out of prison. All of his lands were turned over to his creditors and the final accounting showed he owed almost $3 million.

Morris's speculations at times flirted on the edges of legality, but generally they remained within the bounds of law. Other speculations were outright swindles. Perhaps the biggest scam of the early republican era was the Yazoo controversy. During the 1790s Georgia continued its claim to the Yazoo lands, that area between the western border of the current State of Georgia and the Mississippi River. Several powerful Indian tribes—the Creeks, Choctaws, and Cherokees among them—lived in the area, and until 1795 Spain disputed much of the territory. Undeterred by such niceties of possession, on January 7, 1795, the Georgia legislature sold thirty-five million acres of the Yazoo lands to a group of four land companies, including the Georgia Mississippi Company, for $500,000. All but one member of the Georgia state legislature received a bribe in the process. Like all good land speculators, the new owners of the Yazoo planned to unload their real estate. Over the course of the next year they found a variety of buyers, the largest of which was the New England Mississippi Land Company, which bought eleven million acres for $1,138,000, providing a 650 percent profit for the Georgian Yazoo owners. The problem was that in the meantime a popular movement headed by Jeffersonian politician James Jackson created an outcry that led to a repeal of the initial sale by the Georgia legislature. As the preamble to the repeal legislation proclaimed, the original sale violated "democratical" principles of a "government founded on equality of rights" and threatened to create a "destructive aristocracy" through "proprietary grants or monopolies in favor of a few."[4] The dispute did not end there. The New England Mississippi Land Company and other secondhand purchasers claimed that they were innocent victims, even if the initial sale had been corrupt. Debates and litigation over the Yazoo lands continued for well over a decade, complicated by the fact that the U.S. government took over Georgia's western land claims in 1802. The case went to the Supreme Court (*Fletcher v. Peck,* 1810), which invalidated the repeal, asserting that the Georgia legislature violated the Constitution's provision against repudiating "the Obligation of Contracts." In 1814, Congress offered $5 million in compensation for the secondhand purchasers of Yazoo real estate, providing the investors in the New England Mississippi Land Company, and others, with a nice windfall.

Ultimately the profits from speculation were supposed to come from the settlement of the land by farmers willing to till the soil and reap the harvests to produce agricultural commodities. The relationship between the settler and the speculator was therefore crucial to frontier expansion. Putting aside the anti-Yazoo rhetoric attacking huge land purchases as aristocratic, it was possible for speculator and settler to have a mutually symbiotic relationship. William Cooper offered generous terms of credit, often requiring nothing down, for the purchase of farms in Otsego County in upstate New York. This policy paid social and political dividends, if not financial ones, into the opening decade of the nineteenth century for Cooper. Many speculators offered similar deals, making it easy for settlers to commence farming with almost no capital. Some would offer especially low prices for the first one hundred families to move into an area. Frequently, the only difference between a man who purchased a two-hundred-acre farm and the real estate developer who bought a million acres was in scale. Both gambled on the future increase in property values. Even the first settler disparaged by Rush sought to reap some profit from his "improvements." Although he might run away from debts if he were "a tenant to some rich landholder," if he were "the owner of the spot of land which he began to cultivate, he sells it at a considerable profit to his successor."[5]

Speculators and settlers, however, could also find themselves in conflict. Repeatedly, frontiersmen—Rush's first settlers—hiked into the woods and through dint of their labor carved out a farm for themselves. Many of these men believed that the mere act of squatting on a piece of territory gave them first claim to the land. In 1801 one Maine informant for large landowners reported that squatters declared "that they are the sole owners of such lands as they have made themselves the possession of" and that they were willing to defend their claim; "they have a good right to hold their possessions by the firelock and will kill any person who offers to run a compass [survey] thro' their possession." Throughout the 1790s and early 1800s "white Indians"—settlers who donned Indian costume—in Maine attacked and harassed surveyors who worked for individuals who claimed proprietary rights to vast tracts of land. Squatter's rights reflected a strong current of egalitarianism that spread throughout American society during the early republic. As one leader of the Maine antiproprietor movement explained in 1810, "no proprietor owned any land, and that the government was corrupt in allowing any title." Moreover, "no proprietors had any right, for God gave the earth to the sons of men, and that no man had a right to more land than he could improve," which was about 200 acres.[6]

State land policy at times seemed to support this idea. Several states sold land at low prices and liberal terms. The Pennsylvania Land Act of 1792 offered bargain rates in the northwest portion of the state to any person "who may have settled and improved, or is desirous to settle and improve" the land up to 400 acres.[7] The Kentucky land law of 1800 allowed a settler to buy a 400-acre tract for twenty cents an acre with as many as twelve installments. When purchasers fell behind in payments, the legislature extended the period of the loan. Georgia had a lottery system that offered land for as little as six or eight cents an acre. The creation of military tracts in Ohio, Kentucky, Tennessee, and other states also encouraged the idea that there was free land available for settlement. Land used for payment for military service was not gratis because it had a certain value based on the fact that individuals issued warrants served in the Continental army without previously receiving pay. To the veteran, however, who had lost hope for any compensation for his sacrifice, the idea that there was a tract of land somewhere out west that his military service had earned him made the land grant appear free. Suddenly the Revolution had a whole new meaning—not only had the war been fought for independence from Great Britain, but also for the soldier's individual independence as a farmer. The fact that through the sale of warrants, or, in the case of state land, chicanery, much of this land ended up in the hands of a speculator does little to change the idea that there was a popular image during the early republic combining squatter's rights with the success of the revolution that seemed to promise land for all. Occupancy or betterment laws strengthened the squatters' claim to land. Beginning in 1797, Kentucky compensated settlers for their improvements to property even if they had no clear title to it. Other states, including Tennessee, Pennsylvania, Vermont, and Massachusetts (for Maine), passed betterment acts that often extended occupancy rights to squatters. This legislation sometimes allowed the squatter to purchase land he had settled at the predeveloped price.[8]

Though more restrictive, federal policy at times also encouraged the idea that land was available on the frontier for the taking. In several instances the federal government permitted the right of preemptive purchase by an original settler. Although the U.S. government would not dole out free land until the Homestead Act of 1862, the land acts of 1796, 1800, and 1804 made it progressively easier for a settler to purchase a farm. The Federalists set a relatively high standard price of two dollars per acre in 1796 and a minimum sale of 640 acres. The 1800 law, and even more so the 1804 law, allowed for easy credit with small down payments and decreased the minimum amount of land that could be purchased. After 1804 a settler could buy 160 acres for a down payment of 5 percent, with installments paid over four years. The land might not be free, but a man could begin the process of starting a farm with a $16 investment in land.[9]

The settlement of land on the frontier was part of a great migration unleashed by the American victory in the Revolutionary War. Kentucky went from a few thousand settlers in 1780 to a population of 73,677 in 1790, and 406,511 in 1810. Ohio also experienced phenomenal growth. In 1790 a few hundred European Americans had moved into the region. By 1800 there were 45,365 people, and in 1810, by which time Ohio had become a state, there were 230,760. Upstate New York west of the Hudson went from a land occupied by the Iroquois in 1780 to a booming farm country inhabited by hundreds of thousands of European Americans by 1810. Everywhere, people seemed to be moving. Even in more established areas the population shifted from place to place, creating a new society. As a Kentuckian explained to James Madison in 1792, this mobile population "must make a very different mass from one which is composed of men born and raised on the same spot. . . . They see none about them to whom or to whose families they have been accustomed to think themselves inferior." Because they were "ambitious themselves . . . they suppose all others to be equally so, and that all have self interest in view more than the public good."[10] Whatever castles in the air speculators may have conjured, the settlers focused their attention on their own cabins on the ground in a new individualistic, egalitarian, and competitive world.

There was, of course, a major exception to the idea of equality on the frontier. Expansion to new areas flowed north and south of the Ohio River. In many ways the new communities created in both areas looked the same, and reflected the world of the first settlers described by Rush. Pioneer families built rough-hewn, small log homes, planted a garden patch nearby and a few fields of corn sown amid tree stumps. They were surrounded by forest. For protein they relied on wild game and almost-as-wild cattle and pigs that roamed freely in the countryside. After a few years the half-wild domestic animals provided the first marketable product of the farm. Thereafter the differences between the free territory north of the Ohio and slave territory south of the river became important. Greater availability to transportation, through roads, rivers, or canals, allowed farmers access to overseas markets: Northerners exported grains; southerners had more profitable crops such as cotton and tobacco. To help grow that cotton and tobacco, tens of thousands of African American slaves were compelled to cross the Appalachian Mountains in a forced migration often overlooked in the story of western expansion. This ordeal began in the 1790s and continued throughout the period before the Civil War.

African American slaves had no choice in this move. European American settlers did. American folklore has built on the Jeffersonian vision of the yeoman farmer seeking his independent existence to create a mythology to explain westward expansion. Pursuing a course of rugged individualism, pioneers headed to the frontier to better their lives and fulfill the American dream. Like most myths, there is an element of truth to this idea. Human motivation, however, is often complex and there are probably as many reasons for this great migration as there were people who migrated. Some individuals may have been driven by wanderlust. Others were driven by necessity. Many farmers to the east of the Appalachians confronted dwindling prospects. Depleted soil convinced some families to search for more fertile land elsewhere. Having too many children persuaded others of the need to increase their holding in less populated regions where real estate was less expensive. As the daughter of one early settler later recalled, her father went to Kentucky because "his family was now large, and he wished to locate where his children could find homes around him when they chose."[11] Still others pursued profit. Rather than simply earn a competence, many settlers hoped to make a financial killing through speculation and become a person of "consequence." Even the noted woodsman Daniel Boone aspired to engross as much land as possible on the frontier. Regardless of the individual reasons, the American Revolution had provided new opportunities. The ideal of equality created a world in which every man thought he had the right to scramble toward the top. And a generous peace treaty extended the United States boundary, regardless of the claims of Native Americans, to the Mississippi River.

Louisiana

The boundary of the United States did not remain the Mississippi River. In an incredible stroke of luck, Jefferson's administration purchased from France the vast Louisiana Territory, nearly 830,000 square miles, for $15 million—a price of three cents an acre. With hindsight there is an inevitability in this acquisition, and subsequent American expansion, that obscures the precariousness and uniqueness of the moment. In the new American republic it was not self-evident that the United States would spread across the continent. In fact, there were real questions concerning holding on to the West. Frontiersmen might have decided to strike out on their own and ally themselves with some foreign power. Or, after France regained control of Louisiana, there was the possibility that Napoleon would try to create a new Franco-American empire.

The Mississippi River was the natural outlet for the produce of the Ohio River Valley. Whoever controlled New Orleans could dictate the future of much of the American nation. Spain was weak enough, however, to pose only a small threat to the United States. The Spanish had conceded the right of deposit and access to the port of New Orleans in the Treaty of San Lorenzo of 1795. Every year thereafter flatboats full of pork, grains, tobacco, and cotton floated down the Mississippi for export through New Orleans. There was nothing to guarantee that the frontiersmen would stay loyal to the United States if they saw their interests lay with Spain. As early as 1784 George Washington commented that "The Western settlers . . . stand as it were upon a pivot; the touch of a feather, would turn them any way."[12] Throughout the 1780s and 1790s, westerners in pursuit of the main chance had demonstrated a penchant for independent action. Some of this activity derived from the effort of speculators to gain control of the legal apparatus to secure land titles. Settlers in the hills of North Carolina and the future state of Tennessee had created the short-lived State of Franklin in 1784–90. Some efforts had more serious potential to challenge the integrity of the United States as a nation. In the late 1780s, James Wilkinson swore allegiance to the king of Spain and attempted to establish an independent Kentucky allied with his new sovereign. Wilkinson's efforts failed and he subsequently became the U. S. military commander in the West. Despite his military office, he received a secret annual payment of $2,000 from Spain through the 1790s and into the early 1800s. In 1793 Edmond Genêt persuaded frontier Revolutionary War hero George Rogers Clark to lead a French-supported expedition against the Spanish in Louisiana. When Genêt became discredited with the Washington administration, the plan had to be abandoned. As Tennessee's governor and then senator, William Blount tried to hatch a similar design on both Florida and Louisiana in 1796 and 1797 with British help. He hoped to gain a huge land grant and believed his actions would enhance the value of his extensive speculations in western lands. After a compromising letter fell into the hands of his political enemies and government officials, the Senate voted to expel Blount for his activities. He escaped arrest by going back to Tennessee, where he was still popular enough to be elected as speaker of the state senate. As long as New Orleans remained under the control of other nations, there was no guarantee of the loyalty of anyone in the West.

The situation became more critical with the retrocession of Louisiana from Spain to France in 1800. No sooner had Napoleon put the Quasi War behind him than he plotted to rebuild France's American empire. The first step in this endeavor was a reconquest of St. Domingue, which had

FIGURE 8–2 James Wilkinson
A veteran of the Revolutionary War, Wilkinson served as an important American officer on the frontier during the early republic. His allegiance to the United States was questionable. He plotted to establish an independent Kentucky, was in the secret pay of Spain through the 1790s and into the early 1800s, and was involved in the Burr conspiracy.

been in upheaval since rebellion broke out there in 1791. The second step was to strengthen the French hold on Louisiana. It is unclear if there was a third step involving the United States. The French, however, never got past St. Domingue. By 1801, Toussaint Louverture claimed control over the whole island. Napoleon sent his brother-in-law, Charles Leclerc, to the West Indies with seventeen thousand troops in December 1801. Between yellow fever and a nasty and treacherous guerilla war, Napoleon's plan fell apart. Leclerc was dead within a year, and the French armies had to abandon their campaign in November 1803.

Jefferson recognized the threat posed by French possession of Louisiana. He wrote in 1802 to Robert Livingston, the American ambassador to France, that New Orleans was the "one single spot" on the globe that the "possessor of which is our natural and habitual enemy" as great quantities of American produce passed through the port on the way to market. "France placing herself in that door assumes to us the attitude of defiance" and will generate an "eternal friction with us." It was therefore "impossible that France and the U. S. can continue long friends when they meet in so irritable position." Jefferson believed that the only "arrangements which might reconcile" French possession of Louisiana "to our interests" would be the "ceding to us the island of New Orleans and the Floridas."[13] He therefore sent James Monroe to France and instructed Livingston and Monroe to purchase New Orleans and, if possible, Florida. In the meantime, the situation on the Mississippi worsened when Spanish officials, who had continued to administer the colony after the retrocession, closed the port of New Orleans to Americans on October 16, 1802. The 1795 treaty had promised to keep the port open for only three years and each subsequent year had been at Spanish discretion.

Fortunately for the United States, several international developments now worked in its favor. The French had been able to send an army to St. Domingue only because of the Peace of Amiens, which in 1801 ended hostilities between Great Britain and France. This uneasy truce was little more than a hiatus in the ongoing struggles in Europe. With Leclerc's failure in St. Domingue and with war looming on the horizon, Napoleon saw no need to hold on to a North American wilderness and antagonize the United States. Napoleon also feared that he would not be able to defend Louisiana should war begin, leaving it to become a potential target for the British. Finally, Napoleon needed the money to support his other ambitions for empire. The French therefore responded to the American overture for New Orleans with the offer of all of Louisiana. Although the asking price was far more than the $6 million Livingston and Monroe had been authorized to spend, and the final treaty disregarded other aspects of

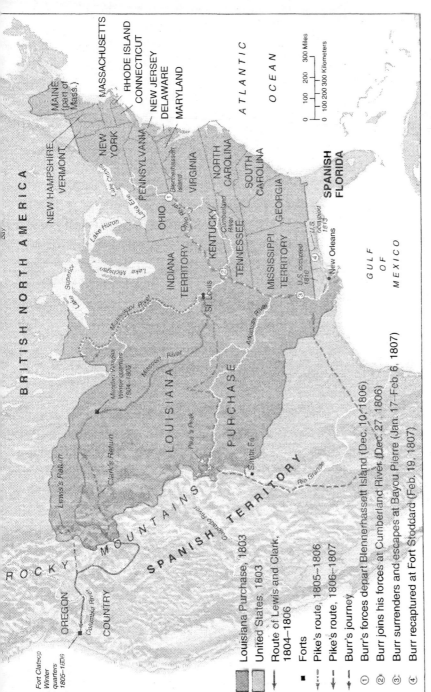

MAP 8-1 Louisiana Purchase Thomas Jefferson doubled the size of the United States with the Louisiana Purchase. Aaron Burr, however, threatened to divide the nation with his conspiracy in 1805 and 1806. Burr's exact plans remain obscure to this day, but he may have hoped to set up a rival empire centered on the Mississippi River. While Burr was plotting, Lewis and Clark were exploring the far west, extending scientific knowledge and American claims to the Pacific Ocean. Many Americans believed that West Florida had been part of the Louisiana Purchase. Although the United States occupied some of this territory before the War of 1812, Spain contested American pretensions to their province.

their written instructions, the two Americans readily agreed to the deal. It took only two weeks to work out all the details of the sale and an agreement was signed on April 30, 1803.

Jefferson had some qualms about the constitutionality of the purchase, but was quick to recognize its significance. Throughout the summer and early fall of 1803 Jefferson shifted back and forth on the need for a constitutional amendment to permit the acquisition of Louisiana. He had lambasted Hamilton's use of the "necessary and proper clause" during the 1790s, and Jefferson probably would have preferred to follow a strict construction of the Constitution in 1803. Although Jefferson never fully put aside his constitutional scruples, by late fall he decided to say nothing publicly about the issue. The United States had only six months to ratify the treaty, and Jefferson realized how important Louisiana would be for the future of the country. The treaty solved a problem that had plagued the nation from its inception by giving Americans complete control over the Mississippi River and opening access to markets for much of the interior. It also eliminated a foreign power from a vital transportation artery and left the western border between Spanish possessions and American settlements hundreds of miles away across territory occupied only by Native Americans. Jefferson did not see any immediate use of this land for European American farmers. He hoped that in the short term it would become an asylum for Indians from the East who could be removed to make way for the advance of the American "civilization." In the long term he believed that "the fertility of the country, its climate and extent, promise in due season important aids to our treasury, an ample provision for our posterity, and a wide-spread field for the blessings of freedom and equal laws."[14]

The Louisiana Purchase, however, also intensified the volatility of American politics and had the potential to tear apart the United States into regional "empires." Federalists decried the addition of Louisiana as unconstitutional because it brought the territory into the United States on equal terms with the rest of the nation. One New York Federalist complained that the framers of the Constitution made no provision for an extension "to the Union of a territory equal to the whole United States, which additional territory might overbalance the existing territory, and thereby the rights of the present citizens of the United States be swallowed up and lost." Federalist Roger Griswold of Connecticut admitted that "A new territory and new subjects" might be annexed to the nation through conquest or purchase, but that they could not be brought into the Union. Instead, "They must remain in the condition of colonies, and be governed accordingly." To do otherwise would be to accept the principle that "the President and Senate may admit at will any foreign nation into this copartnership without the consent of the States."[15] Incorporation of the new territory threatened to further the growing sectional imbalance between New England and the rest of the country. The western states that had been admitted into the Union (Kentucky, Tennessee, and Ohio) were dominated by the Republican Party. New states no doubt would follow suit and guarantee Federalist political oblivion. The Federalists believed that opening the Mississippi encouraged further settlement in the slave South. As a result, future states carved from Louisiana would add to the power of slavery in the United States. This problem so distressed Federalists like Timothy Pickering that they even talked of secession. Pickering imagined an independent country to include New York, New Jersey, and New England because this region shared "a sufficient congeniality of character to authorize the expectation of practicable harmony and a permanent union." Only by separating from the Republican-dominated states could they "rid themselves of Negro Presidents and Negro congresses, and regain their just weight in the political balance."[16]

In an odd twist of circumstances, the Louisiana Purchase contributed to one of the most dramatic episodes in the history of American politics—the Burr–Hamilton duel. Pickering pinned much of his hopes for an independent eastern "empire" on Aaron Burr. Having been deleted from the national ticket by Jefferson, Burr sought to resuscitate his own fading political star by pursuing the governor's office in New York. Burr appealed to his factional base among Republicans, and to disgruntled Federalists. Pickering hoped that once Burr became governor of New York he would head a secession movement. Alexander Hamilton was aghast that Pickering would flirt with Burr and disunion. Hamilton did everything he could to discredit Burr, speaking intemperately, referring to Burr as "a profligate," and a "voluptuary in the extreme," who would ruin any man who followed him.[17] Burr lost the election to the Jeffersonian Morgan Lewis, and blamed Hamilton for sabotaging him with the Federalists. A long-simmering animosity came boiling to the surface as Burr first demanded that Hamilton explain his remarks attacking Burr's character, and then issued a challenge when no explanation was forthcoming. However democratic politics was becoming, in the minds of would-be aristocrats like Burr and Hamilton, honor still ruled. These two men believed that if they did not fight the duel they would lose face in public and weaken themselves in the larger political arena. Hamilton explained before the fatal encounter that he agreed to the duel to ensure his "ability to be in future useful, whether in resisting mischief or effecting good, in those crises of our public affairs."[18] The duel took place in Weehauken, New Jersey, on the morning of July 11, 1804. The exact details of this "affair of honor" are clouded and confused by contradictory reports from the opposing sides. It is not clear if both men shot at each other, or if Hamilton aimed his pistol in the air. We do know that Hamilton was mortally wounded, dying the next day, and that Burr escaped physically unscathed, although politically marred for life.

The purchase of Louisiana formed the backdrop for a New England secession movement, Burr's dalliance with the Federalists, and Hamilton's death. It also provided the context for a more serious threat to the United States that emerged out of Burr's next exploit. The duel may have discredited Burr in his home state of New York, but he still had a personal following elsewhere in the country. For this ambitious man the Louisiana Territory and the West beckoned. As soon as he stepped down from the vice presidency in March 1805, Burr embarked on a tour of the West, traveling down the Ohio and the Mississippi to New Orleans. Along the way he met with a variety of political leaders, including Ohio Senator John Smith, Major General Andrew Jackson of the Tennessee militia, and the ever duplicitous General Wilkinson, who was now governor of the Louisiana Territory. Westerners had previously demonstrated their penchant for independence. Suddenly they had a dynamic man of action to lead them. Ever engaging, Burr had a knack for attracting supporters. He spoke about great land speculations, about invasions of the Spanish empire, about the gold of Mexico, and about creating a new, strong western "empire." He sent out feelers to the British, the French, and even the Spanish, assuring his American listeners of foreign support for his enterprise. Over the course of the next year and a half the plot thickened. By the fall of 1806, Burr had established a cache of weapons and supplies on Blennerhassett Island, not far from Marietta, Ohio. About sixty armed men gathered at this rendezvous, awaiting Burr to lead them down the river on a triumphant conquest—whether it be Louisiana, Florida, Mexico, or wherever.

The conspiracy then began to unravel. Too many people had heard the stories. Smith got cold feet and pretended he knew nothing about Burr's plans. Jackson, who claimed he was merely helping with preparations for a possible war with Spain, sent a letter to Washington and to New Orleans warning of Burr's intentions. Wilkinson, having patched up some border difficulties with the Spanish, decided to abandon Burr and also sent a warning to Jefferson. Jefferson had seen reports about Burr before, but he had decided to ignore the suspicious activity. After receiving Wilkinson's letter, however, Jefferson issued a proclamation on November 27, 1806. Sidestepping the threat to Louisiana, Jefferson stated that "sundry persons" were "conspiring & confederating together to begin & set on foot, provide

& prepare the means for a military expedition or enterprise against the dominions of Spain." These unnamed individuals were "deceiving & seducing honest & well meaning citizens," men like Smith, Jackson, and Wilkinson, "under various pretences to engage in their criminal enterprises." Jefferson demanded that anyone concerned in this affair "cease all further proceedings" and ordered government officials to seize weapons and supplies and prevent any further illegal operations.[19] Ohio militia raided Blennerhassett Island while Wilkinson marched to New Orleans and prepared for Burr's "invasion." Burr's remaining force continued down the Ohio and Mississippi Rivers until stalling at a U.S. military outpost just north of Natchez in early February. Confronted by failure, Burr abandoned his men, but was captured a month later in the Mississippi Territory. Whatever Burr's intentions, and to this day we do not know if he merely intended to invade Mexico or establish a western empire of his own, he was acquitted of any wrongdoing in his treason trial in a federal court presided over by John Marshall.

Although the Burr conspiracy disintegrated quickly, and became merely an interesting footnote to the history of expansion, it demonstrated just how unclear the future of the United States appeared to those who lived through the opening decade of the nineteenth century. Jeffersonian Republicans may have been pushing to unleash the individual in a new world of equality. But it was still possible for an ex–vice president—a man who had almost become president in 1800—to contrive a plot that envisioned a different America. Burr was able, at least for a while, to gain the ear of, among others, a senator, a future president, and a military governor. Adding the vast, ill-defined Louisiana Territory may have been the first step in the U.S. expansion across North America; it could have also been the first step in the dissolution of the American republic. Rather than opt for division, disunion, and destruction implicit in Burr's flirtation with New England's Federalists and his western conspiracy, the United States moved in the direction of exploration, exploitation, and expansion. In this saga of the road taken, just as Burr pursued his various schemes, Meriwether Lewis and William Clark headed a Voyage of Discovery up the Missouri, across the Rocky Mountains and along the Columbia River to the Pacific Ocean. In what can only be seen as curious coincidence, Burr floated down the Ohio and Mississippi in his vain attempt to bring his conspiracy to fruition only a few months after Lewis and Clark floated down the Missouri on the return from their great expedition.

Jefferson began planning for the exploration of the Far West before the purchase of Louisiana. He decided early on that the best man for the job

FIGURE 8–3 Meriwether Lewis as the Explorer Thomas Jefferson chose his secretary, Meriwether Lewis, to lead an expedition into the far west. Lewis and William Clark explored the Missouri River Valley and crossed the Rocky Mountains to the Pacific, and then returned by almost the same route. Their trek lasted from 1804 to 1806.

was his own private secretary, Meriwether Lewis. Jefferson knew that Lewis was intelligent, intrepid, and the kind of individual who would carefully gather and preserve scientific specimens. As a man of the Enlightenment, Jefferson wanted more information that would be further proof that the New World was better than the Old World. Jefferson had written his *Notes on the State of Virginia* in large part to demonstrate the superiority of American nature, and continued his interest in this debate the rest of his life. Jefferson also had geopolitical reasons for the enterprise that shifted with the rapid developments concerning Louisiana between 1801 and 1803. At first Jefferson probably assumed that sooner or later Spain would lose its tenuous grip on the territory and that it would be appropriate to have a better knowledge of the Missouri Valley. As word of the French retrocession arrived in Washington, and with the potential for armed conflict with Napoleon, there was even more reason to send out an exploring party to discern the extent of Louisiana. With the American purchase, which occurred during the planning stages of the Voyage of Discovery, the expedition became a means to provide a better understanding of the new borders of the United States. Moreover, at the end of 1801, Alexander Mackenzie published a two-volume account of his own journey across the Canadian wilderness to the Pacific in 1793. Mackenzie argued for the British to establish outposts that would preempt American intrusion into the Pacific Northwest. An American expedition would be the first step in preventing this development. Jefferson was also aware of the economic benefits that might flow from better knowledge of North American geography. He directed Lewis that his mission was "to explore the Missouri river, & such principle stream of it" that would allow communication with the Pacific in "the most direct & practicable" a manner as possible "for the purposes of commerce." Jefferson was even more explicit when it came to the fur trade. American merchants had developed a thriving business with China that included a stop in the Pacific Northwest for furs. Americans knew that there were great rivers, including the Columbia, that emptied into the Pacific. If this river connected to the Missouri River either directly, or over a short portage, then furs might be funneled toward the United States and the Atlantic, rather then centered on the far-off Pacific. As Jefferson explained to Lewis in his letter of instruction on June 20, 1803:

> Should you reach the Pacific ocean inform yourself of the circumstances which may decide whether the furs of those parts may not be collected as advantageously at the head of the Missouri . . . as at Nootka Sound, . . . and that trade be consequently conducted through the Missouri & U. S. more beneficially than by the circumnavigation now practised.[20]

A journey of this scale needed careful planning and preparation. Jefferson submitted a secret message to Congress on January 18, 1803, asking for an appropriation to support the expedition. Congress provided $2,500; Jefferson ultimately spent between $40,000 and $60,000. Lewis took his time getting ready. He made several trips to Philadelphia to gain scientific training and to learn navigation. He also supervised the construction of an iron, collapsible canoe at Harper's Ferry that never worked. A large keelboat was constructed at Pittsburgh and sailed down the Ohio River. Equipment had to be prepared and brought together, and a party of experienced frontiersman recruited. The most important addition was William Clark, brother of George Rogers Clark, who was an experienced army officer who knew his way around the wilderness and on river transports. Although Lewis agreed to make him coleader, Jefferson never recognized him as such until the two men returned from their journey. On the trip, however, Lewis and Clark worked in tandem with hardly a hitch. By early December 1803, Lewis and Clark were camped on the east bank of the Mississippi River near the mouth of the Missouri. That winter they devoted to further preparations and waiting for spring.

Although Lewis and Clark wanted to depart in mid April, they did not get underway until May 14, 1804. They had with them about forty men, including several French fur trappers who had been West before. In addition to the keelboat they had two smaller vessels to bring over twenty tons of supplies and equipment up the Missouri. Against the current, progress was excruciatingly slow. The keelboat had a mast and sail, but they could only be used when conditions were right. The rest of the time the men dragged the vessels upstream with tow ropes from shore, or used poles to move the boats. On a good day they might make ten to twelve miles. All in all it was a cumbersome and inefficient way to travel. By October 24, 1804, they were at a group of Native American villages—Mandan and Hidatsa—at the bend of the Missouri in modern-day North Dakota. The expedition wintered near the Mandans, recruiting Toussaint Charbonneau, a French fur trader, and his Shoshone wife, Sacagewea, as translators. On April 7, 1805, Lewis and Clark sent the keelboat back down the river with scientific specimens for Jefferson and then continued on their exploration of the upper Missouri. The Mandans and Hidatsa had given them some idea of what to expect. The explorers knew that they would have to portage around the great falls of the Missouri, and also knew that in the mountains they were likely to meet Shoshone Indians who would have horses to help them get across the Rockies. When they finally met the Shoshone in mid August, Sacagewea served as translator, even though all communication had to go from Shoshone to Hidatsa, and then Hidatsa to French, via Charbonneau, and then French to English, via Francois Labiche, a member of the exploration party. With the horses and an old Indian as a guide, they made the arduous trip through the mountains, and to the Pacific. They had hoped to meet with some American merchant vessel, but none was in the offing. Wintering on the coast, they returned much the same way they came—with additional difficulties—making it to St. Louis on September 23, 1806.

Despite the efforts of Lewis and Clark, the United States still had only a vague understanding of the boundaries of the Louisiana Territory, which had been defined in the treaty as comprising the drainage basin of the Missouri and its tributaries and the drainage basin of the rivers that flowed into the western side of the Mississippi River (except for in Florida, rivers on the eastern side already belonged to the United States). Lewis and Clark provided some understanding of how far the Rocky Mountains were and the dimensions of the territory to the northwest. But the other boundaries remained ill defined. General Wilkinson sent his protégé, Zebulon Pike, to clarify the northern boundary at the source of the Mississippi during the winter of 1805–06, and to chart the southwestern boundary along the Red River in 1806–07. Pike's Mississippi expedition suffered terribly and was probably saved by British fur traders in the area. Pike did not find the correct source of the Mississippi. The next summer Wilkinson, in what may have been an effort to scout Spanish territory as a part of the Burr conspiracy, sent Pike into the Great Plains to identify the sources of the Arkansas and Red Rivers. Again, Pike missed the mark as an explorer. And again his men suffered terribly in the following winter. He did see, but failed to climb, the Colorado peak that now bears his name. He also managed to get captured by the Spanish on the northern Rio Grande—an act that probably saved him and his men from dying of cold and hunger. Pike's capture caused a minor international incident, as Spain correctly suspected Pike of spying. Eventually Pike and some of his men were returned to the United States on July 1, 1807. By that time the Spanish had taken Pike through New Mexico, Chihuahua, and Texas, providing him with a personal view of forts and outposts that he could report on.

Compared to Pike, Lewis and Clark achieved a stunning success. They survived their trek across a continent by dint of leadership and preparation rather than being saved by agents of a competing nation. Not only did they travel to the source of the Missouri, they also established an American claim to the Pacific Northwest. On the negative side, the ordeal in the Rockies demonstrated that there would be no easy water route through the continent. Perhaps more important, Lewis and Clark ran a scientific expedition. They identified dozens of new flora and fauna. Their notebooks are packed with illustrations of these findings. They kept meticulous records and maps and took notes on over fifty different Indian tribes. Moreover, at a vulnerable time in the development of the young republic, when men like Burr and Wilkinson could plot its dismemberment, Lewis and Clark provided a great achievement for Americans to celebrate and assert a national identity.

"Civilizing" Native Americans

Lewis and Clark came into contact with several different Native American groups in the Great Plains, the Rockies, and the Pacific Coast. Some of these Indians had already had extensive interaction with European Americans, others had not. Like almost all Native Americans in North America, whatever their direct contact with whites, the European intrusion into North America had initiated a series of changes transforming the Indian world. This impact ranged from the ripple effect of trade and disease to more direct efforts to "civilize" Native Americans by compelling them to adopt the European American way of life. Indians, in turn, shaped both the long-range and immediate consequences of what historian Alfred Crosby has called the "Columbian exchange" along a cultural path uniquely their own.[21]

The people of the Pacific Northwest had interacted with European Americans for a few decades by the time Lewis and Clark had shown up. Traders in pursuit of fur and seal skins had visited the coast throughout the 1790s. Both the Clatsops and Chinooks who lived at the mouth of the Columbia River had bartered with Europeans and had little trouble dealing with Lewis and Clark. These Indians, and those tribes to the north, such as the Coast Salish, Kwakiutl, Bella Coola, Haida, Tsimshian, and Tlingit, lived off a natural bounty of fish, game, nuts, and berries that allowed for relatively dense populations. They stood at the crossroads of empire as Russians, British, Spanish, and Americans competed for their territory in the early nineteenth century. Occasional contact shifted to more permanent relationships in the years after the visit of Lewis and Clark with the establishment of the American fur trading center of Fort Astoria in 1812. The British captured Fort Astoria in 1813. The Russians, seeking to expand their holdings down the coast from Alaska, built a short-lived outpost in what is now northern California in 1812. The Europeans brought new trading goods, but they also brought disease and depopulation.

The Indians in Spanish-held California, New Mexico, and Texas had a more extended exposure to Europeans and as a result experienced greater hardship. California was a relatively new colony, established in 1769 in part to forestall British and Russian designs in the Pacific. The Hispanic population was slow to grow in the area, reaching only about 3,200 by 1821. The Franciscan fathers built a series of missions where they brought thousands of Native Americans to Christianity and "civilization," organizing the Indians as farmers under their auspices. Mortality was very high among the mission Indians and California's native population declined from about 300,000 in 1769 to 200,000 in 1821. The natives in New Mexico and Texas had longer contact with the Spanish, dating to the early seventeenth century. The first Spanish settlement at Santa Fe began in 1609. By 1800, the native population was divided between the more sedentary agriculturalists under the control of the Spanish, like the Pueblo Indians of New Mexico and the mission Indians in Texas, and the more nomadic and hostile groups like the Apaches and Comanches. Beginning in 1786 the Spanish made a concerted effort to pacify the region. They treated Indians captured in war severely, often selling them into slavery in Cuba and elsewhere in the Caribbean.

The centuries-long Spanish intrusion into what later became the Southwest United States had a profound impact on many Native Americans throughout the interior of the continent. By the eighteenth century, Indian trade networks reached from the Rio Grande to Hudson's Bay and even crossed the Rockies to the Columbia River basin. Disease could follow this route as easily as trade goods. During the 1770s and 1780s a smallpox epidemic swept through much of North America, reaching the Great Plains and the Pacific Northwest from Mexico, devastating several tribes: over thirty thousand died on the Great Plains, and twenty-five thousand died on the Northwest Pacific Coast.[22] Another epidemic swept across the plains, halving the population from New Mexico to the Missouri, and striking over the mountains to the Pacific Northwest around 1800.[23] The Spanish also provided the horses that altered life on the Great Plains. The revolt by the Pueblo Indians that drove the Spanish out of New Mexico from 1680 to 1692 made horses available to Indians on a large scale. Thereafter newly mobile Comanches and others raided and traded with Spanish settlements to obtain more horses. Indians became expert horsemen and also raised horses of their own on the rich grasslands of the Great Plains. Within one hundred years horses spread so far north that they were a vital part of the Nez Perce and Shoshone cultures when Lewis and Clark crossed the Rockies. During the eighteenth century, several Indian tribes, including the Comanche and the Sioux, migrated from the periphery of the Great Plains, where they had lived as agriculturalists or hunters and gatherers, to the vast grasslands and created a new culture based on hunting the bison (buffalo). These tribes adopted a decentralized political structure as there was less need for cooperation in a nomadic lifestyle. The status of women declined. Previously, women grew the crops or gathered the food that had fed the tribe and had a relatively powerful voice in tribal councils. A culture molded around hunting buffalo left women with the status of auxiliary labor, tanning hides and dressing meats. Both trade and warfare also became more important and the exclusive province of men. The Great Plains may have been terra incognita for Lewis and Clark, but the mobile Native Americans who lived there knew it well. The Mandans and Hidatsa could tell the two American explorers not only what to expect on the upper Missouri, but also when the Shoshone would be crossing the mountains to hunt for buffalo. The early 1800s were a high watermark for the Plains Indians. The only two hostile tribes met by Lewis and Clark were the Teton Sioux and Blackfeet, who were just then hitting their stride as aggressive nomads who hunted the buffalo. At the same time, sedentary groups like the Mandan and Hidatsa, who helped Lewis and Clark during the winter of 1804–05, were on the decline. Attached to their life of agriculture, they made easy targets for more warlike and mobile neighbors. Extended contact with European Americans also increased their exposure to disease. The group of villages that Lewis and Clark had found on the great bend of Missouri contained about 4,500 people. A few decades later, the villages had disappeared. The Mandan and Hidatsa had either died or joined other tribes on the Plains.

East of the Mississippi, Native Americans experienced cultural disruption as they faced repeated demands for land cessions and an onslaught of European American settlers. The Cherokees ended almost two decades of devastating warfare in 1794. Their population had declined from about 16,000 to 10,000 during those years of conflict. Over the next couple of decades the Cherokees struggled to maintain their cultural identity. Hunting and combat had combined to define Cherokee manhood. With hunting grounds depleted by treaties granting ever more land to the United States, and with war no longer a viable option, many Cherokee men were at a loss as to what to do with themselves. The U. S. government encouraged the Cherokees to "civilize" by turning to European farming methods, which meant that males would till the fields that had been the province of females. This abandonment of traditional gender roles was hard to take. Many women, on the other hand, embraced "civilization." One group of women in 1796 told Indian Agent Benjamin Hawkins "that they rejoiced much at what they had heard and hoped it would prove true" and that the U.S. government would help them to produce more cloth. Hawkins reported that women repeatedly expressed support for "the plan contemplated by the government for the bettering of the condition of the Red people" as it would help them improve in agricultural, livestock, and domestic production, areas in which women traditionally did most of the work.[24] The result was a fractured society. Some Cherokees, especially the increasing number who had part European ancestry, accepted the methods of white "civilization." Others followed a middle course by focusing on raising livestock, renting land to whites, or buying slaves to farm for them. Others strove to adhere to a more traditional path even if it meant removing to the West. Several hundred headed west before 1800, settling in modern-day Arkansas. Moravian and other Christian missionaries appeared after 1799, preaching both the gospel and "civilized" agriculture. The Cherokees divided into two factions: the Lower Town Cherokees, who seemed willing to sign away land for bribes and promises, and the Upper Town Cherokees, who wanted to hold on to their homeland. A crisis began in 1808 over land cessions and the issue of removal, leading to the migration of over one thousand more Cherokees to Arkansas in 1810–11.

The opposition of the Upper Town Cherokees to this action led to a consolidation of power by the national council. In 1810, the Cherokee Council decried the fact that some Cherokees had gone west. They argued that because "The country left to us by our ancestors has been diminished by repeated sales to a tract barely sufficient for us to stand on and not more than adequate to the purpose of supporting our posterity," any Cherokees not living in the homeland had no right to cede tribal lands.[25] By reasserting and redefining Cherokee identity, denying the ideal of private property and insisting on the integrity of their homeland, the Council took an important step toward accepting European American "civilization" on their own terms and leading to the development of Cherokee nationhood.

If the Cherokees represented one response to the European American challenge to Indians east of the Mississippi, the Seneca leader Handsome Lake's revitalized religion represented another. Few Native Americans had lost as much in the last half of the eighteenth century as the Iroquois. Having once extended their reach from the Finger Lakes district in what is now upstate New York to the Great Lakes, the Ohio country, and even to the Cherokees and Creeks in the South, by 1800 they were confined either to exile in Canada or to a few small reservations in New York. Many Iroquois, including Handsome Lake, became despondent, drank too much alcohol, and lived on the fringes of their own or white society. Beginning in 1799, Handsome Lake had a series of visions that became the basis of a Native American religion. He associated alcohol with witchcraft, renouncing both by declaring "that the Whiskey is the great Engine which the bad Spirit uses to introduce Witchcraft and many other evils amongst Indians." He urged his supporters to maintain some aspects of Iroquois ceremony and culture, while embracing European American technology. In 1801 he advised his people

> that they might farm a little and make houses; but that they must not sell anything they raised off the ground, but give it away to one another and to the old people in particular in short that they must possess everything in common.

Handsome Lake believed that educating some members of the tribe would protect them from further exploitation by whites. He wanted to hold on to whatever land and culture was left to his people. As he explained, "there is hardship for those who part with their lands for money."[26] His religion combined Native and Christian practices. He saw himself as the Indian counterpart to the white Jesus and as a prophet preaching for the salvation of his people. He talked about the need to confess sin and lead a wholesome life, urging his followers to cherish marriage, family, and children. Many Iroquois welcomed this message as a halfway house to "civilization"; they rejected European American ideas on capitalism and adopted Handsome Lake's religion as a peaceful means to deal with a changing world.

In the Ohio Valley another revitalization movement had a more bellicose approach. Like the Iroquois, the Shawnees had experienced defeat and a decline in the eighteenth century. Although they were not confined to a reservation, the Shawnees were having a difficult time sustaining their male hunting and female horticultural lifestyle, as more and more European Americans settled north of the Ohio River. A Shawnee who became known as Tenskwatawa (the "Open Door"), or the Prophet, had a vision in 1805 similar to Handsome Lake's a few years earlier. In this vision Tenskwatawa visited the Master of Life, or Great Spirit, and had seen paradise, which he described as "a rich fertile country, abounding in game, fish, pleasant hunting grounds and fine corn fields." The Great Spirit said that Indians had to return to their old ways if they hoped to get to the spirit world. Previously, Tenskwatawa was a drunkard and ne'er-do-well, known more for his prattling and bragging (his prevision name was Lalawethika, or "Noisemaker"). Now he became a holy man whose "sole object was to reclaim the Indians from bad habits and to cause them to live in peace with all mankind." He saw the "Long Knives" (European Americans from the United States) as "the children of the Evil Spirit" who "grew from the scum of the great Water when it was troubled by the Evil Spirit." Tenskwatawa called on Indians to renounce everything belonging to the white man, including alcohol, which he labeled "poison and accursed." He insisted that his followers abandon the pursuit of the accumulation of wealth, which Protestant missionaries had encouraged as an important step toward "civilization." Native Americans who possessed "wealth and ornaments" would "crumble into dust." Indians who shared with their tribesmen would die happy and when they arrived in the afterworld they would "find their wigwam furnished with everything they had on earth."[27]

If Tenskwatawa had never been a great warrior or hunter, his brother Tecumseh was. The two brothers led a pan-Indian movement that had the potential to expand to massive proportions. In 1808 they moved away from white settlements to establish a pristine Native American village on the Tippecanoe River near present-day Lafayette, Indiana. They attracted thousands of followers from many different tribes. As Tecumseh admitted to Governor William Henry Harrison of Indiana Territory in 1810, he and Tenskwatawa had "organized a combination of all the Indian tribes in this quarter to put a stop to the encroachments of the white people and to establish a principle that the lands should be considered common property

TECUMTHA.

FIGURE 8–4   Tecumseh
A Shawnee who lived in the area north of the Ohio River, Tecumseh led a pan-Indian movement in the opening decades of the nineteenth century, even visiting with Native Americans from the South. Although he and his brother rejected much of European American culture, this picture shows Tecumseh wearing a European American military jacket and sporting a European medallion.

and none sold without the consent of all."[28] Any chiefs who violated this idea, like those who had recently ceded lands at the Treaty of Fort Wayne, would be executed. In 1811 Tecumseh went south to get the Creeks and others to join with the effort to push whites back across the mountains. While Tecumseh was on this trip, Harrison marched on Prophetstown. As he approached, Tenskwatawa encouraged his followers to attack by proclaiming that the army's bullets would not harm the Indian warriors. The magic did not work and they were dispersed and driven back. Harrison's men then burned Prophetstown. The Indian defeat at the Battle of Tippecanoe on November 7, 1811, discredited the Prophet's and Tecumseh's movement.

The effort to "civilize" the Indians was central to the story of U.S. expansion during the early republic. Just as men like Benjamin Rush looked on the first settlers on the frontier as white Indians who failed to embrace their European American civilization and develop successful farms, most white Americans viewed the Indian as a "noble savage" whose lifestyle reflected a primitive state. The Indians faced a choice: They could be taught the proper agricultural techniques and domestic arrangements to be fully incorporated into the larger European American world; or they could face extinction. Although the coastal tribes of New England

and Virginia had not totally vanished, American leaders regretted their "disappearance." Secretary of War Henry Knox lamented to George Washington in 1789 that Americans had not "imparted our knowledge of cultivation and the arts to the aboriginals of the country, by which source" their "future life and happiness" could have "been preserved and extended."[29] The U.S. government hoped to avoid a similar fate for the remaining Indians east of the Mississippi by pursuing a policy of philanthropy in an effort to "civilize" Native Americans in the 1790s and early 1800s. As William H. Crawford explained concerning the Cherokees, "they cannot much longer exist in the exercise of their savage rights and customs. They must become civilized, or they will finally . . . become extinct."[30] Crucial to this enterprise was to get Indians to change their culture, accept capitalist notions of individual private property, adopt farming and patriarchal families, and embrace Christianity. If the United States was successful, the benefits would include not only leading the Indian from "savagery" to "civilization," but also, because farming would limit the amount of land Native Americans would need, open up huge amounts of land for speculators to purchase and white farmers to settle. If the United States was unsuccessful, the Louisiana Purchase provided an outlet for Indian removal, leaving the land east of the Mississippi again open to speculators and settlers. Many Indians, including the Cherokees, Iroquois, and Shawnees, resisted these measures and rejected European American notions of property. Sometimes they pursued a path toward war; more often they pursued a path of cultural adaptation and revitalization in an effort to preserve what remained of their land and culture.

Endnotes

1. Benjamin Rush, "An Account of the Progress of Population. Agriculture, Manners, and Government in Pennsylvania, in a Letter to a Friend in England," in Rush, *Essays, Literary, Moral & Philosophical by Benjamin Rush, M. D. and Professor of the Institutes of Medicine and Clinical Practice in the University of Pennsylvania* (Philadelphia: Thomas & Samuel F. Bradford, 1798), 213–15, 218–20.

2. Quoted in Andrew R. L. Cayton, *The Frontier Republic: Ideology and Politics in the Ohio Country, 1780–1825* (Kent, Ohio: Kent State University Press, 1986), 21, 32.

3. Quoted in Cayton, *The Frontier Republic,* 62, 69. Originally in Beverly W. Bond, Jr., ed., *The Intimate Letters of John Cleves Symmes and His Family* (Cincinnati: Historical and Philosophical Society of Ohio, 1956), 51, 52.

4. Quoted in C. Peter Magrath, *Yazoo: Law and Politics in the New Republic, The Case of* Fletcher v. Peck (Providence, R.I.: Brown University Press, 1966), 13.

5. Rush, "An Account of the Progress of Population," 215–16.

6. Quoted in Alan Taylor, *Liberty Men and Great Proprietors: The Revolutionary Settlement on the Maine Frontier, 1760–1820* (Chapel Hill: University of North Carolina Press, 1990),

17–18. Originally from Elisha Sylvestor to Pejepscot Proprietors, Jan. 19, 1801, folder 1800–1801, Pejepscot Proprietors' Papers, box 12, Essex Institute; and "no proprietor . . ." Elliot G. Vaughan to Colonel Thomas Cutts, Oct. 30, 1810, in miscellaneous box 24, "Papers Relating to Lands in Lincoln County," Massachusetts State Archives, Boston.

7. Quoted in Barbara Ann Chernow, *Robert Morris: Land Speculator, 1790–1801* (New York: Arno, 1978), 94.

8. Taylor, *Liberty Men and Great Proprietors,* 220–32. See also Paul W. Gates, *Landlords and Tenants on the Prairie Frontier: Studies in American Land Policy* (Ithaca, N.Y.: Cornell University Press, 1973), 22–24; R. S. Cottrill, "The National Land System in the South: 1803–1812," in Paul Wallace Gates, ed., *Public Land Policies: Management and Disposal* (New York: Arno, 1979), 496.

9. Paul W. Gates, *History of Public Land Law Development* (Washington, D.C.: Public Land Law Review Commission, 1968), 125–36; Daniel Feller, *The Public Lands in Jacksonian Politics* (Madison: University of Wisconsin Press, 1984), 7–13; Malcolm J. Rohrbough, *The Land Office Business: The Settlement and Administration of American Public Lands, 1789–1837* (New York: Oxford University Press, 1968), 18–50; Cayton, *The Frontier Republic,* 56, 115–16; Everett Dick, *The Lure of the Land: A Social History of the Public Lands from the Articles of Confederation to the New Deal* (Lincoln: University of Nebraska Press, 1970), 7–10.

10. Robert A. Rutland, et al., eds., *The Papers of James Madison,* 17 vols. (Chicago and Charlottesville: University of Chicago and University Press of Virginia, 1962–1991), 14: 359.

11. Quoted in Stephen Aron, *How the West Was Lost: The Transformation of Kentucky from Daniel Boone to Henry Clay* (Baltimore: Johns Hopkins University Press, 1996), 69.

12. George Washington to Benjamin Harrison, Oct. 10, 1784, The George Washington Papers online, 1741–1799, Library of Congress.

13. The exact status of East and West Florida was unclear at the time. Spain retained possession of the territories, but Americans thought that they were a part of the Louisiana retrocession. Thomas Jefferson to Robert R. Livingston, Apr. 18, 1802, Thomas Jefferson Papers Series I, General Correspondence, 1651–1827, Digital Archives, Library of Congress, Image 131.

14. Thomas Jefferson, Oct. 17, 1803, Annual Message, Thomas Jefferson Papers Series I, General Correspondence, 1651–1827, Digital Archives, Library of Congress, Image 273.

15. Quoted in Henry Adams, *History of the United States of America,* 9 vols. (New York: Charles Scribner's Sons, 1891–98), 2: 97, 100.

16. Quoted in Gary Wills, *"Negro President": Jefferson and the Slave Power* (Boston: Houghton Mifflin, 2003), 134.

17. Quoted in Joanne B. Freeman, *Affairs of Honor: National Politics in the New Republic* (New Haven: Yale University Press, 2001), 162.

18. Quoted in Freeman, *Affairs of Honor,* 166.

19. Thomas Jefferson, Nov. 27, 1806, Proclamation on Spanish Dominion Expeditions, Thomas Jefferson Papers Series I, General Correspondence, 1651–1827, Digital Archives, Library of Congress, Image 1303.

20. Thomas Jefferson to Meriwether Lewis, June 20, 1803, Instructions, Thomas Jefferson Papers Series I, General Correspondence, 1651–1827, Digital Archives, Library of Congress, Image 636.

21. Alfred W. Crosby, *The Columbian Exchange: Biological and Cultural Consequences of 1492* (Westport, Conn.: Greenwood, 1972).

22. Elizabeth A. Fenn, *Pox Americana: The Great Smallpox Epidemic of 1775–1782* (New York: Hill and Wang, 2001), 274.
23. Bernard W. Sheehan, *Seeds of Extinction: Jeffersonian Philanthropy and the American Indian* (Chapel Hill: University of North Carolina Press, 1974), 228–229.
24. Quoted in Theda Perdue, *Cherokee Women: Gender and Culture Change, 1700–1835* (Lincoln: University of Nebraska Press, 1998), 115–16.
25. Quoted in William G. McLaughlin, *Cherokee Renascence in the New Republic* (Princeton: Princeton University Press, 1986), 162.
26. Quoted in Anthony F. C. Wallace, *The Death and Rebirth of the Seneca* (New York: Alfred A. Knopf, 1969), 259, 281, 260.
27. Quoted in R. David Edmunds, *The Shawnee Prophet* (Lincoln: University of Nebraska Press, 1983), 32–38.
28. Quoted in R. David Edmunds, *Tecumseh and the Quest for Indian Leadership* (Boston: Little, Brown, 1984), 132.
29. Quoted in Sheehan, *The Seeds of Extinction*, 120–21.
30. Quoted in Sheehan, *The Seeds of Extinction*, 248.

Free Trade

Markets

Barbary Pirates

The Failure of Diplomacy

Markets

Throughout the 1790s and early 1800s, Americans became more interested in consumer items. This development had an impact on the material well-being of people as more and more Americans ate off of ceramic plates, instead of wooden platters; as they sat in chairs, instead of on stools; and as they purchased cloth, instead of wove it themselves. The demand for consumer goods also increasingly brought Americans into a market economy and encouraged the development of capitalism. The new society produced by the American Revolution and the rise of equality fostered an entrepreneurial spirit among individual common men who aggressively sought to make money in innovative ways. Interregional and international trade expanded as merchants sought markets to accommodate the consumer impulse of the public and pursued profits. This trade, along with the United States role as a neutral carrier in a time of war, sustained American economic growth. Although the United States had established some tariffs under the Hamiltonian program, Americans clung to the notion of free trade. They believed that American ships should be allowed to sail to any port and be treated at least the same as even the most favored nation. This ideal was not easy to sustain in the early years of the American republic. Problems arose when outside forces threatened American shipping or attempted to limit American trade. The Barbary States along the shore of North Africa demanded that the United States pay tribute to avoid war. The American government, despite its advocacy of free trade, paid these bribes after Algerians captured a few American vessels in the 1780s and 1790s. In 1801 the United States went to war with Tripoli to avoid increased tribute, proclaiming Tripoli a pirate nation. The United States also faced difficulties with both France and Great Britain as they individually tried to control American trade for their own benefit in their ongoing world war. Americans sought a variety of solutions to these impositions, only to find diplomatic failure in the War of 1812.

Although the consumer revolution in America began some time before 1750, by 1800 it had expanded greatly. One reason for this growth was the introduction of new consumer goods, creating demands for items that had not previously existed. There were also changes in production and marketing that transformed other consumer items, spreading the interest in consumerism into all realms of American society. Whether in a city, a New England town, or the Kentucky frontier, Americans increasingly entered the market economy to gain cash to buy consumer goods and became increasingly capitalistic. The tentacles of the monster of consumerism even extended into the slave quarters and Native American villages. To sustain this dynamic consumerism Americans expanded both interregional and international trade.

The relationship between innovation, consumerism, the market, and capitalism can be seen in the development of the broom. Before 1800 the twig broom predominated. In 1797 farmer Levi Dickinson of Hadley, Massachusetts, began experimenting with growing broom corn. Although his neighbors initially ridiculed Dickinson, taunting him that making brooms was "Indian" work, many soon joined him. Broom making was a wonderful way to earn extra cash during the less labor-intensive winter months on a New England farm. The demand for the new household tool was insatiable and set a new standard for cleanliness. Only a few years before there was no interest in a corn broom; by 1810 New England produced seventy thousand corn brooms and a market of eager consumers had been created. Although broom making remained wedded to traditional household production, expanded production relied on larger marketing networks that ultimately made broom corn and finished brooms commodities traded in the capitalist marketplace. The broom was only the entering wedge of a whole new approach to the household. Over the next couple of decades rugs and carpets were introduced to more and more homes, and a separate room—the parlor—developed as a sign of respectability. Specialized furniture, wallpaper, and ornaments to hang on the walls or display on tables were added consumer goods for which there had previously been no market.[1]

The clock was another innovative item that transformed the lives of the American consumer. In the eighteenth century only the rich could own a clock, which would be proudly and conspicuously displayed as a status symbol amid superfluous household goods. Skilled artisans would be lucky to make twenty-five clock movements a year at a cost of $25 each without a case. Beginning around 1802, Connecticut clockmaker Eli Terry began to develop a quicker way to make clocks using water-powered machinery and wooden parts. Such innovation demanded capital investment and new marketing techniques. In 1806 Terry contracted to make four thousand movements with a distributor who used a system of itinerant peddlers to sell the cheaper clocks. Consumers loved the new clocks. Between 1799 and 1820 there was a sixfold increase in the number of timepieces owned in Connecticut. In 1816 Terry created a shelf clock that soon could be found in homes throughout the country. By the 1840s such clocks were a proud possession in some of the most humble abodes in Arkansas, Kentucky, Indiana, Illinois, and Missouri. What had once been a symbol of genteel status became a mark of civility that could be possessed by almost anyone. Equally important, with every home sporting at least one clock, people's lives were reconfigured. Instead of living strictly by the rhythms of sunrise and sunset, distinguishing the parts of the day by the relative position of the sun (forenoon, high noon, and afternoon), Americans could regulate their lives with the hourly precision of time kept by the household clock. As Henry Terry, Eli's son, later commented, "these things"—cheaply manufactured clocks with an extensive distribution network—"taken together *constituted* a *new form* of clock, *a new article* and a *new manufacture*." It also represented a new way of living in and viewing the world.[2]

The same interaction between innovation, consumerism, the market, and capitalism can also be seen in some more traditional areas of production. Printing was a well-established trade, as attested to in the success of Benjamin Franklin, by the mid-eighteenth century. But during the early republic the production of reading matter underwent a dramatic transformation that enhanced the spread of a print culture. Although colonial craftsmen printed newspapers and books, these items had limited readership. Most Americans might have an almanac and a Bible, but little other printed material in their homes. During the years of the early republic, however, more published matter became available to large numbers of Americans. In part because of politics, and in part because of the geographical spread of the population, newspapers proliferated. In 1790 there were about 100 newspapers in the United States; by 1820 there was almost 600.[3] This development meant that more people were reading "news" and obtaining information about far-off places than ever before (local news was seldom reported in newspapers prior to the 1830s). Publishing a newspaper became such a demanding occupation that printers had to dedicate much of their energy to the enterprise, leading to changes in their profession. A newspaper editor became more writer and politician than mechanic working the printing press. Readers of newspapers became part of a national audience and, through the advertisements that dominated every newspaper, they became informed consumers aware of the latest shifts in taste.

Simultaneously, the book publishing business also changed. Men like Matthew Carey in Philadelphia abandoned their artisan roots and became entrepreneurs whose main occupation became publishing and marketing, rather than printing. To be successful the publisher had to have access to capital to invest in the production of books, and he had to have his finger on the pulse of the market. Publishers hired peddlers, often clergymen, who would sally forth into the countryside to sell their wares. These itinerants would travel hundreds of miles. Books published in Philadelphia reached far into the American South and west to the Mississippi. One of the most successful of the booksellers was Parson Mason Weems, who reported to Carey the needs and desires of his consumers. In 1801 Weems wrote to Carey, declaring, "I deem it glory to circulate valuable books. I would circulate millions. This cannot be effected without the character of *cheapness.*" He wanted the public to point to him as he entered a community and say " *'there goes the little Parson that brings us so many clever books and so cheap'.*"[4] The best-selling books remained religious, including the Bible, but educational matter like Noah Webster's spellers and workbooks also sold well. Weems urged Carey to publish a wider range of works, advising that they should be "of the gay and sprightly kind, Novels, decent plays, elegant Histories. . . . Let the Moral and Religious be as highly dulcified as possible."[5] Following his own advice Weems authored a series of biographies on American heroes from the revolution, including, of course, his contrived *A History of the Life and Death, Virtues and Exploits of General George Washington* (1800), with its fabricated story of a young George, hatchet in hand, confessing that he could not tell a lie and that he had chopped down his father's favorite cherry tree. This best-selling biography, along with Franklin's autobiography, carried a didactic message emphasizing honesty, hard work, and the values of the developing middle class. Thousands of young Americans read this literature, as well as more titillating tales like Susannah Rowsan's *Charlotte Temple,* learning how and how not to behave. Reading became both educational and entertaining. By the 1810s and 1820s most American homes sported an assortment of reading material and libraries opened in countless neighborhoods, creating a broader and more intimate intellectual world. This democratization of the mind changed the very meaning of reading from the mere tool of literacy to, as Justice Joseph Story put it, become "among the necessaries of life."[6]

Consumerism meant more than the introduction of new items or the redefinition of old items. It permeated the everyday experience of Americans. A visit to almost any historical house from the colonial and federal periods bears testimony to the importance of consumer goods to early Americans. These museums, abounding with fine and fancy furniture including elegant dinner tables set with the best china and a bounty of plastic food displayed for the tourist, were the residences of the elite. Homes of the more humble seldom have survived the vagaries of time. An 1811 letter signed by "A Tradesman" appearing in the New York *Independent Mechanic,* a newspaper published for artisans, allows a quick peek into the home of an urban workman and the difficulties the new consumerism presented for the laboring class. The "Tradesman" wrote complaining of his wife "squandering" her husband's "substance" through extravagant dress and holding "tea-parties once or twice a week." The problem was that his wife had a new set of friends who seemed to be competing to ornament their houses and themselves in the latest fashion. The "Tradesman's" wife lamented that her "furniture was become too common" and her "*rag carpet* was a disgrace to the floor." One of her friends had a fine "Turkey carpet, and her husband did not make as much money as" the "Tradesman." Her "chairs were not fit for a decent person to sit on, because Mrs. _____ had a set of white and gold, with *painted rush bottoms.*" The "*calico* curtains ought to be burnt" and his wife "was ashamed to look at them, after she had seen Mrs. _____'s white muslin ones with net fringes and *gilt* cornices." She was also "quite ashamed to ask a few ladies to tea, after having spent an afternoon at Mrs. _____'s, whose set of china cost *forty dollars.*" In other words, everything in the house—"our tables and irons, looking glass"—did not measure up to his wife's developing taste as a consumer and "ought to be sent to vendue" as "they were a disgrace to a decent family." Even her clothes were inadequate. She refused "to be seen twice in the same gown or hat" for fear that "she should be *known* by *clothes,* always in the same dress." After watching his wife's friends drive their husbands to bankruptcy, and all their fine possessions sold at the auction block, the "Tradesman" refused to countenance these extravagancies. His wife reacted by dashing "to the other extreme," ignoring her appearance and not maintaining the household in a decent manner. This left the "Tradesman" equally unhappy, suggesting that even he relished the idea of some participation in the new world of the consumer.[7]

These developments extended into rural areas. Although a local exchange network and household production continued to be important in places like rural New England, by 1800 many families spent as much as one-quarter of their disposable income on goods brought in from outside their locality. Families that produced their own cloth, also bought imported textiles. On June 6, 1797, when Ruth Henshaw and her sisters wove woolen shirting, her parents returned from a Boston shopping spree with "fabric for gowns" and "fashionable hats, purple satin lined with straw." Maine midwife Martha Ballard took pride in the cloth production of her daughters, but also frequented the local stores to purchase crockery, knives and forks, and imported cloth.[8] In fact, the sale of the household production of textiles often provided the cash for the consumer goods. Farmers also sent their excess production to distant markets. A Massachusetts teamster in the 1790s carried pork, butter, leather, and tallow to port towns, and returned with textiles, earthenware, rum, sugar, salt, glass, paper, and gin. A Deerfield boatman on the Connecticut River in 1802 delivered barrel staves to Hartford and returned with brandy, sugar, tea, and salt.[9] Ultimately, the emergence of a market economy led to the rise of the New England village as we know it. Crucial to this development was the creation of town centers with multiple businesses. Town centers became more than simply a meetinghouse or a tavern. They became real villages with shops occupied by artisans such as printers, hatters, and blacksmiths; with stores to sell a variety of goods; and with offices of merchants, lawyers, and doctors. Such towns had "more motion, life, and bustle than in the older parts of the country." Merchants would provide the raw materials for home manufacture—the putting out system—to make cloth or items such as palm hats. Local artisans began producing high-quality goods to compete with the artisans of the cities. These towns became the conduit of communication with post offices, regular stagecoach schedules, and the crossroads of an elaborate system of roads.[10]

Consumerism and the market reached the frontier with the first settlers. As men and women crossed the Appalachians to Kentucky they often secreted within their baggage a few choice luxury items such as tea cups, pewterware, or, in the case of Mary Walker Holloway, an imported Chinese punch bowl. What they could not carry with them as proof of "primitive gentility," newcomers could purchase in stores that quickly opened for business. Fort Boonesborough had a store in 1775, and by 1792, there were twenty stores in Lexington alone. By the early 1800s Kentuckians began to spend a significant proportion of their income on consumer goods such as fancy tableware, coffee, tea, sugar, spices, dozens of different types of cloth, hardware, whiskey, shoes, haberdashery, writing paper, and a host of different items. In 1797 one storekeeper advertised he lost "A CRATE OF QUEENS WARE, containing blue edged plates and dishes, coffee pots, tea pots, coffee cups and saucers, tea cups and saucers, bowls, &c." Even the poorest of customers might purchase pewter or a

FIGURE 9–1   Village Tavern The results of the consumer revolution can be seen in this tavern scene with ample glassware, pictures on the wall, newspapers available for reading, and a traveling salesman with his bag of goods entering through the doorway.

teapot. This consumerism involved Kentuckians in an elaborate exchange and market system that reached down the Mississippi River, over the Appalachians, and across the oceans.[11]

Groups on the periphery of mainstream European American society also participated in the market as consumers. One frontier Kentucky store-keeper noted several purchases by African American slaves in the 1790s and even extended credit to these customers. Jack, a slave of Rebecca Hite, bought tea, shoes, buckles, velvet, and thread at the store, making payment in small amounts of cash along with seven racoon skins and other trade items.[12] Slaves in more developed areas also sought consumer goods, paying for them by any means they could. Sometimes they used produce from small gardens, animals they trapped, or cash earned for work done in what little spare time they had. They might also use items pilfered from their owner or others to obtain a few modest consumer goods. Blacks, both slave and free, in urban centers had greater access to markets and additional sources of income. Whites often complained of the flamboyant dress of African Americans. Elizabeth Drinker in 1799 lamented the extravagant clothing her two black servants, Jacob Turner and Sarah Needham, wore to a wedding: "Jacob dressed in a light cloath coat, white cashmere vest and britches, white silk stockings, and a new hat; Sarah, the bridesmaid, in white muslin dizen'd with white ribbons from head to foot, yellow morocco shoes with white bows."[13]

By 1800 many Native Americans had long been involved in their own rising consumerism that they paid for through the fur or skin trade and by selling land. Even the beads the Indians adorned themselves with came from European glassworks. Native taste in clothing depended on imported textiles, and Indians used European weapons and metal in their everyday activities. Almost every painting of a Native American leader from the period demonstrates this consumerism, including Tecumseh wearing a military jacket with epaulets or Handsome Lake, who may have sported a plumed headdress and body piercings, but also wore a European-style overcoat and a red blanket made of European textiles. Not even the effort to revive original Indian culture could completely purge native society of European American consumer goods.

To reach all of these markets the United States had to develop greater interregional trade. Coastal shipping was crucial to this growth. Between 1790 and 1815 there was a near constant increase in coastal tonnage, tripling in its total. This shipping included the movement of cargos from lesser ports to greater ports for both consumption and export, and the distribution of imports from major ports to minor ports. But as the U.S. interior became more populated and developed, coastal trading, though important, was moving goods around the periphery. River traffic helped ease the flow of merchandise within the continent. By 1807 New Orleans received $5,370,555 worth of commodities that had been floated down the Mississippi.[14] An expanding postal system furthered economic connections between regions. Newspapers could be sent from town to town cheaply—editors often copied stories from other papers verbatim with little concern for attribution—and the mail facilitated exchanges between merchants, storekeepers, and other businessmen. In 1792 the United States had seventy-five post offices and 1,875 miles of post roads. By 1812 there were 2,610 post offices and almost 40,000 miles of post roads.[15] Along with turnpikes, the post roads facilitated the movement of products to market. Interregional transportation remained fairly primitive. During the first decade of the nineteenth century the use of the steamboat was in its early stages. Robert Fulton and Robert Livingston sailed the *Clermont* up the Hudson River on August 14, 1807, but full application of the invention to the nation's rivers would take another decade or more and the great expansion of the canal network would only begin in the 1820s.

However limited, interregional trade was important for most Americans. We can get some idea of how this interregional trade worked by examining the intricate web of exchanges Kentuckians needed to obtain their small luxuries. Tobacco, cotton, pork, or similar products of a farm would be shipped down to New Orleans for export, to gain credit and cash in eastern cities like Philadelphia and Baltimore. In turn, those eastern ports would ship the storekeeper's wares over the mountains and down the Ohio River to Kentucky. Through this process the farmer's wife in Kentucky who sported her best dress at a humble tea party was tied to a market system that reached around the globe. The material for her clothing was probably the product of a textile factory in industrializing Britain and items such as queensware came from the potteries of Englishman Josiah Wedgwood. The tea came from China or India, and the teaspoon of sugar from the West Indies.[16]

International trade thus provided consumer goods for Americans in the wilderness of Kentucky. In a port like Baltimore, Americans had access to even greater variety. In 1806, for example, you could purchase different types of coffee from the East and West Indies and the Isle of Bourbon in the Indian Ocean. You could also select from six kinds of tea from China; eight varieties of sugar; spices ranging from cinnamon, cloves, cassia, ginger, mace, nutmeg, pepper, and pimento; and alcoholic spirits such as French brandy and cognac, Spanish cordials, Dutch and American gin, rum from Jamaica, St. Croix, Antigua, and the Windward Islands, a host of assorted wines, and of course, American whiskey. In addition to these items and consumer goods such as glassware and cloth, Americans could obtain some raw materials such as copper, iron, lead, logwoods, cordage canvass, indigo from Britain, Russia, Sweden, Germany, and India.[17] Taken all together, American imports for consumption quadrupled between 1790 and 1807.[18]

American ships sailed the seven seas in search of markets. During the first decade of the nineteenth century Americans sought trade wherever they could, regardless of the war between Great Britain and France. A brief visit to the Baltimore Customs House in May 1806 provides an idea of the range of this mercantile activity. All ships trading abroad had to register at the customs house and indicate their port of destination. Fifty-six vessels cleared Baltimore for foreign ports that May. Thirty-three vessels for a combined tonnage of 3,335 tons headed for the West Indies, destined for British, French, Spanish, and Danish possessions. Fourteen ships with a combined tonnage of 3,438 tons crossed the Atlantic for Northern Europe to ports including Liverpool, Bristol, Hamburg, Amsterdam, Bremen, Antwerp, and Bordeaux. Another seven vessels went to southern Europe and Mediterranean destinations, including Lisbon, Leghorn, Trieste,

Gibraltar, and Smyrna. Two ships were bound for the Far East ports of Manila and Batavia in the Dutch East Indies. These merchantmen, whether they went to the West Indies, Europe, or further afield, would return laden with the goods that consumers, be they on the East Coast or the wilds of Kentucky, so eagerly sought.[19]

In the holds of these ships as they left port could be any number of products. The West Indies, mainly dedicated to cash crops, especially sugar and coffee, were desperate for the foodstuffs of North America. European markets were more complex. Baltimore at this time was a major grain port, tapping into the wheat-producing areas of Pennsylvania, Maryland, and Virginia. A portion of the cargoes of American ships was therefore home-grown products. Baltimore ships might also export tobacco and some naval stores. Other ports would include these items as well as rice, lumber, and even pot and pearl ash (produced from the residue of burned hardwood trees and used to make soap, glass, and gunpowder) among their exports. The largest export item of this time, at least for ports other than Baltimore, was cotton. In 1790 the United States exported almost no cotton. By 1807 Americans sent overseas over sixty million pounds of cotton and were responsible for over half of the cotton imported into Great Britain.[20]

The reexport trade, however, remained central to American shipping. The fact that Baltimore had a thriving trade with both the West Indies and Europe suggests that the holds of the ships that crossed the Atlantic included coffee, sugar, and other products of the Caribbean. In this way either France or Great Britain could obtain goods from their colonies aboard neutral traders. By 1807, the year of the highest value of reexports in this period, American ships carried almost $60 million worth of reex-port goods for the European powers.[21] Most of this trade flowed through the ports of Philadelphia, New York, and Baltimore, leading to the expansion of these cities. From 1790 to 1810 Baltimore and New York almost tripled in population whereas the number of people in Philadelphia and Boston approximately doubled.

The export and reexport trade together had a profound impact on the American economy, especially in the northeast. With France and Great Britain at war, and with most other European nations dragged in on one side or another, the American merchant marine expanded dramatically. Over 90 percent of all American trade in 1807 was aboard American ships. To meet this demand American shipyards hummed with activity. Any trade connected to the sea—sailmaking, ropemaking, blockmaking, coopering, and so on—thrived. Sailors had a relatively easy time finding employment, although the demand for labor aboard American vessels was so great that the amount of work each sailor had to do at sea increased. Per ton,

American ships had fewer men than ships from other nations. In addition, financial services also expanded. Many of the new state banks in the port cities catered to a mercantile clientele. By 1804 there were forty insurance companies, capitalized at a total of $10 million.[22] Merchants reaped the largest profits, building stately Federal-style mansions and spending more on luxury consumer items. The U.S. government also benefitted, because the largest part of its income was derived from impost duties. Not only did the U.S. customs service collect a tax on all imports, but merchants had to pay a partial duty even on goods intended for reexport. If Americans could somehow maintain neutrality and continue with their trade unmolested by outside forces, prosperity appeared to stretch out before them like the horizon on the open ocean.

Barbary Pirates

American trade, however, ran into problems in a world that did not always greet an independent United States with open arms. One of the benefits of colonial status before 1776 had been the protection of the British navy. Colonial ships had entered the Mediterranean without too much concern for the depredations of the Barbary States—Morocco, Algiers, Tunis, and Tripoli. For centuries these rogue nations periodically declared war on one or another European power, capturing merchantmen, enslaving crews and passengers, and exacting ransom and tribute. Even with its powerful navy, Great Britain contributed to the Barbary coffers as a relatively cheap means to protect its shipping. Independence ended the immunity American vessels enjoyed sailing under the British flag.

The trouble began in October 1784 when Morocco captured the brig *Betsy* and her crew of ten seamen. Although this seizure could be considered an act of war, it was really just a cry for attention. The Moroccan emperor, Sidi Muhammad ibn Abd Allah, was something of a fan of the United States, and had been one of the first rulers to recognize American independence in 1778. The Continental Congress, preoccupied with fighting the Revolutionary War, failed to take notice of Morocco's beneficence and did not pursue a treaty with what must have seemed a distant and exotic nation. Taking the *Betsy* and holding the seamen as hostages sent a message: The United States and Morocco needed to talk and come to a trade agreement. Spain interceded to help with the negotiations and by July 1785 the *Betsy* and the hostages had been released as a goodwill gesture. The United States sent Thomas Barclay to negotiate a treaty with Morocco in 1786, which provided the emperor with $10,000 worth of gifts, established trading relations between the two nations, and to the international community's surprise, set no annual tribute. Had all the Barbary States been so amiable, there would not have been any problem with trade in the Mediterranean.

The British, and the greed of the other North African states, ensured rougher waters for the United States. Encouraged by the British, who wished to control American trade with southern Europe, Algiers declared war on the United States in July 1785. Swooping into the Atlantic, the Algerians quickly captured two American merchantmen and twenty-one crew members off the coast of the Iberian Peninsula. Fortunately for the United States, the Algerians also began to attack Portuguese ships, leading the Portuguese to blockade the Strait of Gibraltar and keeping any other Algerian cruisers from entering the Atlantic Ocean. However, for most of the next decade American shipping could only enter the Mediterranean when Algiers was struck by the plague, thus incapacitating most of its fleet, or with false papers from another nation. In the meantime, the twenty-one American seamen endured the ordeal of slavery.

American diplomats were fully aware of the problem. John Adams, as minister to Great Britain, and Thomas Jefferson, as minister to France, disagreed over the best course of action. Adams pragmatically argued that the United States should simply do what the European nations did—pay tribute and thereby encourage the spread of American commerce. He thought that he could obtain a Dutch loan, believing that a "war will cost us more millions of sterling money" than paying tribute, and that it would lead to "the miserable depression of the reputation of the United States, the cruel embarrassment of all our commerce, and the intolerable burthen of insurance, added to the cries of our countrymen in captivity." He optimistically wrote that "If a perpetual peace" were made with the Barbary States, "the character of the United States would instantly rise all over the world." Equally important, "Our commerce, navigation, and fisheries would extend into the Mediterranean, to Spain and Portugal, France and England. The additional profits would richly repay the interest, and our credit would be adequate to all our wants."[23] Jefferson took a more idealistic and bellicose approach. He believed that the United States should break from the corrupt patterns of European diplomacy and refuse compromise. He wanted to go to war with Algiers and compel the Barbary States to exempt the United States from any tribute. Jefferson outlined his reason in a letter to Adams. He contended that both "Justice" and "Honor" favored war and that it would "procure us respect in Europe, and respect is a safe-guard to interest." War would also be less expensive than tribute and "Equally effectual." As a side benefit, war would lead to the creation of a small navy and thereby strengthen the federal government.[24]

Each diplomat followed a course of action in line with his arguments. Adams tried to negotiate with the Tripolitan ambassador to Great Britain, and even convinced Jefferson to come over from France and join him. However, in the end, Triploli's demand for a payment of 30,000 guineas, when added to what would then have to be paid to Tunis and Algiers, came at too high a price. Jefferson, for his part, hoped to build a coalition of powers—including the Scandinavian countries, German and Italian states, and even Russia—to attack Algiers. But these efforts failed in the face of British and French opposition, individual countries coming to their own settlements with the Barbary States, and the American inability to provide any military support without a navy. When Jefferson headed back to the United States in 1789, nothing had been done to end the conflict with Algiers, and the handful of captured seamen—several had died from the plague—continued to wallow in abject bondage.

The situation remained in limbo despite Jefferson's efforts to encourage some action while he was secretary of state. Jefferson submitted a report to Congress in 1790 that connected the health of the American economy to the Mediterranean trade. He pointed out that between eighty and one hundred American ships a year had traded with the region before independence with as much as one-sixth of the exported wheat, one-fourth of American "dried and pickled fish," and a large proportion of the country's rice production sent to southern Europe. The actions of the Barbary States had a direct bearing on the American farmer by closing these markets. Jefferson outlined three possible actions: paying the tribute; abandoning Mediterranean trade; or building a navy.[25] Congress agreed that the navy was a good idea, but felt that the nation's finances needed to be more secure. It therefore voted to negotiate a settlement, allowing $40,000 to ransom the captives and $100,000 in tribute for Algiers, Tunis, and Tripoli (although neither Tunis nor Tripoli had captured any Americans, they claimed to be at war with the United States until a treaty was signed). However, more delays occurred. In an effort to intimidate the Algerians, Jefferson appointed John Paul Jones as his negotiator. Jones died before leaving Paris. Jefferson then assigned the task to Thomas Barclay, who had worked on the Moroccan treaty. But he too died before getting to Algiers. A third diplomat, David Humphreys, accepted the assignment and headed to Algiers in the fall of 1793.

In the meantime, Great Britain sought again to strike at U.S. trade using diplomatic tricks and the Barbary pirates. The British convinced Portugal to sign a treaty with Algiers in October 1793. The peace lasted only a few weeks, but during the interim the Portuguese withdrew their blockade of the Strait of Gibraltar and Algerian cruisers entered the Atlantic and captured eleven American ships and enslaved over one hundred seamen. What had been a minor problem on the diplomatic back burner, now was a major international conflagration.

The plight of American sailors captured by Algiers became a national issue. Showing their interest in suiting the needs of the market, publishers like Matthew Carey turned out books on the history of Algiers and the Barbary Coast that portrayed the North Africans as a bloodthirsty and criminal people who were the antithesis of liberty-loving and republican Americans. Susannah Rowsan's popular play, *Slaves in Algiers,* capitalized on this new interest. The play asserted American values and contrasted what Rowsan saw as libertine sexuality of Muslim plural marriage with American liberty. Asked to join the harem of the Algerian ben Hassan, the American captive Rebecca declined a "liberty in love" and indignantly warned ben Hassan not to "prostitute" the ideal of liberty "by applying it to licentiousness; the sons and daughters of liberty, take justice, truth, and mercy, for their leaders, when they list under glorious banners."[26] Much of the literature on American captivity in North Africa had an antislavery message. Carey's *Short Account of Algiers* confessed that Americans were "not entitled to charge the Algerines with any exclusive degree of barbarity" in the practice of "buying and selling slaves." But the focus of the interest in the Algerian crisis centered on the American tar and his sacrifice for the rest of society. Reports of the condition of the captured American sailors made their slavery appear worse than the enslavement of blacks in North America by describing how they had their heads shaved, were poorly fed and housed in dungeons, wore coarse clothes, and were sent to work in chains. This treatment was especially galling considering that the comfort and prosperity of the United States depended on common seamen sailing ships taking American produce to overseas markets and bringing consumer goods in exchange. Carey made this connection explicit by reminding his readers how much "the people of the United States" relied on trade. Carey wrote that Americans therefore "cannot be unconcerned at knowing the hard fate of those of their countrymen, who, by being exposed to the severe and perilous duties of the sea" have to suffer "the hard condition of slaves, to the most ferocious enemies to humanity."[27]

This hoopla helped to spur the U.S. government to action. A Federalist-dominated Congress passed legislation in March 1794 to create a navy of six frigates to punish Algiers. The United States also was willing to negotiate. A diplomatic team of Humphreys, Joel Barlow, and Joseph Donaldson worked out a treaty with the Dey of Algiers on September 5, 1795, that agreed to pay ransom for the hostages and $21,000 a year in naval supplies as ongoing tribute. The total payment to Algiers, including peace presents and commissions (really bribes), was $642,500. Difficulties in raising the money through loans caused delays that added costs, including the gift of the *Crescent* frigate to the Dey. The final price of peace came to nearly $1 million.[28] The delays also added to the suffering of the American seamen; they were not released until late in 1796. Because Algiers was the most powerful of the Barbary States, and the only one holding American prisoners, treaties with lesser, one-time payments were quickly arranged with Tunis ($107,000 payment with occasional other gifts required), and Tripoli ($56,486 payment and no annual tribute). Also, the United States had to make a gift ($20,000) to the new ruler of Morocco to sustain the treaty of 1786.[29] By the end of 1797 the Mediterranean was at last open to American merchant vessels.

Peace with any of the Barbary States was never a sure thing. Even though the rulers in each state recognized a certain pecking order, with Algiers on top, they constantly eyed one another with a certain jealousy. If one or another of the Barbary rulers felt that they were not being treated appropriately by a nation with merchant ships in the Mediterranean, then they might declare war, capture a few prizes, and see if they could negotiate a better deal. Each Barbary potentate, moreover, liked to be at war with at least one country at all times to keep his corsairs busy and sustain a supply of captive slaves. Sooner or later, therefore, conflict was bound to erupt again between the United States and one of the Barbary States. The Bashaw of Tripoli, Yusuf Qaramanli, who had been building his navy and extracting more tribute from several European nations, decided that it would be sooner. By 1800 he had grown dissatisfied with his arrangement with the United States. He had received far less than Tunis and Algiers from the Americans and believed that his growing power warranted greater gifts and respect. As a symbol of his displeasure, one of Qaramanli's vessels captured an American merchantman in July 1800, but the bashaw later released the vessel and crew. American prestige in the area was on the wane. When the first American warship, the *George Washington* under Captain William Bainbridge, visited Algiers in September 1800, the dey compelled the vessel to serve as his messenger by insisting, under the threat of batteries of cannon, that Bainbridge sail to Constantinople and deliver tribute and presents to the Ottoman sultan for the dey. Encouraged by these actions, the bashaw wanted a new treaty that would include a $225,000 one-time payment and an annual tribute of $25,000. William Eaton, the American consul in Tunis, advised the administration that "If the United States will have a free commerce in this sea they must defend it." Paying the bashaw more tribute would only increase the demands made by Tunis and Algiers. When the United States did not come up with the money, and in fact was still late in the final payment from the previous treaty, the bashaw ordered the flagstaff of the American consul in Tripoli to be cut down on May 14, 1801—the traditional Barbary action proclaiming a declaration of war.[30]

The United States was in a different position in 1801 than it had been in the early 1790s. Although there had been delays, and construction on some of the frigates had even been temporarily suspended after the 1795 treaty with Algiers, the United States not only had a navy, it was already battle-tested in the Quasi War. Thomas Jefferson as the new Republican president may have been committed to smaller government, but he also had a long history dating back to his diplomatic service in Europe of advocating fighting the Barbary States rather than relying on the corrupt diplomacy of the Old World and paying tribute and bribes. Before he even read Eaton's dispatch, Jefferson met with his cabinet and decided "to detach a squadron of observation into the Mediterranean sea, to superintend the safety of our commerce there."[31] Though he hoped that the mere presence of an American naval force would dissuade any Barbary State from going to war with the United States, the sailing orders to Commodore Richard Dale in command of the fleet provided specific instructions concerning operations if one or more Barbary powers had declared war by the time the fleet arrived. If the bashaw alone had declared war, then Dale was to blockade the port of Tripoli as "The force of Tunis & Tripoli are contemptible, & might be crushed with any one of the Frigates under" Dale's command.[32]

However contemptible Tripoli may have been, the war turned out to be more difficult than anyone expected, lasting four years and costing millions of dollars. The conflict included a few spectacular triumphs, one horrendous disaster, and a great deal of wasted time and effort. Part of the problem was geographical. No Tripolitan vessel stood a chance in a sea battle with one of the American superfrigates, and even the smaller U.S. ships demonstrated superior gunnery and fire power. However, attacking a fortified port with a treacherous harbor to negotiate or maintaining a blockade off the coast of North Africa was a complex task that was often beyond the navy's capabilities. Part of the problem was also a failure in leadership. Several American commanders seemed to think that all they had to do was show up in the Mediterranean and fly the American flag and the bashaw, and other Barbary potentates, would capitulate. This approach was a serious underestimation of the flexibility and determination of Tripoli and the other Barbary States.

The American navy achieved very little in the opening two years of the war. The first American squadron in the Mediterranean, which included four frigates and a schooner, managed to bottle the Tripolitan flagship in

Gibraltar, visit Algiers and Tunis to show American determination, and briefly blockade Tripoli. There was also one sea battle in which the American schooner *Enterprise* pulverized the *Tripoli,* a vessel of equal size. But the blockade was ineffectual and had to be abandoned in September 1801 because of short supplies and an expanding sick list. An even larger fleet, under Commodore Richard Morris, was sent to the Mediterranean in the spring of 1802 to relieve Dale and his men, whose enlistments were expiring. Morris achieved even less than Dale, occupying himself with sailing from one Mediterranean port after another, attending balls and seeing the sights. At one point an exasperated William Eaton asked of the naval officers, "What have they done but dance and wench?"[33] The answer was that they also drank, argued, and fought duels with each other. For two months in the summer one American ship, the *Constellation,* lay off Tripoli, and its blockade was so porous that it did not even stop a Tripolitan cruiser and its American prize from entering the harbor. After the *Constellation* left for Malta in mid August, no American ship appeared off Tripoli until May 1803. In the meantime, Morris managed to insult both the Bey of Tunis and the Dey of Algiers while making so-called courtesy calls in the Barbary States not at war with the United States. During the operations in May and June 1803 the American navy engaged in several actions, made a few captures, and even landed a small contingent of marines and navy men on shore in a raid to destroy shipping. However, by the end of June, Morris had called off the blockade and returned to Malta, where his wife had just had a baby. Taken all together, it was not a very impressive showing. When Morris attempted to negotiate with Yusuf Qaramanli, the bashaw demonstrated his contempt for American forces by insisting that the United States pay $200,000 in cash, $20,000 a year in tribute, cover Tripoli's expenses in the war, and provide "A Quantity of Military & Naval Stores Annually."[34] Morris was eventually court-martialed and dismissed from service for his lack of vigor against Tripoli.

The war entered a more active phase with the replacement of Morris on June 21, although the letter informing Morris of this fact took several months to reach him. The new commodore was Edward Preble in command of the *Constitution.* Before sailing to Tripoli with his fleet, Preble first had to intimidate Morocco, which had declared war on the United States. The capture of a Moroccan cruiser and its American prize and the mere appearance of a powerful American fleet in Tangiers convinced the Moroccans to reconfirm the 1786 treaty on October 11, 1803. Before this peace, Preble sent the frigate *Philadelphia* and the schooner *Vixen* out ahead to Tripoli. The main fleet consisting of the frigates *Constitution* and *John Adams,* along with several smaller vessels designed to maintain a blockade close in to shore, would follow after a stop at Algiers. The delay had a fatal consequence for the war. The *Philadelphia* and the *Vixen* arrived off Tripoli on October 7. Captain Bainbridge of the *Philadelphia* sent the *Vixen* to chase some corsairs who were reported 150 miles away, leaving the *Philadelphia* to guard Tripoli alone. On October 31, Bainbridge ordered his large ship too close to shore in pursuit of a Tripolitan vessel making for port. Without proper charts, the *Philadelphia* struck some rocks and was grounded. Tripolitan gunboats surrounded the crippled ship, firing into it as the Americans struggled to free themselves by tossing cannon and supplies overboard, cutting down masts, and lightening ship. Unable to fight back, stranded in Tripoli harbor without any other American vessel in sight, Bainbridge surrendered. Not only did this "unfortunate event" hand the bashaw more than three hundred American seamen as hostages, but it also presented him with 36-gun frigate after a gale a few days later floated the *Philadelphia* free from the rocks.[35]

The capture of the *Philadelphia* was a disaster that threatened to destroy Preble's mission even before he got started. Efforts to blockade Tripoli in the winter failed, given that the storming north winds might push the American vessels ashore. Fortunately, the Americans did capture one Tripolitan vessel in their brief winter operation. Renamed the *Intrepid*, Lieutenant Stephen Decatur, Jr., sailed the vessel with its Barbary rigging and under a British flag into Tripoli harbor on the evening of February 16. In an incredible act of daring that did much to redeem national pride and reputation, the Americans boarded the *Philadelphia* and burned it to the waterline. Only one American sailor received some slight wounds. The rest escaped the harbor unscathed.

Buoyed by this success, Preble not only planned on a spring blockade, but also some more direct military action. While he kept a few ships off Tripoli in the spring and early summer, Preble added a number of gunboats and floating batteries to his fleet, some of which were borrowed from the Kingdom of the Two Sicilies. By the beginning of August he was ready for action. On August 3, 1804, an American fleet bombarded Tripoli, and engaged Tripolitan vessels in fierce combat. Despite the heroics of men like Decatur, who boarded several Tripolitan vessels, little was achieved in this attack. The Americans renewed the assault on August 7 with an effort to bombard the city from a side bay. Again, the results were meager, and one American gunboat was blown up by a direct hit from shore. Although he had some wind taken out of his sails by receiving news that he was to be replaced by Samuel Barron, Preble was nothing if not persistent. He led his squadron on three other forays against Tripoli on August 24, 28, and September 3, in an effort to compel the bashaw to make peace.

BOMBARDMENT OF TRIPOLI.

FIGURE 9–2 Attack on Tripoli In August and early September 1804, the U.S. Navy bombarded Tripoli several times in an effort to free commerce from raids by the Barbary States.

On September 4, Preble sent a fireship into Tripoli harbor, which either was hit by Tripolitan cannon or blew up on its own, killing the volunteer crew. Preble may have destroyed some shipping and lofted shells into the city, but he was unable to shake Tripolitan resolve. In early September he decided to end the attacks and await his replacement.

The war now entered its final and, in many ways, most bizarre stage. After wintering in Malta and Sicily, with its new commodore too ill most of the time to command, the American navy prepared for another assault on Tripoli in the spring. Simultaneously, William Eaton engaged in a project of his own to replace Yusuf Qaramanli with his brother Hammet, who had been overthrown by Yusuf several years earlier. Eaton had managed to get some support for this adventure in the United States, but neither Barron nor Tobias Lear, who was supposed to negotiate with Tripoli, put much faith in the enterprise. Eaton found Hammet in Egypt, recruited a small international force of mercenaries, and some North African Arabs, and along with a parcel of U.S. marines, marched from Egypt to eastern Libya. Somehow Eaton kept this discordant force together despite near mutiny, poor supplies, and minimal naval support. He even defeated the bashaw's forces at Derne, capturing this Libyan town on April 28, 1805. However, he was still hundreds of miles from Tripoli. Yusuf Qaramanli, however, saw the threat as real. The war had finally taken its toll on his state. He had to increase taxes and recruit men into his army, and he had little opportunity to send out cruisers with American ships outside Tripoli. Poor harvests exacerbated his situation. The only advantage he had was the Americans captured from the *Philadelphia*. With an American fleet under John Rodgers, who was serving for the ailing Barron, ready to recommence operations, the bashaw finally signed a peace on June 4. Although the United States agreed to abandon all support for Hammet's insurgency and pay $60,000 for the hostages, Americans claimed victory as there would be no annual tribute and it appeared to be the result of the force of arms.

Trouble with the Barbary States did not completely go away. Rodgers sailed from Tripoli to Tunis, where he promised to use force unless the Bey of Tunis backed off from his threats to attack American shipping. Here, the presence of American arms had its effect. Rodgers wanted to keep his fleet in the Mediterranean to protect American shipping. However, during 1807 more serious threats emerged to American commerce and the American navy was withdrawn to North American waters.

The Failure of Diplomacy

Jefferson was a lucky president in his first term. The war with Tripoli was a minor irritant. Despite years of procrastination and inactivity, the occasional accomplishment, especially Decatur's spectacular raid into Tripoli harbor and the burning of the *Philadelphia*, allowed the war to appear as something of a triumph. Diplomatically, his administration also stumbled into the deal of the century—the Louisiana Purchase. The opening years of his administration were blessed with relatively peaceful relations with Great Britain and France. Adams had seen to it that the Quasi War was over before Jefferson took office. France and Great Britain agreed to the Peace of Amiens (1801), which may have hurt the reexport trade, but also eased international tensions for the United States. Even the British prize courts seemed to smile on Jefferson. The *Polly* decision in 1800 allowed the reexport trade if the goods were landed in a neutral country (the United States), a small duty was paid, and then the goods were shipped to Europe.

After Great Britain and France resumed their war in May 1803, Jefferson's luck began to run out. The renewed conflict only intensified as France expanded its reach throughout continental Europe and Great Britain solidified its control of the seas after the Battle of Trafalgar (October 21, 1805). Faced with a stalemate, each belligerent sought to bring the other to its knees through economic coercion. American merchant ships plying the Atlantic with holds brimming with West Indies products became the target of regulations by both warring nations. Britain signaled a change in policy with the *Essex* decision of 1805, which made it more difficult for Americans to evade British trade restrictions concerning France and its allies. The case involved some wine that had been shipped from Spain, through the United States, to Havana. The British court declared that the reshipment of the wine through the United States had been merely to deceive the British navy and that the duties paid had been minimal. Henceforth, such sham operations were to be illegal. As a result of the decision the British navy seized dozens of American ships that had followed similar procedures. American merchants, however, quickly caught on and devised new stratagems, including the selling of the cargo in the United States, that allowed them to carry out the reexport trade almost as before; total American trade declined only about 1 percent from 1805 to 1806, and then picked up again in 1807.

Beyond the immediate impact on commerce, the *Essex* decision had an important symbolic meaning for Anglo-American relations. The court shifted the burden of proof from the British navy to the American merchant. Previously, a navy captain had to demonstrate that an American vessel had violated regulations; now, the American captain had to prove that he had not violated the regulations. In other words, owners of American merchant vessels were now considered guilty until they could prove themselves innocent. The ruling also added a degree of instability to American commercial enterprise. There had been no warning that a change of policy was about to take place. If Britain could change a policy of five years so abruptly once, who was to say that there would not be another ruling to allow even more captures. The whole procedure seemed to reflect a capriciousness and lack of respect for the American flag. The British demonstrated their arrogance, as well, when ambassador James Monroe protested the *Essex* decision: Monroe was informed that the issue was not "of so pressing a nature" as to warrant any diplomatic discussion.[36]

In 1805 and 1806 the *Essex* decision was only one of several problems with the British for the United States. Perhaps the issue of greatest concern to ordinary Americans was impressment. The British navy desperately needed men to sail its ships and defend the nation. In 1792 there were 36,000 men in the British navy. By 1805 that number had risen to 120,000. After 1805 it took an additional 10,000 men a year just to keep the ships manned at the same level. The British tapped their merchant marine almost to the breaking point for seamen. They eagerly recruited foreign nationals to serve in his majesty's navy. Even Americans who might have been unable to find a regular berth on a merchantmen, or who wanted the recruitment bounty, volunteered. The British also relied on press-gangs in British ports to draft men into the navy. Periodically, press-gangs swept through the waterfront, entering bars and brothels, hoping to catch sailors unaware. These efforts were still not enough. The British searched merchant ships as they entered or left a port, and stopped ships on the high seas in their insatiable thirst for more seamen.

American neutrality presented a problem for the British. As the carrying trade expanded, so, too, did the need for skilled seamen on American ships. A captain anxious to leave a port cared little where a man was from. He was willing to pay good wages, often twelve to fourteen dollars a month, so he could put out to sea. Many merchant seamen exchanged their berth on a British vessel for an American one. Likewise, men in the British navy, in which service was for the duration and the treatment often harsh, would desert to sail aboard an American ship. The British and Americans also had different notions of citizenship. The British insisted that birthplace dictated an inalienable nationality—if a person was born in the British Isles he stayed forever a subject of the king. Americans held that a person could obtain citizenship after a specified number of years of residence. Given these different definitions of citizenship and the British need for seamen, as well as a shared language and culture, there was bound to be confusion over distinguishing between British and American seamen. The British navy included thousands of Americans aboard their ships, many of whom were taken from vessels flying the U.S. flag. To avoid any questions of citizenship, the United States issued certificates called protections that were supposed to declare that a sailor was born in America and should be protected from impressment. But these documents were little more than a sworn affidavit by a sailor offering a description and stating he was born in a particular location. Every British officer knew a protection was easily forged and sometimes sold for as little as a dollar along the waterfront. The British were not unreasonable in all cases of impressment. Sometimes the legal process worked and many an American tar was released from the clutches of a press-gang when he flashed his protection. The U.S. government also stepped in to get Americans released from the British navy. Before 1804 the State Department officially protested over a thousand impressments. The British government released about half of these men as bonafide Americans. After 1804, however, as Britain renewed its struggle with France, fewer than one in three men were released.

There is no question that Americans suffered as a result of impressment. Many Americans found their protections useless when confronted by a British captain in need of seamen. One officer told a group of Americans he was about to press: "men I will not look at your protections—my ship is in distress, and I will have men to carry me to England."[37] The ordeal of American tars in the British navy became a popular concern in the years leading up to the War of 1812, just as the captivity of American sailors by the Barbary pirates had been so important in the 1790s and early 1800s. In 1811, a Boston newspaper referred to impressment as an "atrocity . . . of the blackest and most savage complexion" and a "barbarous" practice tantamount to the theft of American citizens.[38]

Despite such claims, the U.S. government did not do everything it could to resolve the impressment issue. The reason for this failure to compromise was simple—it would hurt American commerce because there were more British subjects working on American ships than Americans who were impressed. In 1805 there were about 64,000 men sailing on U.S. merchant ships and fishing vessels, but only about 18,000 of these men were rated able seamen—the highest level of skilled mariner. Secretary of Treasury Albert Gallatin reported to Jefferson that half of these were probably British subjects even by American standards. There were also quite a few British deserters in the U.S. navy. Any equitable solution to the impressment question would have included forcing these British seamen to serve in his majesty's navy. Jefferson recognized that this action would have crippled American commerce and therefore he would just as soon leave impressment out of any agreement with the British.[39]

Impressment, however, was the type of issue that could bring American blood to a boil. When British ships began to search American vessels as they left U.S. ports, the popular mood could turn ugly very quickly. In April 1806, the captain of the HMS *Leander* ordered a warning shot to be fired across the bow of an American ship outside of New York in an effort to overhaul the vessel to search for British deserters. Unfortunately, the *Leander's* gun crew was not too accurate and accidently killed an American seaman, John Pierce, in the process. When news of this incident reached New York, crowds gathered in outrage. British officers in the city had to be taken into custody for their own safety and mobs seized supplies destined for the British navy. Protest spread through the nation. Jefferson insisted that the British ships leave New York's waters and demanded that the captain of the *Leander* be court-martialed.

The *Leander* affair occurred in the midst of an increasingly difficult international scene for the United States. James Monroe, later joined by special envoy William Pinkney of Maryland, was in London trying to negotiate a new treaty with the British to replace the expiring Jay Treaty. Jefferson wanted the British to allow the reexport trade and to end impressments in exchange for continued American trade. Angered by the increased seizures of American shipping, Congress passed a Non-Importation Act in April 1806. The law threatened to stop the importation of certain commodities—some metal goods, cloth made of hemp or flax, expensive woolens, glass, finished clothing, beer, ale, and a few other items—unless the British agreed to a treaty. It did not proscribe the most significant imports such as cottons, cheap woolens, steel, and iron. To allow the British time to consider the Non-Importation Act, the law set up a November timetable for implementation. Jefferson later extended this date and the law was not invoked until 1807. Extreme Republicans, who were willing to forego all international trade, viewed the measure as too weak. John Randolph of Virginia proclaimed the law "A milk-and-water bill, a dose of chicken broth to be taken nine months hence." The British thought the Americans could never give up their need for consumer items and labeled the law a "foolish and teasing measure" that was mere bluff and bluster.[40]

Despite the Non-Importation Act and the imbroglio over the murder of Pierce, the British had actually become more receptive to the American position with a new government under Charles James Fox and Lord Grenville. In May 1806 they declared a blockade of France and French-controlled ports, but stated that it would be enforced strictly only between the Seine and Ostend. Beyond that limit neutral trade would be allowed. The British also signed a new treaty with the Americans in December 1806. Although the British made some trade concessions, the Monroe-Pinkney Treaty was less than what Jefferson had expected. The British agreed to allow American trade between the French West Indies and unblockaded ports in France, as long as the Americans paid more than a token customs duty in the United States. The British, however, did little concerning impressment other than to provide a note stating that they would try not to impress Americans. Jefferson refused to even send the treaty to the Senate for consideration.

Simultaneously, the screws began to tighten on American commerce. Napoleon countered the British blockade with his own paper blockade in the Berlin Decree of November 1806. The edict prohibited all trade with Britain. In addition, French ports, and the ports under Napoleon's expanding control in his Continental System, were closed to any vessel that stopped in a British port. The British countered in January 1807 with an Order in Council that prohibited trade between French ports or its allies.

On June 22, 1807, the situation reached crisis proportions when the British attacked the U.S. frigate *Chesapeake*. The British had stationed a small squadron off the Chesapeake Bay, trapping two French war vessels that had gained a safe haven in Norfolk, Virginia, in August 1806. During the long wait for the French ships to repair and head to sea, the British navy bought supplies and drinking water in the United States. But any time a British warship came near shore, it was likely to lose a few men to desertion. Several of these deserters promptly enlisted in the American army or navy. As the *Chesapeake* prepared to go to sea that spring to join the American ships stationed in the Mediterranean, at least four British deserters signed on for the cruise. British officers quickly discovered what had happened and lodged formal protests. One deserter even met a British officer in a Norfolk street, damned him, and asserted that "he was in the Land of Liberty; and that he would do as he liked."[41] American officials knew the men were deserters, but believed their stories that they were pressed Americans. (Only one, as it later turned out, had been born in Great Britain. The other three were Americans who may or may not have signed on to the British navy of their own free will.) British naval officers were very unhappy about this position, especially because they returned three deserters from the American army who had just joined the British navy. Aware of this situation, the senior British officer, Admiral George Berkeley in Halifax, ordered the British to stop and search any American warship that left Norfolk that harbored deserters.

As soon as the *Chesapeake* put to sea and reached international waters, the HMS *Leopard* intercepted it. Although the *Leopard* carried more guns, the two ships were relatively evenly matched—at least on paper. But the *Leopard* under Captain Salusbury Humphreys had a seasoned and well-trained crew, whereas the *Chesapeake* was only beginning its voyage with a raw crew that had not even worked the guns. In fact, the *Chesapeake* was poorly prepared for battle; its gun decks were littered with debris and supplies. As the *Leopard* neared, Commodore James Barron did not clear for action, the standard procedure at the approach of a foreign vessel of war. When Humphreys demanded to search the vessel for the deserters he knew were on board, all Barron could do was refuse and try to get his men quietly to their battle stations. Humphreys, however, was not going to give up his advantage. He closed, then opened fire. The *Chesapeake* was a scene of complete confusion and after about fifteen minutes managed to fire only one gun, for the honor of the flag, before Barron surrendered. The British had gotten off at least three broadsides, killing three Americans and wounding another sixteen, including Barron. Humphreys refused the *Chesapeake* as a prize, but did take the four known deserters. The *Chesapeake* limped back to Norfolk a symbol of national dishonor.

Americans reacted with shock and horror to the attack, and clamored for war. In Norfolk citizens attacked a British watering crew and local officials organized a committee of correspondence to prepare for a possible British invasion. Public meetings, sometimes attended by thousands, proclaimed popular outrage in Baltimore, New York, Philadelphia, Charleston, and even in Federalist Boston. At an assembly on July 8 the people of Wilmington, North Carolina, agreed that "our rights as an Independent nation" had been violated and that the attack was "tantamount to a declaration of war, or a flagrant violation of our sovereignty."[42]

If Jefferson wanted a war with the British all he had to do was call a special session of Congress. In July, Republican leader Elbridge Gerry wrote to Madison, "the public indignation is universally excited by the repeated destruction of our unoffending seamen." He believed that "if redress for the present, and prevention for the future, cannot be obtained, will not a state of warfare, be preferable to such a state of national insult and degredation."[43] Although Jefferson ordered all British vessels to leave American waters on July 2, and called on the states to activate 100,000 militiamen to protect the nation, he hesitated to push for immediate war. In the middle of the summer there were too many American merchant ships out to sea. A declaration of war would leave them easy pickings for the British navy. In the process, the United States might lose thousands of sailors who would either be sent to prison or forced to fight for the British. Moreover, the United States was unprepared for war: Its army was small, its port cities virtually defenseless. America needed time to get ready for war. Jefferson also sought a diplomatic solution and instructed Monroe to continue the negotiations, although he now tied Monroe's hands by insisting that Britain agree to end impressment aboard both public and private U.S. vessels.

By the fall of 1807, when Jefferson finally called Congress into session, the furor had quieted. The Republicans who controlled Congress hoped for an alternative to war. The Federalists, who represented the mercantile interests of New England, opposed any thought of war and simply wanted to find a way to keep American commerce afloat. The international situation now became even more difficult. The British admitted that the attack on the *Chesapeake* had been wrong, but also insisted that the Americans were partially to blame for not turning over the deserters before the *Chesapeake* sailed. They refused to reconsider their policy on impressment and reasserted their right to impress any British-born seamen on non-British ships. That fall news arrived in the United States that France had begun to seize American vessels under the Berlin Decree. On November 11, 1807, a new Tory government less sympathetic to the Americans issued an Order in Council that stated that any neutral ship that wanted to trade with Napoleonic Europe must first stop in a British port to obtain a license indicating that the cargo was not contraband. Napoleon responded with the Milan Decree of December 17, 1807, which declared that any neutral ship that stopped in a British port, or was searched by a British ship, would be seized on entering a French port or any port controlled by France's allies. Taken together, the new British and French regulations put American ships in an impossible situation, and liable to confiscation by either or both of the warring nations. Even before this gridlock became apparent, Congress instituted the Non-Importation Act on December 14 and decided to pass an embargo stopping all American international trade. U.S. ships were forbidden to leave port and foreign vessels could depart only in ballast or with the goods already in their holds.

The idea behind the embargo of December 22, 1807, was that Europe needed America more than the United States needed Europe. It harked back to previous American efforts at economic coercion during the resistance movement of the 1760s and 1770s and was based on the belief that the virtue of an agrarian republic in the New World would trump the consumer luxuries of a corrupt Old World. This assumption seriously misconstrued the nature of the American economy. Americans not only dearly loved their consumer goods, but were also dependent on the export market for income. The embargo therefore devastated the American economy. Within months the American docks went from "noise and bustle" where "everything was in motion" to desolation with "Not a box, bale, cask, barrel, or package" to be seen, with grass growing on the wharves.[44] Exports plummeted from about $108 million to $22 million and imports declined from $144 million to $58 million. The reexport trade declined from about $60 million to $13 million.[45] Numbers do not reflect the human cost. Sailors who only a few months before had their choice of good berths at decent wages, now faced unemployment. In Baltimore, Philadelphia, and New York they held mass meetings to petition officials for work. Mechanic shops that had hummed with business now stood idle. Even Jefferson's independent farmers suffered, as they found it difficult to sell their produce. Wheat declined from two dollars a bushel to seventy-five cents a bushel, if a farmer was lucky enough to find a buyer. The tobacco market completely collapsed and the growers of rice and cotton also had difficulty. Bankruptcies spread, foreclosures increased, and sheriff sales were everywhere.

Of course, there were evasions of the law. Coastal voyages were not prohibited and it became all too easy to be blown off course to the West Indies or Halifax, where the ship was unloaded. Goods streamed across the border with Canada in upstate New York, Vermont, and New Hampshire. Jefferson struggled to stop this rampant violation of the law. Congress repeatedly strengthened the enforcement provisions of the embargo, increasing the bonds paid to ensure coastal voyages kept to their U.S. destinations, and enhancing the power of the government to prevent smuggling. Troops were dispatched to the borders with Canada and Florida, and ships were stationed to intercept embargo violators. On April 19, 1808, Jefferson, who once thought "a little rebellion now and then was a good thing," issued a proclamation stating "that sundry persons are combined or combining and confederating together on Lake Champlain and the country thereto adjacent for the purposes of forming insurrections against the authority of the laws of the United States" and evading the embargo.[46] All of these efforts accomplished little. In a convoluted logic, the more successful the embargo became, the more likely it was to lead to evasions as prices soared and the inducements to smuggling increased. If the price of flour in the British West Indies shot up from $8.25 to $40 a barrel, some entrepreneurial merchant would be sure to take advantage and find a way to ship flour illegally to the high-priced market. Lest we think that only sharp Yankee traders sidestepped the law, by the beginning of 1809 the largest single item smuggled out of the United States was cotton produced by Jeffersonian southern farmers seeking to take advantage of skyrocketing prices in England.[47]

Although the embargo hurt the economy overall, it also encouraged increased domestic manufacturing, thus furthering American material independence. Before 1808, fifteen cotton mills had been built in the United States; by 1809, eighty-seven more cotton factories had been added, with a capacity of 31,000 spindles as compared to 8,000 spindles before the embargo. Other industries also experienced some growth. Jefferson and his administration recognized this positive development. In 1810, Albert Gallatin reported that "the injurious violations of the neutral commerce of the United States, by forcing industry and capital into other channels, have broken inveterate habits, and given a general impulse, to which must be ascribed the great increase of manufactures during the last two years."[48] Even before the embargo Jefferson wrote that the diplomatic crisis had encouraged domestic manufacturing, especially in cloth. By April 1808, Jefferson was excited by the strides taken in domestic manufacturing and bragged that the United States would never again have to depend on imported textiles. He asserted that much of the increase in production was in household manufacturing that was "unseen by the public eye" and provided coarse goods for families. His experience in these years taught him to appreciate a more integrated economy that would include "An equilibrium of agriculture, manufactures, and commerce." Even after he retired, Jefferson continued his interest in domestic manufacturing, taking pride in the cloth produced within his own household and bragging to John Adams how only a few slaves could make enough material for his entire plantation.[49]

Whatever silver lining Jefferson may have found in the embargo, it created serious political problems for him. The Federalists did not disappear after their defeat in 1800. They lost the election and faded from political power, but lingered in the wings. Their stronghold was in New England, where they could still garner majorities. Before 1800, the Federalists were nothing more than a loose coalition of like-minded men who might caucus together and even support a slate of candidates. After 1800, they became a more regular political party, with carefully crafted organizational structures on the state level. The embargo offered them an opportunity to regain some lost ground. Federalists attacked the embargo mercilessly, calling it the "dambargo" and publishing political cartoons featuring a turtle called "Ograbme"—embargo spelled backward—threatening American trading vessels. Clever Federalists pushed the anagram even further:

Embargo read backward, O-grab-me appears,

A scary sound ever for big children's ears.

The syllables transformed, Go bar' em comes next

FIGURE 9–3 Ograbme, or the American Snapping Turtle Federalists made fun of the Republican embargo, scrambling the letters and creating a snapping turtle that grabbed anyone who would trade with Britain.

A mandate to keep ye from harm, says my text.

Analyze Miss Embargo, her letters, I'll wage,

If not removed shortly, will make mob-rage.[50]

The Federalist appeal remained limited, but it was strong enough to retake control of Massachusetts and force John Quincy Adams, who had become a Jeffersonian, out of the Senate. The Federalists also increased their presence in the rest of New England, and made some gains in New York and elsewhere. However, they could not seriously challenge the Republicans on the national ticket, and Jefferson's chosen successor, James Madison, handily won the presidency in 1808.

By the beginning of 1809, nearly everyone recognized that the embargo was a failure. Britain had not been brought to her knees and France, it seemed, could not care less about the U.S. trade. Evasion had reached proportions that almost made the law a dead letter. And the Federalists continued to gain ground as the law became increasingly unpopular. Jefferson left office under a cloud of derision for pursuing an ineffectual policy. Although some politicians clamored for war, most still hoped to avoid it. Congress repealed the embargo in February, to be effective March 4, 1809 (inauguration day), and simultaneously passed the Non-Intercourse Act. This legislation prohibited all export and import trade with England and France and closed American ports to their warships. It also promised to resume normal trade with either belligerent if it lifted its trade restrictions. American ships could trade with any other nation. The law was ridiculous. As John Randolph sourly explained, "We have trusted our most precious interests in this leaky vessel."[51] American merchants could easily sidestep the law by sailing illegally to either Great Britain or France directly, or by going to some neutral port and then, ironically, engaging in a new kind of reexport trade whereby the cargo could be shipped to the prohibited nations. Given that the law had even less impact on either Britain or France than the embargo, it was replaced in 1810 with Macon's Bill Number Two. Under this legislation the United States would trade with France and Great Britain regardless of the trade regulations. However, if either power accepted American conditions for free trade, then the United States would reinstitute nonintercourse with the other power. Diplomatically, this measure was also a failure. Napoleon shrewdly suggested he might repeal the Berlin and Milan decrees. Although Napoleon never followed through on his suggestion, the United States foolishly believed him, reinstating nonintercourse with Great Britain in February 1811. This action helped bring on the debacle of the War of 1812.

Endnotes

1. Richard L. Bushman, *The Refinement of America: Persons, Houses, Cities* (New York: Alfred A. Knopf, 1992); Gregory H. Nobles, "Commerce and Community: A Case Study of the Rural Broommaking Business in Antebellum Massachusetts," *Journal of the Early Republic*, 4 (1984), 287–308.

2. Quoted in David Jaffee, "Peddlers of Progress and the Transformation of the Rural North, 1760–1860," *Journal of American History*, 78 (1991), 517.

3. Jeffrey L. Pasley, *"The Tyranny of Printers": Newspaper Politics in the Early Republic* (Charlottesville: University Press of Virginia, 2001), 403.

4. Quoted in Rosalind Remer, *Printers and Men of Capital: Philadelphia Book Publishers in the New Republic* (Philadelphia: University of Pennsylvania Press, 1996), 128.

5. Quoted in Jaffee, "Peddlers of Progress," *Journal of American History*, 78 (1991), 519.

6. Quoted in William J. Gilmore, *Reading Becomes a Necessity of Life: Material and Cultural Life in Rural New England, 1780–1835* (Knoxville: University of Tennessee Press, 1989), 20.

7. Paul A. Gilje and Howard B. Rock, eds., *Keepers of the Revolution: New Yorkers at Work in the Early Republic* (Ithaca, N.Y.: Cornell University Press, 1992), 264–69.

8. Laurel Thatcher Ulrich, *The Age of Homespun: Objects and Stories in the Creation of an American Myth* (New York: Alfred A. Knopf, 2001), 298.

9. Christopher Clark, *The Roots of Rural Capitalism: Western Massachusetts, 1780–1860* (Ithaca, N.Y.: Cornell University Press, 1990), 28–38.

10. Quoted in David Jaffee, *People of the Wachusett: Greater New England in History and Memory, 1630–1860* (Ithaca, N.Y.: Cornell University Press, 1999), 219.

11. Elizabeth A. Perkins, "The Consumer Frontier: Household Consumption in Early Kentucky," *Journal of American History*, 78 (1991), 486–510. Quotations from ibid., 489, 499.

12. Perkins, "The Consumer Frontier," *Journal of American History*, 78 (1991), 496–97.

13. Quoted in Gary B. Nash, *Forging Freedom: The Formation of Philadelphia's Black Community, 1720–1840* (Cambridge: Harvard University Press, 1988), 220.

14. Douglass C. North, *The Economic Growth of the United States, 1790–1860* (New York: Prentice-Hall, 1966), 32–35.

15. David Jaffe, "The Village Enlightenment in New England, 1760–1820," *William and Mary Quarterly*, 3rd ser., 47 (1990), 339.

16. Perkins, "The Consumer Frontier," *Journal of American History*, 78 (1991), 486–510.

17. *Baltimore Weekly Price Current*, May 1, 1806.

18. North, *The Economic Growth of the United States*, 28.

19. Baltimore Entrances and Clearances, Vols. 15–21 (1802–06), Bureau of Customs, United States, Entry 1149, RG 36, National Archives, Washington, D.C.

20. North, *The Economic Growth of the United States*, 24–58.

21. North, *The Economic Growth of the United States*, 25.

22. North, *The Economic Growth of the United States*, 46–58.

23. Charles Francis Adams, ed., *The Works of John Adams, Second President of the United States*, 10 vols. (Boston: Little, Brown, 1853), 8: 379.

24. Jefferson to Adams, July 11, 1786, Thomas Jefferson Papers Series 1, General Correspondence, 1651–1027, Digital Archives, Library of Congress, Image 1146.

25. Claude A, Swanson, ed., *Naval Documents Related to the United States Wars with Barbary Powers: Naval Operations*, 6 vols. (Washington, D.C.: U.S. Government Printing Office, 1939), 1: 22–26.

26. Quoted in Robert J. Allison, *The Crescent Obscured: The United States and the Muslim World, 1776–1815* (New York: Oxford University Press, 1995), 68.

27. Carey, *A Short Account of Algiers* . . . (Philadelphia: J. Parker for M. Carey, 1794), 16, 44. Allison suggests that the American sailors who were slaves in North Africa were not as poorly treated as black slaves in North America. Allison, *The Crescent Obscured*, 110–13.

28. *American State Papers: Foreign Relations,* 6 vols. (Washington, D.C.: Gales and Seaton, 1832–61), 1: 555.

29. *American State Papers: Foreign Relations,* 1: 525; American State Papers: Foreign Relations, 2: 18–19, 125.

30. Swanson, ed., *Naval Documents Related to the United States Wars with Barbary Powers,* 1: 430–31.

31. *American State Papers: Foreign Relations,* 2: 348–49.

32. Swanson, ed., *Naval Documents Related to the United States Wars with Barbary Powers,* 1: 463–69.

33. Quoted in William M. Fowler, Jr., *Jack Tars and Commodores: The American Navy, 1783–1815* (Boston: Houghton Mifflin, 1984), 75.

34. Swanson, ed., *Naval Documents Related to the United States Wars with Barbary Powers,* 2: 449.

35. Swanson, ed., *Naval Documents Related to the United States Wars with Barbary Powers,* 3: 171.

36. Quoted in Bradford Perkins, *Prologue to War: England and the United States, 1805–1812* (Berkeley: University of California Press, 1968), 82.

37. Joshua Penny, *The Life and Adventures of Joshua Penny, A Native of Southold, Long Island . . . Who Was Impressed Into the British Service . . .* (New York, 1815), 11.

38. Quoted in Perkins, *Prologue to War,* 85.

39. Burton Spivak, *Jefferson's English Crisis: Commerce, Embargo, and the Republican Revolution* (Charlottesville: University Press of Virginia, 1979), 65.

40. Quoted in Perkins, *Prologue to War,* 112–13.

41. Quoted in Spencer C. Tucker and Frank T. Reuter, *Injured Honor: The Chesapeake–Leopard Affair* (Annapolis, Md.: Naval Institute Press, 1996), 72.

42. Quoted in Tucker and Reuter, *Injured Honor,* 108.

43. Quoted in Reginald Horsman, *The Causes of the War of 1812* (Philadelphia: University of Pennsylvania Press, 1962), 103.

44. Quoted in Henry Adams, *History of the United States of America,* 9 vols. (New York: Charles Scribner's Sons, 1891–98), 4: 278.

45. North, *The Economic Growth of the United States,* 221, 228.

46. James D. Richardson, *A Compilation of the Messages and Papers of the Presidents, 1789–1897,* 20 vols. (Washington, D.C.: Government Printing Office, 1896–1914), 1: 450–51.

47. Spivak, *Jefferson's English Crisis,* 167–68, 200–03.

48. North, *The Economic Growth of the United States,* 56–57. Quote is on p. 57.

49. Andrew A. Lipscomb, ed., *The Writings of Thomas Jefferson,* 20 vols. (Washington, D.C.: Thomas Jefferson Memorial Association, 1903–1904), 11: 97–98, 427; ibid., 12: 271, 293–96.

50. Quoted in John Bach McMaster, *A History of the People of the United States, From the Revolution to the Civil War,* 8 vols. (New York: D. Appleton and Company, 1901–1914), 3: 292n.

51. Quoted in Perkins, *Prologue to War,* 232.

The Debacle of War

Origins

The United States did not have to fight the War of 1812. Two days before President James Madison signed the declaration of war on June 18, 1812, the British decided to suspend the Orders in Council and withdraw all restraints on American trade. Given that it took weeks for word to cross the Atlantic, by the time news of these concessions reached Washington it was too late. When the United States went to war, however, many Americans believed they had good reasons to fight Great Britain. The United States wanted to defend the commerce that sustained the growing consumer revolution. Madison and Congress concluded that the diplomatic failures of the previous decade had left the nation with few options to secure its trade and to prevent the impressment of American seamen other than war. Americans also wanted to open new lands for speculators and entrepreneurial farmers. War hawks cried out for conquering Canada and even Florida, while many blamed the British for encouraging Native Americans to oppose the United States. Finally, some Americans wanted to prove that their republican government, along with its egalitarian society and unrestrained economy, was powerful enough to meet the challenges posed by a world dominated by kings and emperors.

The war itself did not go as expected. Although the United States ultimately dealt a crushing blow to the Native Americans east of the Mississippi, the fighting against Great Britain brought few great victories and failed to lead to the conquest of new territory. In fact, the conflict almost proved critics right by demonstrating how ineffective a diffuse and weak republic could be in a prolonged crisis. Repeatedly, Americans experienced

273

miscues, mishaps, and missed opportunities. Invasions of Canada either ended in failure or were abandoned before they ever got started. Early naval victories gave way to an effective British blockade that prevented American warships from getting to sea. In 1814 a British attack in the Chesapeake included the burning of Washington D.C. The war ended in a stalemate. With both nations recognizing the futility of the war, peace was agreed to at the Treaty of Ghent. Jackson's victory at the Battle of New Orleans only confirmed the war's end. The United States ignored the Dartmoor Massacre in April 1815, when British troops fired on rioting American naval prisoners of war, killing six, but the United States also acted quickly to secure its trade in a final action against the Barbary pirates in 1815.

The diplomatic situation between the United States and Great Britain deteriorated seriously in 1810 and 1811 on several fronts. To the south the United States asserted its claim to Florida on the basis of a questionable interpretation of the extent of the Louisiana Purchase. Between the French occupation of Spain and the chaos of the European war, the Spanish hold on Florida, which had never been strong, began to loosen even more. In 1810 a group of American expatriates, mainly deserters, debtors, and land speculators, led a revolt in West Florida along the Mississippi River. Throughout the summer and fall the situation remained confused, with some of these rebels seeking to establish their own independent nation, whereas others sought to join the United States. Great Britain, which allied itself with Spain after its revolt against Napoleon in 1808, warned the United States several times not to occupy any part of Florida. Americans feared that the British themselves might seize Florida, and believed that continued disorder on its borders would disrupt "the tranquillity and security" in the neighboring American territories of Orleans and Mississippi. President Madison therefore issued a proclamation on October 27, 1810, ordering the military occupation of West Florida to the Perdido River.[1] American control, however, barely reached to the Pearl River. Beyond that point, confusion persisted, with some expatriates contesting Spanish rule. Early in 1812, Congress admitted the new state of Louisiana with the Pearl as its eastern boundary south of the 31st parallel, and granted the Mississippi Territory the remainder of West Florida to the Perdido even though the Spanish still had an outpost at Mobile. Efforts to break up smuggling from Amelia Island on the Atlantic coast of East Florida led to the occupation of that island by American forces just as the War of 1812 broke out in June. Many Americans hoped that war with Great Britain would provide an excuse to seize all of Florida.

To the north, Americans blamed the British for promoting Native American resistance in these years. Although British officials tried to

FIGURE 10–1   The British Encouraging the Indians Many Americans believed that the British encouraged Native American attacks on the frontier before and during the War of 1812.

maintain a delicate balance of ensuring Indian support without provoking war, British agents in Canada had encouraged Tecumseh and his brother, the Prophet, in their pan-Indian movement that culminated in the Battle of Tippecanoe on November 7, 1811. Weakened by this defeat, Tecumseh still had an important influence among Indians in both the Old Northwest and among the Creeks to the south. British fur traders also had extensive contacts with Native Americans in modern Wisconsin, Minnesota, and Iowa and worked to agitate animosity toward the United States in the region. Early in 1812 hostilities broke out along the frontier of the American northwest. Indians killed ten men within three miles of Fort Dearborn (modern Chicago); other settlers were murdered along the Mississippi and Ohio Rivers. That spring refugees heading for the safety of Kentucky streamed into Vincennes. Others retreated to nearby blockhouses to await what they knew would be a British-inspired Indian onslaught. Given this explosive situation, many westerners called for war and for the conquest of Canada. In 1810, Henry Clay argued that the United States could easily capture Canada and thereby "extinguish the torch that lights up savage warfare." Other westerners picked up on the same theme. One editor complained of the influence of "British intrigue and British gold" on the Indians and Andrew Jackson lambasted "Secrete agents of Great Britain" among the Indians. In December 1811, William Duane in Philadelphia made a similar comment when he declared that "war has been begun with British arms and by the Indians instigated by British emissaries."[2] Americans considered Canada an easy target. Its population, at a half million, was only a fraction of the seven and a half million in the United States. Americans thought that much of Canada's population had a dubious loyalty to the British crown. There were still tens of thousands of French Canadians around Quebec, and many of the settlers of Upper Canada came from the United States, lured by cheap land and low taxes. Americans were brimming with confidence. Clay proclaimed to the Senate, "I verily believe that the militia of Kentucky are alone competent to place Montreal and Upper Canada at your feet."[3] Advocates of war hoped that if the British could be driven from the continent, new territory could be added to the United States and the Indians could be easily subdued.

The greatest irritants in Anglo–American relations, however, were on the "maritime frontier." In his 1810 speech, Clay declared that Britain stood "pre eminent in her outrage on us" in "the mercantile spoliations inflicted and menaced" and "by her violation of the sacred personal rights of American freemen, in the arbitrary and lawless imprisonment of our seamen," and in "the attack on the Chesapeake."[4] During the opening session of the Twelfth Congress, which Madison had called early in November 1811 to deal with the diplomatic impasse with Great Britain, Indian atrocities were often mentioned. But the focus of discussion remained "free trade and sailors' rights." The report of the Committee on Foreign Relations to the House of Representatives on November 29, 1811, could not have been more explicit about the economic root of the conflict. It summarized "the great causes of complaint against Great Britain" by highlighting the right of the United States "as a sovereign and independent Power . . . to use the ocean . . . for the purposes of transporting, in their own vessels, the products of their own soil and the acquisitions of their own industry, to a market in the ports of friendly nations, and to bring home, in return, such articles as their necessities or convenience may require." The report decried against American ships being "seized on our own coasts, at the very mouths of our harbors, condemned and confiscated." It also pointed out that "If it be our duty to encourage the fair and legitimate commerce of this country by protecting the property of the merchant; then, indeed, by as much as life and liberty are more estimable than ships and goods," the government should "shield the persons of our seamen" from the "barbarity" of "the loss of . . . their liberty" through impressment.[5] These sentiments were echoed by several congressmen who supported legislation to prepare the nation for war. Felix Grundy of Tennessee may have been more interested in the West generally, and have argued that British "baubles and trinkets" had convinced Indians to attack the United States, but he supported fully the emphasis on maritime issues. He argued that it was no longer the carrying trade that was the problem, but "the right of exporting the productions of our own soil and industry to foreign markets" and saw the origins of the controversy in "the rapid growth of our commercial importance" that had "awakened the jealousy of the commercial interests of Great Britain." He also called impressment an "unjust and lawless invasion of personal liberty."[6]

Grundy made another important argument for the war. National honor and reputation demanded it. Grundy recalled that, in 1808, Congress had agreed that the United States had three alternatives: the embargo, war, or submission. The United States chose the embargo and that failed. Grundy exclaimed, "we now have no embargo, we have not declared war. I then say it, with humiliation produced by the degradation of my country, we have submitted."[7] To prove American independence, and to prove the viability of the republic, the United States had to go to war. A month after the declaration of war, Congressmen Hugh Nelson of Virginia expanded on this idea as he explained the war to his constituents. The trade restrictions of France and Great Britain demonstrated that neither power had any respect for the United States and that they had concluded that the American republic was "inefficient and incompetent to exert power and energy of the nation, and to assume the attitude and posture of war." To

> repel these unfounded imputations, to demonstrate to the world and especially to the belligerents, that the people of these states were united, one and indivisible in all cases of concern with foreign nations, to shew that our republican government was competent to assert its rights, to maintain the interests of the people, and to repel all foreign aggression.

war had become a necessity.[8]

By the closing months of 1811, Madison and the Republican-dominated Congress had come to think that war might be inevitable with England. Efforts to get the British to remove their restrictions on trade, as U.S. officials falsely believed Napoleon had done, met with intransigence that the Americans viewed as arrogance. The Twelfth Congress, sometimes referred to as the War Congress, therefore began to get ready for armed conflict. However, the Republicans in Congress found themselves hampered by the ideals that had carried them to power; a commitment to small government and low taxes did not make it easy to put the nation on a war footing. Congress therefore moved in fits and starts through the winter of 1811–12. By early spring it had passed several measures that some thought were mere bluff and bluster, but that others saw as serious preparation.

First, Congress increased the recruitment bounty to encourage full enlistment of the army to the previously mandated size of 10,000 men (the
army had been only about half its official size). Congress also authorized
an increase of 25,000 men to the regular army, and the enlistment of
50,000 short-term volunteers. The problem with the last two measures was
that they were unrealistic; it was physically impossible for the United States
at that time to recruit and train 25,000 men, and the volunteers would
probably be drawn from state militias and could not leave their home
states. Congress also turned its attention to the navy. Republican parsimony prevented any efforts to set up a well-planned expansion, but Congress did pass a bill to fit out the navy for combat at sea. The nation's
harbors were in dire need of fortifications to stifle a British attack. After
much debate, Congress allocated only $500,000 for coastal defense. Paying
for a war was a real problem for the Republicans. At Secretary of Treasury
Albert Gallatin's advice, Congress agreed to raise $11 million in loans.
With some reluctance, Congress also agreed to raise taxes in the event of
an outbreak of war. Having built itself on an ideology emphasizing a mini-
malist government, the Republican Party had difficulty in reversing course
and expanding government to meet the needs of war.

Another symptom of this problem of allowing the principle of limited
government to run counter to the interests of the larger public good on the
eve of war can be seen in the earlier demise of the Bank of the United
States on March 4, 1811. This Federalist-created engine of the economy
had long been despised by Republicans, who had cut their political teeth by
opposing its charter in 1791. In 1811, the Republicans, ignoring the fact
that the BUS had helped regulate the economy and had led to government
profits through the sale of stock, let the BUS expire as its twenty-year charter came to an end. Republican opponents to the BUS argued that only
states could charter banks and there was no constitutional power permitting
a national bank. They saw the BUS as an agent for the British—perhaps
two-thirds of the stock was owned in England in 1811—and that it was "a
splendid association of favored individuals . . . invested with exemptions
and surrounded by immunities and privileges."[9] Whoever profited from the
BUS, it would have been a useful instrument as the United States faced war
because it had the potential to help the government raise loans quickly and
meet its bills in an effective manner. Without the BUS, the Treasury had difficulty subscribing the $11 million loan authorized in early 1812, and con-
tinued to have fiscal problems throughout the war.

As Congress prepared for war, the British position began to shift.
Throughout 1811 and into 1812 the British did not take American saber
rattling seriously. They knew that Napoleon had not followed up on the

suggestion that he would repeal the Berlin and Milan decrees, and expected a more reasoned American approach once the United States realized Bonaparte's duplicity. Even a provocative incident on the high seas did not alter their attitude. In early May 1811, the American frigate *President* under Commodore John Rodgers had been ordered to patrol the U.S. coast to prevent further seizures of American ships trading with France and to stop impressments. Mistaking the British sloop-of-war *Little Belt* for a larger ship, and encountering the vessel at night, the 44-gun *President* pulverized the smaller British vessel in a brief engagement on May 16, 1811, killing thirteen and wounding nineteen British seamen; one American was slightly injured. Although the British government protested this affront, the origin of which was buried in the haze of contradictory testimony, the British government did not follow popular sentiment and go to war. In fact, the British had even decided to apologize and offer reparations for the earlier *Chesapeake* affair. Just as the War Congress began its special session in November, Augustus John Foster, the British ambassador to the United States, indicated his government's willingness to pay compensation for the men killed in the attack and promised to return two of the four seamen taken from the American frigate (the other two were dead: One had been executed as a deserter; the other had died of natural causes). Madison saw this concession as ill timed and a mere sop to American grievances. He wrote that it "takes one splinter out of our wounds" and had "the appearance of a mere anadyne to the excitements in Congress and the nation."[10] Given the tardy nature of the offer, the fact that many Americans believed that the attack on the *Little Belt* had avenged the assault on the *Chesapeake*, and the accumulated ill will, the United States asserted that no amount of money could compensate for the loss of American life and liberty. Madison rejected any reparations, but did accept the return of the two seized seamen.

If the United States was oblivious to any softening of the British position, it was in part a reflection of mixed signals. Foster had arrived in the United States in May 1811, but waited until November to explain the British concessions on the *Chesapeake* question. In the meantime, he had protested the American incursion into Florida, and refused to provide any movement on the Orders in Council. The British navy also increased its presence in North American waters to intercept ships headed to France. However, throughout the spring of 1812 the British debated and discussed repeal of the Orders of Council. Leading British manufacturers of consumer goods such as cutlery, hardware, pottery, dishware, and woolen and cotton textiles, wanted to export their products to America. As the cutlers of Sheffield explained, "of all foreign markets yet discovered for the sale of our manufactures the U.S.A. has been the most important."[11] Unemployment, disorder, and riots marked the industrial regions of Great Britain. The manufacturers therefore urged their government to abandon the Orders to relieve all of this distress and revive the American trade. As parliamentary debates raged, Prime Minister Spencer Perceval remained unmovable. His murder on May 11, 1812, by a deranged and disappointed office seeker dramatically changed the situation. After about a month of confusion and upheaval a new government emerged under Lord Liverpool that was finally willing to repeal the Orders in mid June.

It was too late. On April 1, Madison had requested a sixty-day embargo as a precursor to war. Congress, extending the embargo to ninety days, quickly passed the measure. The idea was to limit the amount of American shipping at sea once hostilities commenced. The last American hope for peace hinged on dispatches from Europe due to arrive in May. When they arrived on May 22, the British offer to share licenses for trade with Europe (which the British had previously issued exclusively to their own ships) was not enough of a concession to delay war further. The British, still believing that the Americans would see through Napoleon's sham revocation of the Berlin and Milan decrees, did not recognize the seriousness of the situation. As Madison later explained, he now had a simple choice "between war and degradation." Degradation would only invite "fresh provocation" and render "war sooner or later inevitable," and so he decided to act immediately.[12] On June 1, 1812, he sent his message to Congress calling for a declaration of war on Great Britain. Congress debated and passed the measure by June 17 and Madison made the war official when he signed the declaration the next day.

Throughout the process of moving toward war the Federalists could do little. With only six senators and a handful of congressmen, there were not enough Federalists in the national legislature to mount a concerted opposition. Indeed, Madison had more difficulty convincing some members of his own Republican Party, especially the so-called Quids led by John Randolph, to support his policies than he did the Federalists. Some Federalists, like the British, did not take the warmongering seriously. For years the Republicans had been threatening war to gain concessions, and these Federalists believed that Madison was simply bluffing again. Others secretly hoped for the war because they thought it would lead to the downfall of the Republican Party. These Federalists argued that there was no way the United States could win against Great Britain and that the taxes the Republicans would be forced to raise, coupled with military defeat, would mean Federalist victory at the polls. The Federalists therefore followed a contradictory and inconsistent path in the Twelfth Congress, voting for some war measures, especially for strengthening the navy, but obstructing other measures. However, in June, faced with the declaration of war, Federalists did all they could to stop congressional action. The Federalists in the House of Representatives issued a circular address attacking the war, and proclaimed that it put the United States on the side of France, exposing "us to the vassalage of States serving under the banners of the French Emperor."[13] Senate Federalists, joined by a few disgruntled Republicans, almost defeated the war bill. As it was, they obstructed and delayed final congressional approval of war for several days. The closeness of the vote indicates that the nation was not united as it entered the war. Although a majority of Americans probably supported the war, a significant minority was against it. There was a regional base to how Americans stood: New England adamantly opposed the war; the South and the West supported the war; and the middle Atlantic states were more divided.

Two Baltimore publications provide some indication of the kind of rhetoric used on both sides. Hezekiah Niles, editor of a weekly newssheet, championed the war. Niles referred to England as "our ancient and inveterate foe" and stated that the United States had for years "endured what no independent nation ought to have suffered for a moment." Efforts at negotiation, Niles pointed out, had come to naught and simply led to more "insults and injuries." He claimed that "In the valley of humiliation, at the foot of the throne of her ideot monarch, at the threshold of the palaces of the knaves who administer the government in his name, we sought justice and begged for peace." For Niles, as was true for many Americans, impressment was the most salient issue. He referred to British press gangs as "*Algerines*" who "kidnapped" American seamen. This "indignity, abuse and destruction of our seamen, and through them, the violent assault on the sovereignty of the country itself, has long cried for revenge." Niles further asserted that "*It is the law of the land that we fight England*—it is also the will of the people, goaded by insults and injuries." He therefore called on all Americans to put aside their differences and support the war. Anyone who persisted in opposing the war and who wanted to see "the defeat of their own government and the triumph of a *foreign enemy*" would be viewed as Tories. Niles, however, recommended "forbearance and temper" and concluded his commentary with "*Long live America, the asylum of freedom—sovereign, independent and happy*."[14]

Alexander Contee Hanson, the editor of the Baltimore *Federal Republican,* saw the war differently. Hanson denounced the bellicose actions of the Madison administration and the War Congress. When rumors spread through Baltimore that the paper would be attacked by a mob if it did not change its tune after the outbreak of war, Hanson was defiant. He declared that Federalists would not be intimidated into accepting an unjust and unwise war; otherwise, "a war would put the constitution and all civil rights to sleep. Those who commenced it, would become dictators and despots, and the people their slaves." Hanson condemned the declaration of war in the June 20, 1812, edition of the *Federal Republican*. He labeled the war "unnecessary," "inexpedient," and reflecting the "marks of undisguised foreign influence." Proclaiming that the paper would use "every constitutional argument and every legal means" to oppose the war, Hanson stated that the editors would "hazard every thing most dear" to oppose "a system of terror and proscription."[15]

Hanson might have gotten away with this vitriolic language in Federalist New England. But Baltimore was a Republican city that supported the war. On the night of June 22, a group of thirty to forty men, cheered on by a larger crowd, proceeded with "sang froid" to dismantle the offices of the *Federal Republican*. The crowd went about its business "as regularly as if they had contracted to perform the job for pay."[16] Local Republican officials did little to stop the mob. At one point, Mayor Edward Johnson approached one rioter and asked him to desist. The man responded:

> Mr. Johnson, I know you very well, no body wants to hurt you: but the laws of the land must sleep, and the laws of nature and reason must prevail; that house . . . is the Temple of Infamy, it is supported with English gold, and it must and shall come down to the ground!

The Baltimore mob had registered its support of the war and its determination not to countenance "traitors."[17]

The gulf that separated Federalist and Republican, however, was more than political. Baltimore was a dynamic city that had grown from being a small village fifty years earlier, to becoming the third largest city in the United States in 1812. Federalists operated from assumptions derived from a more traditional world of hierarchy and deference in which everyone was assumed to share the same, larger interest. They expected the people would simply follow the leadership of the well born and talented. In the early nineteenth century that world was rapidly disappearing, especially in a place like Baltimore that was churning with new people who represented many interests. The city had merchants, middling artisans, native-born and immigrant laborers, rough seamen on the waterfront, free and slave blacks. There was also a rising level of unskilled labor—often youths, women, immigrants, and blacks—challenging the security of journeymen tradesmen. In the wake of this first attack on the office of the *Federalist Republican,* there was a wave of popular disorder reflective of this new divided society. Night after night crowds scoured the streets, threatening

Federalists, harassing free blacks, attacking an Irishman, and dismantling several ships loaded with grain destined for the British army in Spain (this trade was legal, but seemed to many a form of profiteering).

Into this explosive atmosphere stepped Hanson, scion of the aristocracy and Federalist agitator. Hanson was not going to be intimidated by a mob. He reopened the *Federal Republican* in Georgetown and set up an office at Number 45 Charles Street in Baltimore to distribute the paper. Almost in response to the rioter who addressed Mayor Johnson, Hanson declared that the "empire of laws" had been "overthrown" and that society had been "unhinged" and "degraded to a state of nature." Determined to protect his "natural and constitutional rights" to publish the paper, Hanson and about fifty Federalists barricaded themselves in the paper's new Baltimore headquarters on July 27.[18] That night a huge crowd appeared outside and began pelting rocks and hurling insults at the defenders. The Federalists warned the crowd to keep away, and even fired a blank volley to intimidate the mob. Still, the crowd raged and finally charged the building. As several men burst in the door, the Federalists fired again, killing one man and wounding several others. After the mob retreated a running gun battle erupted, with both sides firing at each other. The crowd eventually brought up a cannon and prepared to use it against the building. At this point a small body of militia appeared and negotiated a settlement whereby the Federalists surrendered to their protective custody. The Federalists were disarmed and taken through the jeering crowd to the jail.

The Baltimore common people were not quite finished with the aristocratic Federalists. Tempers simmered all the next day, erupting into an assault on the jail that night. Mayor Johnson again attempted to intercede, only to get a lesson in the new political science of democracy. He stood in the jailhouse doorway and pleaded, "I am the Mayor of your city; they are my prisoners, and I must and will protect them." One rioter viciously responded: "you damn'd scoundrel don't we feed you, and is it not your duty to head and lead us on to take vengeance for the murders committed."[19] There were to be no natural aristocratic leaders, either Federalist or Republican, of the new society; only servants of the people at their beck and call. Several Federalists escaped in the darkness and confusion. The mob captured the rest and beat them mercilessly, tearing the fine aristocratic clothing off of their victims, dropping hot candle grease into their eyes, and inflicting other tortures. When Federalist James Maccuban Lingan attempted to tell the crowd he had been a general in the Revolutionary War, he was attacked with renewed fury until he stopped moving. By that time he was dead. Neither Hanson, nor another Revolutionary War general, Light-Horse Harry Lee, ever fully recovered from their wounds.

At the end of the "massacre," the jail was strewn with the "foreign dress" of the elite—"Montgomery coats" and "Virginia Boots"—and the Federalist victims were piled in an indistinguishable heap.[20] The mob turned the bodies over to a few doctors who falsely promised to use the remains (all but one was still alive) as cadavers for dissection.

The Baltimore riots were an inauspicious beginning to a war. They revealed how deep political divisions ran, and showed a society that had moved a long way from the ideals of the eighteenth century. In the fall elections, the Federalists would capitalize on this attack on the right of free speech and the unpopularity of the war in some regions to make important gains in Congress and several states. They even came within one state—Pennsylvania—of recapturing the White House. Republicans blamed the Federalists for the riots, claiming Hanson and his followers provoked "violence from the people by ill-timed abuse" and were nothing more than "cold blooded and deliberate murderers!" They were "a lawless band of political incendiaries" and a "gang of desperadoes" who "impiously attempted to plunge the country into all the horrors and desolating cruelties of a civil war."[21] Whatever their political rhetoric, the Republicans were eager to put the riots behind them and vainly hoped that victory in Canada would strengthen their political hold on the nation.

Fighting the War

The war, however, did not go as easily as many Americans had thought. Repeatedly, campaigns along the Canadian border either came to little or ended in disaster along three fronts: the West, the Niagara frontier, and the Lake Champlain corridor. During the first year of the war the greatest catastrophes occurred in the West. British forces combined with Native American allies handed the United States defeat after defeat. The British captured a small American garrison at Fort Mackinac, which guarded the straits between Lakes Huron, Michigan, and Superior, on July 17, 1812. The U.S. troops at Mackinac became the conflict's first prisoners of war before their commander even knew that war had been declared. The men stationed at Fort Dearborn fared worse. Throughout the summer, General William Hull, a veteran from the Revolutionary War and in command of the western forces, became increasingly morose at his headquarters in Detroit. He decided that the loss of Mackinac made the position at Fort Dearborn untenable. He therefore ordered its sixty-five-man garrison and couple of dozen civilians to abandon the outpost. As the soldiers evacuated the fort on August 15, they were attacked by the Indians who had granted them safe passage. All but a few European Americans were killed

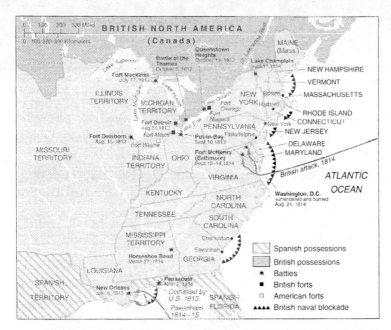

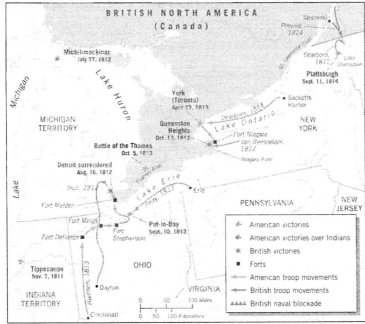

MAP 10–1 The War of 1812 The war was fought to a stalemate on three major fronts on the Canadian border: in the west near Detroit, along the Niagara River, and on the Lake Champlain to Montreal corridor. In the later stages of the war, American forces defeated the Creeks and then defended against a British invasion from the south at the Battle of New Orleans. The British also were able to raid the coast with impunity, burning Washington D.C. and occupying much of Maine in 1814.

in the massacre. In the meantime, Hull had begun to panic. Despite having a numerical advantage over the British, Hull did not press the attack after crossing into Canada. Instead, he worried over his long supply lines to the Ohio River. Unable to secure those lines, he retreated to Detroit, frustrating and demoralizing his men. In August he found himself besieged by the British and Indians. Without putting up much of a fight he surrendered his entire garrison of 2,200 men, along with huge quantities of equipment and ammunition. For this act of incompetence and cowardice, Hull was court-martialed and sentenced to death. He was later given a reprieve by Madison on account of his age and his service in the Revolutionary War.

The Niagara campaign went almost as poorly. The Niagara command was divided between General Stephen Van Rensselaer, of the New York militia, and General Alexander Smyth of the regular army. Neither had combat experience; each had difficulty cooperating with the other. With 6,000 men, the Americans should have been able to advance against a combined force of 2,000 British and Indians. It did not work out that way. Smyth watched from the sidelines as Van Rensselaer launched an attack across the Niagara River on October 13. Once the Americans gained hard-fought control of Queenstown Heights, the New York militia refused to cross into Canada as reenforcements (other militia units would behave similarly throughout the war) because they claimed to be only a defensive force. Without the extra men, the Americans were overwhelmed in a counterattack. Before the battle was over, almost one thousand Americans were captured and hundreds more were killed or wounded. Van Rensselaer resigned and command fell to Smyth, who failed in his effort to capture Fort Erie in November.

The third thrust at Canada was directed at Montreal and fell under the command of Henry Dearborn, who was no more capable than the other American commanders. With six to eight thousand men he finally marched his army from Albany to Plattsburgh on Lake Champlain in November. The late fall was not the best time to launch an attack from northern New York. Militia units again refused to cross the border, hampering operations. Dearborn's troops fought an inconclusive skirmish with the British on the Canadian side of the border before retreating back to the United States. An outright disaster was avoided, but nothing was accomplished, either. Taken together, all three campaigns were an embarrassment. As Albert Gallatin admitted: "The series of misfortunes . . . in our military land operations exceeds all anticipations made even by those who had least confidence in our inexperienced officers and undisciplined men."[22]

The "war hawks" had imagined that the "land operations" would be easy and expected that the sea operations, facing the most powerful navy in the world, would be impossible. To everyone's surprise it was on the high seas that Americans gained their greatest success in 1812. The British made a strategic error at the beginning of the war. On hearing that a squadron under Commodore John Rodgers had left port, the British concentrated their ships and went in pursuit of Rodgers, rather than blockading every major port. The result was that returning American merchant shipping came back to the United States relatively unscathed, and many of the remaining American ships-of-war could get to sea. The cruising American warships sunk or captured several British merchant vessels and won a series of sea battles against the British. Three of the battles involved American frigates that were the best designed and most heavily armed vessels of their class. On August 19, 1812, the *Constitution* battered the HMS *Guerriere* into surrender. About a third of the British crew was killed or wounded (15 dead, 63 wounded), compared to only seven Americans killed and seven wounded. After the battle, the *Guerriere* was in such bad shape that it had to be sunk rather than brought back to the United States as a prize. So many British cannonballs bounced off the hard oak of the *Constitution*'s sides during the engagement that one American sailor reportedly yelled out during the battle, "Huzzah, her sides are made of iron," earning the vessel the nickname "Old Ironsides." Two months later, on October 25, the *United States* met the HMS *Macedonian* in the mid Atlantic. The Americans again out gunned the British. The casualties were also lopsided: The British lost 103 killed and wounded; the Americans only 12. This time, however, the Americans were able to make repairs to the captured British frigate and return with her to the United States. On December 29 the *Constitution* gained its second victory over a British frigate off the coast of Brazil, sinking the HMS *Java*. Along with a few smaller ship engagements, the American navy gave the nation something to be proud of in the face of the disasters on land. The British, on the other hand, could not believe that their vaunted navy had been so embarrassed, although they also complained that none of the frigate engagements were really an even match.

Land operations improved slightly in 1813, thanks in part to a major naval success on the Great Lakes. In the western theater there was a complete reversal of fortunes. Oliver Hazard Perry put together a fleet of ships on Lake Erie that defeated a British squadron on the western end of the lake on September 10, 1813. This victory, which Perry reported with the famous phrase "We have met the enemy and they are ours," secured American supply lines and compelled the British to abandon Detroit. General William Henry Harrison, now in command of the western forces, pursued the British into Canada and defeated a combined Native American and

FIGURE 10–2 The Battle of the Thames American forces under General William Henry Harrison defeated British and Indians at the Battle of the Thames in Canada on October 5, 1813. During the battle, Americans killed Tecumseh and struck a mortal blow to Indian resistance east of the Mississippi River.

British force at the Battle of the Thames on October 5, 1813. Perhaps equally important was the fact that the Shawnee leader Tecumseh died in the battle, striking a final blow to the pan-Indian movement. Although Harrison did not push farther into Canada, he and Perry had removed much of the Indian threat to the Old Northwest.

The stalemate continued on the other two Canadian fronts. The campaign began on a promising note when, in late April, the Americans sailed across Lake Ontario, captured York, burned the public buildings, and then returned to the United States. (This raid was later used by the British to justify their burning Washington, D.C.). On May 24, 1813, Americans captured Fort George on the Canadian side of the Niagara River, gaining an important foothold on British territory. But when the Americans did not follow up this victory, the British were able to rally and counterattack through the summer, fall, and into the winter. The British won several battles and not only recaptured Fort George, but also seized Fort Niagara on December 18. Along the northern border of New York, the United States planned a two-pronged attack. General James Wilkinson, the same man who had been in the pay of Spain and who probably had plotted with Aaron Burr, was to take a force up the St. Lawrence River from Lake Ontario; General Wade Hampton was to march through the Lake Champlain Valley. Wilkinson's reputation preceded him, and Hampton refused to obey or cooperate with him. The British gained control of Lake Champlain in June when they captured two American warships that had foolishly sailed too close to a British position in shallow water. Hampton delayed his advance until October. He managed to get some of his troops across the border (about a thousand militia again refused to leave the United States), only to be driven back by a smaller British force. Wilkinson had an even later start and did not begin to head down the St. Lawrence until early November. His army ran into some resistance and soon withdrew to winter quarters. The net result of both invasions was a few hundred casualties, a lot of sore feet, and a great deal of disillusionment.

In 1813 a fourth front opened in the South. Without declaring war against Spain, a small American force occupied Mobile in early 1813, bringing all of West Florida under U.S. jurisdiction. The big conflict, however, was with a part of the Creek nation. The trouble harked back to Tecumseh's visit to the region in 1811. Many young Creeks were inspired by his call for a return to native ways and wished to join in the pan-Indian movement. Calling themselves Red Sticks, they began a civil war with the older leadership of the Creeks who wanted to continue to seek accommodation with the United States. By the summer of 1813, the Red Sticks appeared to have gained the upper hand against their more conservative elders. Angered by a skirmish with Mississippi militia in late July, the Red Sticks captured Fort Mims on August 30 and massacred most of its 250 inhabitants. The skirmish and the massacre brought the United States into the conflict. The Americans launched a three-pronged assault into Creek territory. One army with about 1,500 men approached from Georgia, another force of 1,200 men invaded from the south, while an army of 3,000 men, including about 500 Creeks and Cherokees, came from the north under General Andrew Jackson. Pressed by each of these forces, the Red Sticks lost several engagements, climaxed by the Battle of Horseshoe Bend (or Tohpeka) on March 27, 1814, where Jackson's forces killed about a thousand Indians, including women and children. In a few short months, from July 1813 to April 1814, the Red Sticks lost about half of their 4,000 warriors and were driven to seek refuge in Florida. Declaring victory in the Creek War, Jackson then dictated terms to the Creek Nation, including those who had supported him against the Red Sticks. At the Treaty of Fort Jackson on August 9, 1814, the Creeks surrendered over twenty million acres, half of the present state of Alabama and a significant chunk of southern Georgia, to the United States. The accomodationalist Creeks had to bow to the military might of Jackson's army, but immediately protested. The Creek leaders reminded the U.S. government that "we have adhered faithfully in peace and war to our treaty stipulations with the United States" and pointed out that the treaty was unfair because it took so much of their land. They vainly hoped that the United States would "cause justice to be done us."[23] When it came to land that furthered settlement and speculation, European Americans were not going to do justice to Native Americans. The United States kept the land ceded in the treaty even though the Treaty of Ghent ending the war with Great Britain specifically called for the restoration to the Indians of "all the possessions, rights, and privileges" that existed before the outbreak of hostilities.[24]

Besides the fighting in the South in 1814, the United States attempted to further secure the Old Northwest by retaking Fort Mackinac and again invading Canada across the Niagara. The United States effort to recapture Fort Mackinac failed when a combined British and Indian force surprised the advancing Americans in northern Michigan on August 4. In the meantime, the U.S. troops crossed the Niagara River, winning the Battle of Chippewa (July 5), fighting the British to a draw at Lundy's Lane (July 25) and successfully defending Fort Erie (August 15). After all the bloodshed and hardship there was little gain on this front for either side.

The impending defeat of Napoleon in Europe changed the strategic situation for the British in 1814, who could now devote more resources to the war against the United States. Yet, even though reenforcements brought the British army to a total of 40,000 men in North America by the end of 1814, the war continued as a stalemate. The same characteristics that made it difficult for the United States to win the war—a weak central government and a sprawling geographic area with a dispersed population—also made the country almost impossible to subdue. The British planned a major advance through the Lake Champlain corridor. Although the British beat an American army at the Battle of Plattsburgh on September 11, Lieutenant Thomas Macdonough's naval victory on Lake Champlain on the same day compelled the British to withdraw. British troops also occupied about half of the District of Maine during the summer, but this action merely left them in control of a few scattered settlements and vast tracts of woods. The British made a more serious thrust at the very center of the nation with a combined naval and land attack in the Chesapeake. On August 24, 1814, they beat back a hodgepodge American force at the Battle of Blandensburgh and then occupied and burned Washington, D.C. The destruction of the capital was a blow to American prestige, but given the decentralized nature of the government, and the fact that Washington had not really become much of a city, it did not have a serious impact on the war. When the British then attacked Baltimore, which was both a commercial hub and a population center, they ran into greater resistance and were beaten back. The British also launched an attack against the United States from the south. A small British force arrived in Spanish Florida in August to support what was left of the Red Sticks and black runaway slaves who had joined them. Jackson drove the British from Pensacola in early November before withdrawing to Mobile, where he expected a larger British invasion. Jackson then belatedly went to New Orleans, arriving on December 1, after he realized the British planned to send a veteran army to Louisiana to seize control of the Mississippi. Drawing on his own troops, local militia, and a group of pirates and smugglers under the command of Jean Laffite, Jackson put together a force of about 5,000 men to meet a British force of roughly the same size. Jackson established a defensive line south of New Orleans behind earthworks, with a swamp anchoring one side of the line and the Mississippi River on the other. If the British were to take New Orleans, they had to advance across an open field. When they attempted to do so on the morning of January 8, 1815, they came under a withering fire that shattered their army. Before the battle was over, the British lost almost half their men, including commanding general Edward Packenham, in the most complete American victory of the war.

After 1812 the war at sea became more difficult. U.S. warships still won occasional ship-to-ship battles, but the tally no longer was so one-sided. The British finally redeemed themselves in a frigate action in the victory of the HMS *Shannon* against the *Chesapeake* off the coast of Massachusetts on June 1, 1813. The British also expanded the navy stationed in American waters, tightening a blockade that made it more difficult for American vessels to get to sea. By the end of the war, when the frigate *President* attempted to escape from New York harbor, the odds were daunting. Despite giving the British a run for their money, Stephen Decatur had to surrender the *President* as several British warships overtook him off the coast of Long Island. British command of the seas also meant that they could raid the American coast with impunity. Not only did the British capture Washington, but they launched an extensive raid in the Chesapeake the year before, and periodically bombarded harbors in New England and elsewhere, destroying shipping, capturing supplies, and leaving destruction in their wake.

Despite the British supremacy on the seas, American privateers continued to be effective commerce raiders. During the war there were twenty-three vessels in the American navy, which captured 254 enemy craft. As impressive as this number is, the 517 authorized American privateers captured 1,345 British prizes worth over $45 million. Insurance rates skyrocketed even in the waters around Great Britain. Individual successes of American privateers could be spectacular. In 1813, the privateer *Thomas* captured two ships that netted $214,531 in the prize courts. The owner made over $92,000 and the least any crew member was awarded was a princely $800—all for a few weeks' cruise. The privateers tended to be smaller schooners and sloops, known for their fast sailing. They did not pack a powerful broadside. Instead, they carried plenty of men and just enough armament to overwhelm merchant ships. The last thing a true privateersman wanted was a ship-to-ship engagement with a British man-of-war.

Whatever type of service men engaged in, motives were not always patriotic. Most crews aboard privateers signed on for adventure and profit. These men were dissatisfied with their jobs on shore, in which they were "not making money fast enough." As one sailor explained, he intended to "cruise for dollars, where they were to be found in greater plenty than in the place of his birth."[25] Similar mercenary motives appeared among the regular navy, the army, and the militia throughout the war. If enlistments lagged, bounties and enticements were increased. Sailors in the navy also earned prize money and gained a few months' advance on salary when they signed aboard a naval warship. Soldiers were given cash payments for joining the army, and were promised land at the end of the conflict. Before the outbreak of the war, Congress had advanced the recruitment bounty from $12 to $31 and 160 acres of the land. Thereafter Congress repeatedly upped the ante, raising the bounty to $124 and 320 acres of land, increasing the pay, and offering three months' salary in advance as well as protection from arrest for debt.[26] A survey of the men who enlisted in the army found them to be young men in their early twenties who were neither poor nor destitute. Most came from agricultural or artisanal backgrounds, who, though respectable, were on the edges of that respectability. They were individuals who had experienced the economic disruptions of the period—the results of overpopulation in settled rural areas and the restructuring of crafts that compelled them to move to seek opportunity wherever they could find it.[27] Militia were also given inducements to serve, although some men resented being called for military duty and paid substitutes as high as $100 to take their place.

Given the financial motivation of many common men for fighting the war, and the fact that, once sworn into service, pay and supplies were often in short supply, discipline remained a persistent problem. The militia, in particular, was poorly trained and armed. Not only did they often balk at crossing into Canada during an invasion, but they were frequently unreliable in battle. Privateersmen were also very unruly. One crew refused duty for two days because the captain had cut their rum ration. When the weather became foul, the captain, finding "that his government was democratical," had to bow "to the large and fearful majority; and the New England spirit carried the day."[28] Insubordination and lack of discipline plagued all the services and often hindered military operations. Men deserted in droves. For the entire war, the overall desertion rate was 12.7 percent and the army executed 181 recaptured deserters.[29] Sometimes deserters ran away to avoid combat, or were simply disgusted with the hard life of the military. Some returned home to civilian life. Others reenlisted to collect a new bounty, or even joined the British. Soldiers and sailors were not above plundering both the enemy and their fellow countrymen. Serving with the navy on Lake Ontario, Ned Myers related how he and his gun crew went ashore and helped themselves to some tea, sugar, and, of course, whiskey. Myers explained: "It seemed to us to be a scrape, and that was a sufficient excuse for disobeying orders, and for committing a crime."[30]

Patriotism was not entirely absent from the military. Many on both the land and sea believed that they were defending their nation against repeated insults and aggression. Sailors knew that impressment had threatened their well-being and their lives before the outbreak of the war. Repeatedly, American naval vessels displayed banners with the inscription "free trade and sailors' rights," a phrase that every common seamen had heard and understood. During the war, over one thousand Americans serving in the British navy determined that they would rather be incarcerated as prisoners of war than fight against the United States. American soldiers, too, could take pride in fighting for their flag. Many westerners realized that hostile Indians were ready to drive them back across the Appalachians. These men were fighting not only for their country, but for hearth and home. After witnessing the bombardment of Fort McHenry in the 1814 attack on Baltimore, Francis Scott Key penned "The Star-Spangled Banner." Although the song did not become the national anthem until the twentieth century, it was an immediate sensation as a tribute to American bravery and patriotism.

Part of the problem with maintaining the patriotism and loyalty of the troops was a weak central government that appeared reluctant to take strong measures in support of the war. The same congressmen who voted enthusiastically for war in 1812 refused to pass enough taxes to pay for the war. At the beginning of the conflict Congress was willing to double the import duty and increase fees on foreign ships trading with the United States, but it would not establish any internal taxes. In 1813, Congress finally enacted a limited internal tax to raise a little over $5 million. It did so with trepidation. The Republicans knew that similar taxes had led to protest and rebellion in the past: A tax on bank notes resembled the British Stamp Act; taxes on imported salt and sugar were similar to the British Sugar Act and Townshend Duties; a tax on stills harked back to the Federalist whiskey tax; and a direct tax on land looked like the house tax that triggered Fries Rebellion. Having hesitatingly swallowed this bitter pill, Congress delayed implementation until the end of the year. Even so, the money raised fell far short of government needs. In 1814, these taxes had to be increased significantly, including a tax on all liquor sold and on manufactured goods to bring in $13.5 million in revenue in 1815.

Congress also was reluctant to act against trading with the enemy throughout the war. Republicans in Congress in 1812 passed a law prohibiting trade with Great Britain, but allowed the use of British licenses to bring grain to the British army in Spain. The following year Congress banned the use of these licenses. Similarly, British merchants sent about $18 million worth of goods to the United States after the repeal of the Orders in Council in June 1812, expecting the United States to end nonimportation and the war. Although this trade was illegal and all of the goods liable for seizure, Congress and the courts ultimately allowed the American merchants to keep the merchandise. The United States was thus denied the revenue from selling confiscated goods (worth $30 million on the market), but the customs duties on what should have been an illegal trade raised a $5 million windfall for the Treasury. Smuggling and illegal trade with the British persisted throughout the war. In fact, the blockading British fleet depended on supplies sold to them by enterprising Americans. Madison did his best to stifle this illicit commerce and even instituted another embargo in December 1813 to prohibit American ships from leaving port and banning the importation of all goods traditionally received from Great Britain. The measure had little real effect and Madison agreed to its repeal in April. The profit motive seemed to outweigh the importance of the common good for many Americans. As one British officer observed: "Self, the great ruling principle" was "more powerful with Yankees than any people I ever saw." Another commented that "You may always buy a Yankee" regardless of "rank and station." As late as August 1814, a British general admitted that "Two thirds of the army in Canada" were "eating beef provided by American contractors."[31]

Self-interest also seemed to guide Congress's actions regardless of the administration's intent. Confronted with serious problems financing the war, many Republicans came to see the utility of a national bank. A first effort to charter a new Bank of the United States failed in early 1814 amid rumors of peace and the belief that it was just a scheme to create paper money. In the fall of 1814, however, Secretary of Treasury Alexander J. Dallas submitted an elaborate plan for a national bank that would be closely tied to the U.S. government and that would absorb at least $20 million in war bonds. By the time Congress finished amending and altering the plan, government control had been practically eliminated and it became more of a vehicle for private investment. An exasperated Dallas exclaimed: "I asked for bread" and Congress "gave me a stone. I asked for a Bank to serve the Government during the war; and they have given me a commercial Bank, to go into operation after the war."[32] Madison vetoed the bank bill on January 30, 1815, declaring that it did not "answer the purposes of reviving the public credit, of providing a national medium of circulation, and of aiding the Treasury by facilitating the indispensable anticipations of the revenue and by affording to the public more durable loans." Instead, "the proposed establishment" would "enjoy a monopoly of the profits of a national bank" for twenty years, without providing "a greater security for attaining the public objects of the institution."[33]

The nation's moneyed men shared the lack of enthusiasm for sacrifice and continued to pursue the main chance. Repeatedly, the request for loans to the government were undersubscribed, even when the loans were offered at a discount. The $11 million loan authorized in March 1812 raised only $6.5 million; the rest had to be made up in Treasury bills, which were short-term loans to the government. These certificates were not legal tender, but were often used as currency. Financiers such as Stephen Girard and John Jacob Astor drove hard bargains before doing their patriotic duty and lending the nation money. The $16 million loan authorized in 1813 was discounted by 12 percent ($88 bought a loan of $100), providing instant profits for the lenders. Another $7.5 million loan later that year was discounted almost as much. Public credit was even more tenuous in 1814. Loans offered at 20 percent discount were undersubscribed. By the closing months of 1814, the situation had reached crisis proportions when the government defaulted on the national debt by not paying interest on notes in specie as required by law. War bonds fell to 75 percent of face value and treasury notes were offered at 15 to 25 percent discount.

Economic conditions deteriorated for the nation generally during the war, although the situation varied from region to region. New England and the South, both of which were more directly tied to the Atlantic economy, suffered the greatest hardship, whereas the middle Atlantic states and the region west of the Appalachians at first prospered as a result of war expenditures. Initially, the British had treated New England kindly in an effort to encourage opposition to the war in the region. But after the opening year of the war the British extended their blockade to include New England and began to raid coastal towns. The result was that shipping and fishing, industries that New England had most depended on, shrank to almost nothing. Hundreds of ships sat rotting in New England ports. Property values dropped and fortunes disappeared. The only commercial activities open to merchants and seamen were smuggling and privateering. Both were high-risk enterprises in which the rewards could be great, but in which it was just as easy to lose not only your investment, but your life. Southerners who had been dependent on the export of a commodity crop, such as tobacco or cotton, also suffered. Prices dropped precipitously as it became impossible to send ships to sea. Jefferson wrote in 1814 that tobacco was "not worth the pipe it is smoked in."[34] Cotton exports in 1814 were one-fifth of what they had been in 1810. Even the price for wheat in Virginia fell so low that it almost became not worth the bother to grow. On the other hand, both Pennsylvania and New York, closer to the theater of military operations, experienced something of a wartime boom as contracts to feed and supply American armies, as well as illegal trade to supply British armies, led to a rise in agricultural prices and even an increase in manufacturing. Western states also enjoyed prosperity. A Boston merchant visiting Lexington, Kentucky, in 1813 wrote that "the war, so far from depressing the people of the Western States, is making the greater proportion of them rich."[35]

As the war dragged on, however, economic distress spread. Foreign trade plummeted as the British blockade tightened in 1813 and 1814. Exports dropped from $61,317,000 in 1811 to $6,927,000 in 1814; imports fell from $57,887,000 in 1811 to $12,967,000 in 1814 (customs duties decreased as well). Overall, the price of imports almost doubled during the war.[36] The British blockade also hobbled interregional trade along the coast. Inland transportation remained relatively primitive and expensive, creating gluts and shortages throughout the country. Sugar cost almost three times as much in Baltimore as in New Orleans. Consumers encountered disparities in prices in other goods as well. Wily merchants hoarded commodities in the hope that the price would rise. The New York *Columbian* reported late in 1813 that the "*mania* for *commercial speculations and monopolies*" had grown "extensive" and was increasing.[37] Banking also suffered. Without the BUS to regulate the banking industry the number of new banks proliferated after 1811. Several of these new institutions were not run carefully enough and they printed an excess of notes to help customers and to buy war bonds. Simultaneously, there was a drain on specie from the nation, much of it caused by the illicit purchase of consumer goods from abroad. The British invasion of the Chesapeake led to a run on the banks in Baltimore and Washington. With customers demanding more gold than was in their vaults, these banks suspended specie payment. A ripple effect ensued and most banks in the nation soon refused to redeem their notes in specie. Within months, bank notes were being discounted 15 to 30 percent and both public and private credit teetered on the brink of insolvency.

In the face of economic and military crisis in 1814, the U.S. government began to show new resolve. In the fall of 1814, the administration estimated that it would need 100,000 men to fight the war in 1815. The army had only about 30,000—another 70,000 men were needed. This was an unprecedented increase for the American military. To raise this number of men Madison initially considered a conscription law. When that idea did not meet with congressional approval, the government increased the enlistment bounty and passed a law allowing the signing of minors. Madison also accepted the recruitment of 40,000 volunteers and the use of up to another 40,000 state militia in the federal service for local defense. Congress authorized an expansion of the navy with a navy board of commissioners to oversee further construction of warships and the purchase of twenty schooners to raid British commerce. In addition, Congress approved more loans and taxes and passed serious measures to curtail trading with the enemy. Before this legislation could be fully implemented, news of peace arrived in early 1815.

Finding a Peace

The Federalists were right. The War of 1812 was a useless and expensive conflict that wasted lives, material, and treasury. The official tally of 2,260 killed and 4,505 wounded in action tells only a part of the story. In addition to the battlefield casualty rate, many died from accident and disease, raising the total number of lives lost to about 20,000. Add to this the civilian casualties, largely at the hands of Indians, and the suffering and agony of about 20,000 prisoners of war, and we begin to get some sense of the dimensions of the war's human cost. The financial cost is easier to assess. The nation's economy was about to collapse by the beginning of 1815. Putting aside property damage such as the destruction of Washington and the loss of economic opportunities, the cost of the war was $158 million: $93 million was spent on the army and navy; $16 million was for interest on war loans; and $49 million would be spent on veterans benefits. From 1812 to 1815 the national debt ballooned from $45 million to $127 million, more than erasing the gains Jeffersonian parsimony had made in paying off the debt. Discounts and paper currency meant that, although the government borrowed a total of $80 million during the war, it yielded only $34 million in specie. The Republican Party, just as the Federalists predicted, had to pass a host of unpopular internal taxes. The Republicans not only abandoned long-standing ideological positions on taxes and debt, but also discussed seriously other measures that ran counter to their beliefs, including the creation of a new national bank, the use of conscription, and the strengthening the central government's control over state prerogative.

Being right may have brought some political gains, but it did not sweep the Federalists into national office, nor did it guarantee protection from political oblivion in the years after the war. In 1812 and 1814, the Federalists increased their numbers in the House of Representatives to about one-third, and reduced the Republican majority in the Senate from 82 percent before the war broke out, to 78 percent after the election in 1812, to 67 percent after the election in 1814. Republicans, when they could agree, retained working majorities in both houses. Federalists also managed to regain control of all the New England state governments and made significant inroads elsewhere. As a party the Federalists opposed most war measures, except legislation for defense and strengthening the navy, and voted in a block. New England Federalists were adamant in opposing Madison's government. They saw the war as a partisan effort to strengthen the hand of the Republicans and weaken the influence of New England. Federalists believed that the war hawks were more concerned with conquest than commerce, and they thought that the Republicans wanted to ally the nation with evil incarnate—Napoleon Bonaparte. Throughout the conflict the radical Federalists talked of secession and making a separate peace with Great Britain. More moderate Federalists opposed such talk and agreed to a convention in Hartford, Connecticut, to discuss New England's grievances. As moderate Federalist Harrison Grey Otis explained, the convention was to be "a medium for obtaining from the General Government if possible security against Conscription, taxes & the danger of invasion by being allowed to take care of ourselves." Federalist Party leaders also hoped to restrain "the tendency to excess manifested in some of the petitions," which had gone so far as to urge nullification, and even a declaration of independence.[38]

The Hartford Convention met from December 15, 1814, to January 5, 1815, with delegates from Massachusetts, Connecticut, and Rhode Island. Neither Vermont nor New Hampshire sent an official representation, but three counties from these states sent delegates. The moderates, headed by Otis, controlled the agenda. Their report did not advocate secession as some had feared. Instead, the convention recommended seven amendments to the

FIGURE 10–3 The Hartford Convention Republicans portrayed the Federalist Hartford Convention, which met from December 15, 1814 to January 5, 1815, as an act of betrayal to the United States as depicted in this cartoon.

Constitution that addressed the grievances of New England Federalists. To correct what the Federalists saw as the overrepresentation of the South in Congress because of the three-fifths clause, they wanted to base representation on the "numbers of free persons" in a state. With the Federalists holding about one-third of the seats in the national legislature, the convention also called for amendments insisting on a two-thirds majority vote on several crucial issues. These included the admission of new states into the union, embargoes (which would be limited to only sixty days), the interdiction of "the commercial intercourse" with other nations, and declaring war, except if a U.S. territory was threatened directly. To limit foreign influence, the Federalists wanted an amendment to prohibit naturalized citizens from holding government office or sitting in Congress. To break up the Virginia dynasty, the Federalists wanted amendments limiting a president to a single term, and preventing the election of a president from the same state as his predecessor.

In politics, timing and image often count more than substance. Had the war continued, the Federalists might have managed to push their agenda further. But even as the Hartford Convention deliberated, a peace treaty was finally agreed on. By the time commissioners from the convention made it to Washington in February 1815, news of Jackson's victory at

New Orleans had preceded them. The day after they arrived at the nation's capital, official reports of the Treaty of Ghent sent the city into joyous celebration. The Federalist complaints now had a hollow ring, and the amendments fell on deaf ears. The whole convention process contaminated the Federalist Party with the taint of treason. Despite the moderate nature of its outcome, Republicans portrayed the Hartford Convention as encouraging "rancorous animosities" that tended "to a dissolution of the union." From this perspective, "the Hartford Convention was to commence a course of measures calculated to destroy our union, destroy our constitution, and consumate the views of opposition leaders."[39] Amid the jubilation that greeted the end of the war, and the emergence of a strident nationalism that claimed victory in the contest against Great Britain, few Americans wanted to be reminded of tribulations and near disaster. The Federalists may have been right about the war, but their convention's protests were ill timed and their image forever tarnished. They managed to sustain themselves as a local party in Massachusetts and a few other places, but nationally they became almost invisible.

More than opposition to the war ruined the Federalists. However correct they were concerning policy, they failed to understand the American people. The Federalists clung to an eighteenth-century notion of society in which the people deferred to their betters. They mistrusted the people and could not comprehend the ideal of equality. Although the upper crust of the Republican Party had not yet abandoned the notion that the elite should rule, they had more faith in the people. Men like Jefferson and Madison appealed to the common man. They created a political structure that was open to those from below. As the next generation asserted itself, a new political reality was emerging; office holders were no longer public servants, but men who were hired by the public to do its bidding. Federalists could never accept this reality. The men who attended the Hartford Convention could be tarred with the brush of treason because the fundamental ideas of the Federalist Party appeared alien to the mass of Americans.

The Treaty of Ghent caught Federalists and Republicans alike by surprise. The British had agreed to direct negotiations for peace as early as November 1813, but it had taken until August 1814 for the talks to actually begin. The United States had sent a stellar team of diplomats and politicians, including John Quincy Adams and Henry Clay. The British envoys were a less talented group: Their country's best minds were settling the business of reordering Europe after the defeat of Napoleon. The British opened the discussions by insisting on the creation of a permanent and large reservation for the Indians in the Old Northwest, land concessions in Maine and present-day Minnesota, the demilitarization of the

Great Lakes, and limits on American fishing in Canadian waters. These conditions were unacceptable to the Americans. By October, the British had abandoned their Indian allies and were willing to settle for ending the war, with both sides keeping whatever territory their troops currently occupied. Because the British held on to Mackinac Island, Fort Niagara in New York, and much of Maine, whereas the United States had only toe-holds in Canada at Forts Erie and Malden, the Americans rejected this offer as well. When news of this impasse reached the United States every-one expected the war to last for a long time. But the British government had good reason to end the war. After decades of struggle, Great Britain wanted to save the expense of another invasion of the United States and keeping a fleet posted in distant waters. The American navy and privateers continued to take prizes and hurt the British economy. Besides, being tied down in North America limited British diplomatic and military maneu-verability in Europe as each of the victors over France sought advantage at the Congress of Vienna. On Christmas Eve, December 24, 1814, Great Britain and the United States signed an agreement that simply returned all borders and conditions to the situation before the war. The peace became official on February 17 after the United States ratified the treaty.

Most Americans viewed the treaty as a great triumph. Less than a year after the burning of Washington, Americans believed they had prevailed over the British. In part, this sense of victory came from an odd coincidence. In most of the United States, news of the Battle of New Orleans arrived shortly before word of the peace treaty. First, Americans read of the annihilation of the British at New Orleans, then within days they read that a peace treaty had been signed. There was more to the belief in American success than the juxtaposition of two unrelated news stories. The Native American threat had been all but eliminated. Tecumseh was dead and the Red Sticks driven to the swamps of Florida. Never again would Indians mount a serious threat to the United States east of the Mississippi. Perhaps even more important was prov-ing the viability of a republic—even if that republic nearly imploded—in fighting the British to a draw. Just surviving the contest with the most pow-erful empire on earth was an achievement. Canada may not have been con-quered (although a part of Florida was), but the republic had endured.

What about "free trade and sailors' rights"? Much of the diplomatic brouhaha leading up to the war focused on American commerce and British impressment. But neither issue was mentioned in the Treaty of Ghent. In many ways, geopolitical circumstances made the issues moot. With the European war over, there was also little reason for the British to impress anyone on American ships and no need for the Orders in Council. In the years after the war, however, Americans did not forget "free trade and sailors' rights," although the U.S. government was more eager to protect commerce than it was to provide justice for its seamen.

Only a few months after the end of the war, American diplomats were willing to whitewash an atrocity committed against American seamen held as prisoners of war. The Treaty of Ghent stipulated that all prisoners of war "shall be restored as soon as practicable after the Ratifications of this Treaty."[40] For the 6,000 American sailors held in the dismal prison in southwest England called Dartmoor, "as soon as practicable" meant interminable delay. Like the other Americans who fought for their country in the war, these sailors were an unruly lot and had repeatedly demonstrated and even rioted in protests about food and treatment. As one prisoner explained, the sailors' behavior could often be "provoking," although he did not think that it was "malignant, much less, bloody." This sailor traced the rowdiness and taunting to a "spirit of *fun* and frolic, which our people indulge in beyond all others in the world." In short, this behavior should be seen "as one of the luxuriant shoots of our *tree* of *liberty*," showing "the strength, depth and extent of its roots, and the richness of the soil."[41] On April 6, 1815, months after the ratification of the treaty of peace, "the luxuriant shoots of our *tree* of *liberty*" sprouted into a confrontation between the British guard and American prisoners. Taunted by the prisoners, who seemed to be ready to break out of the prison en masse, British soldiers began to fire at the Americans clustered in the prison yard. Twenty minutes later, six Americans lay dead and many more were wounded in an episode that came to be known as the Dartmoor Massacre. Despite the protests of the sailors in Dartmoor that the shooting was unwarranted, and despite a public uproar among the American people, both the U.S. and British governments did not want this incident—this violation of sailors' rights— to interfere with their diplomatic rapprochement. A joint British and American commission met and, although they found the incident lamentable, they ultimately blamed "the unfortunate transaction" on the prisoners' behavior and the garrison soldiers who continued to fire at the sailors "from the state of individual irritation and exasperation."[42]

The U.S. government was more willing to take action when there was a threat to commerce. The American navy at the end of the War of 1812 was more powerful and confident than ever. Moreover, the Republicans had decided that they needed a strong navy and were willing to use it. No sooner had Congress ratified peace with the British than the United States declared war on Algiers, which had taken advantage of the War of 1812 to commit depredations on American commerce. In May 1815, a fleet of several frigates and other vessels sailed under Stephen Decatur for the Mediterranean. The American navy won two sea battles against Algerian

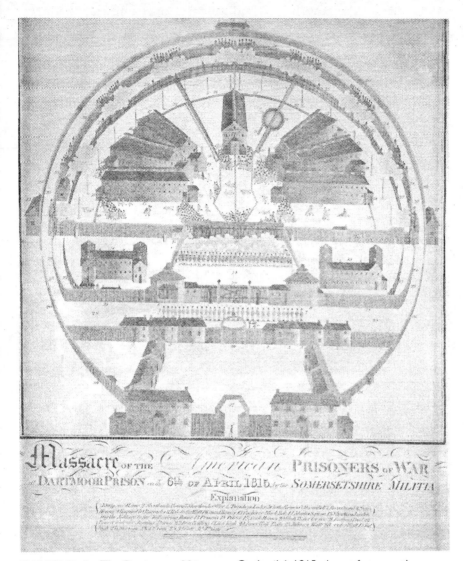

FIGURE 10–4   The Dartmoor Massacre On April 6, 1815, almost four months after the Treaty of Ghent was agreed upon, British soldiers fired into a rowdy crowd of American sailor prisoners of war in Dartmoor prison in southwest England. Diplomats, anxious to maintain peace, sidestepped the incident, despite the popular uproar in many parts of the United States.

ships and dictated peace terms, which included no tribute, to Algiers at gunpoint. The other Barbary States quickly agreed to similar treaties.

The United States emerged a stronger nation after the War of 1812. Regardless of the divisions within the country and the often pathetic performance of the government and military, Americans gained a new swagger and a strident sense of nationalism. Madison captured this spirit in the message he sent to Congress when he submitted the Treaty of Ghent for approval. In complete denial of reality, Madison congratulated the American people "upon an event which is highly honorable to the nation" and that "terminates with peculiar felicity a campaign signalized by the most brilliant successes." He went even further to praise "the wisdom of the Legislative Councils," "the patriotism of the people," "the public spirit of the militia", and "the valor of the military and naval forces of the country." There can be little doubt that Madison believed that the United States had triumphed and had asserted "the rights and independence of the nation." Madison also pointed to the economy, marking the war as an important moment in the rise of American capitalism. He declared that the nation's resources, which "were at all times competent to the attainment of every national object . . . will now be enriched and invigorated by the activity which peace will introduce into all the scenes of domestic enterprise and labor."[43] In other words, surviving the war not only meant that Americans believed that they had beaten the British, it also meant that Americans could run rampant across a continent, to settle, to speculate, to invest, and to look to the future.

Endnotes

1. James D. Richardson, *A Compilation of the Messages and Papers of the Presidents, 1789–1897,* 20 vols. (Washington, D.C.: Government Printing Office, 1896–1914), 1: 480–81.
2. Quoted in Bradford Perkins, *Prologue to War: England and the United States, 1805–1812* (Berkeley: University of California Press, 1968), 283–84.
3. *Annals of the Congress,* 11th Congress, 2nd sess., 580.
4. *Annals of the Congress,* 11th Congress, 2nd sess., 579–80.
5. *Annals of the Congress,* 12th Congress, 1st sess., 375–76.
6. *Niles' Weekly Register,* I (Dec. 28, 1811), 313–14.
7. *Annals of the Congress,* 12th Congress, 1st sess., 426.
8. Quoted in Roger H. Brown, *Republic in Peril: 1812* (New York: Norton, 1971), 77.
9. From Henry Clay's speech against the BUS, *Annals of the Congress,* 11th Congress, 3rd sess., 213.
10. J. C. A. Stagg, et al., eds., *The Papers of James Madison: Presidential Series,* 1–vols. (Charlottesville: University Press of Virginia, 1984–), 4: 17.
11. Quoted in Reginald Horsman, *The Causes of the War of 1812* (Philadelphia: University of Pennsylvania Press, 1962), 249.
12. Quoted in Perkins, *Prologue to War,* 401.
13. Quoted in Donald R. Hickey, *The War of 1812: A Forgotten Conflict* (Urbana: University of Illinois Press, 1989), 55.
14. *Niles' Weekly Register,* II (June 27, 1812), 283–85.

15. Quoted in Hickey, *The War of 1812,* 57–59.
16. Annapolis, *Maryland Republican,* July 1, 1812.
17. Maryland, General Assembly, House of Delegates, Committee on Grievances and Courts of Justice, *Report of the Committee of Grievances . . . on the Subject of the Recent Riots in the City of Baltimore, Together with the Depositions taken for the Committee* (Annapolis, Md.: Jonas Green, 1813), 242, 160–61, 199, 336, 344–45.
18. Georgetown *Federal Republican,* July 27, 1812.
19. Maryland General Assembly, *Report of the Committee of Grievances . . . ,* 170, 48, 190.
20. Maryland General Assembly, *Report of the Committee of Grievances . . . ,* 275, 295.
21. Annapolis, *Maryland Republican,* Aug. 12, 1812.
22. Albert Gallatin to Thomas Jefferson, Dec. 18, 1812. Thomas Jefferson Papers Series 1. General Correspondence, 1651–1827, Digital Archives, Library of Congress, Image 408.
23. Quoted in Gregory Evans Dowd, *A Spirited Resistance: The North American Indian Struggle for Unity, 1745–1815* (Baltimore: Johns Hopkins University Press, 1992), 189–90.
24. Treaty of Ghent, The Avalon Project at Yale Law School, www.yale.edu/lawweb/ avalon/diplomacy/britain/ghent.htm.
25. Josiah Cobb, *A Green Hand's First Cruise: Roughed Out From the Log-Book of Memory, of Twenty Five Years Standing . . .* (Boston: Otis, Broaders and Company, 1841), I, 40–55.
26. Hickey, *The War of 1812,* 33, 76–77, 111, 164, 243.
27. J. C. A. Stagg, "Enlisted Men in the Army, 1812–1815: A Preliminary Survey," *William and Mary Quarterly,* 3rd ser., 48 (1986), 615–45.
28. Benjamin Waterhouse, *A Journal of a Young Man of Massachusetts, Late a Surgeon on Board an American Privateer Who Was Captured at Sea by the British . . .* (Lexington, Ky.: Worsely and Smith, 1816), 6–7.
29. Hickey, *The War of 1812,* 222.
30. J. Fenimore Cooper, ed., *Ned Myers; or, A Life Before the Mast* (Annapolis, Md.: Naval Institute Press, 1989; orig. pub., 1843), 63–64.
31. Quoted in Hickey, *The War of 1812,* 216, 305, 226.
32. Quoted in Hickey, *The War of 1812,* 251. Originally in Dallas to William Jones, Jan. 29, 1815, Uselma Clarke Smith Collection (Coll.1378A), William Jones Correspondence, Historical Society of Pennsylvania.
33. Richardson, ed., *A Compilation of the Messages and Papers of the Presidents,* 1, 555–57.
34. Quoted in Hickey, *The War of 1812,* 230.
35. Quoted in Hickey, *The War of 1812,* 229.
36. Douglass C. North, *The Economic Growth of the United States, 1790–1860* (New York: Prentice-Hall, 1961), 26, 221, 228, 229.
37. Quoted in Hickey, *The War of 1812,* 153.
38. Quoted in James M. Banner, Jr., *To the Hartford Convention: The Federalists and the Origin of Party Politics in Massachusetts, 1789–1815* (New York: Alfred A. Knopf, 1970), 323. Originally in Letter from Harrison Gray Otis to Noah Webster, May 6, 1840, Noah Webster Papers, The New York Public Library Astor, Lenox and Tilden Foundations.
39. *New Hampshire Gazette,* December 26, 1815.
40. Treaty of Ghent, The Avalon Project at Yale Law School, www.yale.edu/lawweb/ avalon/diplomacy/britain/ghent.htm.
41. Waterhouse, *A Journal of a Young Man of Massachusetts,* 239.
42. *Annals of the Congress,* 14th Congress, 1st sess., 1511–17.
43. Richardson, ed., *A Compilation of the Messages and Papers of the Presidents,* 1: 552–54.

EPILOGUE:
BEN FRANKLIN, AGAIN

Benjamin Franklin lived many different lives. He was an artisan, colonial office seeker, imperial spokesman, revolutionary, diplomat, and a Founding Father. But perhaps his most remarkable life occurred after his death. In the minds of generations of Americans, he became the epitome of the self-made man and has lived on as the quintessential American. This legacy emerged out of his *Autobiography,* which began to appear in print almost as soon as Franklin died on April 17, 1790. Pieces of his life story surfaced in magazines in England and the United States in 1790. A French translation of his *Autobiography* was printed in Paris in 1791 from a copy Franklin had sent to a friend. Then the deluge began. Between 1794 and 1828, there were at least twenty-two editions of the Franklin autobiography, including grandson William Temple Franklin's "official" version in 1818.[1] The story was too good for others not to add their own retelling of Franklin's life. Perhaps the most popular biography was by Parson Mason Weems, of cherry-tree fame. Weems's book, which appeared in 1818, probably even outsold the *Autobiography* and was explicit in the moral lessons Franklin's life held for young boys. Weems ignored Franklin's deism and made young Ben a "true" Christian. He admonished his readers to follow Franklin's example and "stick to the *main chance*" by focusing on "BUSINESS AND EDUCATION."[2]

The *Autobiography* was written in four parts. Franklin penned the first half of his life story in 1771. Although he would remain in England until 1775, Franklin was already coming to realize that he might never obtain high office in Great Britain. The first part of the autobiography is the saga of a poor boy who made good despite the odds, and can be viewed as an assertion of his own self-worth in the face of rejection by the British court. Franklin wrote the three other parts after the Revolutionary War (the second section was written in France in 1784; the remaining two sections were composed in Philadelphia within two years of his death in 1790). These later additions emphasized the application of Enlightenment

principles to remaking the individual as he strove to do good, live virtu-
ously, and contribute to the greater benefit of society. Americans reading
about Franklin's life did not focus on either the wounded pride of
a would-be aristocrat, nor the musings of an Enlightened philosophe;
instead, they relished the story as the prototype of the American businessman. In this misreading, we can see the beginnings of the rise of capitalism
and the creation of a new society.

By viewing Franklin as the self-made man, Americans almost erased
from their collective memory any recollection of the true nature of colonial society. They thereby obscured a complete understanding of the great
revolution that gave birth to the American nation. Gone was any notion of
the world in which all men were created unequal. English society had
been hierarchical and by definition that hierarchy was corrupt. The idea
that anyone would be comfortable in a corporate society, with paternalism
and deference uniting those on the bottom with those on the top of society, was unthinkable. Starting in the years of the early republic, Americans
believed that colonial society had always been the land where a poor boy
like Honest Ben could travel from Boston to Philadelphia and, beginning
with only a few loaves of bread in his pocket, work his way to fame and
fortune. The American Revolution thus became not a radical break from
the past; instead, it was merely an effort to protect that which Americans
always had—equality and opportunity.

**FIGURE EP–1 Benjamin
Franklin** The wily Franklin came
to symbolize the self-made man in
the early nineteenth century as his
Autobiography became a blueprint
for generations of American
entrepreneurs.

Reality was more complex. There were many different currents churning within Anglo-American society before 1776. Some of those currents reflected the more traditional society and some pointed the way to new directions. A series of unexpected and contingent events—a combination of internal, social, economic, and imperial crises—catapulted Americans into a revolution no one expected. Many of those who joined in this revolution hoped merely to create a republican society that included hierarchy and would eliminate the corruption of individuals pursuing their own interest at the expense of the public good. Instead, through the process of fighting a war, designing governments, and living through the formative years of the early republic, they generated a whole new world in which working for one's own interest contributed to the public good. This process was not complete in 1815, but the path was clearly marked and the direction unmistakable.

By the early nineteenth century, Franklin's life story had become the model of the American entrepreneur and his Poor Richard sayings the mantra of a new middle-class morality that emphasized hard work, sobriety, industriousness, and delayed gratification. As Horace Greeley would later write:

> Of the men whom the world currently terms *Self-Made*—that is, who severally fought their life-battles without the aid of inherited wealth, or family honors, or educational advantages, perhaps our American FRANKLIN stands highest in the civilized world's regard.

For Greeley, Franklin was "the consummate type" and showed the "flowering of human nature under the skies of colonial America."[3] Closer to the period covered by this book were the words of Henry Mercein, a master baker who gave an address on November 25, 1820, the day New York opened an "APPRENTICES' LIBRARY." He told the apprentices that, like Franklin, "Industry, ardour, sobriety, and perseverance in your different pursuits, will lead to successful competition in the world." Mercein reminded these young men that

> The life of Franklin will tell you with what privations he struggled in early life; how his young and daring ambition ascended the rough and forbidding steps of knowledge, until he attained the summit of a celebrity where the sun of glory never sets.

And he asked the assembled crowd, "Who can tell how many Franklins may be among you?"[4] Like Mercein and the New York apprentices, generations of Americans have been inspired by Franklin's life and words to espouse the capitalist and egalitarian ethos that emerged from the making of the American republic.

Endnotes

1. For a discussion of the different manuscript and published texts see J. A. Leo Lemay and P. M. Zall, *The Autobiography of Benjamin Franklin: A Genetic Text* (Knoxville: University of Tennessee Press, 1981), xv–lviii; and Leonard W. Labaree, et al., eds., *The Autobiography of Benjamin Franklin* (New Haven: Yale University Press, 1964), 1–40.
2. Quoted in Gordon S. Wood, *The Americanization of Benjamin Franklin* (New York: Penguin, 2004), 239.
3. Quoted in Labaree, et al., eds. *Autobiography,* 12.
4. Paul A. Gilje and Howard B. Rock, eds., *Keepers of the Revolution: New Yorkers at Work in the Early Republic* (Ithaca, N.Y.: Cornell University Press, 1992), 53–54.

SUGGESTED READING

CHAPTER I

There are several recent biographies of Benjamin Franklin. The most insightful is Gordon S. Wood, *The Americanization of Benjamin Franklin* (New York: Penguin, 2004). See also Edmund S. Morgan, *Benjamin Franklin* (New Haven: Yale University Press, 2002); Walter Isaacson, *Benjamin Franklin: An American Life* (New York: Simon & Schuster, 2003); H. W. Brands, *The First American: The Life and Times of Benjamin Franklin* (New York: Random House, 2000). There has been less work on J. Hector St. de Crèvecoeur. See Gay Wilson Allen and Roger Asselineau, *St. John De Crevecoeur: The Life of an American Farmer* (New York: Viking, 1987); Victor Davis Hanson, *The Land Was Everything: Letters from an American Farmer* (New York: Free Press, 2000); Thomas Philbrick, *St. John de Crevecoeur* (New York: Twayne, 1970). The literature on the relationship between capitalism and colonial American society is immense. Particularly useful are J. E. Crowley, *This Sheba, Self: The Conceptualization of Economic Life in Eighteenth-Century America* (Baltimore: Johns Hopkins University Press, 1974); James A. Henretta, *The Origins of American Capitalism: Collected Essays* (Boston: Northeastern University Press, 1991); Allan Kulikoff, *The Agrarian Origins of American Capitalism* (Charlottesville: University Press of Virginia, 1992); Carol Shammas, *The Pre-Industrial Consumer and America* (Oxford: Oxford University Press, 1990).

For social conditions in the colonies on the eve of the revolution see Gordon S. Wood, *The Radicalism of the American Revolution* (New York: Random House, 1993); Gary B. Nash, *The Urban Crucible: Social Change, Political Consciousness, and the Origins of the American Revolution* (Cambridge, Mass.: Harvard University Press, 1979); T. H. Breen, *The Marketplace of Revolution: How Consumer Politics Shaped American Independence* (New York: Oxford University Press, 2004). Jackson Turner Main, *The Social Structure of Revolutionary America* (Princeton: Princeton University Press, 1965);

John J. McCusker and Russell R. Menard, *The Economy of British America, 1607–1789* (Chapel Hill: University of North Carolina Press, 1985). There are also many good studies of individual colonies and states. See Rachel N. Klein, *Unification of a Slave State: The Rise of the Planter Class in the South Carolina Backcountry, 1760–1808* (Chapel Hill: University of North Carolina Press, 1990); Marjoleine Kars, *Breaking Loose Together: The Regulator Rebellion in Pre-Revolutionary North Carolina* (Chapel Hill: University of North Carolina Press, 2002); Rhys Isaac, *The Transformation of Virginia, 1740–1790* (Chapel Hill: University of North Carolina Press, 1982); Richard R. Beeman, *The Evolution of the Southern Backcountry: A Case Study of Lunenburg County, Virginia, 1746–1832* (Philadelphia: University of Pennsylvania Press, 1984); T. H. Breen, *Tobacco Culture: The Mentality of the Great Tidewater Planters on the Eve of Revolution* (Princeton, N.J.: Princeton University Press, 1985); Ronald Hoffman, *A Spirit of Dissension: Economics, Politics, and the Revolution in Maryland* (Baltimore: Johns Hopkins University Press, 1973); Brendon McConville, *These Daring Disturbers of the Public Peace: The Struggle for Property and Power in Early New Jersey* (Ithaca, N.Y.: Cornell University Press, 1999); Edward Countryman, *A People in Revolution: The American Revolution and Political Society in New York, 1760–1790* (Baltimore: Johns Hopkins University Press, 1981); Thomas J. Humphrey, *Land and Liberty: Hudson Valley Riots in the Age of Revolution* (DeKalb: Northern Illinois Press, 2004); Robert A. Gross, *The Minutemen and Their World* (New York: Hill and Wang, 1976); Jere R. Daniel, *Experiment in Republicanism: New Hampshire Politics and the American Revolution* (Cambridge: Harvard University Press, 1970).

For the resistance movement see Edmund S. and Helen M. Morgan, *The Stamp Act Crisis: Prologue to Revolution* (Chapel Hill: University of North Carolina Press, 1952); Pauline Maier, *From Resistance to Revolution: Colonial Radicals and the Development of American Opposition to Britain, 1765–1776* (New York: Random House, 1972); Paul A. Gilje, *The Road to Mobocracy: Popular Disorder in New York City, 1763–1834* (Chapel Hill: University of North Carolina Press, 1987); Richard L. Bushman, *King and People in Provincial Massachusetts* (Chapel Hill: University of North Carolina Press, 1985); Marc Egnal, *A Mighty Empire: The Origins of the American Revolution* (Ithaca, N.Y.: Cornell University Press, 1988); Peter D. G. Thomas, *British Politics and the Stamp Act Crisis: The First Phase of the American Revolution, 1763–1776* (New York: Oxford University Press, 1975); Thomas, *The Townshend Duties Crisis: The Second Phase of the American Revolution, 1767–1773* (New York: Oxford University Press, 1987), Thomas, *Tea Party to Independence: The Third Phase of the American Revolution, 1773–1776* (New York: Oxford University Press, 1991); David Ammerman, *In Common*

Cause: American Response to the Coercive Acts (Charlottesville: University Press of Virginia, 1974); Benjamin Woods Labaree, *The Boston Tea Party* (New York: Oxford University Press, 1966); Ian R. Christie and Benjamin W. Labaree, *Empire or Independence, 1760–1776: A British–American Dialogue on the Coming of the American Revolution* (New York: Norton, 1976).

CHAPTER 2

The best place to begin an understanding of the ideology of the American Revolution is with Bernard Bailyn, *The Ideological Origins of the American Revolution* (Cambridge: Harvard University Press, 1967). Gordon S. Wood traces republicanism through the revolution to the writing of the Constitution in *The Creation of the American Republic, 1776–1787* (Chapel Hill: University of North Carolina Press, 1969). The literature examining republicanism is huge and scholars have debated whether the ideology reflected Lockean liberalism emphasizing the individual or classical republicanism centered on the common good. Of special note are Joyce Appleby, *Liberalism and Republicanism in the Historical Imagination* (Cambridge: Harvard University Press, 1992); Isaac Kramnick, *Republicanism and Bourgeois Radicalism: Political Ideology in Late Eighteenth-Century England and America* (Ithaca, N.Y.: Cornell University Press, 1990); John L. Brooke, *The Heart of the Commonwealth: Society and Political Culture in Worcester County, Massachusetts* (Cambridge: Cambridge University Press, 1989); and Milton M. Klein, et al., eds., *The Republican Synthesis Revisited: Essays in Honor of George Athan Billias* (Worcester, Mass.: American Antiquarian Society, 1992). For Thomas Paine see Eric Foner, *Tom Paine and Revolutionary America* (New York: Oxford University Press, 1976). For the Declaration of Independence see Carl Becker, *The Declaration of Independence: A Study in the History of Political Ideas* (New York: Vintage, 1958; orig. pub. 1942); Gary Wills, *Inventing America: Jefferson's Declaration of Independence* (New York: Random House, 1978); and Pauline Maier, *American Scripture: Making the Declaration of Independence* (New York: Alfred A. Knopf, 1997).

There are libraries full of books on the Revolutionary War. The best single volumes on the entire conflict are Don Higginbotham, *The War of American Independence: Military Attitudes, Policies, and Practice, 1763–1789* (New York: Macmillan, 1971); and Robert Middlekauff, *The Glorious Cause: The American Revolution, 1763–1789* (New York: Oxford University Press, 1982). For a short history of the conflict see Gordon S. Wood, *The American Revolution: A History* (New York: The Modern Library, 2003). See also the essays in John Shy, *A People Numerous and Armed: Reflections on the Military Struggle for American Independence*, rev. ed. (Ann Arbor: University of Michigan Press, 1990). Useful narratives on particular aspects of the war include David Hackett Fischer, *Paul Revere's Ride* (New York: Oxford University Press, 1994); Fischer, *Washington's Crossing* (New York: Oxford University Press, 2004); Stephen R. Taffe, *The Philadelphia Campaign, 1777–1778* (Lawrence: University of Kansas Press, 2003); Richard M. Ketchum, *Saratoga: Turning Point of America's Revolutionary War* (New York: Henry Holt, 1997); Ketchum, *Victory at Yorktown: The Campaign That Won the Revolution* (New York: Henry Holt, 2004). There are many biographies of George Washington. See Joseph J. Ellis, *His Excellency: George Washington* (New York: Alfred A. Knopf, 2004); Marcus Cunliffe, *George Washington: Man and Monument* (Boston: Little, Brown, 1958); and James Thomas Flexner, *Washington: The Indispensable Man* (New York: New American Library, 1984). For the Continental army see Charles Royster, *The Continental Army and American Character, 1775–1783* (Chapel Hill: University of North Carolina Press, 1979); Charles Patrick Neimeyer, *America Goes to War: A Social History of the Continental Army* (New York: New York University Press, 1996); E. Wayne Carp, *To Starve the Army at Pleasure: Continental Army Administration and American Political Culture, 1775–1783* (Chapel Hill: University of North Carolina Press, 1984). For British generals see Ira D. Gruber, *The Howe Brothers and the American Revolution* (Chapel Hill: University of North Carolina Press, 1972); George Athan Billias, ed., *George Washington's Opponents: British Generals and Admirals in the American Revolution* (New York: William Morrow, 1969).

For the impact of the Revolutionary War on everyday Americans see J. Franklin Jameson, *The American Revolution Considered as a Social Movement* (Princeton: Princeton University Press, 1967; orig. pub., 1926); Robert A. Gross, *The Minutemen and Their World* (New York: Hill and Wang, 1976); Woody Holton, *Forced Founders: Indians, Debtors, Slaves, and the Making of the American Revolution in Virginia* (Chapel Hill: University of North Carolina Press, 1999); Ronald Hoffman, *A Spirit of Dissension: Economics, Politics, and the Revolution in Maryland* (Baltimore: Johns Hopkins University Press, 1973); Judith Van Buskirk, *Generous Enemies: Patriots and Loyalists in Revolutionary New York* (Philadelphia: University of Pennsylvania Press, 2002); Richard Buel, Jr., *Dear Liberty: Connecticut's Mobilization for the Revolutionary War* (Middletown, Conn.: Wesleyan University Press, 1980); Rachel N. Klein, *Unification of a Slave State: The Rise of the Planter Class in the South Carolina Backcountry, 1760–1808* (Chapel Hill: University of North Carolina Press, 1990); Wayne E. Lee, *Crowds and Soldiers in Revolutionary North Carolina: The Culture of Violence in Riot and War* (Gainesville: University Press of Florida, 2001). For Loyalists see William H. Nelson, *The American Tory* (New York: Oxford University Press, 1961); Bernard Bailyn,

The Ordeal of Thomas Hutchinson (Cambridge: Harvard University Press, 1974); and Janice Potter, *The Liberty We Seek: Loyalist Ideology in Colonial New York and Massachusetts* (Cambridge: Harvard University Press, 1983).

For foreign policy see Felix Gilbert, *To the Farewell Address: Ideas of Early American Foreign Policy* (Princeton: Princeton University Press, 1961); James H. Hutson, *John Adams and the Diplomacy of the American Revolution* (Lexington: University of Kentucky Press, 1980); Ronald Hoffman and Peter J. Albert, eds., *Diplomacy and Revolution: The Franco-American Alliance of 1778* (Charlottesville: University Press of Virginia, 1981); Jonathan R. Dull, *A Diplomatic History of the American Revolution* (New Haven: Yale University Press, 1985); Richard B. Morris, *The Peacemakers: The Great Powers and American Independence* (New York: Harper & Row, 1965).

CHAPTER 3

The best study on the state and federal Constitution remains Gordon S. Wood, *The Creation of the American Republic, 1776–1787* (Chapel Hill: University of North Carolina Press, 1969). For the state constitutions see also Allan Nevins, *The American States During and After the Revolution, 1775–1789* (New York: A. M. Kelley, 1969; orig pub. 1924); Willi Paul Adams, *The First American Constitutions: Republican Ideology and the Making of the State Constitutions in the Revolutionary Era*, translated by Rita and Robert Kimber, with a foreword by Richard B. Morris (Chapel Hill: University of North Carolina Press, 1980); Donald Lutz, *Popular Consent and Popular Control: Whig Political Theory in the Early State Constitutions* (Baton Rouge: Louisiana State University Press, 1980); Marc Kruman, *Between Authority and Liberty: State Constitution Making in Revolutionary America* (Chapel Hill: University of North Carolina Press, 1997). See also Elisha P. Douglas, *Rebels and Democrats: The Struggle for Equal Rights and Majority Rule During the American Revolution* (Chapel Hill: University of North Carolina Press, 1955).

There are many studies on the Confederation period. For studies that argue that the Articles were not a failure see Merrill Jensen, *The New Nation: A History of the United States During the Confederation, 1781–1789* (New York: Alfred A. Knopf, 1950); Jensen, *The Articles of Confederation: An Interpretation of the Social-Constitutional History of the American Revolution, 1774–1781* (Madison: University of Wisconsin Press, 1970; orig. pub. 1940); Jackson Turner Main, *The Sovereign States, 1775–1783* (New York: New Viewpoints, 1973); E. James Ferguson, *The Power of the Purse: A History of American Public Finance, 1776–1790* (Chapel Hill: University of North Carolina Press, 1961).

For approaches more critical to the Confederation see Richard B. Morris, *The Forging of the Union, 1781–1789* (New York: Harper & Row, 1987); Jack Rakove, *The Beginnings of National Politics: An Interpretive History of the Continental Congress* (New York: Alfred A. Knopf, 1979); Cathy D. Matson and Peter S. Onuf, *A Union of Interests: Political Economic Thought in Revolutionary America* (Lawrence: University of Kansas Press, 1990); Onuf, *The Origins of the Federal Republic: Jurisdictional Controversies in the United States, 1776–1787* (Philadelphia: University of Pennsylvania Press, 1983); Roger H. Brown, *Redeeming the Republic: Federalists, Taxation, and the Origins of the Constitution* (Baltimore: Johns Hopkins University Press, 1993). See also the essays in Richard Beeman, ed., *Beyond Confederation: Origins of the Constitution and American National Identity* (Chapel Hill: University of North Carolina Press, 1987); Ronald L. Hoffman and Peter J. Albert, eds., *The Sovereign States in an Age of Uncertainty* (Charlottesville: University Press of Virginia, 1981). On the Northwest Ordinance see Peter S. Onuf, *Statehood and Union: A History of the Northwest Ordinance* (Bloomington: Indiana University Press, 1987). For Shays's Rebellion see David P. Szatmary, *Shays' Rebellion: The Making of an Agrarian Rebellion* (Amherst: University Press of Massachusetts, 1980); Leonard L. Richards *Shays's Rebellion: The American Revolution's Final Battle* (Philadelphia: University of Pennsylvania Press, 2002); Robert A. Gross, ed., *In Debt to Shays: The Bicentennial of an Agrarian Rebellion* (Charlottesville: University Press of Virginia, 1993).

On the Constitution, besides Gordon Wood's *Creation of the American Republic*, see Jack Rakove, *Original Meanings: Politics and Ideas in the Making of the Constitution* (New York: Viking, 1996); Forrest McDonald, *Novus Ordo Seclorum: The Intellectual Origins of the Constitution* (Lawrence: University of Kansas Press, 1985); Lance Banning, *The Sacred Fire of Liberty: James Madison and the Founding of the Federal Republic* (Ithaca, N.Y.: Cornell University Press, 1995). For the Constitution in American culture see Michael Kammen, *A Machine That Would Go of Itself: The Constitution in American Culture* (New York: Alfred A. Knopf, 1987).

On the Antifederalist/Federalist debate it is best to read the original essays. See Ralph Ketchum, ed., *The Anti-Federalist Papers and the Constitutional Convention Debates* (New York: New American Library, 1986); Alexander Hamilton, et al., *The Federalist* (New York: Modern Library, n.d.). For the Antifederalists see Jackson Turner Main, *The Antifederalists: Critics of the Constitution, 1781–1788* (Chapel Hill: University of North Carolina Press, 1961); Saul Cornell, *Anti-Federalism and the Dissenting Tradition in America, 1788–1828* (Chapel Hill: University of North Carolina Press, 1999); Herbert J. Storing, *What the Anti-federalists Were For* (Chicago: University of Chicago Press, 1981). For the Federalist Papers see Albert Furtwangler, *The Authority of Publius: A Reading of the Federalist Papers* (Ithaca, N.Y.: Cornell University Press, 1984); Garry Wills, *Explaining America: The Federalist* (Garden City, N.Y.: Doubleday, 1981). For the Bill of Rights see R. A. Rutland, *The Birth of the Bill of Rights, 1776–1791* (Chapel Hill: University of North Carolina Press, 1955); Akhil Reed Amar, *The Bill of Rights: Creation and Reconstruction* (New Haven: Yale University Press, 1998).

CHAPTER 4

Discussion of the impact of the American Revolution on Native Americans can be found in Colin G. Calloway, *The American Revolution in Indian Country: Crisis and Diversity in Native American Communities* (New York: Cambridge University Press, 1995); Calloway, *Crown and Calumet: British–Indian Relations, 1783–1815* (Norman: University of Oklahoma Press, 1987); James H. Merrell, "Declarations of Independence: Indian–White Relations in the New Nation," in Jack P. Greene, ed., *The American Revolution: Its Character and Limits* (New York: New York University Press, 1987), 197–223; Merrell, *The Indians' New World: Catawbas and Their Neighbors From European Contact Through the Era of Removal* (Chapel Hill: University of North Carolina Press, 1989); Tom Hatley, *The Dividing Paths: Cherokees and South Carolinians through the Revolutionary Era* (New York: Oxford University Press, 1995); Alan Taylor, "Land and Liberty on the Post-Revolutionary Frontier," in David Thomas Konig, ed., *Devising Liberty: Preserving and Creating Freedom in the New American Republic* (Stanford, Cal.: Stanford University Press, 1995), 81–108. For more general developments among Indians in the late eighteenth century see Gregory Evans Dowd, *A Spirited Resistance: The North American Indian Struggle for Unity, 1745–1815* (Baltimore: Johns Hopkins University Press, 1992); Daniel K. Richter, *Facing East from Indian Country: A Native History of Early America* (Cambridge: Harvard University Press, 2001); Bernard W. Sheehan, *Seeds of Extinction: Jeffersonian Philanthropy and the American Indian* (Chapel Hill: University of North Carolina Press, 1973); Richard White, *The Middle Ground: Indians, Empires, and Republics in the Great Lakes Region, 1650–1815* (Cambridge: Cambridge University Press, 1991); Frederick E. Hoxie, et al., eds., *Native Americans and the Early Republic* (Charlottesville: University Press of Virginia, 1999). See also Wiley Sword, *President Washington's Indian War: The Struggle for the Old Northwest, 1790–1795* (Norman: University of Oklahoma Press, 1985).

Over the past twenty years, historians have come to appreciate what a turning point the American Revolution was for African American history. For an early study of this issue see Benjamin Quarles, *The Negro in the*

American Revolution (Chapel Hill: University of North Carolina Press, 1961). More recent works include Sylvia R. Frey, *Water From the Rock: Black Resistance in a Revolutionary Age* (Princeton: Princeton University Press, 1991); Ira Berlin, *Many Thousand Gone: The First Two Centuries of Slavery in North America* (Cambridge: Harvard University Press, 1998); Gary B. Nash, *Race and Revolution* (Madison Wis.: Madison House, 1990); Nash, *Forging Freedom: The Formation of Philadelphia's Black Community, 1720–1840* (Cambridge: Harvard University Press, 1988); Nash and Jean R. Soderland, *Freedom by Degrees: Emancipation in Pennsylvania and its Aftermath* (New York: Oxford University Press, 1991); and Ira Berlin and Ronald Hoffman, eds., *Slavery and Freedom in the Age of the American Revolution* (Charlottesville: University Press of Virginia, 1983).

In 1980 two books appeared that emphasized the importance of the American Revolution for women: Linda K. Kerber, *Women of the Republic: Intellect and Ideology in Revolutionary America* (Chapel Hill: University of North Carolina Press, 1980); and Mary Beth Norton, *Liberty's Daughters: The Revolutionary Experience of American Women, 1750–1800* (Boston: Little, Brown, 1980). As important as those books were in identifying republican motherhood, scholarship since then has been more guarded in tone. See the essays in Ronald Hoffman and Peter J. Albert, eds., *Women in the Age of the American Revolution* (Charlottesville: University Press of Virginia, 1989); Susan Branson, *These Fiery Frenchified Dames: Women and Political Culture in Early National Philadelphia* (Philadelphia: University of Pennsylvania Press, 2001). For a discussion of the daily lives of women during this period see Joy Day Buel and Richard Buel, Jr., *The Way of Duty: A Woman and Her Family in Revolutionary America* (New York: Norton, 1984); Laurel Thatcher Ulrich, *A Midwife's Tale: The Life of Martha Ballard, Based on Her Diary, 1785–1812* (New York: Random House, 1990). See also Rosemarie Zagarri, *A Woman's Dilemma: Mercy Otis Warren and the American Revolution* (Arlington Heights, Ill.: Harlan Davidson, 1995); and Edith B. Gelles, *Portia: The World of Abigail Adams* (Bloomington: Indiana University Press, 1992).

For developments in American culture see Joseph J. Ellis, *After the Revolution: Profiles of American Culture* (New York: Norton, 1970); Neil Harris, *The Artist in American Society; the Formative Years, 1790–1860* (New York: G. Braziller, 1966); Robert E. Shalhope, *The Roots of Democracy: American Thought and Culture, 1760–1800* (Boston: Twayne, 1990); Kenneth Silverman, *A Cultural History of the American Revolution: Painting, Music, Literature, and the Theatre in the Colonies and the United States . . .* (New York: Columbia University Press, 1987); Emory Elliott, *Revolutionary Writers: Literature and Authority in the New Republic, 1725–1810* (New York: Oxford

University Press, 1986). On education see Lawrence A. Cremin, *American Education: The Colonial Experience, 1607–1783* (New York: Harper and Row, 1970); Cremin, *American Education: The National Experience, 1783–1876* (New York: Harper and Row, 1980); Carl F. Kaestle, *Pillars of the Republic: Common Schools and American Society, 1780–1860* (New York: Hill and Wang, 1983). For reform see Michael Meranze, *Laboratories of Virtue: Punishment, Revolution, and Authority in Philadelphia, 1760–1835* (Chapel Hill: University of North Carolina Press, 1996).

CHAPTER 5

The best work on the politics of the 1790s is Stanley Elkins and Eric McKitrick, *The Age of Federalism* (New York: Oxford University Press, 1993). Also useful are Richard Buel, Jr., *Securing the Revolution: Ideology in American Politcs, 1789–1815* (Ithaca, N.Y.: Cornell University Press, 1972); Joseph P. Ellis, *Founding Brothers: The Revolutionary Generation* (New York: Random House, 2000); Drew R. McCoy, *The Elusive Republic: Political Economy in Jeffersonian America* (Chapel Hill: University of North Carolina Press, 1980). For honor in politics see Joanne B. Freeman, *Affairs of Honor: National Politics in the New Republic* (New Haven: Yale University Press, 2001).

For Alexander Hamilton see Ron Chernow, *Alexander Hamilton* (New York: Penguin, 2004); Gerald Stourzh, *Alexander Hamilton and the Idea of Republican Government* (Stanford, Ca.: Stanford University Press, 1970); Forrest McDonald, *Alexander Hamilton: A Biography* (New York: Norton, 1979).

For James Madison see Jack Rakove, *James Madison and the Creation of the American Republic* (Glenview, Ill.: Scott, Foresman and Company, 1990); Lance Banning, *The Sacred Fire of Liberty: James Madison and the Founding of the Federal Republic* (Ithaca, N.Y.: Cornell University Press, 1995).

For popular politics during the 1790s see Simon P. Newman, *Parades and the Politics of the Street: Festive Culture in the Early American Republic* (Philadelphia: University of Pennsylvania Press, 1997); David Walstreicher, *In the Midst of Perpetual Fetes: The Making of American Nationalism, 1776–1820* (Chapel Hill: University of North Carolina Press, 1997); Alfred F. Young, *The Democratic Republicans of New York; The Origins, 1763–1797* (Chapel Hill: University of North Carolina Press, 1967). For the Whiskey Rebellion see Thomas P. Slaughter, *The Whiskey Rebellion: Frontier Epilogue to the American Revolution* (New York: Oxford University Press, 1986); Leland D. Baldwin, *Whiskey Rebels: The Story of a Frontier Uprising* (Pittsburgh: University of Pittsburgh Press, 1939).

For issues of finance, E. James Ferguson, *The Power of the Purse: A History of American Public Finance, 1776–1790* (Chapel Hill: University of North Carolina Press, 1961) is indispensable. Douglass C. North, *The Economic Growth of the United States, 1790–1860* (New York: Prentice-Hall, 1966) is similarly crucial in understanding overall trade and trends in the economy. See also Thomas M. Doerflinger, *A Vigorous Spirit of Enterprise: Merchants and Economic Development in Revolutionary Philadelphia* (Chapel Hill: University of North Carolina Press, 1986). For the entrepreneurs discussed in the text see Alan Taylor, *William Cooper's Town: Power and Persuasion on the Frontier of the Early American Republic* (New York: Alfred A. Knopf, 1995); Robert F. Jones, *"The King of the Alley": William Duer, Politician, Entrepreneur, and Speculator, 1768–1799* (Philadelphia: American Philosophical Society, 1992); Barbara M. Tucker, *Samuel Slater and the Origins of the American Textile Industry, 1790–1860* (Ithaca, N.Y.: Cornell University Press, 1984); Constance McL. Green, *Eli Whitney and the Birth of American Technology* (Boston: Little, Brown, 1956). Also on early industrialization see Lawrence A. Peskin, *Manufacturing Revolution: The Intellectual Origins of Early American Industry* (Baltimore: Johns Hopkins University Press, 2003); Doron S. Ben-Atar, *Trade Secrets: Intellectual Piracy and the Origins of American Industrial Power* (New Haven: Yale University Press, 2004). For banks see Bray Hammond, *Banks and Politics in America: From the Revolution to the Civil War* (Princeton: Princeton University Press, 1957). For corporations see Hendrik Hartog, *Public Property and Private Power: The Corporation of the City of New York in American Law, 1730–1870* (Chapel Hill: University of North Carolina Press, 1983).

CHAPTER 6

Most studies of politics seek to explain the ultimate triumph of the Jeffersonians. The biggest exception to this approach is Stanley Elkins and Eric McKitrick, *The Age of Federalism* (New York: Oxford University Press, 1993). Good accounts of the 1796 election can also be found in Joanne B. Freeman, *Affairs of Honor: National Politics in the New Republic* (New Haven: Yale University Press, 2001) and Joseph P. Ellis, *Founding Brothers: The Revolutionary Generation* (New York: Random House, 2000). See also Richard H. Kohn, *Eagle and Sword: The Federalists and the Creation of the Military Establishment in America, 1783–1802* (New York: Free Press, 1975). John Adams's reputation has been resuscitated recently by David McCullough, *John Adams* (New York: Simon & Schuster, 2001). Other useful accounts are Peter Shaw, *The Character of John Adams* (Chapel Hill: University of North Carolina Press, 1976); and Joseph J. Ellis,

Passionate Sage: The Character and Legacy of John Adams (New York: Norton, 1993); John Howe, *The Changing Political Thought of John Adams* (Princeton: Princeton University Press, 1966); Stephen G. Kurtz, *The Presidency of John Adams: The Collapse of Federalism, 1795–1800* (Philadelphia: University of Pennsylvania Press, 1957). The international scene is covered in William Stinchcombe, *The XYZ Affair* (Westport, Conn.: Greenwood, 1981); Alexander DeConde, *The Quasi-War: Politics and Diplomacy of the Undeclared War with France, 1797–1801* (New York: Scribner, 1966). For the Alien and Sedition Acts see James Morton Smith, *Freedom's Fetters: The Alien and Sedition Laws and American Civil Liberties* (Ithaca, N.Y.: Cornell University Press, 1956); Leonard W. Levy, *Legacy of Suppression: Freedom of Speech and Press in Early American History* (Cambridge: Harvard University Press, 1960). For Fries Rebellion see Paul Douglas Newman, *Fries Rebellion: The Enduring Struggle for the American Revolution* (Philadelphia: University of Pennsylvania Press, 2004).

The election of 1800 is often viewed as a watershed event in American history. See Daniel Sisson, *The American Revolution of 1800* (New York: Alfred A. Knopf, 1974). More recent appraisals of the significance of 1800, covering a variety of different issues, can be found in James Horn, et al., eds., *The Revolution of 1800: Democracy, Race and the New Republic* (Charlottesville: University Press of Virginia, 2002). See also John Ferling, *Adams vs. Jefferson: The Tumultuous Election of 1800* (New York: Oxford University Press, 2004). For the Jeffersonians leading up to the election of 1800 see Connor Cruise O'Brian, *The Long Affair: Thomas Jefferson and the French Revolution* (Chicago: University of Chicago Press, 1996); Lance Banning, *The Jeffersonian Persuasion: The Evolution of a Party Ideology* (Ithaca, N.Y.: Cornell University Press, 1978). For some local developments see Alfred F. Young, *The Democratic Republicans of New York: The Origins, 1763–1797* (Chapel Hill: University of North Carolina Press, 1967); Carl Prince, *New Jersey's Jeffersonian Republicans: The Genesis of an Early Party Machine, 1789–1817* (Chapel Hill: University of North Carolina Press, 1967); Norman K. Risjord, *Chesapeake Politics, 1781–1800* (New York: Columbia University Press, 1978). For newspapers and politics see Jeffrey L. Pasely, *"The Tyranny of Printers": Newspaper Politics in the Early Republic* (Charlottesville: University Press of Virginia, 2001).

The literature on Thomas Jefferson is immense. In more recent years Jefferson has undergone more critical scrutiny by historians because of the apparent contradictions between his ideals and his life. The two most balanced and careful accounts are Peter S. Onuf, *Jefferson's Empire: The Language of American Nationhood* (Charlottesville: University Press of Virginia, 2000); Joseph J. Ellis, *American Sphinx: The Character of Thomas Jefferson*

(New York: Alfred A. Knopf, 1996). See also the essays in Peter Onuf, ed., *Jefferson's Legacies* (Charlottesville: University Press of Virginia, 1993). For an examination of the evidence of the Jefferson's relationship with Sally Hemmings see Annette Gordon-Reed, *Thomas Jefferson and Sally Hemmings: An American Controversy* (Charlottesville: University Press of Virginia, 1997); Jan Ellen Lewis and Peter S. Onuf, eds., *Sally Hemmings and Thomas Jefferson: History, Memory, and Civic Culture* (Charlottesville: University Press of Virginia, 1999). For other useful recent examinations of Jefferson see Herbert E. Sloan, *Principle and Interest: Thomas Jefferson and the Problem of Debt* (Charlottesville: University Press of Virginia, 1995); Andrew Burstein, *The Inner Jefferson: Portrait of a Grieving Optimist* (Charlottesville: University Press of Virginia, 1995). For an example of a recent hostile approach to Jefferson see Garry Wills, *"Negro President": Jefferson and the Slave Power* (Boston: Houghton Mifflin, 2003). For more traditional approaches to Jefferson see Merrill D. Peterson, *The Jeffersonian Image in the American Mind* (New York: Oxford University Press, 1960); Peterson, *Thomas Jefferson and the New Nation: A Biography* (New York: Oxford University Press, 1970); and the multivolume biography by Dumas Malone, *Jefferson and His Time,* 6 vols. (Boston: Little, Brown, 1962–81).

CHAPTER 7

For the life of the yeoman farmer see Barbara Clarke Smith, *After the Revolution: The Smithsonian History of Everyday Life in the Eighteenth Century* (New York: Random House, 1985); Jack Larkin, *The Reshaping of Everyday Life: 1790–1840* (New York: Harper and Row, 1988); Christopher Clark, *The Roots of Rural Capitalism: Western Massachusetts, 1780–1860* (Ithaca, N.Y.: Cornell University Press, 1990); Alan Taylor, *Liberty Men and Great Proprietors: The Revolutionary Settlement on the Maine Frontier, 1760–1820* (Chapel Hill: University of North Carolina Press, 1990); Laurel Thatcher Ulrich, *A Midwife's Tale: The Life of Martha Ballard, Based on Her Diary, 1785–1812* (New York: Alfred A. Knopf, 1990); Allan Kulikoff, *From British Peasants to Colonial American Farmers* (Chapel Hill: University of North Carolina Press, 2000); David Jaffe, *People of Wachusett: Greater New England in History and Memory, 1630–1860* (Ithaca, N.Y.: Cornell University Press, 1999); Reeve Huston, *Land And Freedom: Rural Society, Popular Protest, and Party Politics in Antebellum New York* (New York: Oxford University Press, 2000).

The most helpful reading on artisans is Howard B. Rock, *Artisans of the New Republic: The Tradesmen of New York City in the Age of Jefferson* (New York: New York University Press, 1978). See also Rock, et al., eds.,

American Artisans: Crafting Social Identity, 1750–1850 (Baltimore: Johns Hopkins University Press, 1995); Bruce Laurie, Working People of Philadelphia, 1800–1850 (Philadelphia: Temple University Press, 1980); Laurie, Artisans into Workers: Labor in Nineteenth-Century America (New York: Noonday Press, 1989); Paul E. Johnson, A Shopkeeper's Millennium: Society and Revivals in Rochester, New York, 1815–1837 (New York: Hill and Wang, 1978); Ronald Schultz, The Republic of Labor: Philadelphia Artisans and the Politics of Class, 1720–1830 (New York: Oxford University Press, 1993); Charles G. Steffen, The Mechanics of Baltimore: Workers and Politics in the Age of Revolution, 1763–1812 (Urbana: University of Illinois Press, 1984); Donna J. Rilling, Making Houses, Crafting Capitalism: Builders in Philadelphia, 1790–1850 (Philadelphia: University of Pennsylvania Press, 2001); Rosalind Remer, Printers and Men of Capital: Philadelphia Book Publishers in the New Republic (Philadelphia: University of Pennsylvania Press, 1996); Sean Wilentz, Chants Democratic: New York City and the Rise of the American Working Class, 1788–1850 (New York: Oxford University Press, 1984).

For discussion of the poor in this period see Ruth Wallis Herndon, Unwelcome Americans: Living on the Margin in Early New England (Philadelphia: University of Pennsylvania Press, 2001); Simon P. Newman, Embodied History: The Lives of the Poor in Early Philadelphia (Philadelphia: University of Pennsylvania Press, 2003); Billy G. Smith, The "Lower Sort": Philadelphia's Laboring People, 1750–1800 (Ithaca, N.Y.: Cornell University Press, 1990); Robert E. Cray, Jr., Paupers and Poor Relief in New York City and Its Rural Environs, 1700–1830 (Philadelphia: Temple University Press, 1988); John K. Alexander, Render Them Submissive: Responses to Poverty in Philadelphia, 1760–1800 (Amherst: University of Massachusetts Press, 1980); Barbara L. Bellows, Benevolence Among the Slaveholders: Assisting the Poor in Charleston, 1670–1860 (Baton Rouge: Louisiana University Press, 1993); Susan Grigg, The Dependent Poor of Newburyport: Studies in Social History, 1800–1830 (Ann Arbor: UMI Research Press, 1984); Raymond A. Mohl, Poverty in New York, 1783–1825 (New York: Oxford University Press, 1971). For European American bound labor see Sharon V. Salinger, "To Serve Well and Faithfully": Labor and Indentured Servants in Pennsylvania, 1682–1800 (Cambridge: Cambridge University Press, 1987); W. J. Rorabaugh, The Craft Apprentice: From Franklin to the Machine Age in America (New York: Oxford University Press, 1986).

Slavery is one of the most studied subjects in American history, but there are not many works that center on the early republic. Useful books include Ira Berlin, Many Thousand Gone: The First Two Centuries of Slavery in North America (Cambridge: Harvard University Press, 1998); Philip D. Morgan, Slave Counterpoint: Black Culture in the Eighteenth-Century Chesapeake and Low

Country (Chapel Hill: University of North Carolina Press, 1998); Douglas R. Egerton, *Gabriel's Rebellion: The Virginia Slave Conspiracies of 1800 and 1802* (Chapel Hill: University of North Carolina Press, 1993); James Sidbury, *Ploughshares into Swords: Race, Rebellion, and Identity in Gabriel's Virginia, 1730–1810* (Cambridge: Cambridge University Press, 1997); Sylvia R. Frey, *Water From the Rock: Black Resistance in a Revolutionary Age* (Princeton: Princeton University Press, 1991); Allan Kulikoff, *Tobacco and Slaves: The Development of Southern Cultures in the Chesapeake, 1680–1800* (Chapel Hill: University of North Carolina Press, 1986); Graham Russell Hodges, *Root & Branch: African Americans in New York and East Jersey, 1613–1863* (Chapel Hill: University of North Carolina Press, 1999); Shane White, *Somewhat More Independent: The End of Slavery in New York City, 1770–1810* (Athens: University of Georgia Press, 1991).

The best study on religion in the early republic remains Nathan O. Hatch, *The Democratization of American Christianity* (New Haven: Yale University Press, 1989). For an overview of religion through the colonial period and into the early republic see Frank Lambert, *The Founding Fathers and the Place of Religion in America* (Princeton: Princeton University Press, 2003). Other useful studies include Susan Juster, *Doomsayers: Anglo-American Prophecy in the Age of Revolution* (Philadelphia: University of Pennsylvania Press, 2003); Dee E. Andrews, *The Methodists and Revolutionary America: The Shaping of an Evangelical Culture* (Princeton: Princeton University Press, 2000); Christine Leigh Heyrman, *Southern Cross: The Beginnings of the Bible Belt* (Chapel Hill: University of North Carolina Press, 1997); Jon Butler, *Awash in a Sea of Faith: Christianizing the American People* (Cambridge: Harvard University Press, 1990); and for the colonial background Patricia U. Bonomi, *Under the Cope of Heaven: Religion, Society, and Politics in Colonial America* (New York: Oxford University Press, 1986).

CHAPTER 8

The settlement of the frontier has attracted historians for over a century. Frederick Jackson Turner's frontier thesis emphasizing the relationship between American democracy and the frontier can be found in Turner, "The Significance of the Frontier in American History," in *The Frontier in American History*, with a foreword by Ray Allen Billington (New York: Holt, Rinehart and Winston, 1962) and in his larger work on the early nineteenth century, Turner, *The United States, 1830–1850: The Nation and Its Sections*, with an introduction by Avery Craven (New York: Norton, 1965). More recent works include Andrew R. L. Cayton, *The Frontier Republic: Ideology and Politics in the Ohio Country, 1780–1825* (Kent, Ohio: Kent State University Press,

1986), Cayton, *Frontier Indiana* (Bloomington: Indiana University Press, 1996); John Mack Faragher, *Daniel Boone: The Life and Legend of an American Pioneer* (New York: Henry Holt, 1992); Faragher, *Sugar Creek: Life on the Illinois Prairie* (New Haven: Yale University Press, 1986); Christopher Morris, *Becoming Southern: The Evolution of a Way of Life, Warren County and Vicksburg, Mississippi, 1770–1860* (New York: Oxford University Press, 1995); Alan Taylor, *William Cooper's Town: Power and Persuasion on the Frontier of the Early American Republic* (New York: Alfred A. Knopf, 1995); Taylor, *Liberty Men and Great Proprietors: The Revolutionary Settlement on the Maine Frontier, 1760–1820* (Chapel Hill: University of North Carolina Press, 1990); Stephen Aron, *How the West Was Lost: The Transformation of Kentucky from Daniel Boone to Henry Clay* (Baltimore: Johns Hopkins University Press, 1996); Malcolm J. Rohrbough, *The Trans Appalachian Frontier: People, Societies, and Institutions, 1775–1850* (New York: Oxford University Press, 1978); Charles E. Brooks, *Frontier Settlement and Market Revolution: The Holland Land Purchase* (Ithaca, N.Y.: Cornell University Press, 1996); Martin Brueghel, *Farm, Shop, Landing: The Rise of a Market Society in the Hudson Valley, 1780–1860* (Durham, N.C.: Duke University Press, 2002); Elizabeth A. Perkins, *Border Life: Experience and Memory in the Revolutionary Ohio Valley* (Chapel Hill: University of North Carolina Press, 1998); Gregory H. Nobles, *American Frontiers: Cultural Encounters and Continental Conquest* (New York: Hill and Wang, 1997).

For studies on speculations and land policy see Malcolm J. Rohrbough, *The Land Office Business: The Settlement and Administration of American Public Lands, 1789–1837* (New York: Oxford University Press, 1968); Paul W. Gates, *Landlords and Tenants on the Prairie Frontier: Studies in American Land Policy* (Ithaca, N.Y.: Cornell University Press, 1973); Shaw Livermore, *Early American Land Companies: Their Influence on Corporate Development* (New York: Octagon, 1968). For Robert Morris see Barbara Ann Chernow, *Robert Morris: Land Speculator, 1790–1801* (New York: Arno, 1978); Eleanor Young, *Forgotten Patriot: Robert Morris* (New York: Macmillan, 1950). On Yazoo see C. Peter Magrath, *Yazoo: Law and Politics in the New Republic, The Case of Fletcher v. Peck* (Providence, R.I.: Brown University Press, 1966).

The diplomacy of the Louisiana Purchase is covered by Alexander DeConde, *This Affair of Louisiana* (New York: Charles Scribner's Sons, 1976); Jon Kukla, *A Wilderness so Immense: The Louisiana Purchase and the Destiny of America* (New York: Alfred A. Knopf, 2003); James E. Lewis, Jr., *The Louisiana Purchase: Jefferson's Noble Bargain?* (Monticello, Va.: Thomas Jefferson Foundation, 2003). For Aaron Burr see Buckner F. Melton, Jr., *Aaron Burr: Conspiracy to Treason* (New York: John Wiley, 2002). Lewis and Clark have received a great deal of popular and scholarly attention. For a sampling of the popular literature see Stephen E. Ambrose, *Undaunted*

Courage: Meriwether Lewis, Thomas Jefferson, and the Opening of the American West (New York: Simon & Schuster, 1996); David Freeman Hawke, Those Tremendous Mountains: The Story of the Lewis and Clark Expedition (New York: Norton, 1980). For more scholarly work see James P. Ronda, Finding the West: Explorations with Lewis and Clark (Albuquerque: University of New Mexico Press, 2001); Rhonda, Lewis and Clark Among the Indians (Lincoln: University of Nebraska Press, 1984).

For an overview of Native Americans in this period see Gregory Evans Dowd, A Spirited Resistance: The North American Indian Struggle for Unity, 1745–1815 (Baltimore: Johns Hopkins University Press, 1992); Reginald Horsman, Expansion and American Indian Policy, 1783–1812 (Norman: University of Oklahoma Press, 1992; orig. pub., 1967); Bernard W. Sheehan, Seeds of Extinction: Jeffersonian Philanthropy and the American Indian (Chapel Hill: University of North Carolina Press, 1974). For the southwest borderlands see David J. Weber, The Spanish Frontier in North America (New Haven: Yale University Press, 1992). For the West's Indians before Lewis and Clark see Colin G. Calloway, One Vast Winter Count: The Native American West Before Lewis and Clark (Lincoln: University of Nebraska Press, 2003). For studies on Indians east of the Mississippi see William G. McLaughlin, Cherokee Renascence in the New Republic (Princeton: Princeton University Press, 1986); McLaughlin, Cherokees and Missionaries, 1789–1839 (New Haven: Yale University Press, 1984); Theda Perdue, Cherokee Women: Gender and Culture Change, 1700–1835 (Lincoln: University of Nebraska Press, 1998); Anthony F. C. Wallace, The Death and Rebirth of the Seneca (New York: Alfred A. Knopf, 1969); R. David Edmunds, The Shawnee Prophet (Lincoln: University of Nebraska Press, 1983); and Edmunds, Tecumseh and the Quest for Indian Leadership (Boston: Little, Brown, 1984).

CHAPTER 9

On the consumer revolution see Neil McKendrick, John Brewer, and J. H. Plumb, The Birth of a Consumer Society: The Commercialization of Eighteenth-Century England (Bloomington: Indiana University Press, 1982); Carol Shammas, The Pre-Industrial Consumer in England and America (New York: Oxford University Press, 1990); Richard L. Bushman, The Refinement of America: Persons, Houses, Cities (New York: Alfred A. Knopf, 1992); T. H. Breen, The Marketplace of Revolution: How Consumer Politics Shaped American Independence (New York: Oxford University Press, 2004); Cary Carson, Ronald Hoffman, and Peter J. Albert, eds., Of Consuming Interests: The Style of Life in the Eighteenth Century (Charlottesville: University Press of

Virginia, 1994). On the patterns of American trade see Douglass C. North, *The Economic Growth of the United States, 1790–1860* (New York: Prentice-Hall, 1966).

The Barbary Wars are often considered a sidelight to American history. For a good discussion of the importance of the conflict to the United States see Robert J. Allison, *The Crescent Obscured: The United States and the Muslim World, 1776–1815* (New York: Oxford University Press, 1995). A recent narrative of the conflict is Joseph Wheelan, *Jefferson's War: America's First War on Terror, 1801–1805* (New York: Carrol & Graf, 2003). A fine account of the naval war can be found in William M. Fowler, Jr., *Jack Tars and Commodores: The American Navy, 1783–1815* (Boston: Houghton Mifflin, 1984). See also Richard B. Parker, *Uncle Sam in Barbary: A Diplomatic History* (Gainesville: University Press of Florida, 2004); A. B. C. Whipple, *To the Shores of Tripoli: The Birth of the U.S. Navy and Marines* (New York: William Morrow, 1991).

Diplomatic history has long been the staple of historians of the early republic. Henry Adams's multivolume *History of the United States of America*, 9 vols. (New York: Charles Scribner's Sons, 1891–98) remains an indispensable narrative. A useful short account is Reginald Horsman, *The Diplomacy of the New Republic, 1776–1815* (Arlington Heights, Ill.: Harlan Davidson, 1985). Other useful surveys are Bradford Perkins, *Prologue to War: England and the United States, 1805–1812* (Berkeley: University of California Press, 1968); Reginald Horsman, *The Causes of the War of 1812* (Philadelphia: University of Pennsylvania Press, 1962). For more specific studies see Spencer C. Tucker and Frank T. Reuter, *Injured Honor: The Chesapeake–Leopard Affair* (Annapolis, Md.: Naval Institute Press, 1996); Burton Spivak, *Jefferson's English Crisis: Commerce, Embargo, and the Republican Revolution* (Charlottesville: University Press of Virginia, 1979). The classic study of the development of the Federalist Party in the early 1800s is David Hackett Fischer, *The Revolution of American Conservatism: The Federalist Party in the Era of Jeffersonian Democracy* (New York: Harper and Row, 1965). See also Morton Bordon, *Parties and Politics in the Early Republic, 1789–1815* (Arlington Heights, Ill.: AHM, 1967).

CHAPTER 10

Historians have strained to explain the origins of the War of 1812. See Bradford Perkins, *Prologue to War: England and the United States, 1805–1812* (Berkeley: University of California Press, 1968); Reginald Horsman, *The Causes of the War of 1812* (Philadelphia: University of Pennsylvania Press, 1962); Roger H. Brown, *Republic in Peril: 1812* (New York: W. W. Norton,

1971); Julius W. Pratt, *Expansionists of 1812* (New York: Macmillan, 1925). For relations with France during the same time period see Clifford L. Egan, *Neither Peace Nor War: Franco-American Relations, 1803–1812* (Baton Rouge: Louisiana State University Press, 1983). I have written about the Baltimore riots in two articles, "The Baltimore Riots of 1812 and the Breakdown of the Anglo-American Mob Tradition," *Journal of Social History*, 13 (1980), 547–64; and "'Le Menu Peuple' in America: Identifying the Mob in the Baltimore Riots of 1812," *Maryland Historical Magazine*, 81 (1986), 50–66.

The best account of the War of 1812, covering military, political, and economic material, is Donald R. Hickey, *The War of 1812: A Forgotten Conflict* (Urbana: University of Illinois Press, 1989). See also Reginald Horsman, *The War of 1812* (New York: Alfred A. Knopf, 1969); J. C. A. Stagg, *Mr. Madison's War: Politics, Diplomacy, and Warfare in the Early American Republic, 1783–1830* (Princeton: Princeton University Press, 1983). The war has not been forgotten quite as much as Donald Hickey suggests and there are many books on a number of campaigns. See David Curtis Skaggs and Gerard T. Altoff, *A Signal Victory: The Lake Erie Campaign, 1812–1813* (Annapolis, Md.: Naval Institute Press, 1997); William Jeffrey Welsh and David Curtis Skaggs, eds., *War on the Great Lakes: Essays Commemorating the 175th Anniversary of the Battle of Lake Erie* (Kent, Ohio: Kent State University Press, 1991); Pierre Berton, *Flames Across the Border: The Canadian–American Tragedy, 1813–1814* (Boston: Little, Brown, 1981); Richard Barbuto, *Niagara 1814: America Invades Canada* (Lawrence: University Press of Kansas, 2000); Robert V. Remini, *The Battle of New Orleans* (New York: Viking, 1999); Frank Lawrence Owsley, Jr., *Struggle for the Gulf Borderlands: The Creek War and the Battle of New Orleans, 1812–1815* (Gainesville: University Press of Florida, 1981); John Sugden, *Tecumseh's Last Stand* (Norman: University of Oklahoma Press, 1985). See also the relevant sections in James M. Fowler, Jr., *Jack Tars and Commodores: The American Navy, 1783–1815* (Boston: Houghton Mifflin, 1984). For a discussion of the militia see C. Edward Skeen, *Citizen Soldiers in the War of 1812* (Lexington: University Press of Kentucky, 1999).

For the Federalists and the Hartford Convention see James M. Banner, Jr., *To the Hartford Convention: The Federalists and the Origins of Party Politics in Massachusetts, 1789–1815* (New York: Alfred A. Knopf, 1970). The Treaty of Ghent is covered in most general histories of the war. For specific studies see Fred L. Engelman, *The Peace of Christmas Eve* (New York: Harcourt, Brace & World, 1962); Bradford Perkins, *Castlereagh and Adams: England and the United States, 1812–1823* (Berkeley: University of California Press, 1964). The Dartmoor Massacre has not been included in most histories of the period. For a discussion of life in Dartmoor and the massacre see W. Jeffrey Bolster, *Black Jacks: African American Seamen in the Age of Sail* (Cambridge: Harvard University Press, 1997), 102–30; and my *Liberty on the Waterfront: American Maritime Culture in the Age of Revolution* (Philadelphia: University of Pennsylvania Press, 2004), 183–91.

COPYRIGHT
ACKNOWLEDGMENTS

329

PHOTOGRAPHS

INDEX